ROBERT ELFGEN

DISTANZ

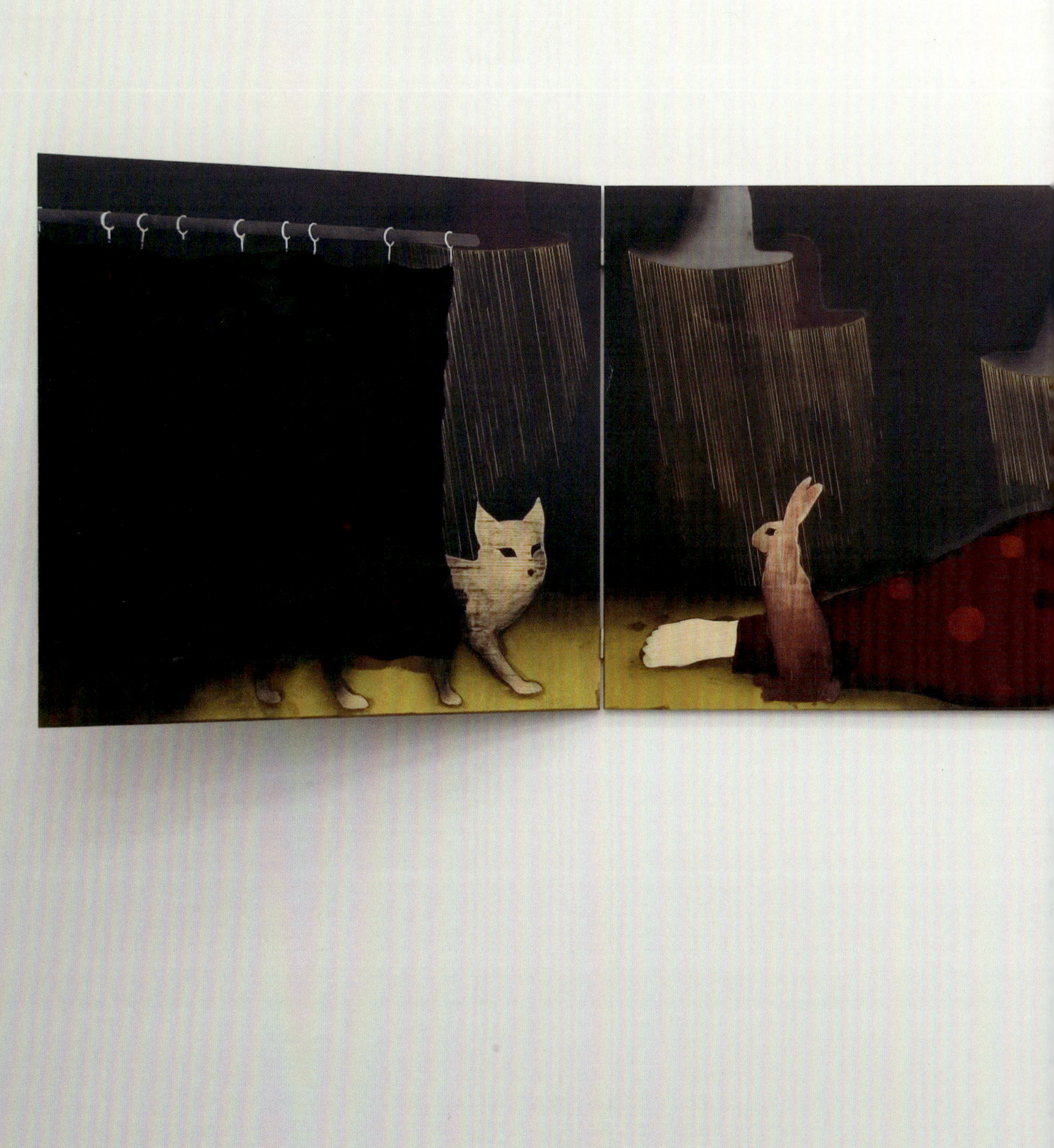

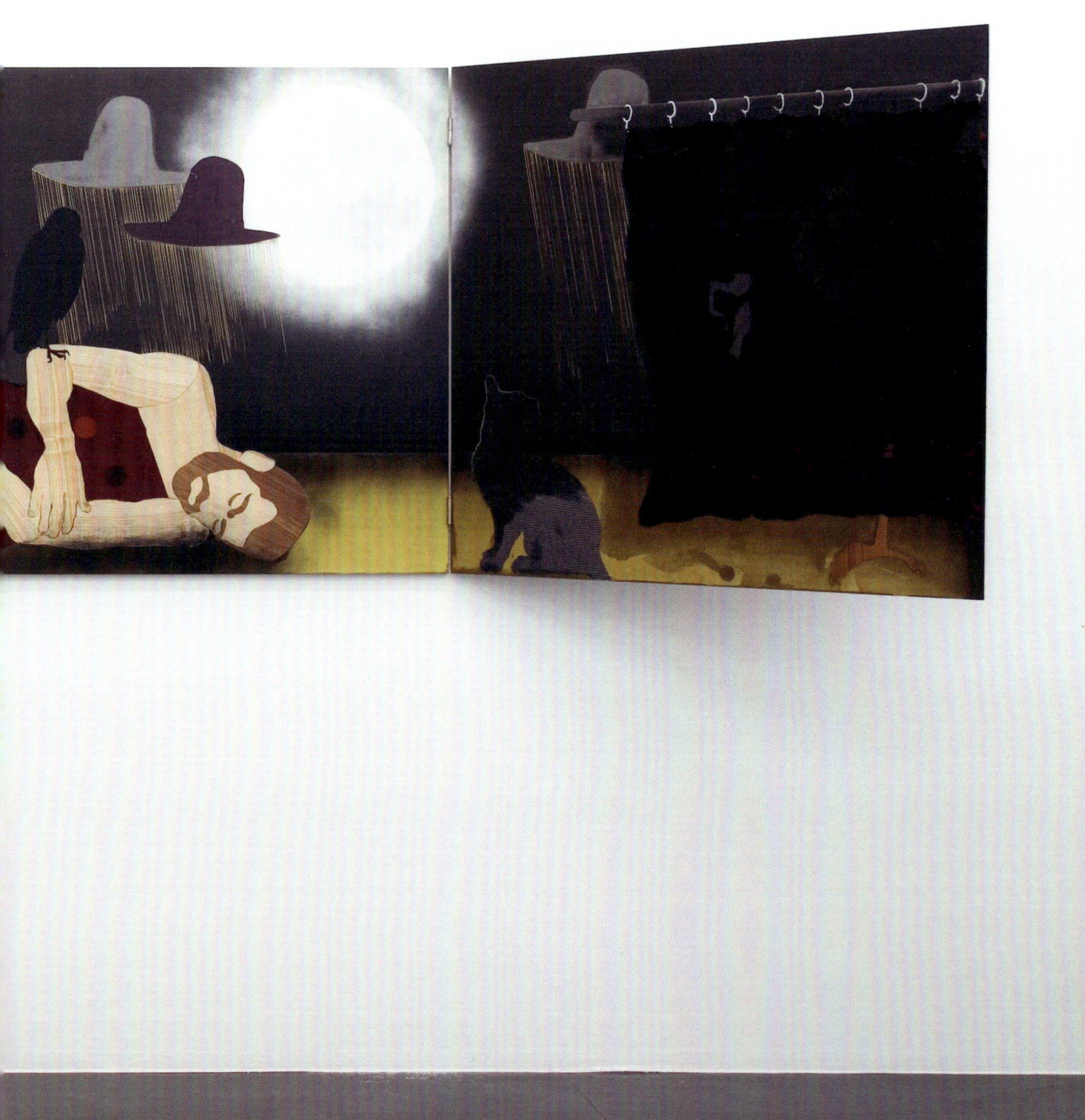

ROBERT ELFGEN

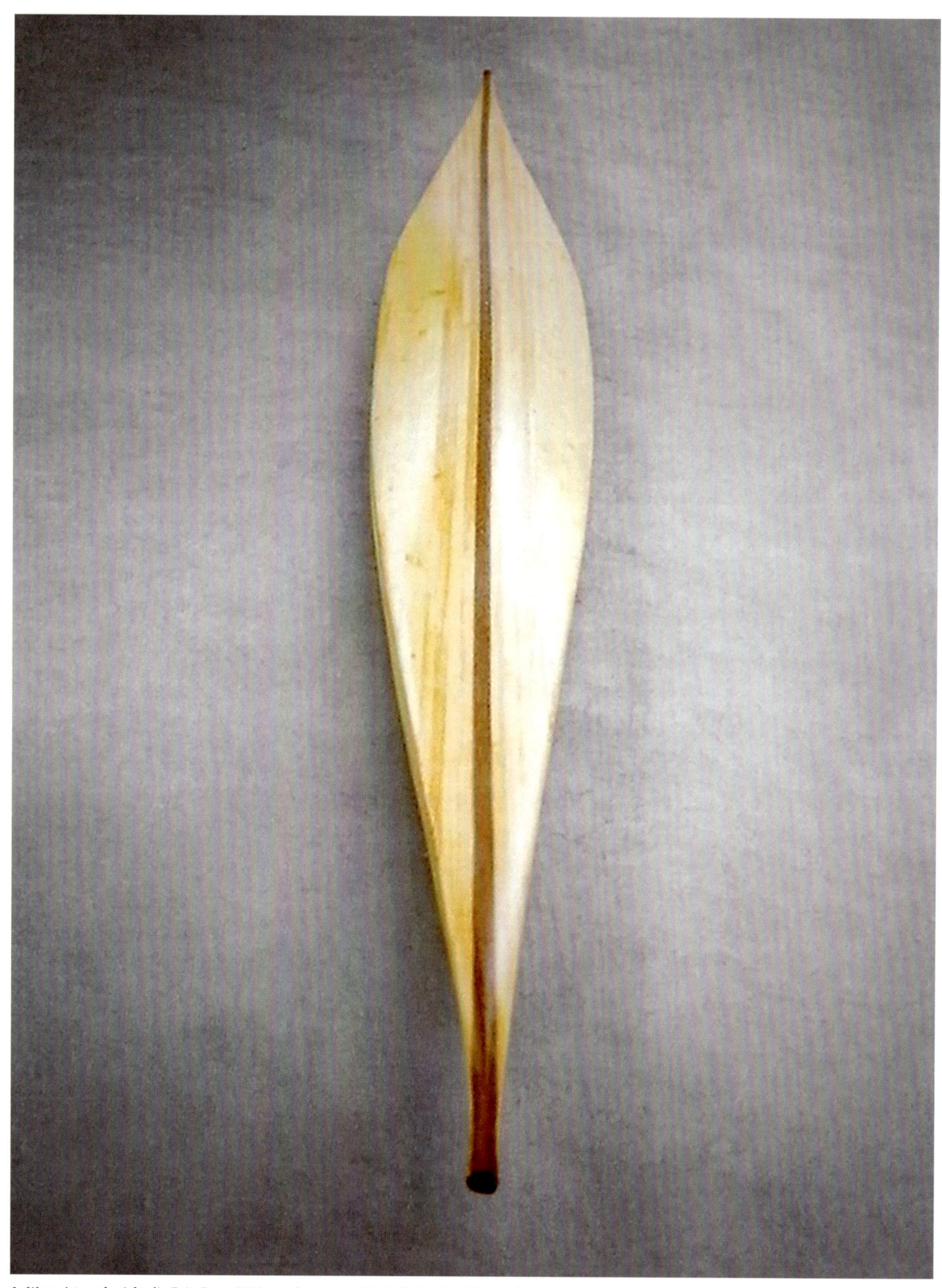

1 *Wann ist noch nicht die Zeit: Boot*, 2004, wood, resin, gold leaf, 29.5 x 56 x 521 cm; Sender Collection

WILDES, MYTHISCHES DENKEN DES BRICOLEURS

Zu Robert Elfgens Raumkunstwerken

Text von Lilian Haberer

Zu Beginn: Ein Kanu ist das einzige Objekt im leeren Ausstellungsraum. Schmal und mit langgezogenem Korpus durchschneidet es die zentrale Türflucht des Ausstellungsraums im Mitteltrakt der barocken, schlossähnlichen Reichsabtei Kornelimünster in Aachen. Seine Oberfläche wurde mit weißer Farbe behandelt und ein Teil der Öffnung mit purpurfarbenem Stoff bespannt, der andere Teil mit dunklen, gegeneinander aufgeschichteten Platten bedeckt. Zwischen Fundstück und Artefakt, gleichsam gestrandet, aber auch zum Aufbruch bereit, bleibt das Boot ein Fremdkörper im Raum, dennoch fügt es sich mit seiner axialen Ausrichtung in seine Fluchten ein (Abb. 2). Als Mittel der Fortbewegung, der Erkundung und Reise, ist es den Betrachtenden hingegen vertraut. Trotz der künstlerischen Eingriffe und Veränderungen insbesondere der herrschaftlich wie klerikal konnotierten Farbigkeit, die diesem Objekt einen erratischen Charakter verleihen, bleibt das Kanu ein Readymade. So stellen sich unmittelbare Assoziationen wie das Überwinden von Distanzen, die

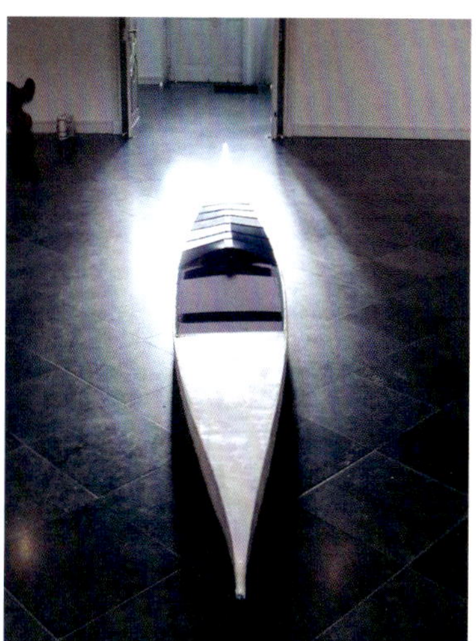

2 *Boot*, 2008, plastic combs, epoxy resin, wood, fabric, wax, approx. 30 × 55 × 530 cm; Private collection, Cologne

WILD, MYTHIC THOUGHT OF A BRICOLEUR

On Robert Elfgen's Spatial Works of Art

Text by Lilian Haberer

At the beginning: A canoe is the sole object in an otherwise empty exhibition space. With its narrow, elongated body, it transects the central door alignment of the exhibition space in the middle section of the Baroque, palace-like Reichsabtei Kornelimünster in Aachen. Its surface has been treated with white paint; purple cloth is stretched across one part of the opening, and dark, perpendicularly stacked panels cover the other. Oscillating between found object and artifact, as if it were stranded but also ready for departure, the boat remains a foreign object in the space even as it aligns itself harmoniously with its axial orientation (illus. 2). Yet it is familiar to its viewers as a means of locomotion, travel, and exploration. In spite of the artistic interventions and alterations — in particular, the coloration with its stately and clerical connotations — which imbue this object with a solitary character, the canoe remains a readymade. It gives rise to direct associations such as overcoming distances, touring by water, embarking on an expedition into unfamiliar territory.

1

Tour zu Wasser und die Expedition in unbekanntes Terrain ein.

Robert Elfgen hatte bereits zuvor ein elegant geschwungenes, glattgeschliffenes Holzobjekt in Form eines Kanus ausgestellt, in der Neuen Bügelei Wuppertal 2003 und ein Jahr später auf der Rheinschau in Köln. Bei letzterer hat er in Blattgold und Bleistift ein konzentrisches Kreismotiv auf den Korpus aufgebracht. Die Form sich ausbreitender Kreise in dünner und kräftiger Linienkontur zeichnet sich in Elfgens Werk mehrfach ab: in seinen Assemblagen, Collagen (Abb. 3) und Bildwerken, aber auch als Bleistiftspur auf dem Akademieboden bei seiner Abschlussausstellung und als Blattgoldemblem auf der Karosserie einer Vespa in *Motorschaden im Oktober* (2004) (Abb. 4). Evoziert die den Blick irritierende, vielfache Kreisform eine Drehbewegung, ein Ausstrahlen oder Zusammenziehen, einem Kraftfeld in ständiger Veränderung gleich, so gehört das Boot, ähnlich wie ein alter Leichenwagen, den der Künstler mehrfach umbaute und ausstellte, ein Floß als Gemeinschaftsarbeit mit Kai Althoff, oder eine Vespa zu den oftmals wiederverwendeten Motiven des Unterwegsseins als Form der Erkundung. Dabei erfordert diese Entdeckungsfahrt bei Elfgen meist keinen großen Radius: Er thematisiert mit dem Umbau seiner Gefährte zudem die Umwidmung einer alltäglichen Nutzung sowie das Überwinden von

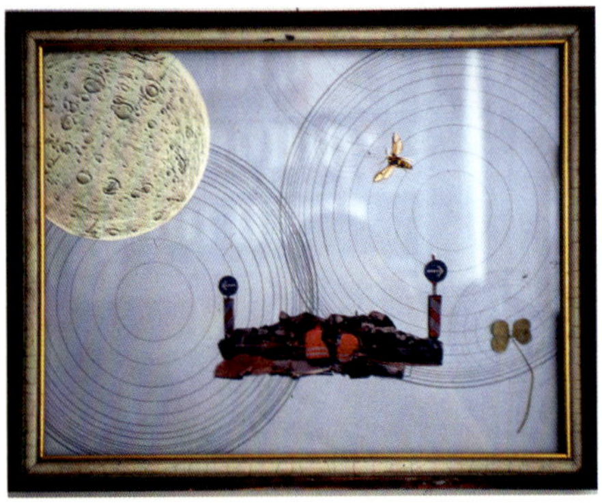

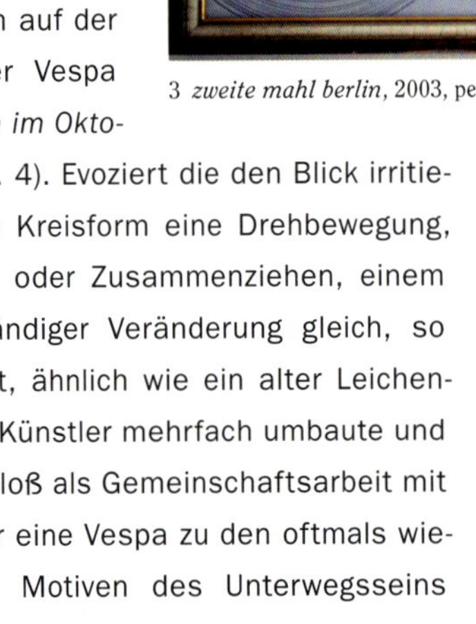

3 *zweite mahl berlin*, 2003, pencil, paper, MDF, 40 × 30 cm

Robert Elfgen had already exhibited an elegantly curved, smoothly polished wooden object in the form of a canoe in 2003 at the Neue Bügelei Wuppertal, and one year later at the Rheinschau in Cologne (illus. 2), where he attached a concentric motif in gold leaf and pencil to the body of the canoe. The concentric circle motif with thinly or thickly delineated contours is evident throughout Elfgen's oeuvre: in his assemblages, collages (illus. 3), and pictorial works, but also as a penciled trace on the floor of the Art Academy in his graduation exhibition and as a gold-leaf emblem on the bodywork of a Vespa in *Motorschaden im Oktober* ('Engine Trouble in October'), both from 2004 (illus. 4). If the visually irritating multiple circles evoke a rotation, radiation, or contraction suggestive of a constantly changing energy field, then the boat — similarly to the old hearse that the artist remodeled and exhibited several times, a raft in collaboration with Kai Althoff, or the Vespa — is one of the motifs of transit Elfgen uses as a form of exploration. For the most part, this voyage of discovery does not require a large radius. When Elfgen reconfigures his vehicles, he redirects their everyday usage and overcomes the distances of their predetermined route: his video *Schutzmann* ('Constable') (2003), for example, which was shown in his first solo exhibition *Raumtaucher* ('Space Diver', 2003) (illus. 5) at the Simultanhalle in Cologne, features a figure

Distanzen einer vorgegebenen Strecke – etwa in seinem Video *Schutzmann* (2003) mit einer Figur, die im Boot den Rhein hinunter geschickt wird, das der Künstler anlässlich seiner ersten Einzelausstellung *Raumtaucher* (Abb. 5) in der Simultanhalle in Köln 2003 zeigte. So spielt die imaginäre Seite dieses Sich-Fortbewegens eine zentrale Rolle, da Robert Elfgens Fahrzeuge und schiffbare Objekte aufgrund ausgebauter Motoren, fehlender Paddel oder lackierter Bodenarbeiten – als Sockelzonen angelegt und Öllachen gleich– arretiert scheinen. Als Objets trouvés beflügeln sie ein imaginatives Umherschweifen und weniger das Sujet des Reisens

sent down the Rhine in a boat. The imaginary aspect of movement plays an essential role as Robert Elfgen's vehicles and navigation objects, with their removed engines, missing paddles, or enameled floor works, are set up as pedestal zones that resemble oil spills and seem to be locked in place. As objets trouvés, they spark the imagination more than they serve as the subject of journeying in itself, which has undergone many changes since the Middle Ages, from pilgrims and the conquerors of early modern times to travel writers on the move, all of whom pursued a goal that does not seem to apply to Elfgen's objects. This aimless wandering could be termed a

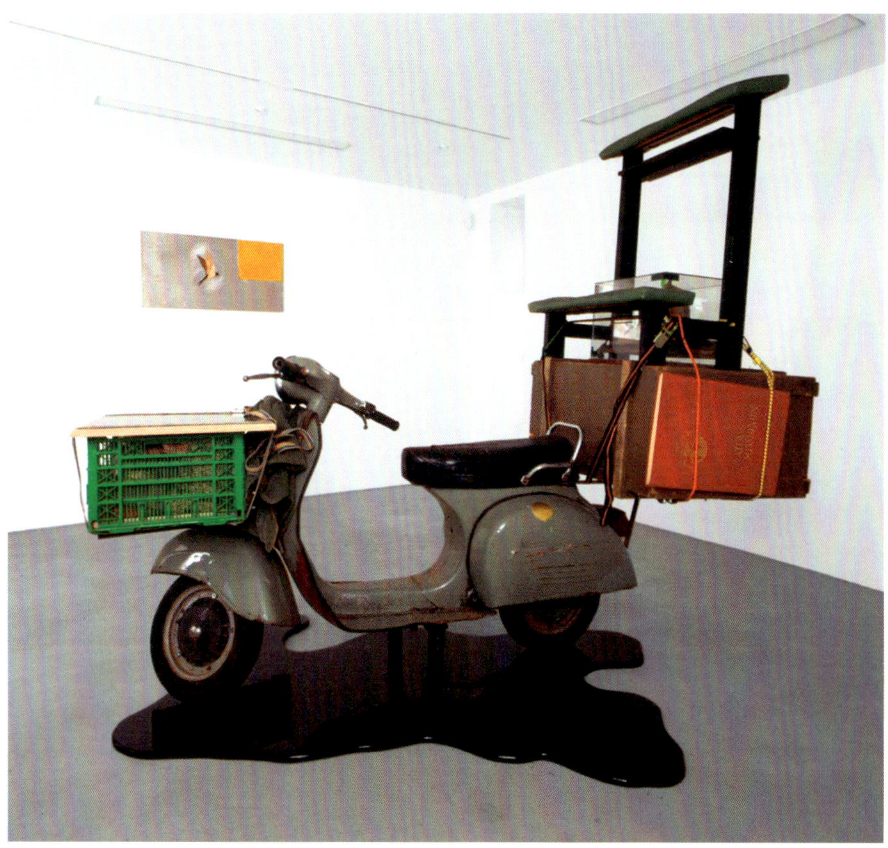

4 *Motorschaden im Oktober*, 2004, sculpture and painting on aluminium, dimensions variable; Goetz Collection

per se, welches seit dem Mittelalter von den Pilgern, den neuzeitlichen Eroberern bis hin zu den umherschweifenden Reiseschriftstellern vielen Wandlungen unterlag, aber vor allem ein Ziel verfolgte, das bei Elfgens Objekten hingegen nicht greifbar scheint.

Dieses nicht ausgerichtete Schweifen ließe sich vielmehr mit einer „nicht vorgezeichneten Bewegung" umschreiben: einer Aktivität, die Abweichungen, Aus- und Irrwege nicht auslässt. Denn diese sind aus der Perspektive des Bricoleurs, wie Claude Lévi-Strauss ihn definierte, näherliegend, da er sich nicht das wissenschaftliche, sondern ein mythopoetisches Denken zueigen macht.[1] Lévi-Strauss unternimmt die Exegese des Bricoleur-Begriffs, der auf die ihm zur Verfügung stehenden, begrenzten wie heterogenen Materialien im Kontrast zum naturwissenschaftlichen Forschen als zweierlei Aspekte wissenschaftlicher Erkenntnis zurückgreift. Thomas W. Kuhn hatte Elfgens Arbeiten bereits mit dem signifikanten Bricolage-Verfahren in Verbindung gebracht, allerdings sieht er in dieser eigenständigen kulturellen Technik neben einer „philosophischen", „prozessual-ritualistischen", eine „hermetische" Produktionspraxis[2] gegeben, die sicherlich anhand einer Reihe von ihm genannter künstlerischer Positionen der Gegenwart nachvollziehbar ist, für Robert Elfgens Werke jedoch nicht den Kern trifft. Insbesondere scheint die mitunter an narratologische Prozedere erinnernde Geschlossenheit seiner frühen Rauminstallationen, und die Auseinandersetzung mit Formen des Abwesenden, Inkommensurablen hier mit einer Hermetik verwechselt zu werden, die sich weder ästhetisch noch thematisch

'non-presaged movement', an activity that does not preclude deviations, escapes, or labyrinths. For these are more plausible from the perspective of the bricoleur who, as defined by Claude Lévi-Strauss, internalizes not a scientific but a mythopoetic mode of thought.[1] Lévi-Strauss undertakes an exegesis of the concept of the bricoleur, who accesses the limited, heterogeneous materials available to him in contrast to the investigations of the natural sciences, thus defining two different aspects of scientific knowledge. Thomas W. Kuhn had already recognized a connection between Elfgen's works and the significant bricolage procedure; however, alongside a 'philosophical' and 'processual-ritualistic' aspect, he also sees a 'hermetic' production practice[2] in this independent cultural technique that is without a doubt applicable to the series of contemporary artistic positions he cites, but does not get to the heart of Elfgen's oeuvre. In particular, the closed form of his early spatial installations, occasionally reminiscent of narratological procedure, and their investigation of forms of absence and incommensurability seem to be confused here with a hermeticism that is not evident in either aesthetic or thematic terms. In contrast, in Robert Elfgen's work, multiple open, aesthetic modes of thoughts and their reorganizations and various thematic strands overlap one other, as Lévi-Strauss expressed it: 'the elements are collected or retained on the principle that 'they may always come in handy'[3], hence they certainly cannot be considered hermetic. This is already clear in his 2005 stipendiary exhibition at the

abzeichnet. Vielmehr sind es bei Robert Elfgen vielfach offene ästhetische Ordnungen und Neuordnungen sowie verschiedene thematische Stränge, die sich überlagern, wie Lévi-Strauss es formulierte, als „gesammelte oder reorganisierte Botschaften"[3], die gerade nicht hermetisch aufzufassen sind. Dies zeichnet sich bereits in seiner Stipendiatenausstellung im Bonner Kunstverein 2005 ab, bei welcher der Künstler Collagen, Bodenarbeiten und Installationen zu lose kombinierten, motivischen Sequenzen und einem großen situativen Raumkunstwerk zusammenfügte.

Bonner Kunstverein, in which the artist combined collages, floor works, and installations into loosely joined, motific sequences and a large, site-specific spatial work of art.

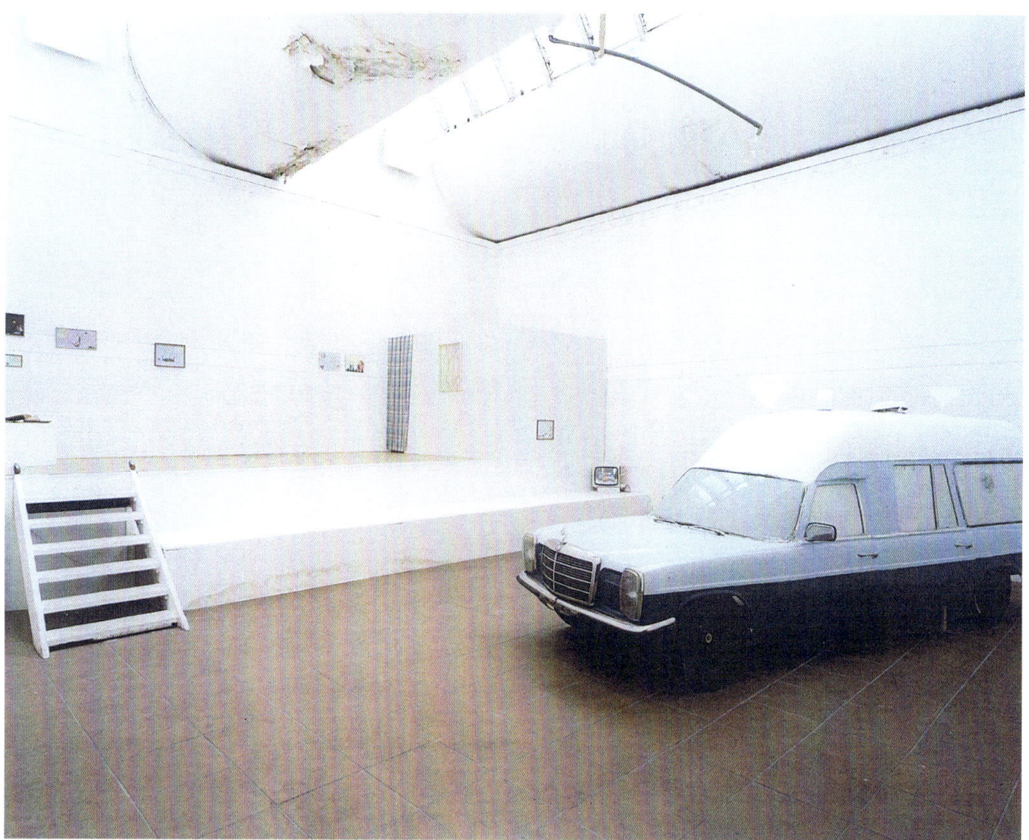

5 *Raumtaucher*, 2003, installation view Simultanhalle, Cologne

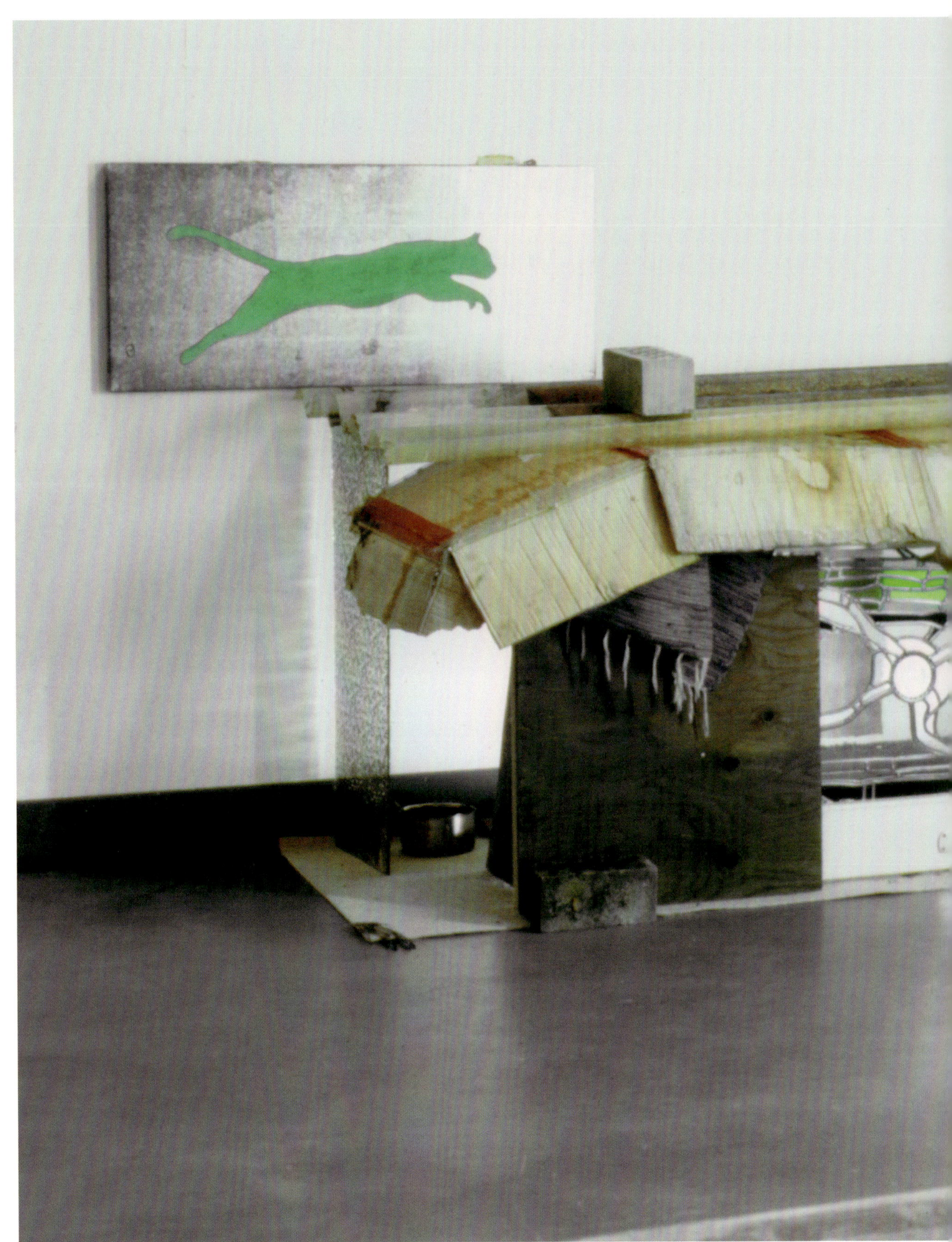

6 *Bude 1*, 2005, installation composed of several sculptures and collages, mixed media, dimensions variable, Bonner Kunstverein; Rubell Family Collection

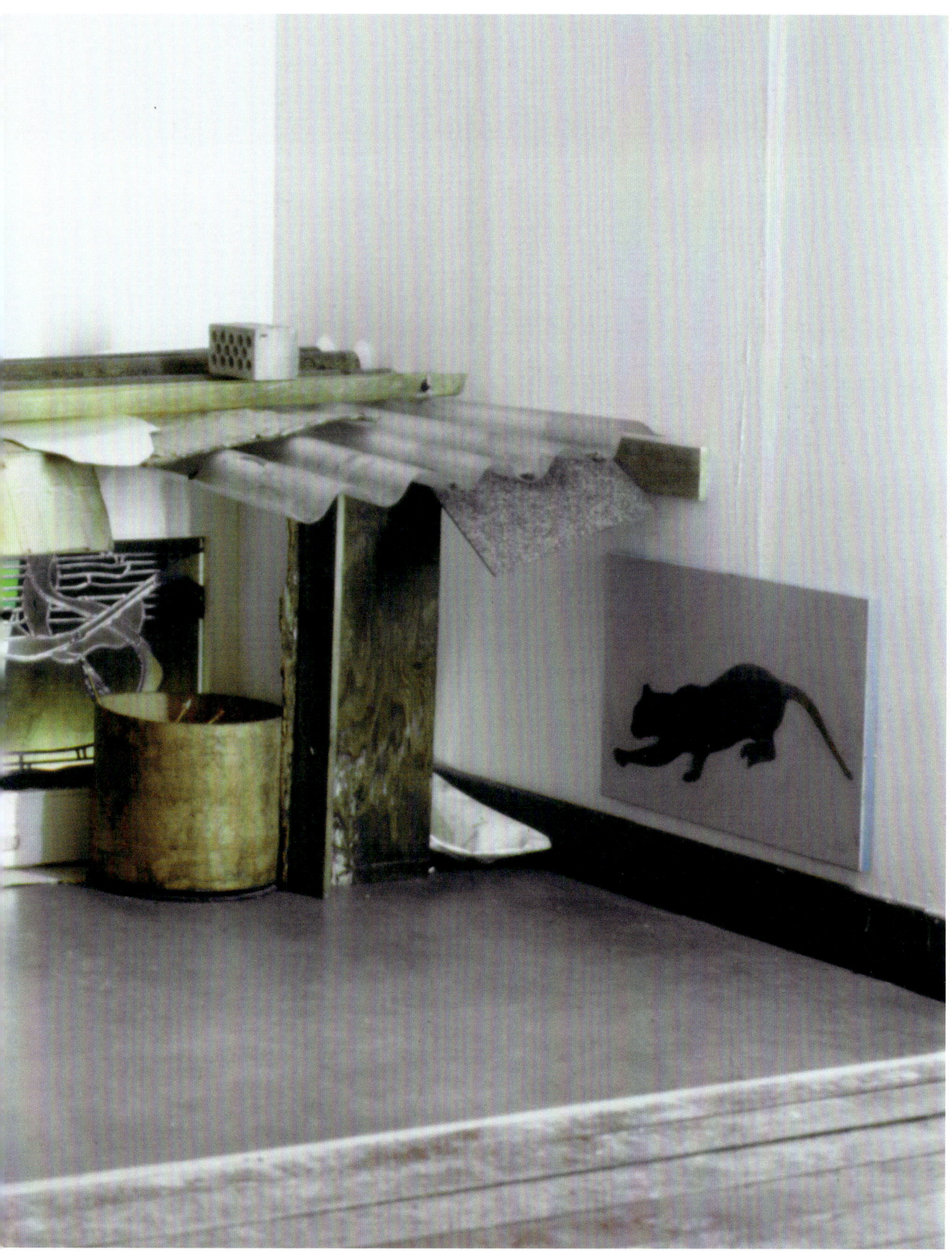

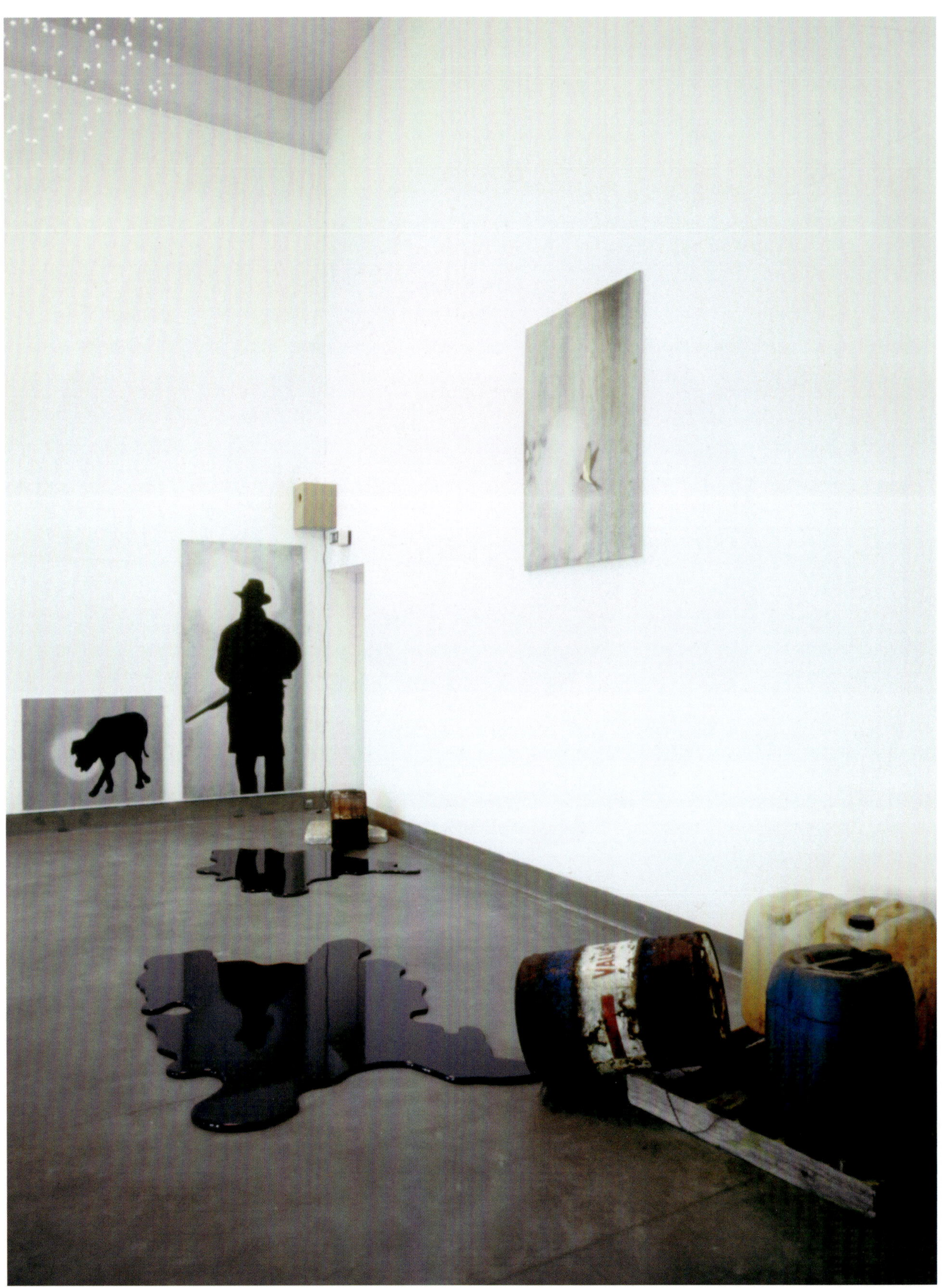

7 *1+1=3 Elfgen Technik*, 2005, installation view Bonner Kunstverein

„GLAUB ICH, WAS ZU WISSEN? WEISS ICH WAS ZU GLAUBEN?"

Ein mobiler Stand, wie er auf Veranstaltungen und Messen zu sehen ist, bildet das Entree der Ausstellung Robert Elfgens im Kunstverein (Abb. 8). Die Tafel oberhalb der Theke des Werkzeugherstellers mit Plakaten von Konstruktionszeichnungen und einem farbig unterlegten Werbeslogan ist ein Blickfang innerhalb der reduzierten Kunstvereinsarchitektur von Haus Rucker & Co. Doch der Stand ist menschenleer und dies scheint sich in dem angrenzenden, riesigen Ausstellungsraum fortzusetzen, der nur zu den Wänden und Ecken hin bespielt ist: An der linken Wand vom Eingang ist eine aus Brettern gezimmerte, leere Bühne zu sehen, die einzig von zwei langen Neonröhren erhellt wird (Abb. 9). Oberhalb an der Wand befindet sich ein Ensemble aus stilisierten schwarzen Wolkenformen und einer beigen, als Mond angedeuteten Lampe. Flankiert wird das Plateau von zwei provisorisch zusammengefügten Unterständen an den Raumecken, unter anderem aus Holzplatten, Stoff, Pappkartons, Glas, Fundstücken und Teppich

"DO I BELIEVE MYSELF TO KNOW SOMETHING? DO I KNOW MYSELF TO BELIEVE SOMETHING?"

A mobile stand of the kind seen at program events and trade fairs is erected at the entrance to Robert Elfgen's exhibition at the Bonner Kunstverein (illus. 8). The panel above the counter of the tool manufacturer, with posters featuring construction drawings and an advertising slogan highlighted in color, is an eye-catcher within the reduced Kunstverein architecture by Haus Rucker & Co. But the stand is deserted, and this emptiness seems to continue into the gigantic adjoining exhibition space, which only contains objects along the walls and in the corners. Beside the left wall of the entrance is an empty, imperceptibly raised stage made of wooden boards and illuminated only by two long neon tubes (illus. 9). Up on the wall is an ensemble of stylized black nebular forms and a beige lamp resembling a moon. The stage is flanked by two shelters provisionally assembled out of wooden panels, cloth, cardboard boxes, glass, found objects, and carpets, and serves as a refuge for cats, as is indicated by the scattered wall works made of wooden inlays on a metallic

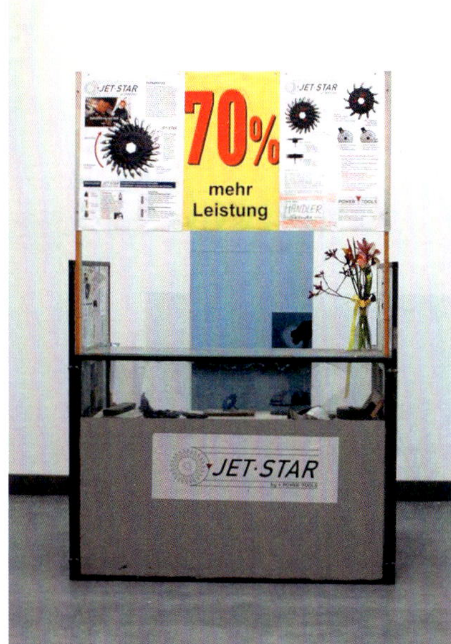

8 *1+1=3 Elfgen Technik*, 2005, Bonner Kunstverein

gefertigt, welche einen Unterschlupf für Katzen bieten, wie die verstreuten Wandarbeiten aus Intarsien und Metallgrund als farbig gefasste Umrisslinien der Tiere andeuten (Abb. 6). An weiteren Wänden gesellen sich, frei angeordnet, diverse Vogelarten und ein Totenkopf hinzu (Abb. 10–11). Verschiedenartige Ölfässer und Tanks, deren ausgelaufene Inhalte sich als spiegelnde, schwarz lackierte Holzflecken auf dem Boden ausbreiten, säumen die Blickachse bis zur Stirnwand, an der als figuratives Einsprengsel die Intarsienarbeiten eines Jägers als Rückenfigur mit seinem Hund sichtbar werden (Abb. 7). Der Raum ist bis auf die Lichtbänder unterhalb der Decke und ein Oberlicht der Architektur nur von den Lichtquellen der Rauminstallation erleuchtet. So liegen die Katzenbuden im Dämmerlicht und evozieren eine nächtliche Hinterhofszene, welche

base displaying colored contours of the animals (illus. 6). Joining in free arrangement on further walls are various species of birds along with a skull (illus. 10–11). Miscellaneous oil drums and tanks whose leaked contents spread across the floor as reflective black-enameled patches of wood fringe the visual axis all the way to the end wall, where wood-inlay works featuring the rear-view figure of a hunter and his dog appear as a figurative sprinkling (illus. 7). Except for the bands of light beneath the ceiling and a skylight in the architecture, the space is illuminated only by the light sources of the installation itself; thus, the cat shelters are only faintly lit and summon up a nocturnal, back-courtyard scene that is supported by the dark silhouettes of the animals and other motifs.

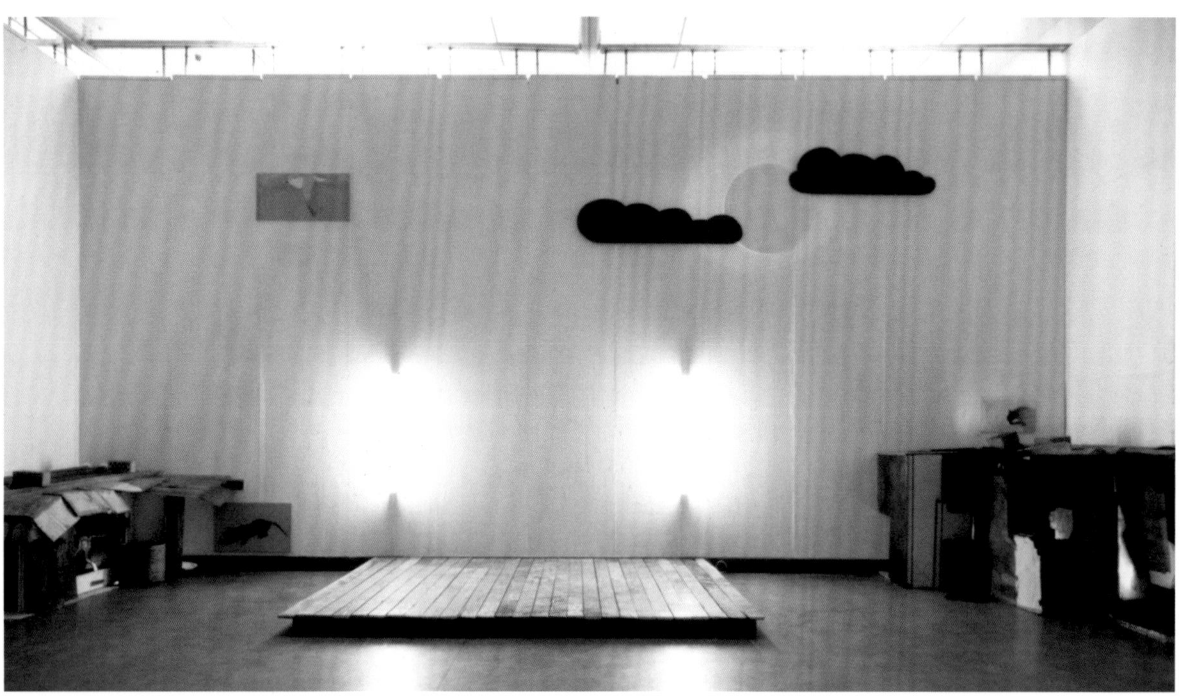

9 *1+1=3 Elfgen Technik*, 2005, installation view Bonner Kunstverein

von den dunkel gehaltenen Schattenrissen der Tiere und Motive unterstützt wird.

Konterkariert die atmosphärische Szenerie des hinteren Raumes den nüchternen Zugang, so verstärkt sich dieser Eindruck mit dem bündigen wie prägnanten Ausstellungstitel *1 + 1 = 3 Elfgen Technik*. Offenbar überlagern sich in der Folge und Gestaltung der Räume verschiedene, aus plastischen Einzelsequenzen zusammengefügte Stränge: zum einen das biographisch motivierte Erinnerungsbild in der Nähe der Werkstatt seines Vaters, bei dem ein im Katalog ebenfalls abgebildeter Hinterhof als genius loci für die Rauminstallation fungiert, auf dem eine alte Frau herrenlosen Katzen ein Obdach bot; zum anderen der auf genauem Tier- und Naturstudium beruhende Forschergeist, welcher sich in den kauernden und lauernden Bewegungen der Tiersilhouetten niederschlägt.

Hinzu kommt die im Titel angedeutete Tätigkeit von Elfgens Vater als Erfinder und Tüftler, die ihren Wiederhall in den Erkundungen lebensweltlicher Zusammenhänge seiner eigenen künstlerischen Produktion findet. In Elfgens Wandarbeiten zeigt sich, was bereits bei Leonardo da Vinci als Kern für die Malerei formuliert wurde: dass der Grund des künstlerischen Ingeniums die Ausdeutung und das

If the atmospheric scenery of the back room contrasts with the cool, reduced design of the stand at the entrance, this impression is enhanced by the exhibition's succinct and striking title, *1 + 1 = 3 Elfgen Technik*. Apparently overlapping in the sequence and design of the spaces are various strands assembled out of individual plastic sequences: on the one hand, the biographically motivated, commemorative image in the proximity of his father's workshop, in which a back courtyard, likewise reproduced in the catalogue with an old woman offering refuge to stray cats, functions as a genius loci for the spatial installation; on the other hand, a spirit of research based on a precise study of nature and animals, which finds expression in the crouching and lurking movements of the silhouetted animals. In addition, the activities of Elfgen's father as inventor

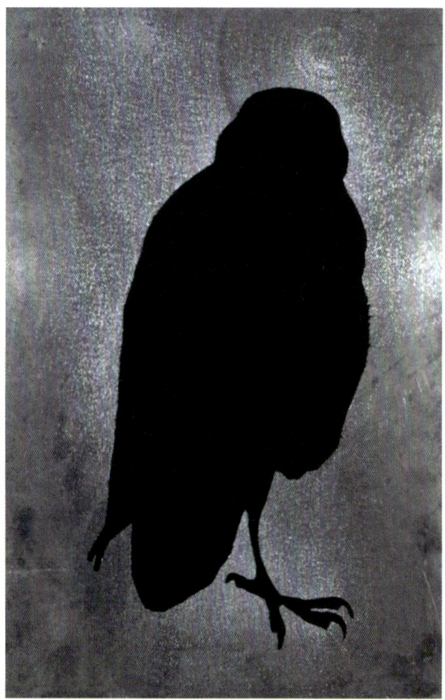

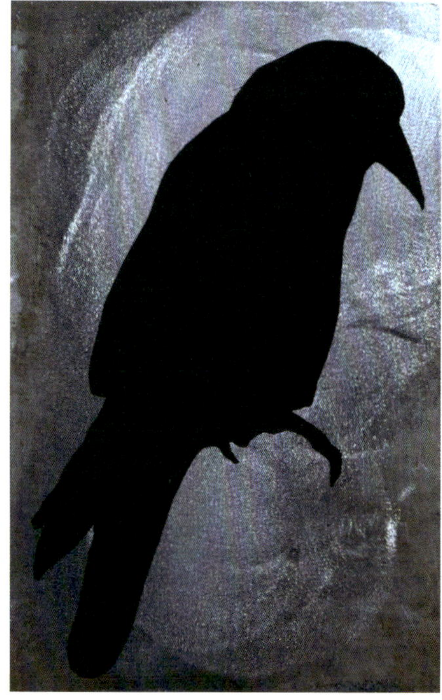

10 *Krähe: Labe*, 2005, fabric on aluminium, 47 × 30 cm   11 *Krähe: Norte*, 2005, fabric on aluminium, 44.5 × 29 cm

Studium der Natur selbst sei.[5] Dabei aktivieren seine sich an bildnerisch-malerischen Fragen abarbeitenden Intarsiendarstellungen und Collagen eine lebendige Erinnerungsfunktion, insofern sie sowohl die Ursprungsmythen von Malerei und Skulptur als Schattenrisse aufrufen als auch ihre phantasmatischen Vorstellungsbilder thematisieren, die darin zeitenthoben Vergängliches der Natur aufheben.[6]

Die bildhafte und anschauliche Erinnerung des Ortes (dasjenige, was genius loci meint) ist es, die bei Robert Elfgens Raumkunstwerken mit dem Erkennen und Erforschen der Natur zusammenkommt. Dies wird ebenso in seinen großformatigen Bildtafeln – jeweils an drei Seiten

and tinkerer alluded to in the title are echoed in the son's explorations of environmental interconnections in his own artistic production. Elfgen's wall works offer a demonstration of that which Leonardo da Vinci already formulated as the essence of painting — namely that the basis for artistic creativity lies in the study and interpretation of nature itself.[5] Elfgen's intarsia representations and collages investigate visual and painterly issues and activate a living function of memory, inasmuch as they thematize not only the myths about the origin of painting and sculpture, but also their phantasmal, imaginative images which, unconstrained by temporal succession, preserve what is ephemeral in nature.[6]

In Robert Elfgen's spatial works of art, the pictorial and illustrative remembrance of the site (that which is meant by genius loci) merges with a cognition and investigation of nature. This likewise comes to light in his large-format picture panels, which are arranged on three sides of the space like a stage, *Norden–Westen–Süden–Osten* ('Germany 2005. North–West–South–East') and *Waldlichtung im Nebel* ('Forest Glade in Fog') from 2005, in which the luminous reflections of the shiny support material

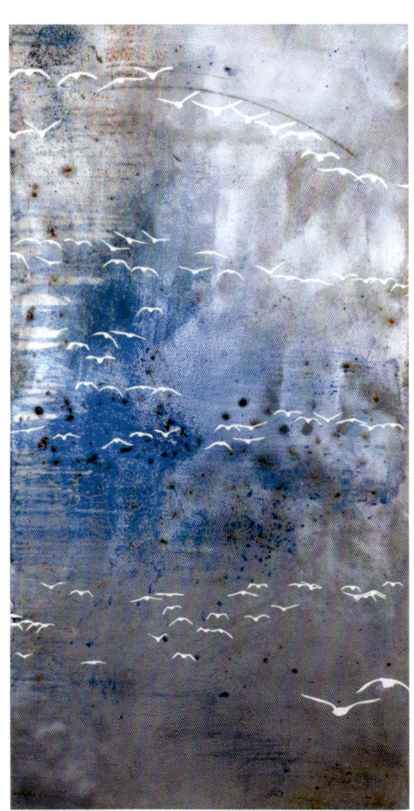

12 *Deutschland 2005. Norden–Westen–Süden–Osten,* 2005, fabric, acrylic on aluminium

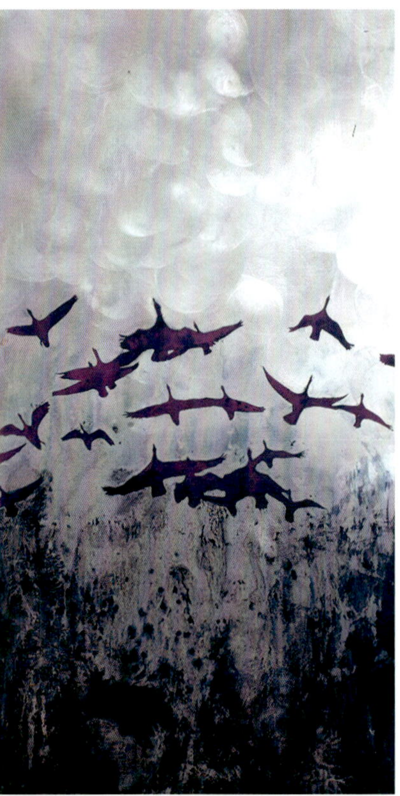

13 *Deutschland 2005. Norden–Westen–Süden–Osten,* 2005, fabric, acrylic on aluminium

im Raum bühnenhaft angeordnet und mit einer zentralen, selbstgebauten Neonlichtquelle ausgestattet – in *Deutschland 2005. Norden – Westen – Süden – Osten* und *Waldlichtung im Nebel* von 2005 sichtbar, bei denen die Lichtreflexionen des glänzenden Trägermaterials Vogelschwärme und Naturschauspiele enthüllen (Abb. 14).

„Glaub ich, was zu wissen? Weiß ich was zu glauben?" – dieser Chiasmus auf den letzten Seiten des Kunstvereinskatalogs von Robert Elfgen, mit der Intarsienarbeit eines in die Höhe blickenden, jungen Mannes, und einer Fotografie seines Vaters an der Werkbank, verzahnt die Fragen nach Wissen und Erkenntnis, nach Annahme und

reveal flocks of birds and spectacles of nature (illus. 14).

'Do I believe myself to know something? Do I know myself to believe something?' — this chiasmus on the final pages of Robert Elfgen's Kunstverein catalogue with the intarsia work of a young man gazing upwards and a photograph of his father at the workshop bench interweaves the issues of knowledge and cognition, supposition and intuition, such that the open formulation of these questions render any avowal and certainty doubtful. In the artistic search, the investigation of objects and nature is inseparably linked to the questioning subject and his/her thought, along

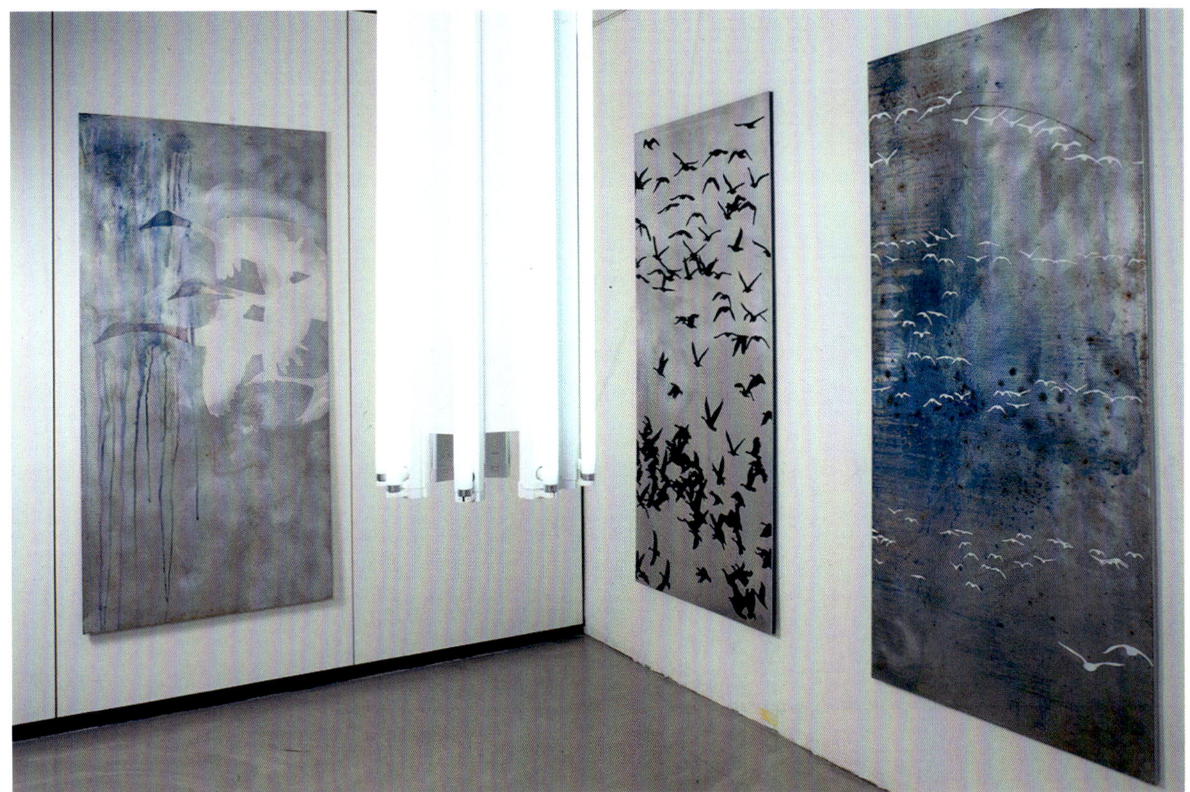

14 *Deutschland 2005. Norden – Westen – Süden – Osten*, 2005, four paintings and lamp, fabric, acrylic on aluminium, dimensions variable; Collection Pervan Willocx, Frankfurt/Ghent

Ahnung miteinander, so dass jedwede Bekenntnis und Gewissheit durch die formulierte Offenheit dieser Fragen in Zweifel gezogen wird. Dergestalt ist in der künstlerischen Suche die Erforschung der Dinge und der Natur untrennbar mit dem fragenden Subjekt und seinem Denken verbunden, und dasjenige, was es aus diesen Erkenntnissen heraus destilliert. So lassen sich die Ebenen der wissenschaftlichen Erkenntnis und des mythischen Denkens, die Lévi-Strauss beim Bricoleur miteinander in Verbindung gebracht hatte und die beide in der Ordnung von Ereignissen bestehen[7], sich insofern verschränken, als die künstlerische Produktion Mittlerfunktion einnimmt: „Wenn das mythische Denken auf spekulativem Gebiet nicht ohne Analogien zur Bastelei auf praktischem Gebiet ist und wenn die künstlerische Schöpfung in der Mitte zwischen diesen beiden Formen der Tätigkeit einerseits und der Wissenschaft andererseits liegt, so bestehen zwischen Spiel und Ritus Beziehungen gleicher Art"[8]. Die elfgensche Produktionsästhetik verbindet somit das frei schweifende, von eigenmythischen Vorstellungsbildern geprägte Denken mit einer bildgewordenen Raumkunst, die sich aus heterogenem Material, Assemblagen, Installationen, Wand- und Bodenarbeiten, Fundstücken und Readymades zusammenfügt.

with that which he/she distills out of these discoveries. Thus, the levels of scientific knowledge and mythic thought that Lévi-Strauss linked together in the concept of the bricoleur and both of which exist in the order of events[7] may be interwoven to the extent that artistic production takes on a mediatory function: 'We have seen that there are analogies between mythical thought on the theoretical, and 'bricolage' on the practical plane and that artistic creation lies mid-way between science and these two forms of activity. There are relations of the same type between games and rites'[8]. Elfgen's production aesthetic thus combines freely roaming thought marked by his own mythic images with a pictorially formulated spatial art which arises out of heterogeneous material, assemblages, installations, wall and floor works, found objects, and readymades.

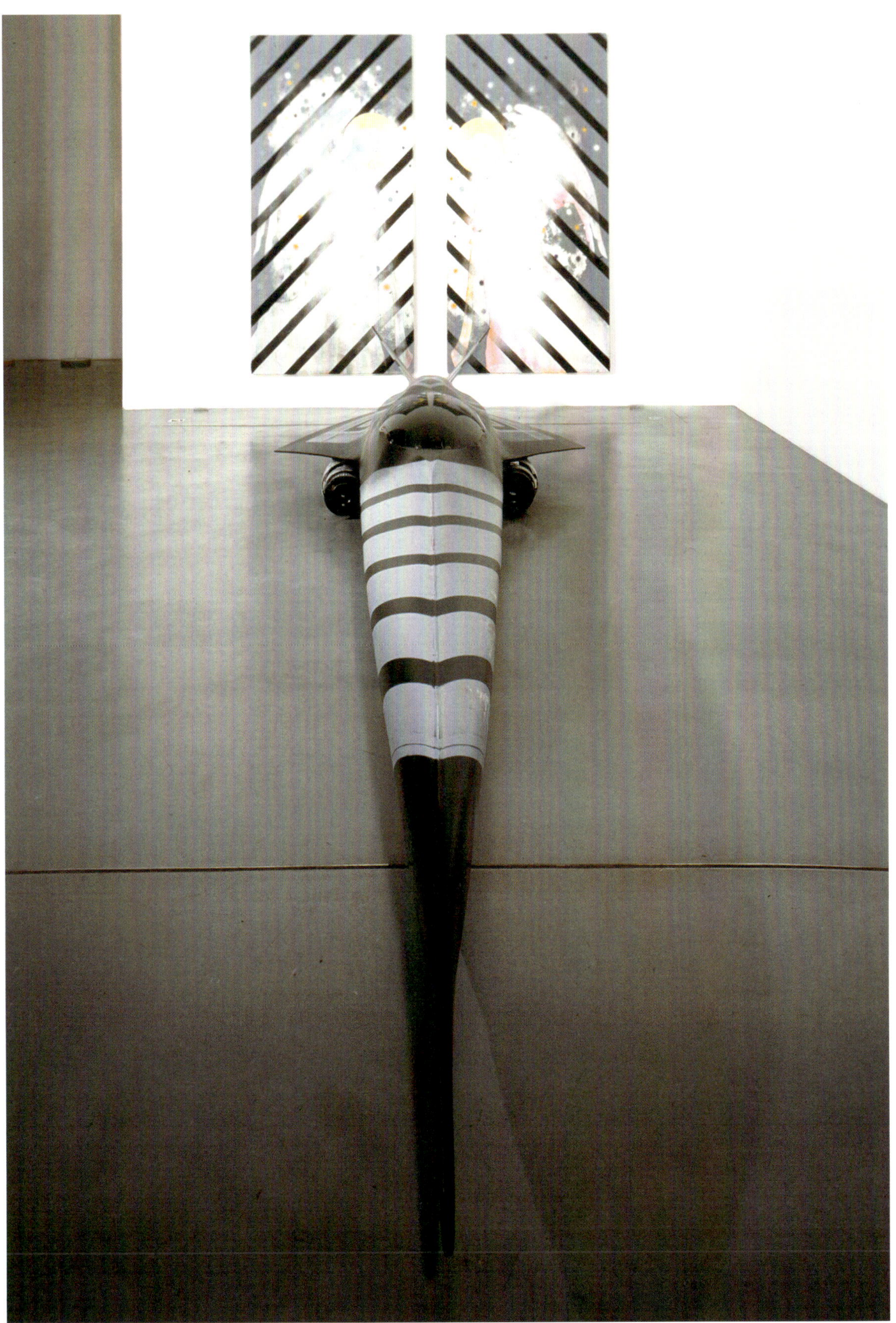

Zweieck, 2005, two paintings: fabric, car finish on aluminium, each 200 × 100 cm, rocket: polyester, polystyrene, wood, lacquer, plaster, 60 × 150 × 550 cm;
Zabludowicz Collection

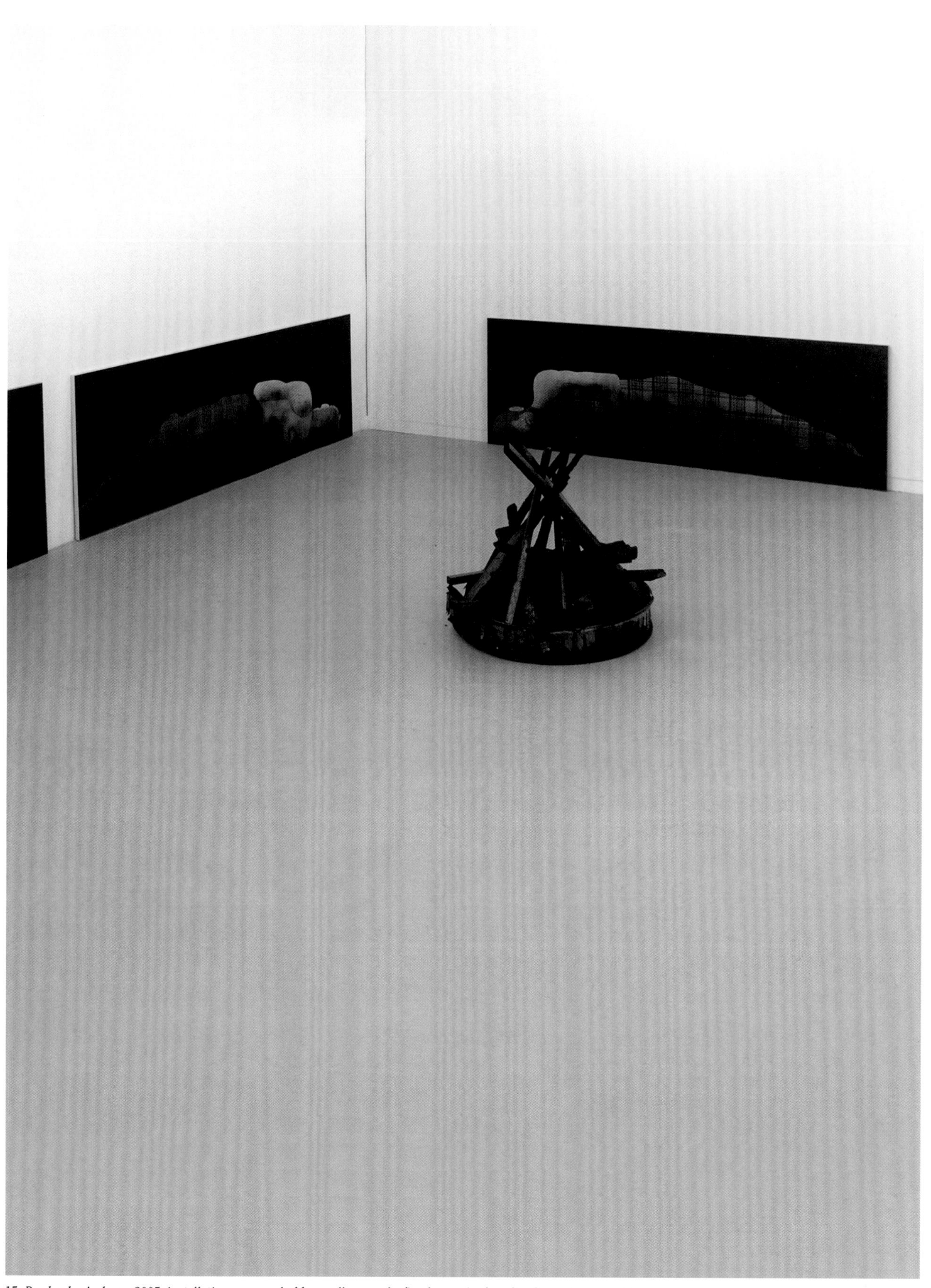

15 *Bruder des Anderen*, 2005, installation composed of four collages and a fireplace, mixed media, dimensions variable, installation view Fuhrwerkswaage, Cologne; Rubell Family Collection

Neben den großformatigen Naturansichten entstanden in den Jahren 2005 und 2006 Rauminstallationen mit ganzfigurigen Personendarstellungen,

In addition to the large-format views of nature, the years 2005 and 2006 saw the creation of spatial installations with whole-figure representations

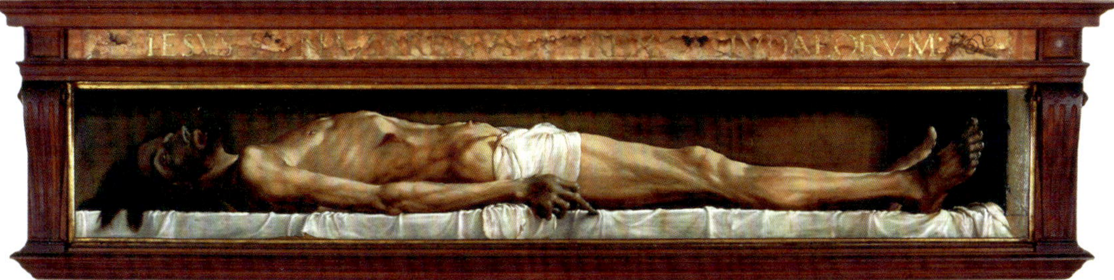

16 Hans Holbein (the Younger), *Der tote Christus im Grabe*, tempera on wood, 1521/22, 30.5 × 200 cm, Kunstmuseum Basel

die der Künstler oftmals nach erinnerten Ereignissen oder Szenen in Rauminstallationen vergegenwärtigte. Signifikant ist hierbei die geschlossene Struktur einer Gruppe von vier liegenden männlichen Schlafenden, in Decken oder Schlafsäcke gehüllt, den Betrachtenden zu- oder abgewandt als querformatige Tafeln, auf deren dunklem Bildgrund der MDF-Platten die Figuren als Intarsien mit Stoff realisiert sind (Abb. 18–21).[9] Sie sind um das Objekt einer erloschenen Feuerstelle angeordnet (Abb. 15). Neben der Lebensgröße sticht das Querformat mit ihrer Darstellung als Liegende ins Auge, da diese statt eines Portraits vor allem auf die Verfasstheit der Personen hinweisen. Seine Arbeit lässt an das Referenzwerk *Der tote Christus im Grabe* von Hans Holbein d. J. aus dem Kunstmuseum Basel (1521/22) denken: Dabei handelt es sich um die an frühneuzeitlicher Detailtreue und

of people whom the artist often envisioned in accordance with remembered events or scenes. What is significant here is the closed structure of a group of four recumbent, sleeping men covered in blankets or sleeping bags and turned towards or away from the viewer as horizontal panels upon which their figures are depicted in cloth intarsia on a dark MDF background (illus. 18–21).[9] They are arranged around the object of an extinguished fireplace (illus. 15). What is striking in addition to the life-sized forms is the horizontal format with the representation in a lying position, for instead of rendering a portrait, this alludes to the persons' physical state. Elfgen's work is reminiscent of *Der tote Christus im Grabe* ('The Body of the Dead Christ in the Tomb' 1521/22) in the collection of the Kunstmuseum Basel, whose Christ figure in the box of a shrine is inimitable

Realismus unnachahmliche Darstellung einer im Schreinkasten platzierten Christusfigur (Abb. 16). Elfgens Menschenbilder sind bis auf die schlafenden oder leblosen Gesichter hingegen nur schemenhaft ausgeführt und bleiben Brüder des Ungewissen.[10] Eben diesen Titel *Brüder Ungewiss* wählte der Künstler für vier großformatige Tafeln im Rahmen der gemeinsam konzipierten Abschlussausstellung der Cusanus-Werk-Stipendiaten *Lieber Friedrich* im Kasseler Kunstverein 2006 (Abb. 22). Dort platzierte er in einer Fensterlaibung vier männliche Rückenfiguren. Zwei lebensgroße, bärtige Wanderer mittleren Alters, auf ihren Stock gestützt, hat Elfgen desgleichen in Holzfurnier und Stoff auf MDF-Platte

in its early modern realism and attention to detail (illus. 16).

Elfgen's images of persons, on the other hand, except for the sleeping or lifeless faces, are only dimly executed and remain brothers of the uncertain.[10] *Brüder Ungewiss* ('Brothers Uncertain') is, in fact, the title the artist selected for the four large-format panels he showed in the jointly conceived concluding exhibition *Lieber Friedrich* ('Dear Friedrich') of the Cusanus-Werk stipendiaries at the Kasseler Kunstverein in 2006 (illus. 22), where he placed four male figures, viewed from the back, in a window embrasure. Elfgen likewise realized—in wood inlay and cloth on MDF board and metal ground—two life-sized,

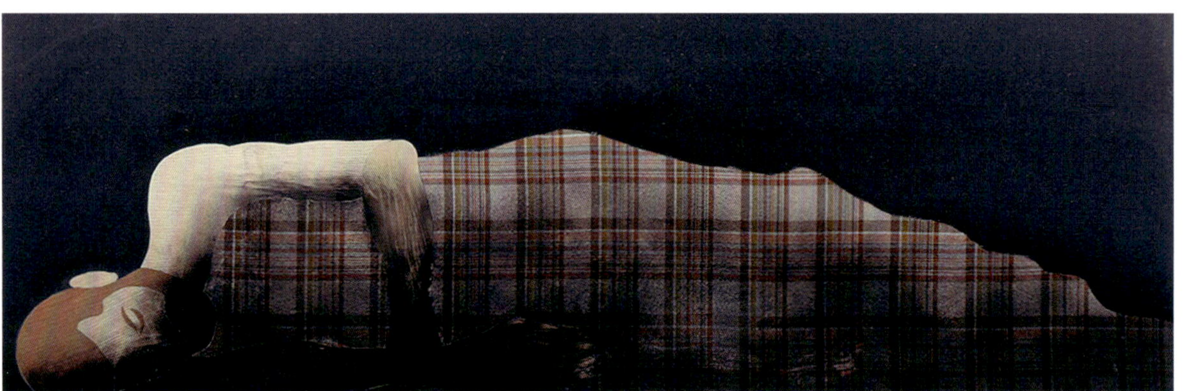

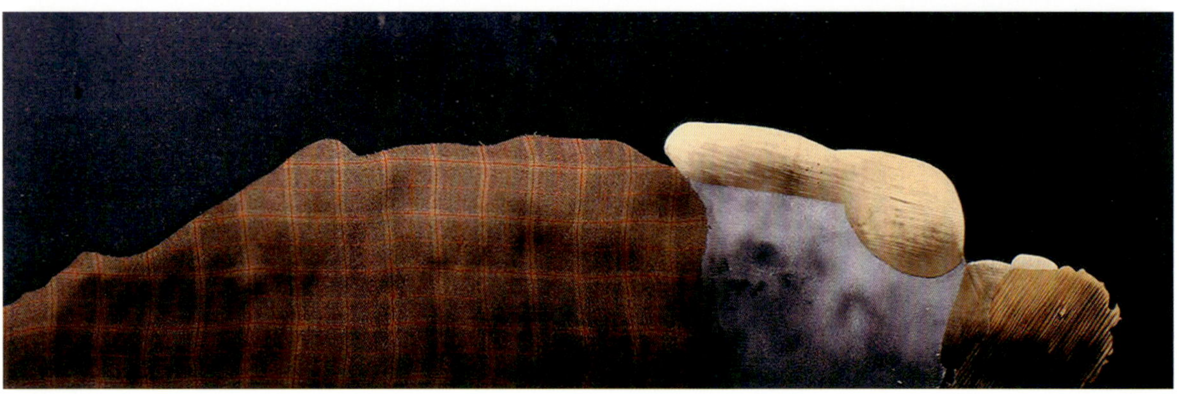

18 + 19 *Bruder des Anderen* (Detail), 2005, veneer, fabric, acrylic on MDF, 61.5 × 186 cm; Rubell Family Collection

und Metallgrund realisiert – sie öffnen sich wie Flügeltüren zum Fenster hin. Ihnen vorgeblendet sind, die Laibung waagerecht rechts und links verschließend, zwei Glasscheiben freistehend angebracht, auf denen zwei sitzende junge Männer mit Stöcken und Hüten platziert sind. Alle blicken – von den Betrachtern abgewandt – nach vorn aus dem Fenster, wie Rastende während einer großen Tour. Der Künstler hat hier erstmals Glas verwendet, um die Personen räumlich zu staffeln und als Identifikationsfiguren aus der Fläche heraustreten zu lassen: eine Technik, die er in weiteren Rauminstallationen aufgreift. Das romantische Sehnsuchtsmotiv – aufgrund der Referenz an Caspar David Friedrich als ein

bearded, middle-aged wanderers resting on their staffs; the two panels open like double-wing doors towards the window. In front of them, seemingly superimposed and closing off the embrasure vertically on the right and left, two freestanding glass panels are mounted that feature two seated young men with staffs and hats. All are turned away from the viewer and gaze out of the window, as if they were resting during a long excursion. The artist used glass for the first time here in order to stagger the persons spatially and to cause them to emerge from the surface as figures of identification — a technique that he takes up in further spatial installations. The motif of Romantic yearning in

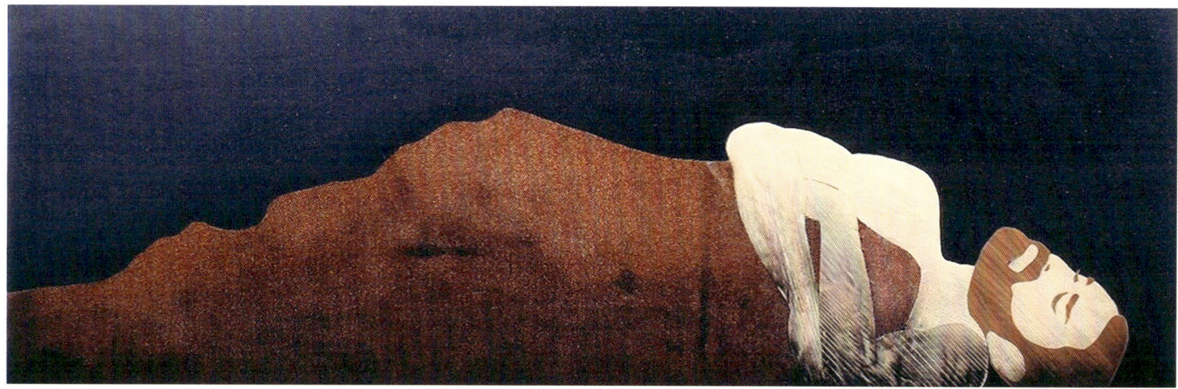

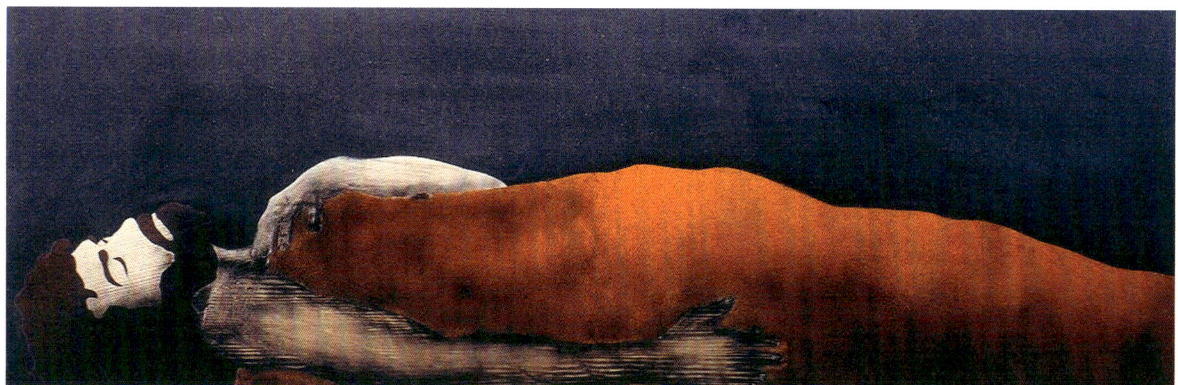

20 + 21 *Bruder des Anderen* (Detail), 2005, veneer, fabric, acrylic on MDF, 61.5 × 186 cm; Rubell Family Collection

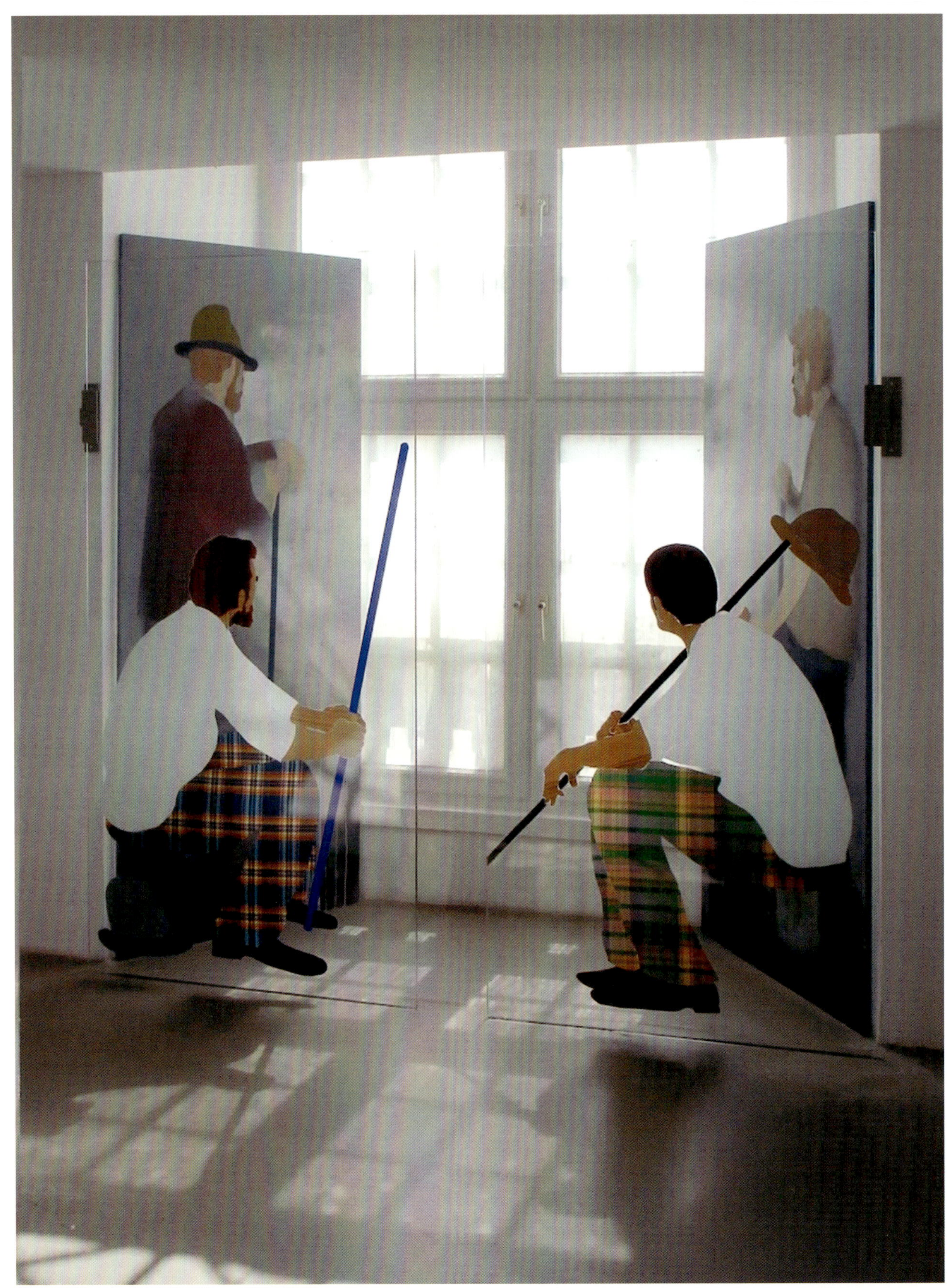

22 *Brüder Ungewiss*, 2006, four panels, fabric, veneer, acrylic on MDF and glass, 207 × 88 cm; 200 × 100 cm, installation view Kunstverein Kassel; Private collection, Cologne

Orientierungspunkt der Ausstellung gegeben— wird hier mit den hintereinander angeordneten Rückenfiguren aufgegriffen und lässt sich zudem im buchstäblichen Betrachterblick aus dem Fenster in die Ferne nachverfolgen. Anders als bei Friedrichs *Wanderer über dem Nebelmeer* (Abb. 23), der eine erhabene Landschaft überblickt, die sich ihm gleichsam zu Füßen ausbreitet, wagen die vier Personen einen Blick über die Grenze des Raumes hinaus in das Unbekannte.

Das Brudermotiv wird hier als offen angelegte Installation mit dem Schäfermotiv verquickt, denn die Wanderer mit den langen Stöcken sind ebenso als Hüter und Torwächter ausgewiesen. Sie überschreiten zwar eine imaginäre Grenze mit ihrem Blick, schaffen jedoch mit der neu errichteten, transluzenten Grenze einen unzugänglichen Raum, in den

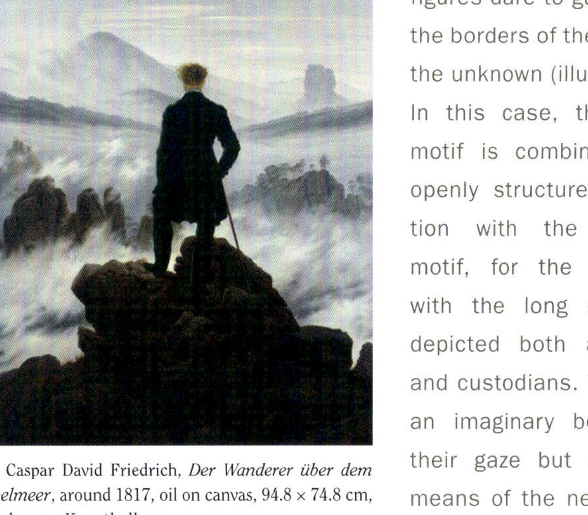

23 Caspar David Friedrich, *Der Wanderer über dem Nebelmeer*, around 1817, oil on canvas, 94.8 × 74.8 cm, Hamburger Kunsthalle

sich die Rezipienten zwar einspiegeln können, der jedoch nur von den Figuren selbst besetzt wird. Die Bildträger aus Glas nehmen somit eine Zwitterstellung ein, als verbindendes, aus der Bildebene heraustretendes Element zur Betrachterperspektive hin und zugleich als unsichtbare Grenze zum Bildgeschehen.

Diese Rolle wird noch deutlicher in Robert Elfgens Installation *Die Nacht des Jägers*, welche er erstmalig 2006 auf der Messe Frankfurt für

reference to Caspar David Friedrich serves as a point of orientation for the exhibition and is taken up here with the back view of the staggered figures; moreover, it can be literally followed into the distance with the viewer's gaze out of the window. In contrast to Friedrich's *Wanderer über dem Nebelmeer* ('Wanderer above the Sea of Fog'), in which the figure surveys a sublime landscape spreading out before him, here the four figures dare to gaze beyond the borders of the room into the unknown (illus. 23).

In this case, the brother motif is combined as an openly structured installation with the shepherd motif, for the wanderers with the long staffs are depicted both as guards and custodians. They cross an imaginary border with their gaze but create, by means of the newly established, translucent border, an inaccessible space in which the recipients can find themselves reflected, a space, however, that is occupied only by the figures themselves. The glass image supports thereby assume a hybrid position — on the one hand as connecting elements emerging from the pictorial plane into the viewing perspective, and on the other as an invisible border to the pictorial event.

This character becomes even clearer in Robert Elfgen's installation *Die Nacht des Jägers* ('The

skulpturale Einzelpositionen zeigte (Abb. 25). Die Arbeit gründet auf ein zunächst diffuses Erinnerungsbild an eine plastische und bilderreiche Tierwelt an einem Fluss. Letztere stellte sich in seiner künstlerischen Recherche als eine filmische Memoria heraus: und zwar an den gestalterisch ebenso eigenwilligen wie dramaturgisch spannungsvollen, gleichnamigen amerikanischen Thriller von 1955, die einzige Regiearbeit von Charles Laughton, mit Robert Mitchum in der Hauptrolle als psychopathischer und perfider Prediger und Verfolger zweier Kinder, denen er ein Geheimnis zu entlocken trachtet. Die filmischen Sequenzen der Flucht dieser beiden Kinder entlang des Gewässers sind durch eine üppige und expressionistisch anmutende Fauna repräsentiert, die sich im Vordergrund des düsteren Settings mit abgründig märchenähnlichen Zügen entfaltet. Mit dem Fokus auf die Tierwelt wird eine mikrokosmische Perspektive auf den Plot gewagt. Diese spezifische Atmosphäre des Films überträgt Robert Elfgen in eine räumlich gestaffelte Installation, die sich von einer Wand aus in den Raum hinein und über eine Ecke hinweg entfaltet. Die Wand ist in grüngrau gehalten, auf der in

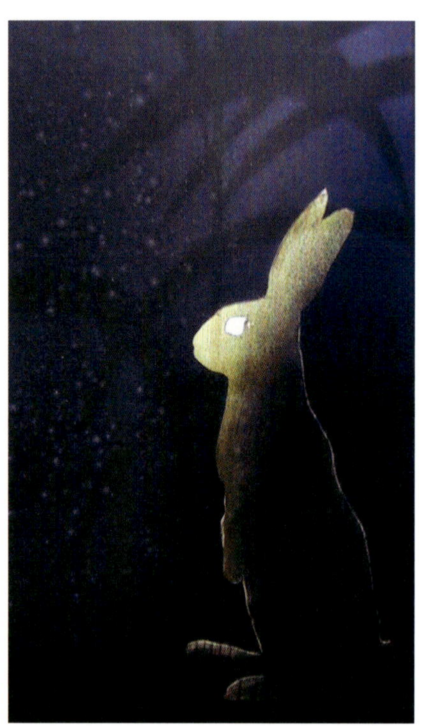

24 *Die Nacht des Jägers* (Detail), 2006, veneer, acrylic on MDF, 70.5 × 40.2 cm; Goetz Collection

Night of the Hunter'), which he first showed in 2006 at the Frankfurt Art Fair focusing on individual sculptural positions (illus. 17). The work is based upon an initially diffuse, remembered image of a sculptural and richly pictorial animal world along a river which his artistic research revealed to be a filmic recollection, namely the eponymous American thriller from 1955 which, both creatively idiosyncratic and dramaturgically energetic, was Charles Laughton's only work as director and which starred Robert Mitchum as a psychopathic and perfidious preacher in pursuit of two children he wants to draw a secret from. The film sequences of the flight of the two children along the river feature a prolific, expressionistic vegetation growing in the foreground of the bleak, profoundly fairytale-like setting. The focus on the animal world creates a microcosmic perspective of the plot; Robert Elfgen transfers this specific atmosphere of the film into a spatially staggered installation that spreads from one wall into the space and around a corner. The wall is painted in greengray; upon it are placed in various formats riparian and nocturnal animals such as a heron, a frog, a hawk, and an owl. A round, beige-colored disc

verschiedenen Formaten Fluss- und Nachttiere, wie ein Reiher, ein Frosch, ein Habicht, eine Eule platziert sind. Eine runde beigefarbene Scheibe repräsentiert – wie schon bei der Bonner Kunstvereinsausstellung– den fahlen Mond, und auf Bodenhöhe ist die Figur des Jägers als Intarsienarbeit im Querformat mit durchdringendem Blick realisiert, deren signifikante Fingertätowierungen wie bei Mitchum im Film die Worte „Love" und „Hate" zeigen. Drei Glasscheiben am Boden, freistehend fixiert und versetzt in den Raum hinein angeordnet, zeigen in Sandstrahltechnik Schilf, Seerosenblätter und einen Frosch. Gleichwohl

represents, as earlier in the exhibition at the Bonner Kunstverein, the pale moon, while placed at ground level is the figure of the hunter as an intarsia work in horizontal format. His gaze is penetrating; tattooed on his finger, just as with Mitchum in the film, are the words 'Love' and 'Hate'. Three freestanding glass panels affixed to the floor and staggered into the space etched in sandblasting technique depict reeds, water-lily leaves, and a frog. Even though this scene unfolds visually and narratively in reference to the feature film, the plot nonetheless provides an occasion both to shift the perspective from

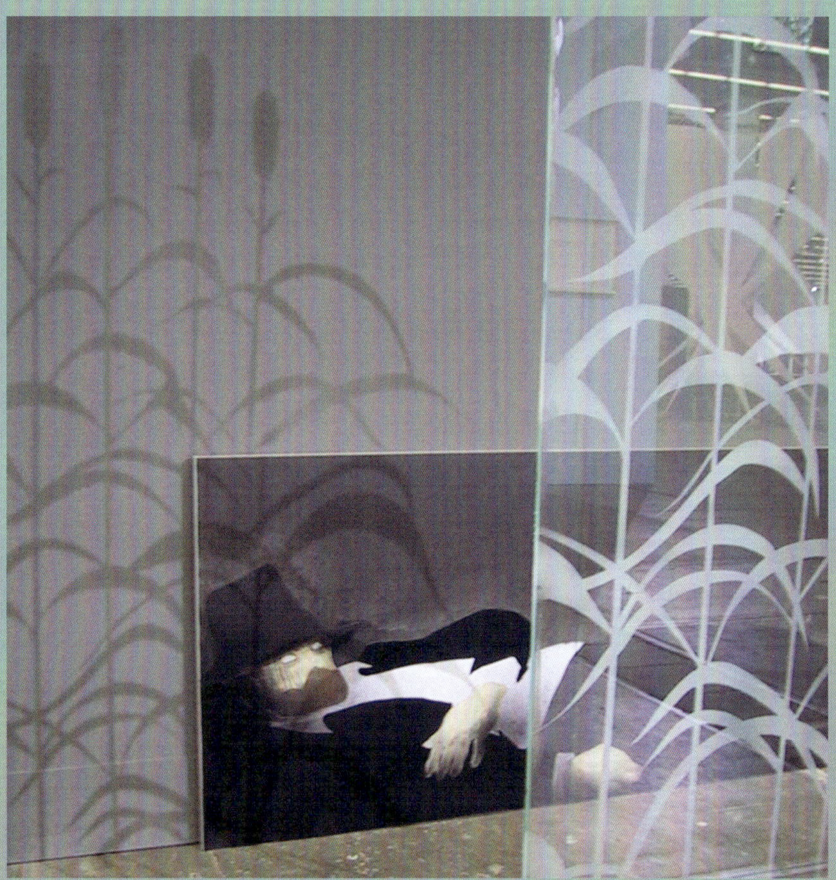

25 *Die Nacht des Jägers* (Detail), 2006, veneer, acrylic, fabric on MDF, 67 × 197 cm; Goetz Collection

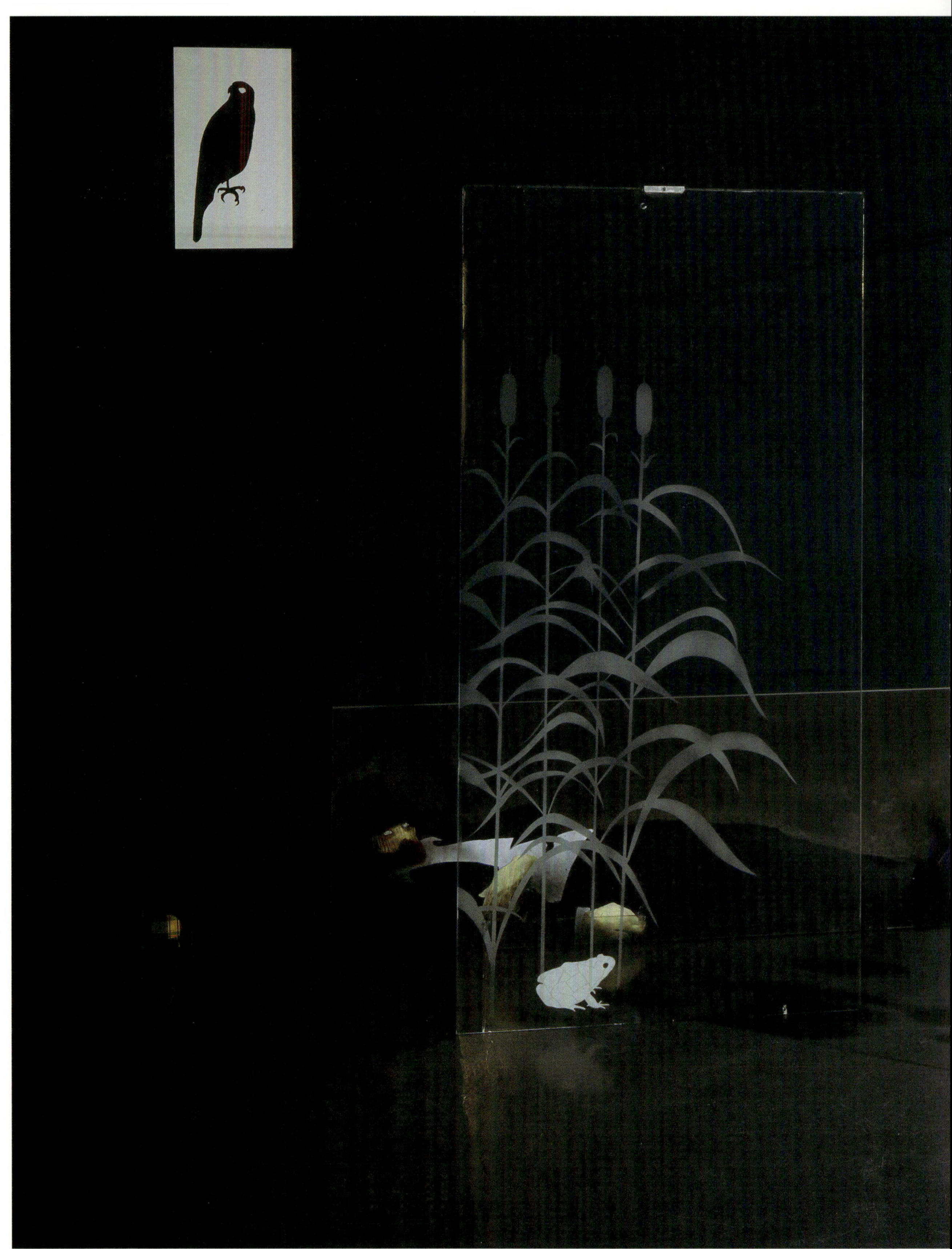

26 *Die Nacht des Jägers*, 2006, installation composed of ten collages and three sand blasted panes of glass, mixed media, dimensions variable, installation view Sprüth Magers Munich; Goetz Collection

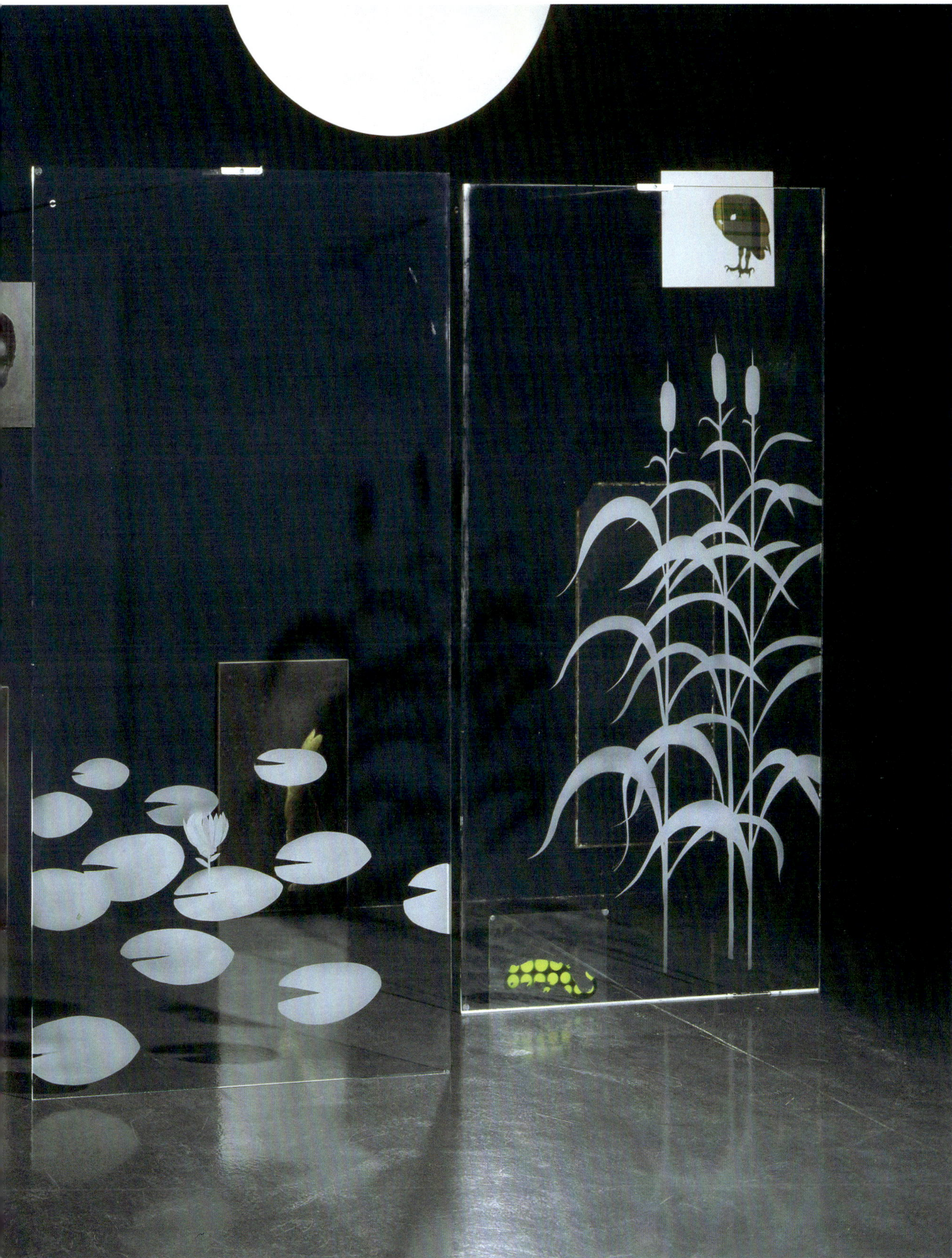

wie anschaulich und narrativ sich diese Szene in Gedanken an den Spielfilm entfaltet, so stellt der Plot doch nur einen Anlass dar, eine eigentümliche wie eindringliche Perspektivverschiebung von den Protagonisten auf die Tierwelt als Erinnerungsbild aufzugreifen, und den Elementen darin eine eigene Ordnung zuzuweisen, welche die Person faktisch in den Hintergrund treten lassen. In Elfgens Reflexion der Szene zeigt sich nicht nur ein formaler Spiegelungseffekt durch den Einsatz von Glas, sondern dieser wird auf die Frage nach der Naturnachahmung, ihrer Aneignung und der Überwindung des Bild-Abbild-Verhältnisses durch Fiktionalisierung ausgeweitet. So greift seine Installation in den Raum aus und lässt sich darüber hinaus als eigene Verbildlichung dieser Erinnerung charakterisieren.

Mit seiner Einzelausstellung *Expedition* bei westlondonprojects 2006 in London intensiviert Elfgen die Fokussierung auf die Tier- und Pflanzenwelt, die nun die Ausstellung maßgeblich bestimmt (Abb. 27 – 28). Als visuelle wie thematische Hintergrundfolie dient eine europäische Amazonas-Expedition. Zwei gesandstrahlte Pflanzenmotive auf zwei symmetrisch an den Raumseiten angeordneten Glasscheiben bilden den Auftakt für eine schrittweise zu durchschreitende Installation, die eine wirkliche Raumschwelle mit einbezieht. Die gesamte Stirnwand zur nächsten Wand ist mit achsensymmetrisch angeordneten Tierdarstellungen bestückt, allesamt vor schwarzem Grund. Die Wand selbst wurde mit schwarzen Farbschlieren und einem von der Decke abgehängten schmalen Tuchband abgedunkelt. Der Stoff dient als Sichtblende, hinter der Strahler Lichtakzente auf die Motive werfen und

the protagonist to the animal world as an image of memory in an insistent and peculiar way. The elements contained therein are assigned an order of their own that visually render the person a part of the setting. In Elfgen's reflection of the scene, the formal effect of reflection is not only achieved through the use of glass, but is also expanded metaphorically into a question with respect both to the imitation and appropriation of nature and a transcendence of the relationship between image and copy through fictionalization. Thus the artist's installation encompasses the space; essentially, it can be read as a significant visualization of this memory.

With his 2006 solo exhibition *Expedition* ('expedition') at westlondonprojects, Elfgen intensifies the focus on the zoological and botanical world, which now comes to define the exhibition (illus. 27 – 28). Serving as a visual and thematic background is a European expedition to the Amazon. Two sandblasted plant motifs on two glass panels arranged symmetrically on the sides of the room constitute the prelude to an installation which is to be moved through step by step, and which includes a genuine spatial threshold. The entire wall facing the next wall is covered with animal depictions arranged in axial symmetry upon a black ground. The wall itself is darkened with streaks of black paint; a narrow strip of cloth hangs from the ceiling. The cloth serves as a screen behind which spots highlight the motifs and create shadows upon the depictions of plants. The picture panels facing the opening to the next space contain nothing other than dim profiles and faces. The palely shining surface of

einen Schattenwurf der Pflanzendarstellungen entstehen lassen. Die der Öffnung zum nächsten Raum zugewandten Bildtafeln sind nur noch mit schemenhaften Profilen und Gesichtern ausgestattet. Die fahl leuchtende Oberfläche der Tiere wie der Menschenköpfe lassen sie als geisterhafte Erscheinungen erkennbar werden, möglicherweise totemistischen Ursprungs, zwischen Imaginärem und Realem.[11] Mittig vor der Türöffnung ist ein Grabstein platziert. Hinter der Tür im Durchgang zum Nebenraum wird eine Videoprojektion erkennbar, mit in Tücher gehüllten, Eurythmiebewegungen vollführenden weiblichen Personen, in ein bläuliches Licht getaucht, die wie Geisterscheinungen anmuten (Abb. 29). Von allen Rauminstallationen Elfgens ist diese die unheimlichste, da das

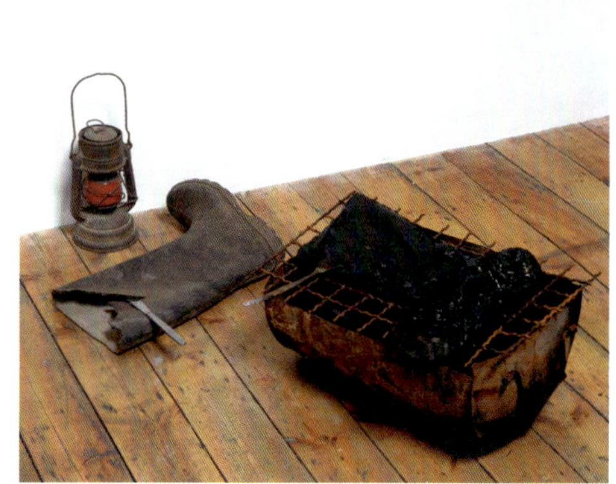

27 *Expedition* (Detail), 2006, mixed media, dimensions variable; Sender Collection

Unbekannte und Erahnte als Leerstelle der anderen Kunstwerke in die Mitte der Darstellung geholt wird. Doch ist der entscheidende Moment der Installation derjenige der Schwellenüberschreitung und einer Überwindung des in die Tiefe des Raumes weisenden Weges. Denn gemäß der rite de passage, wie sie der Ethnologe Arnold van Gennep mit seiner Ritualtheorie vergegenwärtigte, ist das räumliche Überschreiten der Schwellen analog zu den Übergangsriten zu sehen, wie etwa die Phasen von Tod, Transformation und Wiedergeburt; und die Schleier weisen die Tanzenden

the animals and the human heads make them recognizable as ghostly appearances, possibly of totemistic origin, hovering between the imaginary and the real.[11] A tombstone is placed in the middle in front of the door opening. Visible beyond the door in a corridor to an adjoining room a video projection shows women wrapped in scarves performing eurythmy; bathed in a bluish light, they resemble ghosts (illus. 29). Among all of Elfgen's spatial installations, this is the most eerie, for the unknown and surmised element, a void in his other works of art, is now brought to the center of the representation. But the essential aspect of the installation is that it crosses a threshold and overcomes the path leading into the depths of the space. For in accordance with the rites de passage such as the ethnologist Arnold van Gennep described in his theory of ritual, the crossing of spatial thresholds is analogous to rites of transition such as the phases of death, transformation, and rebirth; the veils indicate that the dancers are performing a ritual.[12] The piquant detail therein is simply that the Amazonian mythology finds its ritualistic resonance in an anthroposophical, eurhythmic dance. Here the artist weaves in a further level through regional aspects of his own biographical experience. It links distance and direct proximity and focuses

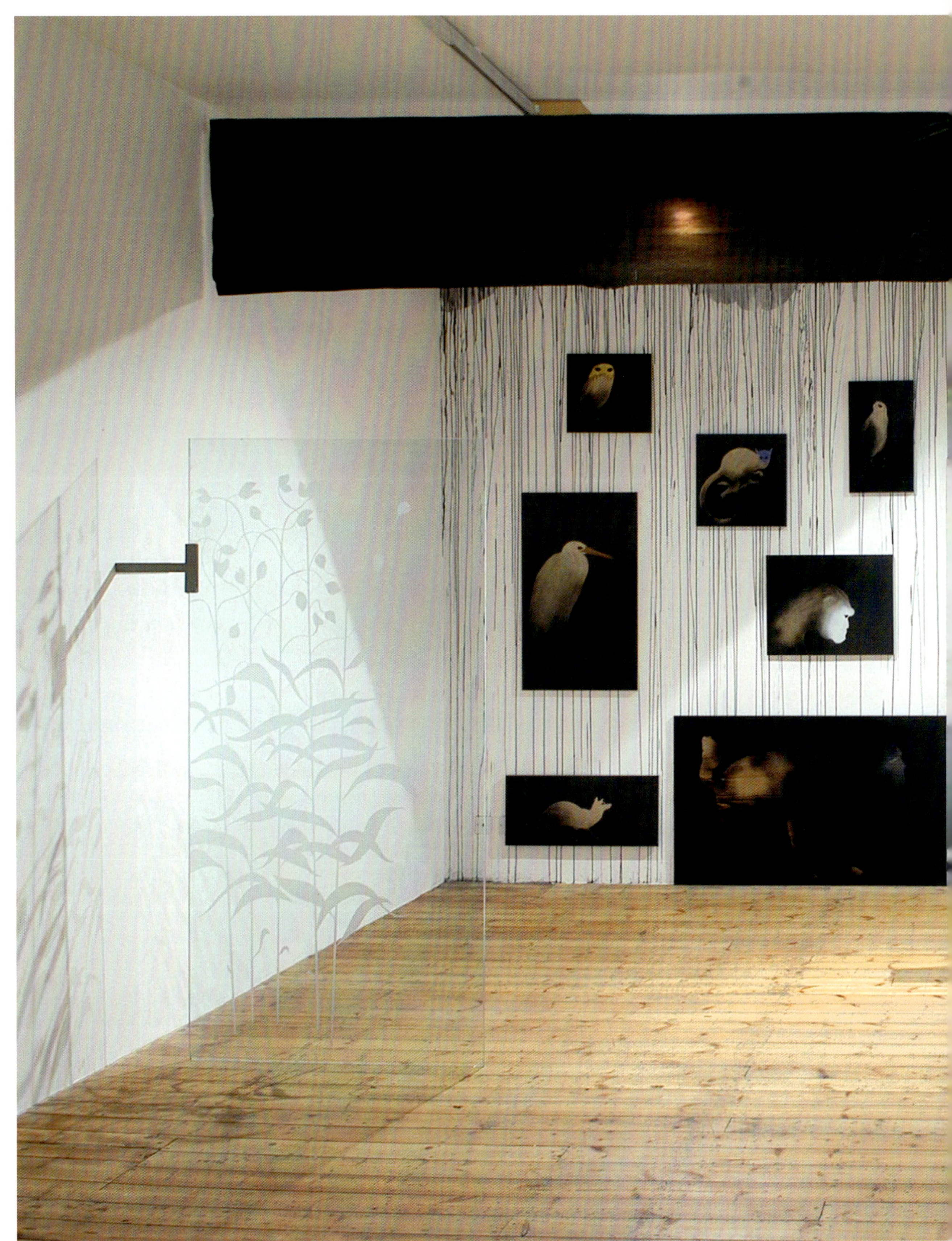

28 *Expedition*, 2006, installation composed of several sculptures, collages and video installation, mixed media, installation view westlondonprojects, London; Sender Collection

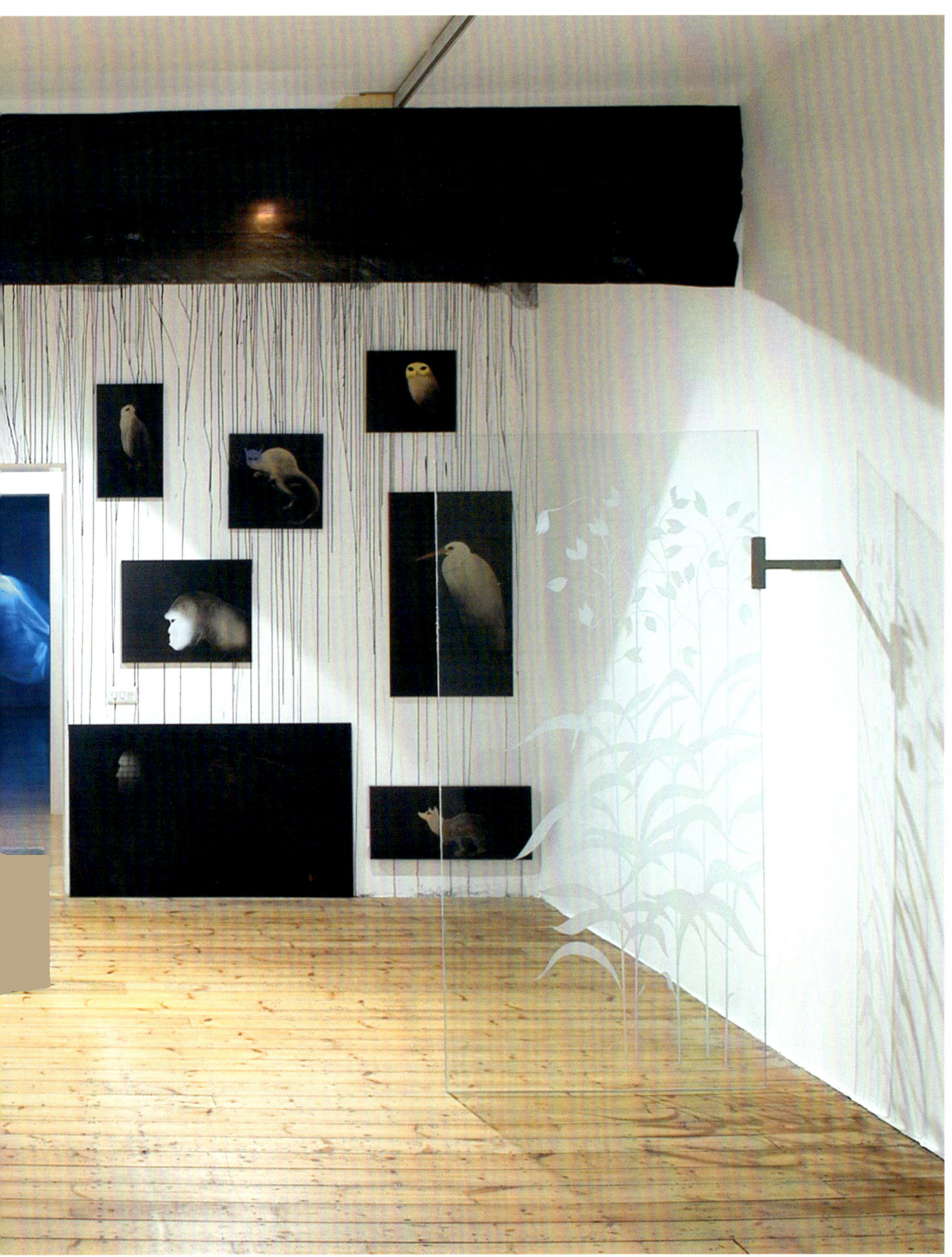

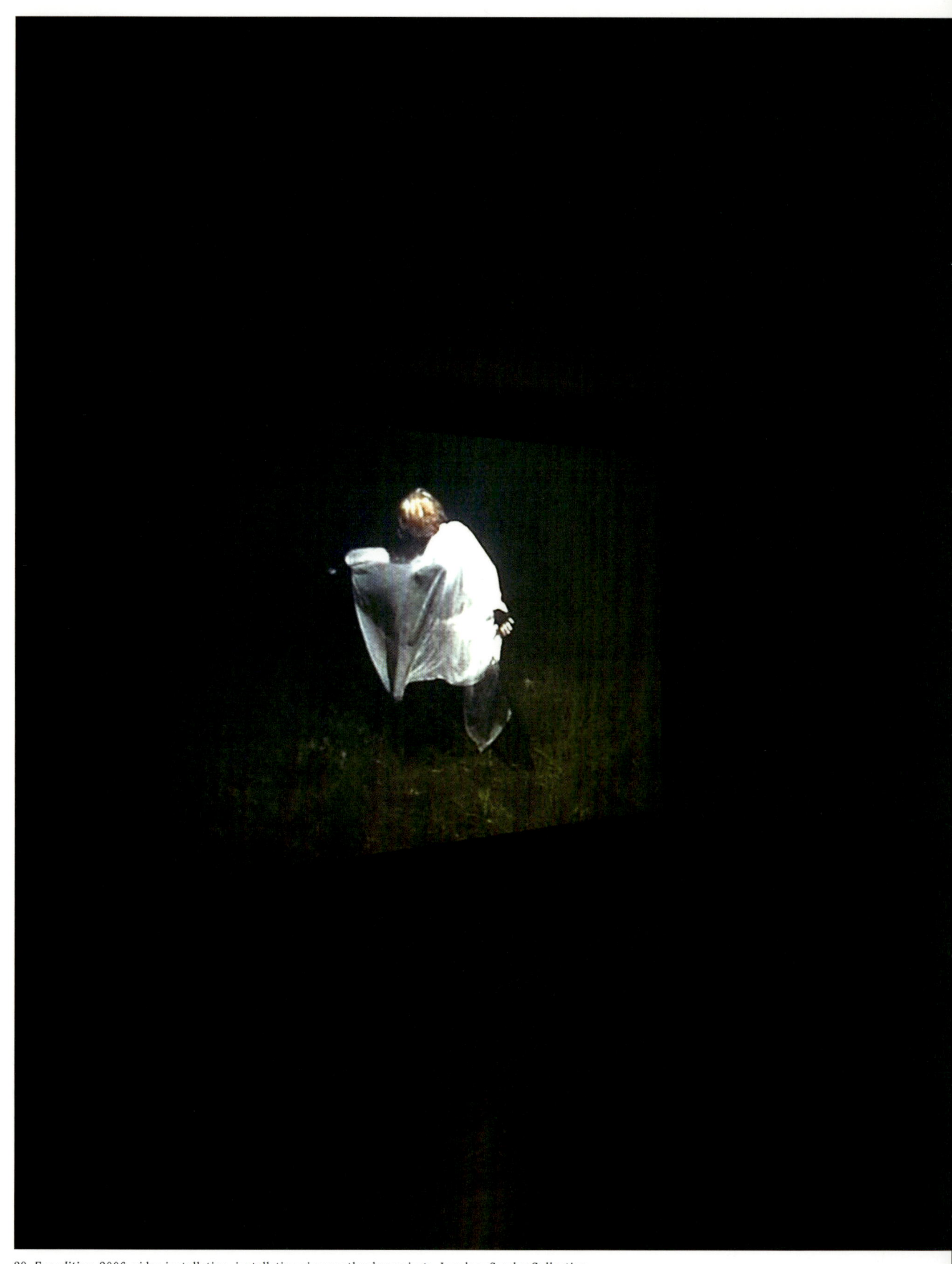

29 *Expedition*, 2006, video installation, installation view westlondonprojects, London; Sender Collection

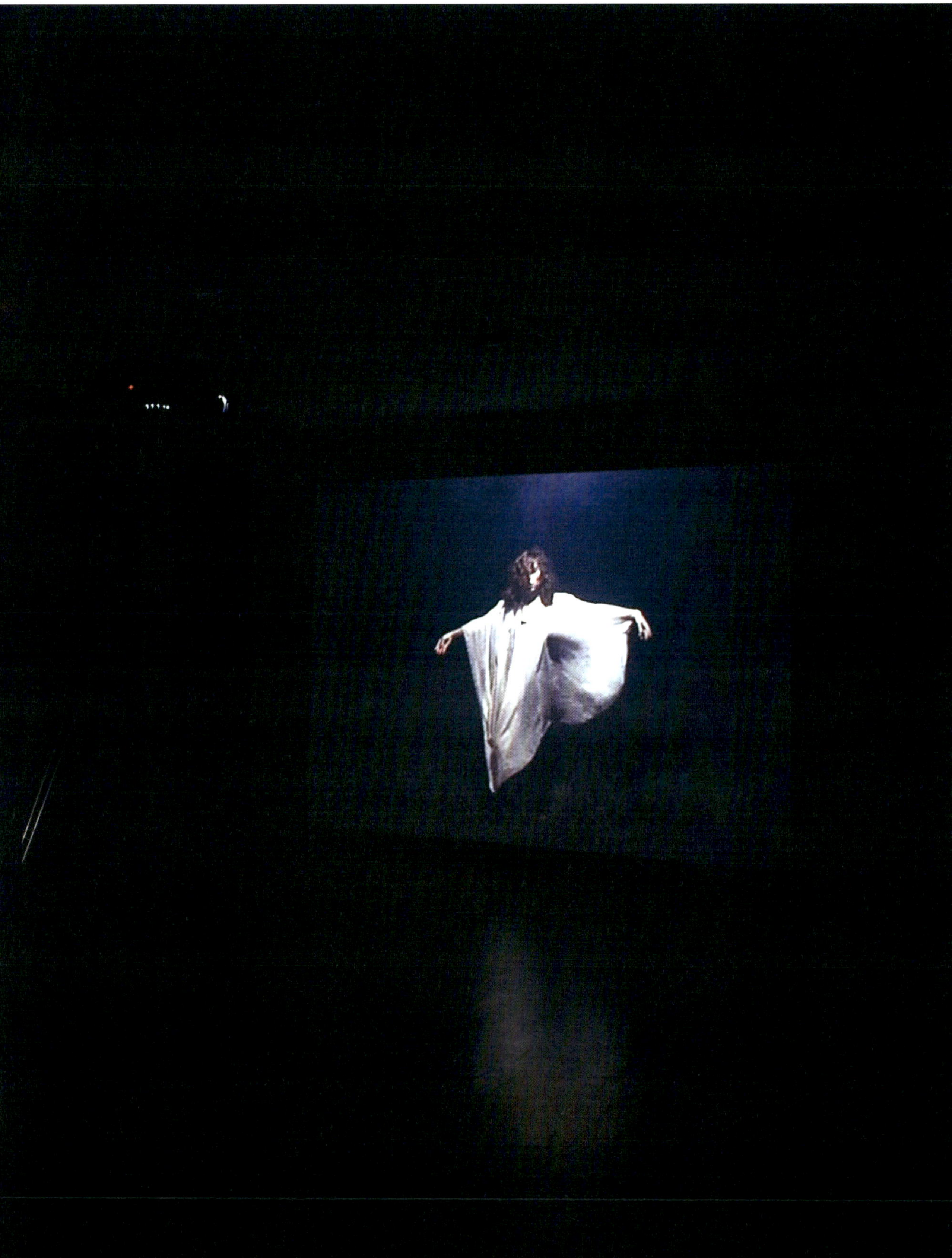

als Vollführer des Rituals aus. Pikantes Detail daran ist nur, dass die Amazonas-Mythologie ihren ritualistischen Wiederhall in einem anthroposophischen Eurythmietanz findet. Hier flicht der Künstler mit regionalen Aspekten seiner biographischen Auseinandersetzung eine weitere Ebene ein. Diese bringt die Ferne und die unmittelbare Umgebung miteinander in Verbindung und nimmt dabei die jeweils eigenen Riten in den Blick, ohne diesen selbst zu erliegen, sondern sie vielmehr anschaulich auszugestalten, um ihre Funktion im Sinne eines Bricoleurs zu untersuchen.

Der Spiegelmetapher kommt in den zuvor behandelten Raumkunstwerken und Installationen eine zentrale Doppelrolle zu: einerseits als Memoria und Reflexion bestimmter Erinnerungsbilder, die zum Teil eng an das Vorgewusste anschließen; andererseits fungieren die lebensgroßen Figurentafeln auch formalästhetisch mit einem bestimmten Abstraktionsgrad als Spiegelungen der dargestellten Personen und Tiere. Sie erfüllen damit dasjenige, was Leonardo für die Funktion der Malerei als Spiegel konstatiert – und deren direkte Gegenüberstellung er als Vergleichsverfahren etabliert hatte –, die beide dem natürlichen Vorbild ähnlich zu sein haben.[13] Aufschlussreich ist, wie Frank Fehrenbach prägnant

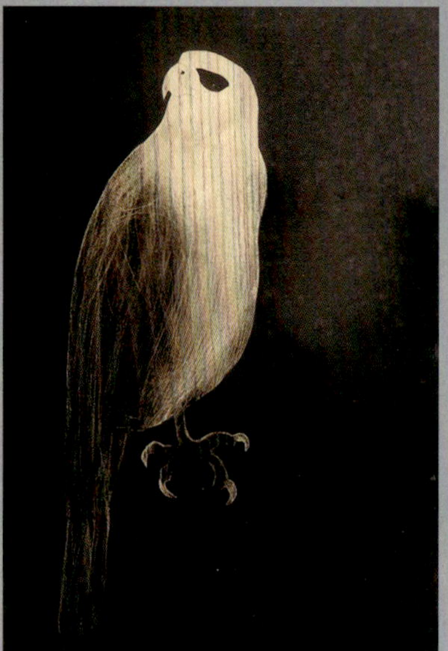

30 *Expedition* (Detail), 2006, veneer, acrylic on MDF; Sender Collection

on the respective rituals without succumbing to them itself, instead imparting vivid shape to them in order to investigate their function in the sense of a bricoleur.

In the previously discussed spatial artworks and installations, the mirror metaphor plays an important double role. On the one hand, it serves as the memory and reflection of certain images of remembrance which to some extent are closely connected to the preconscious. On the other hand, the life-sized, figurative panels function in formal aesthetic terms as mirror images of the depicted persons and animals with a certain degree of abstraction. They accordingly fulfill that which Leonardo stated to be the function of painting as a mirror — and whose direct juxtaposition he established as a comparative procedure —, both of which are required to be similar to their model in nature.[13] It is revealing, as Frank Fehrenbach has persuasively elaborated, that the early modern artist anticipated photography with the investigation as to how objects and depictions of landscapes should be applied to a panel of glass. As I would add with regard to Robert Elfgen's work, the procedure with the glass panel expands the mirror motif, inasmuch as the support itself becomes immaterial and

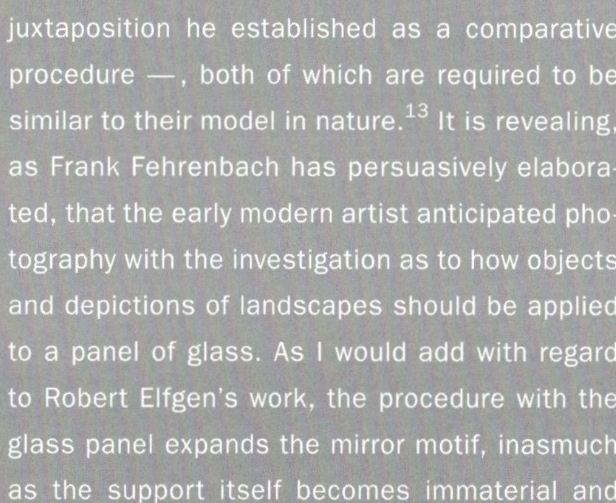

herausgearbeitet hat, dass der frühneuzeitliche Künstler die Fotografie antizipiert hat mit der Untersuchung, wie Objekte und Landschaftsdarstellungen auf eine Glasscheibe appliziert werden sollten. Wie ich für Robert Elfgens Kontext hinzufügen würde, erweitert das Verfahren mit der Glasscheibe das Spiegelmotiv dadurch, dass der Bildträger selbst immateriell wird und einen anderen Realitätsgrad erzeugt. Zudem wird die Glasscheibe und die Darstellungen in *Expedition* symmetrisch gespiegelt, indem sie vom Künstler verdoppelt wurden. Sie ahmen das Spiegelmotiv nach und irritieren durch Symmetrie und die bei der Naturnachahmung gestellte Frage von Bild und Abbild, indem es nur noch Abbilder gibt.

generates another degree of reality. Moreover, the panel of glass and the representations are symmetrically reflected in *Expedition*, inasmuch as they have been duplicated by the artist. They imitate the mirror motif and irritate through their symmetry and the question their imitation raises with regard to image and likeness, inasmuch as there are only likenesses.

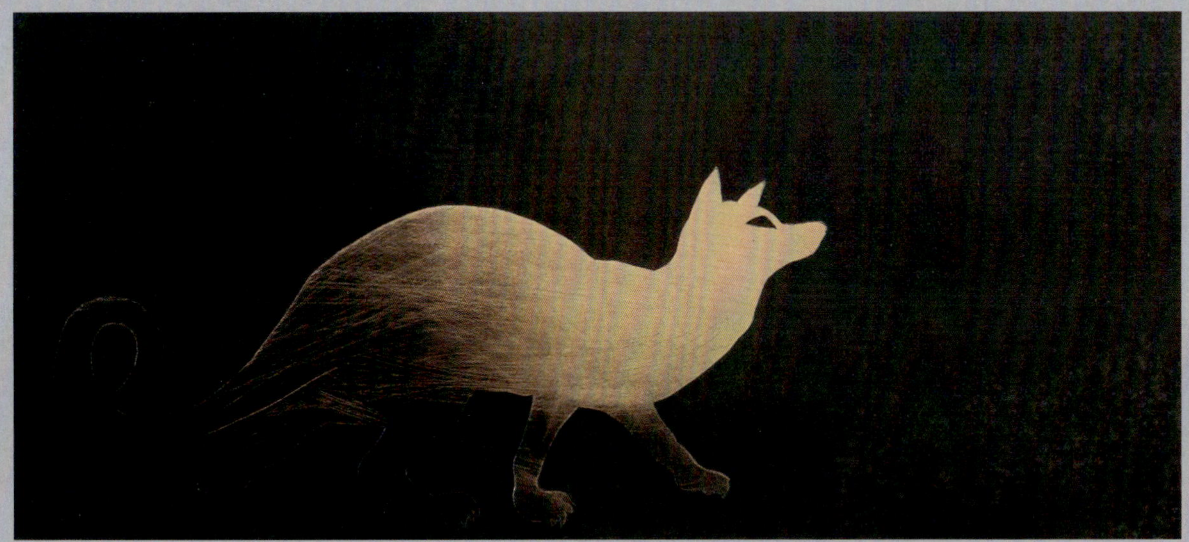

31 *Expedition* (Detail), 2006, veneer, acrylic on MDF; Sender Collection

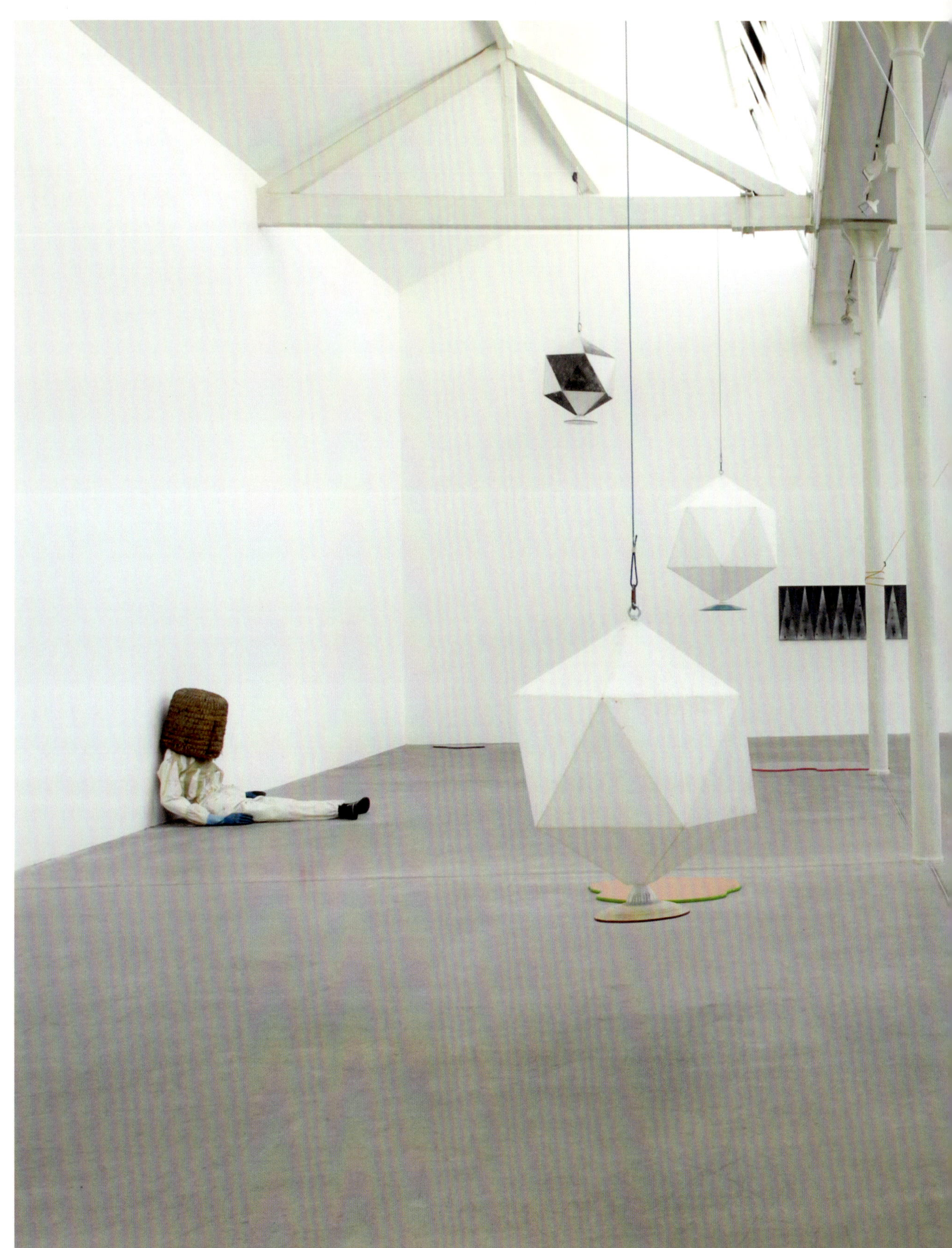

32 *des bien ich*, 2008, installation view Sprüth Magers Cologne

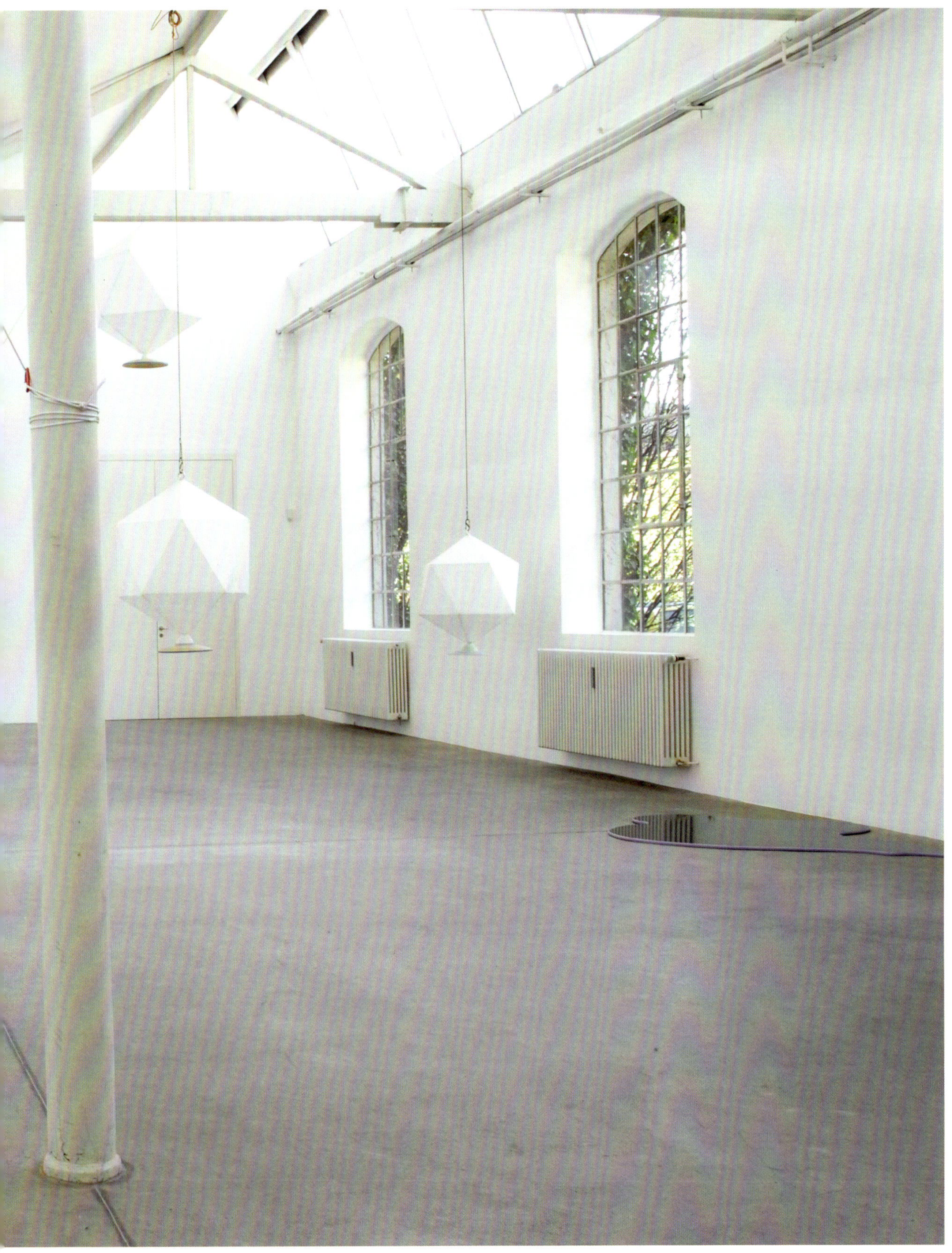

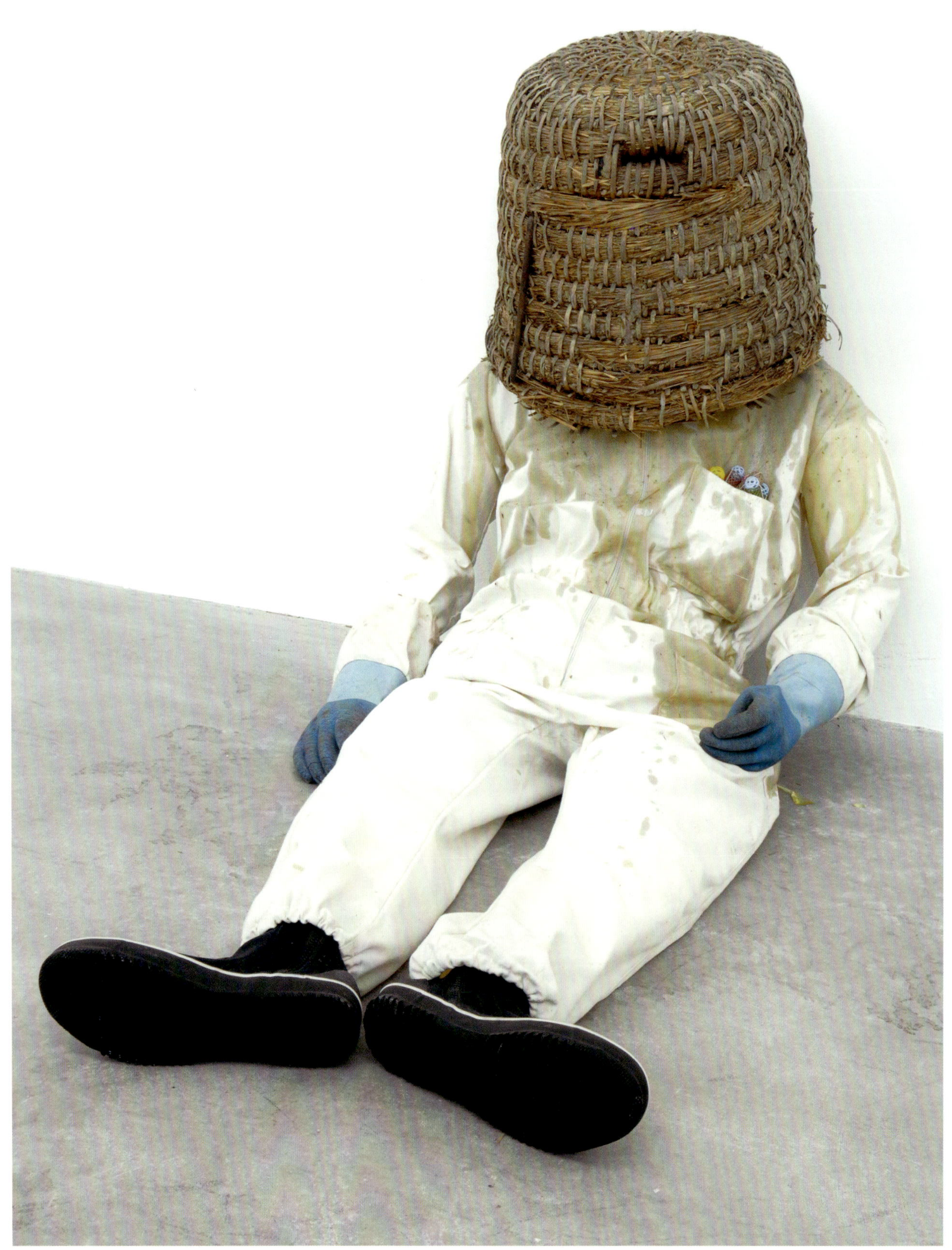

32 *Bienenmann*, 2008, cotton overall, rubber boots, rubber gloves, beehive, curler, polyester resin, 150 × 90 × 70 cm; Goetz Collection

Robert Elfgens erste Einzelausstellung in den Räumen der Galerie Sprüth Magers in Köln nimmt eine Zäsur vor – obwohl sie parallel zu *Expedition* entstanden ist und dort bestimmte Motive wie diejenige der Symmetrien als ästhetische Ordnungen sichtbar werden: Der Künstler taucht in die Bienenwelt und ihre Strukturen mit einer Fülle an Bienen-Wandarbeiten, an Stäben herabhängenden und die geodätischen Modelle des Architekten Buckminster Fuller aufrufenden, stilisierten Bienenkörben (Abb. 20) ein. Das Herzstück bildet ein sitzender Bienenmann, der einen Bienenkorb auf dem Kopf trägt (Abb. 21). Ursprünglich sollte er, in symmetrischer Anordnung, von Tierdarstellungen umringt

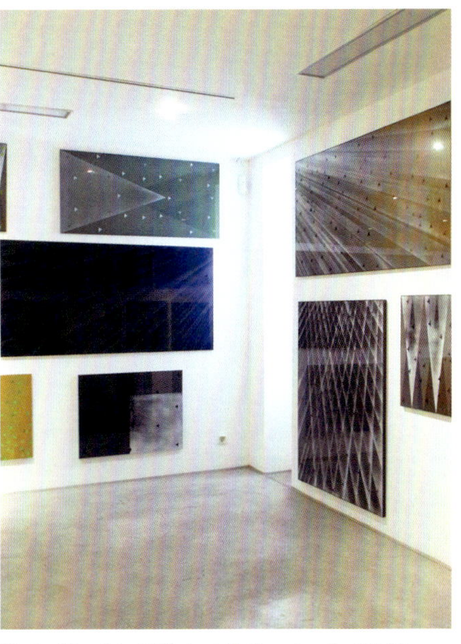

33 *des bien ich*, 2008, installation view Sprüth Magers Cologne

sein, die Elfgen jedoch durch eine leere Fläche ersetzt. Stattdessen hat er in ein angrenzendes Kabinett der Galerie grafisch abstrahierte Bienenassemblagen mit symmetrischen Lichteffekten dicht an dicht gehängt, wo den Bildern die nötige Nähe und Sichtbarkeit zuteil wird (Abb. 22). Obwohl das Eintauchen in die Strukturen und Lebensgewohnheiten der Bienen eine sehr lange künstlerische Tradition hat, umso ungewöhnlicher ist die Darstellung des Imkers, der

Although it was created parallel to *Expedition* and brings to light certain themes, such as that of symmetries as aesthetic arrangements, Robert Elfgen's first solo exhibition in the spaces of the gallery Sprüth Magers in Cologne undertakes a caesura. The artist enters into the apiary realm and its structures with an abundance of wall works picturing bees; in addition, stylized beehives hang down from poles and allude to the geodesic models of the architect Buckminster Fuller (illus. 20). The centerpiece is a seated Bienenmann ('Bee-Man') carrying a beehive on his head (illus. 21). He was originally intended to be surrounded by depictions of animals in symmetrical arrangement, but Elfgen left only an empty surface. Instead, in an adjoining cabinet of the gallery he placed graphically abstract bee assemblages closely together with symmetrical light effects, providing the images with the necessary proximity and visibility (illus. 22). Although an immersion in the structures and habits of bees has a long artistic tradition, the image of the beekeeper is unusual; furthermore, in a succession of symmetries, he carries two hair curlers for capturing the queen bee. He

im übrigen in der Symmetriefolge zwei Locken-wickler in der Schutzanzugtasche trägt, da hier-mit die Königin eingefangen werden kann. Denn er ruft die bis heute rätselhafte Federzeichnung Pieter Bruegel d. J. der drei Imker auf, deren Rolle und Deutung des Blattes nur in Annäherung voll-zogen wurden, da mehr Fragen als Antworten bleiben (Abb. 23).[14] Diese tragen zum Schutz ebenfalls Körbe aus Weidengeflecht und befinden sich in drei verschiedenen Haltungen ihrer Tätig-keit; nur der Mittlere ist im Begriff, in steifer Haltung nach vorn zu schreiten. Sie bleiben, wie Marijnissen betont, anonym, und Versuche, den mittleren Imker in Verbindung mit der Inschrift als „Wissenden" zu thematisieren, erweisen sich als haltlos.[15] Die Rolle des Bienenzüchters bei Elfgen ist etwas weniger rätselhaft, er ist zur

summons up Pieter Brueghel the Elder's pen drawing of three beekeepers, enigmatic even today, whose role, along with the drawing's inter-pretation, can only be surmised given that more questions than answers remain (illus. 23).[14] They likewise wear protective baskets of wattle-work and embody three different aspects of their activity; only the middle figure is in the process of bending forward in a stiff pose. As Marijnissen emphasizes, they remain anonymous; attempts to link the middle beekeeper to the inscription of a 'knowing one' turn out to be unfounded.[16] In Elfgen's case, the role of the beekeeper is some-what less puzzling: condemned to passivity, he is represented in a helpless seated posi-tion leaning against the wall, and possibly sees less than his three predecessors, but remains

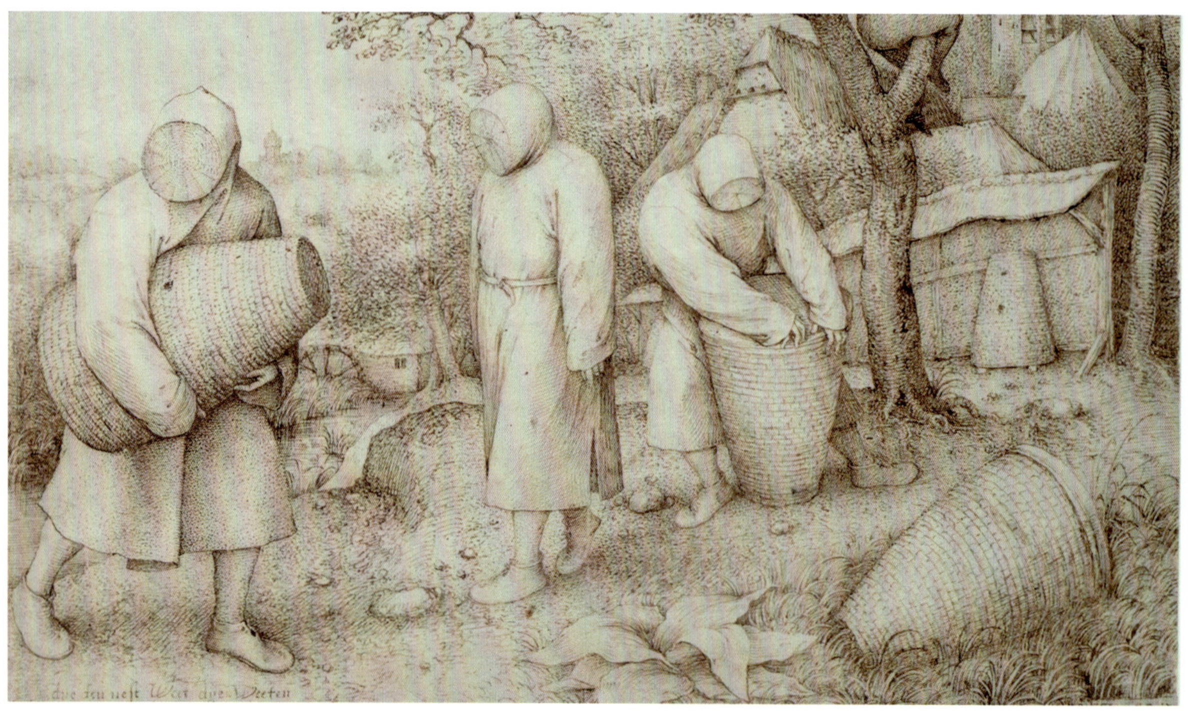

34 Pieter Bruegel (the Elder), *Die Imker*, 2nd Third 16. cent., drawing, 20.3 × 30.9 cm, Kupferstichkabinett, Staatliche Museen zu Berlin

Passivität verurteilt, ohnmächtig sitzend an die Wand gelehnt dargestellt, möglicherweise weniger sehend als seine drei Vorläufer, aber ebenso anonym. Aufschlussreich ist die für den Ausstellungstitel *des bien ich* verwendete Verbform des „bien", welche mit dem Begriff des eigenen Seins, wie auch mit dem Bienen-Sein spielt, gleichzeitig aber eine Vielheit[16] andeutet, die analog zum Bienenschwarm die Aufsplittung der Selbstwahrnehmung hervorruft. Der Imker als derjenige, der mit diesem Tierstaat, seinen Strukturen, umzugehen weiß, indem er sich diese zu eigen macht, bleibt nach wie vor eine spannungsvolle wie mysteriöse Identifikationsfigur auf der Suche nach Erkenntnis und den verdeckten Ordnungen, den pulsierenden Energiekreisläufen und der Koexistenz von Mensch und Tier.

equally anonymous. Some insights are conveyed by the verb form of bien (resembles the German word 'Biene,' or 'bee', but sounds the same as 'bin', or 'I am') used in the exhibition title *des bien ich* ('that I bee'), which plays with the notion of one's own being as well as with apiary existence, while at the same time alluding to a multiplicity[16] which, in analogy to the swarm of bees, summons up the splitting of self-perception. The beekeeper as the one who knows how to handle this animal kingdom and its structures by making them his own continues to remain a fascinating and mysterious figure of identification in the search for knowledge along with the concealed systems of order and modes of thought, the pulsating circulations of energy, and the coexistence of humans and animals.

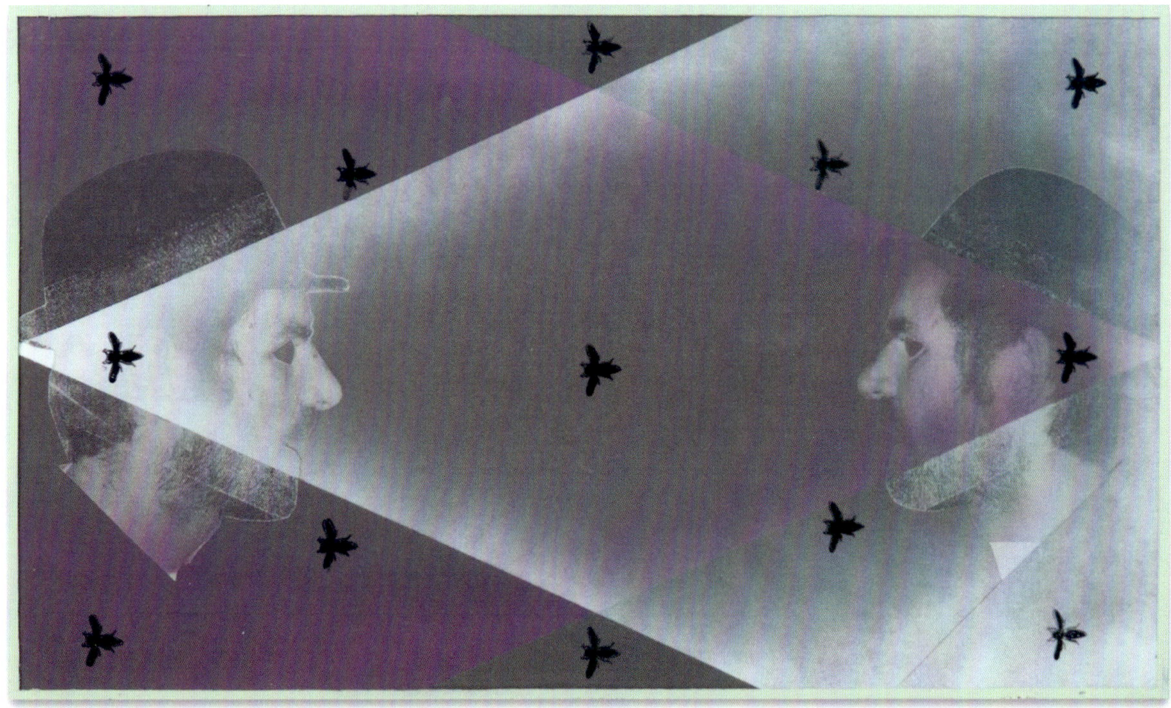

des bien 21, 2008, MDF, wood, paint, 40 × 69 × 2,1 cm; Pervan Collection, Frankfurt

Wie lässt sich die skulpturale und raumkunstwerkorientierte Auseinandersetzung Robert Elfgens, die dennoch bildhaft bleibt, weiter analysieren? Welche Fäden greift sie auf und welche bleiben im weit verzweigten, produktiven Geflecht an Ort und Stelle? Das Motiv des Recycelns und Assemblierens im Raum taucht erneut auf: etwa aus ursprünglich geplanten weiteren Bienenbehausungen, deren Materialien als rohe und fragil balancierte Skulpturen erscheinen oder als Fundstücke, als Relikte alter Arbeiten für den öffentlichen Raum. Und zuletzt? Fallskulpturen auf der Grundlage eines perpetuum mobiles: Überraschendes und Konstruiertes, Vorgewusstes und zufällig Erahntes.

What further analysis is possible with Robert Elfgen's artistic investigation which, with its orientation towards both sculpture and spatial works of art, nonetheless remains pictorial? Which strands does it take up, and which remain in a finely ramified, productive web on the ground? The motif of recycling and assembly in space comes to light once again — for instance, as further, originally planned bee domiciles whose materials appear as rough, delicately balanced sculptures, or as found pieces, relics of old works for public spaces. And last of all? Falling sculptures on the basis of a perpetuum mobile — surprising and constructed aspects, elements of preconsciousness and coincidental intuition.

1. Claude Lévi-Strauss, Das wilde Denken, Frankfurt am Main, 1968 [frz. 1962], S. 29 f.
2. Thomas W. Kuhn, „Robert Elfgen: des bien ich", in: Kunstforum International, Bd. 192 (2008), S. 312–314, hier S. 313.
3. Lévi-Strauss (1968), S. 33.
4. Fragen des Künstlers auf den letzten beiden Seiten seines Kataloges in: Robert Elfgen. 1+1=3 Elfgen Technik, Ausst.-Kat. anlässlich des Peter Mertes Stipendiums und der Ausstellung Robert Elfgen, Gert & Uwe Tobias, Bonner Kunstverein, Bonn 2005, nicht paginiert.
5. „La pittura rappresenta al senso con più verità e certezza le opere di natura, che non fanno le parole o ‚le lettere'", in: Leonardo da Vinci, Trattato § 7, zitiert nach Frank Fehrenbach, Licht und Wasser. Zur

1. Claude Lévi-Strauss, The Savage Mind, Chicago/London 1968 [French original 1962], p. 17 ff.
2. Thomas W. Kuhn, 'Robert Elfgen: des bien ich', in: Kunstforum International, vol. 192, 2008, pp. 312–314, here p. 313.
3. Lévi-Strauss (1968), p. 18.
4. Questions of the artist on the last two pages of his catalogue in: Robert Elfgen. 1+1=3 Elfgen Technik, exh. cat. on the occasion of the Peter Mertes Stipend and the exhibition Robert Elfgen, Gert & Uwe Tobias, Bonner Kunstverein, Bonn 2005, n.p.
5. '[...] painting is to be placed before all other activities because it contains all forms that are and those that are not to be found in nature, and it is more to be magnified and exalted than is music, which concerns only the voice.' Leonardo da Vinci, 'Trattato della

Dynamik naturphilosophischer Leitbilder im Werk Leonardo da Vincis, Tübinger Studien zur Archäologie und Kunstgeschichte hg. von Klaus Schwager Bd. 16, Tübingen 1997, S. 42.

6. Darin schließt sie an Leonardos Untersuchungen zu den memorativen und bewahrenden Fähigkeiten der Malerei an, die bereits mit der Schöpferanekdote des Töpfers Butades bei Plinius thematisiert wurde und mit der aristotelischen Erkenntnislehre zu den imagines. Ebd. S. 51–53.

7. Lévi-Strauss (1968), S. 35.

8. Ebd. S. 45.

9. Vgl. Lilian Haberer, „Bruder des Anderen", in: Köln Quartett 05, Ausst.-Kat. Fuhrwerkswaage Kunstraum, Köln 2005, S. 8–10.

10. Ebd. S. 10.

11. Vgl. Pressetext der Ausstellung *Expedition*, 8. Juni – 30. Juli 2008, westlondonprojects, nicht paginiert.

12. Vgl. Arnold van Gennep, Les Rites de passage, Paris 1909, dt. Augabe ders., Übergangsriten, Frankfurt am Main 1999, S. p. 21–22, 30–33, 175–176, 179–180, 183–186.

13. „...la tua pittura parrà ancora lei una cosa naturale vista in uno grande specchio", Leonardo da Vinci, Trattato § 4, A 104 v, zitiert nach Fehrenbach (1997), S. 63.

14. Für den Hinweis und die Diskussion danke ich Anna Pawlak. Zu Pieter Bruegels *Die Imker*, um 1568, Feder und braune Tinte, 20,3 × 30,9 cm siehe vor allem Roger H. Marijnissen, Bruegel. Das vollständige Werk, Köln 2003, S. 342–345, siehe auch Christian Vöhringer, Pieter Bruegel 1525/30 – 1569, Köln 1999, S. 129 und Max J. Friedländer, Pieter Bruegel, Berlin 1921, S. 72–73.

15. Ebd. S. 345.

16. Siehe auch Kuhn (2008), S. 313.

pittura,' Part One, 17v, in ibid., Treatise on Painting (Codex Urbinas Latinus 1270), translation and commentary by Philip McMahon, vol. 1, Princeton 1956, p. 15. See also Frank Fehrenbach, Licht und Wasser. Zur Dynamik naturphilosophischer Leitbilder im Werk Leonardo da Vincis, Tübinger Studien zur Archäologie und Kunstgeschichte, edited by Klaus Schwager, vol. 16, Tübingen 1997, p. 42.

6. In this respect, they are associated with Leonardo's investigation of the remembering and preserving capabilities of painting, which were already thematized by the anecdote about the creator recounted by the potter Butades in Pliny, and by Aristotelian epistemology with regard to the imagines. Ibid., pp. 51–53.

7. Lévi-Strauss (1962), pp. 21–22.

8. Ibid., p. 30.

9. Cf. Lilian Haberer, 'Bruder des Anderen', in Köln Quartett 05, exh. cat. Fuhrwerkswaage Kunstraum, Cologne 2005, pp. 8–10.

10. Ibid., p. 10.

11. Cf. press release for the exhibition *Expedition*, June 8 – July 30, 2008, westlondonprojects, n.p.

12. Cf. Arnold van Gennep, Les rites de passage, Paris 1909; German edition, ibid., Übergangsriten, Frankfurt am Main 1999, pp. 21–22, 30–33, 175–176, 179–180, 183–186.

13. '[...] You have among your colors shadows and lights more powerful than those of the mirror, certainly, if you know how to put them together well, your painting will also seem a thing in nature, seen in a large mirror.' Leonardo da Vinci, Trattato, Part Three, 132v, in ibid. (1956), pp. 160–161.

14. I thank Anna Pawlak for the reference and the discussion. On Pieter Bruegel's *Die Imker*, circa 1568, pen and brown ink, 20.3 × 30.9 cm, see especially Roger H. Marijnissen, Bruegel. Das vollständige Werk, Cologne 2003, pp. 342–345; see also Christian Vöhringer, Pieter Bruegel 1525/30 – 1569, Cologne 1999, p. 129, and Max J. Friedländer, Pieter Bruegel, Berlin 1921, pp. 72–73.

15. Ibid., p. 345.

16. See also Kuhn (2008), p. 313.

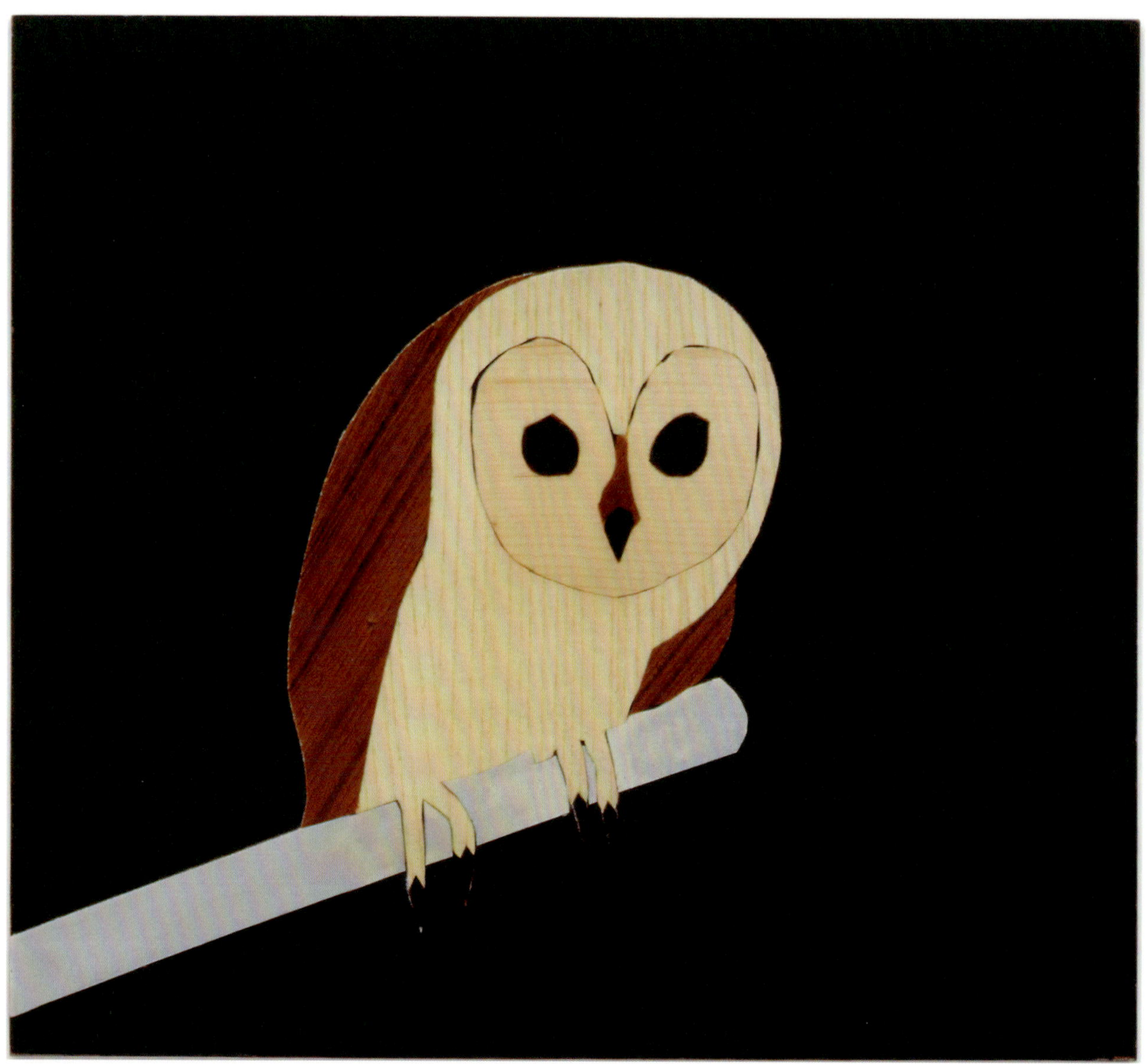

Goldhähnchens Ende (Detail), 2004, press board, veneer, gold leaf, acrylic, 32 × 38 cm; Sender Collection, London

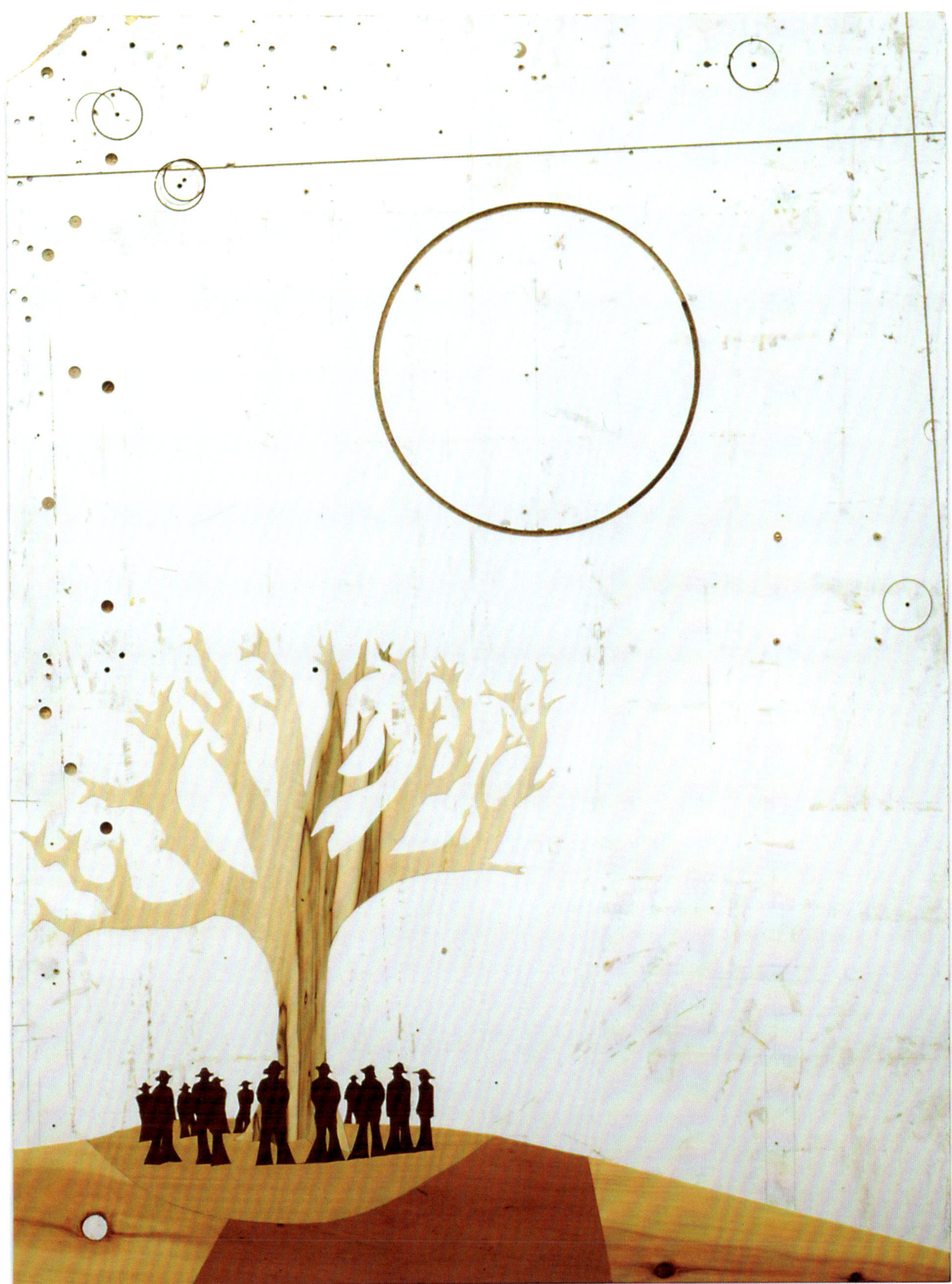

Goldhähnchens Ende (Detail), 2004, veneer on press board, 170 × 130 cm; Private collection

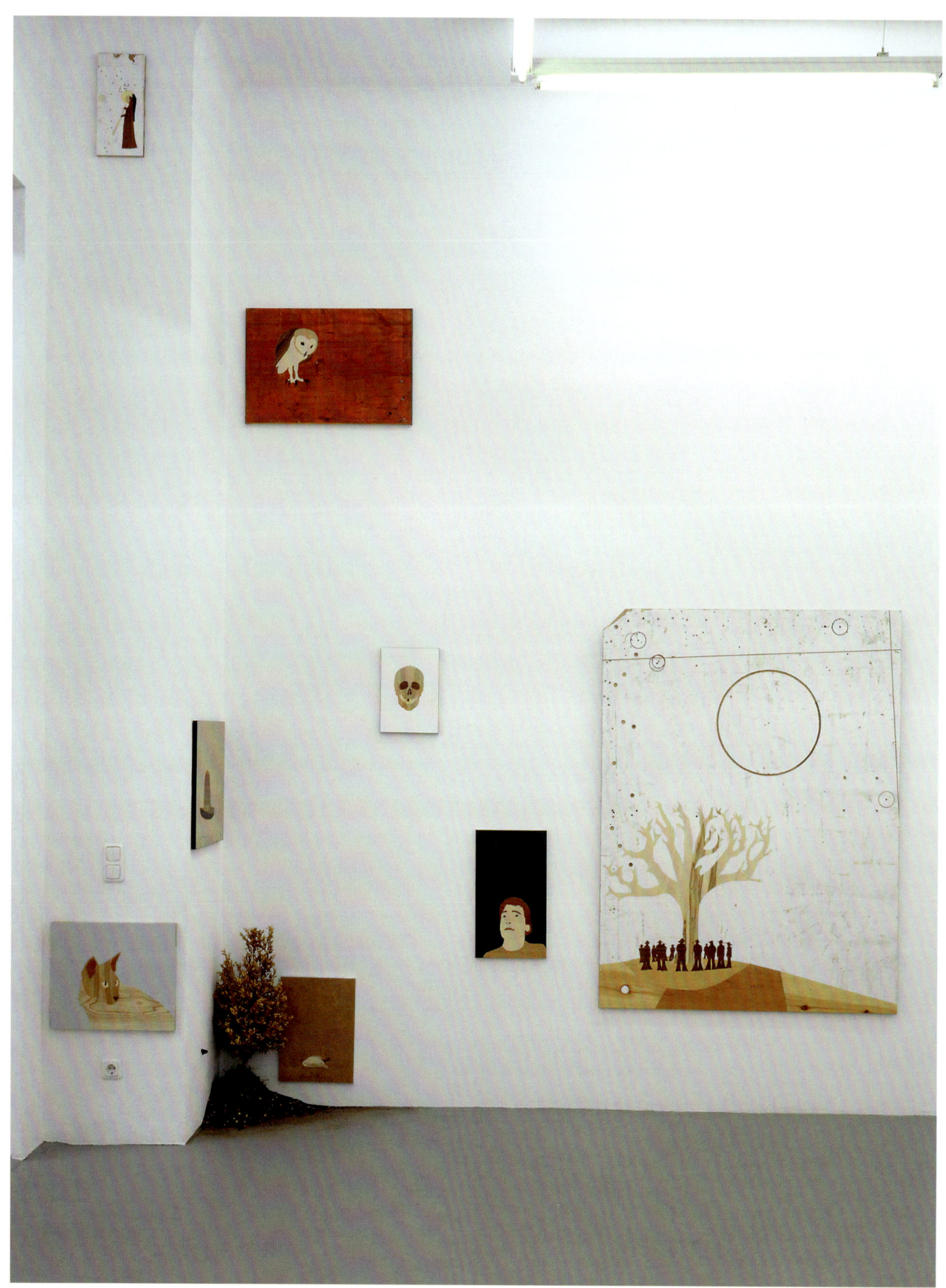

Goldhähnchens Ende, 2004, installation composed of seven collages, mound and sapling, dimensions variable, installation view Sprüth Magers Projekte, Munich

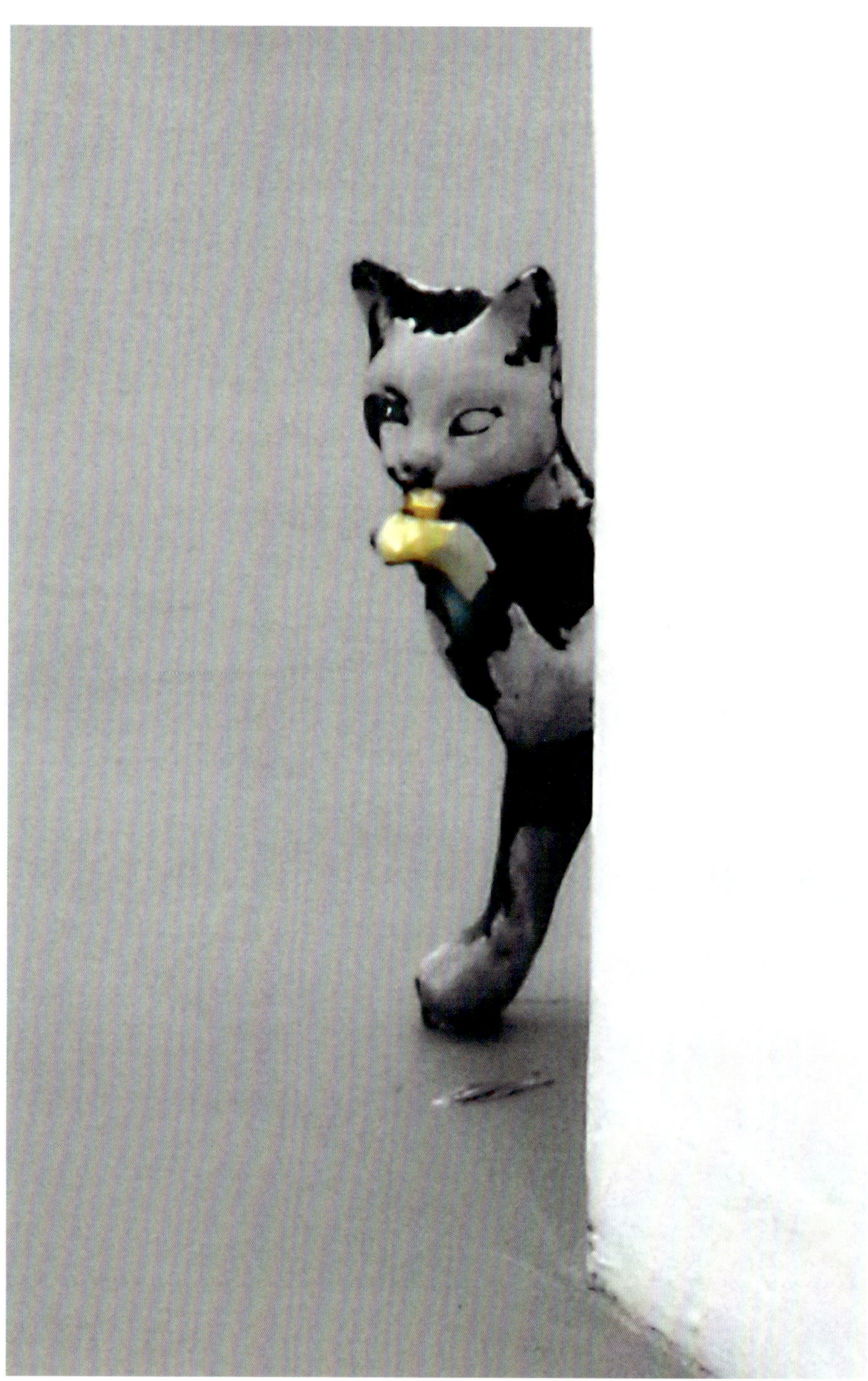

Goldhähnchens Ende: Goldhähnchen, 2004, press board, plastics, wood, in parts gold leaf, dimensions variable;
Private collection, Cologne

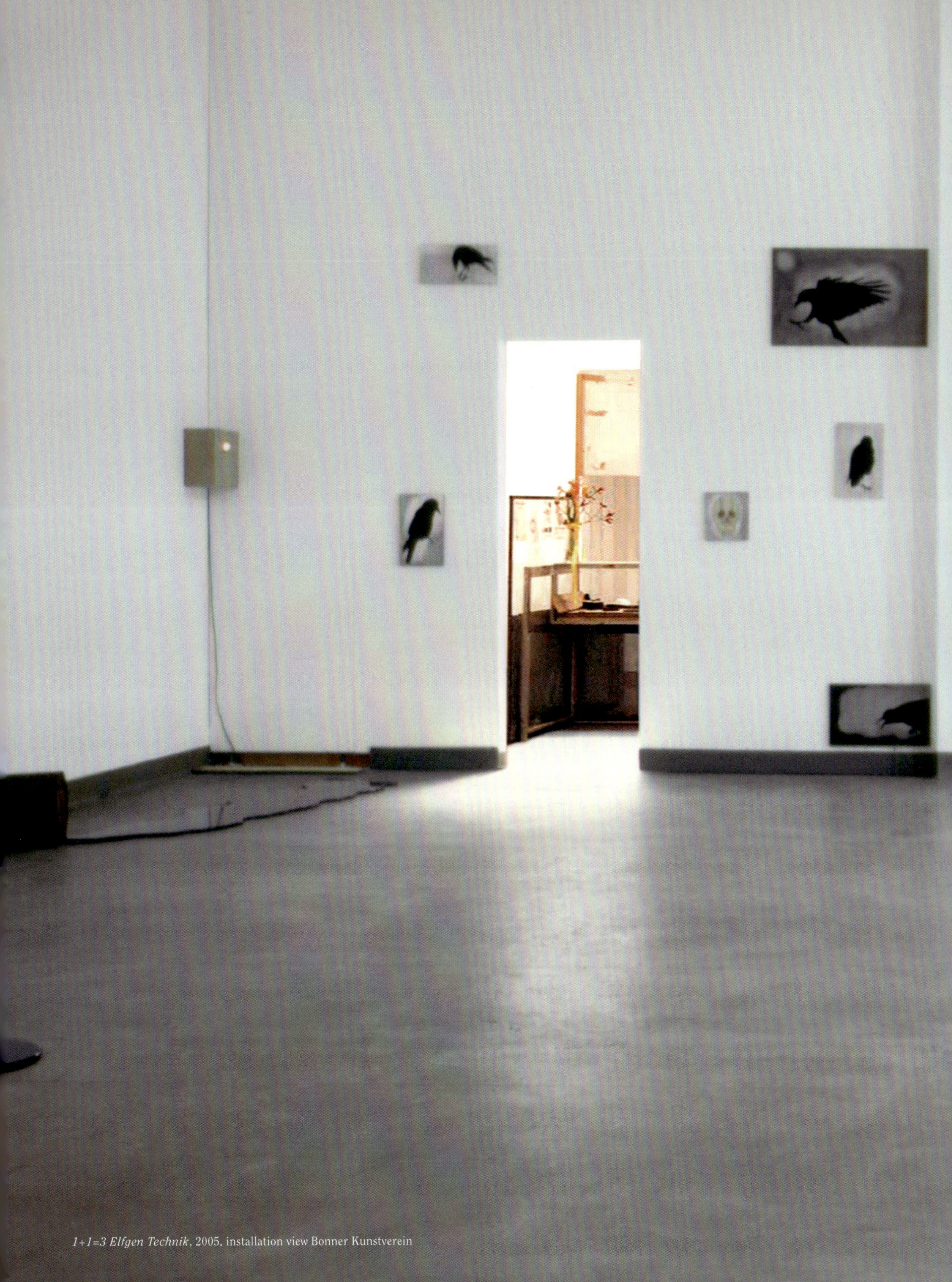

1+1=3 Elfgen Technik, 2005, installation view Bonner Kunstverein

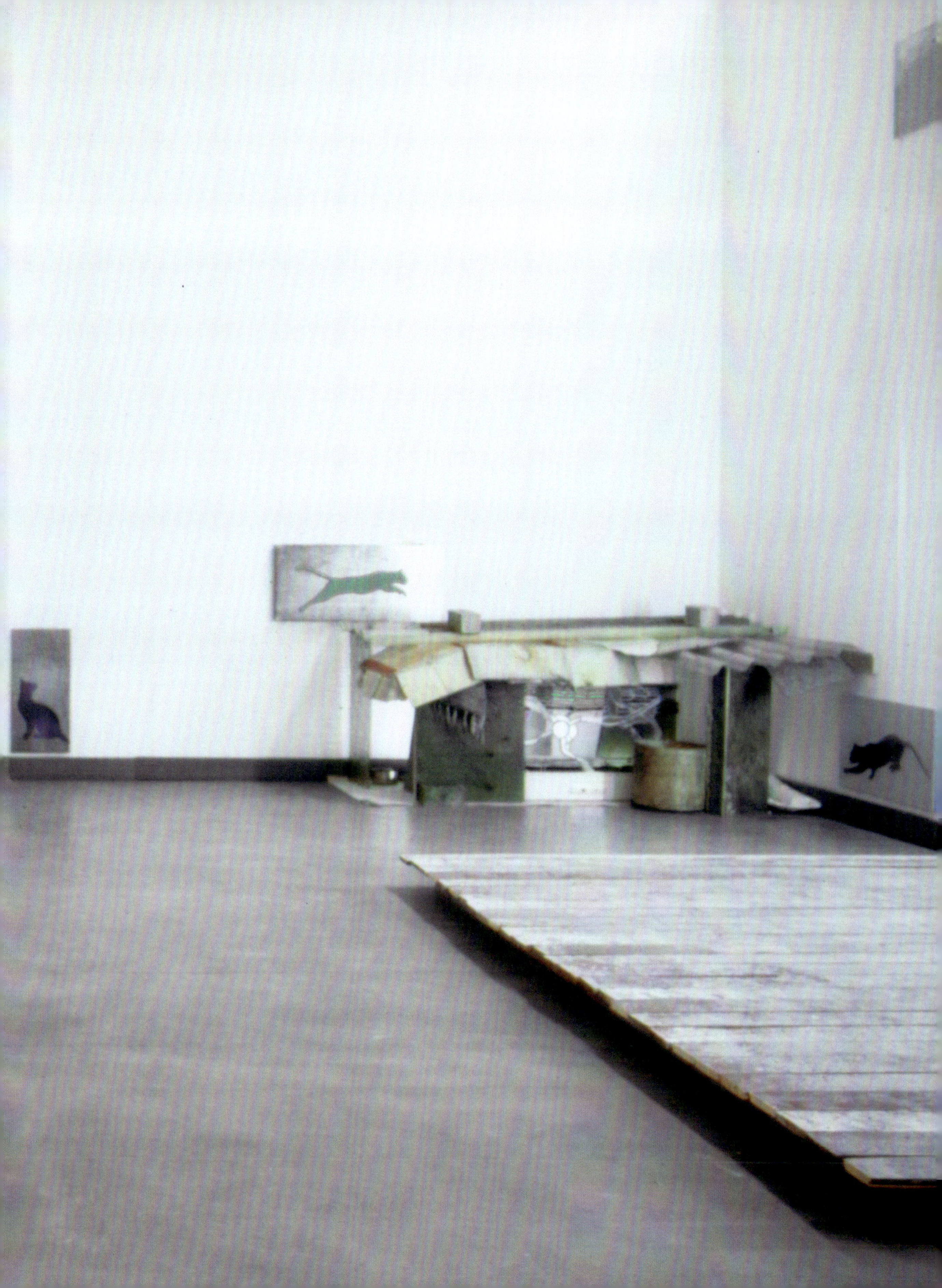

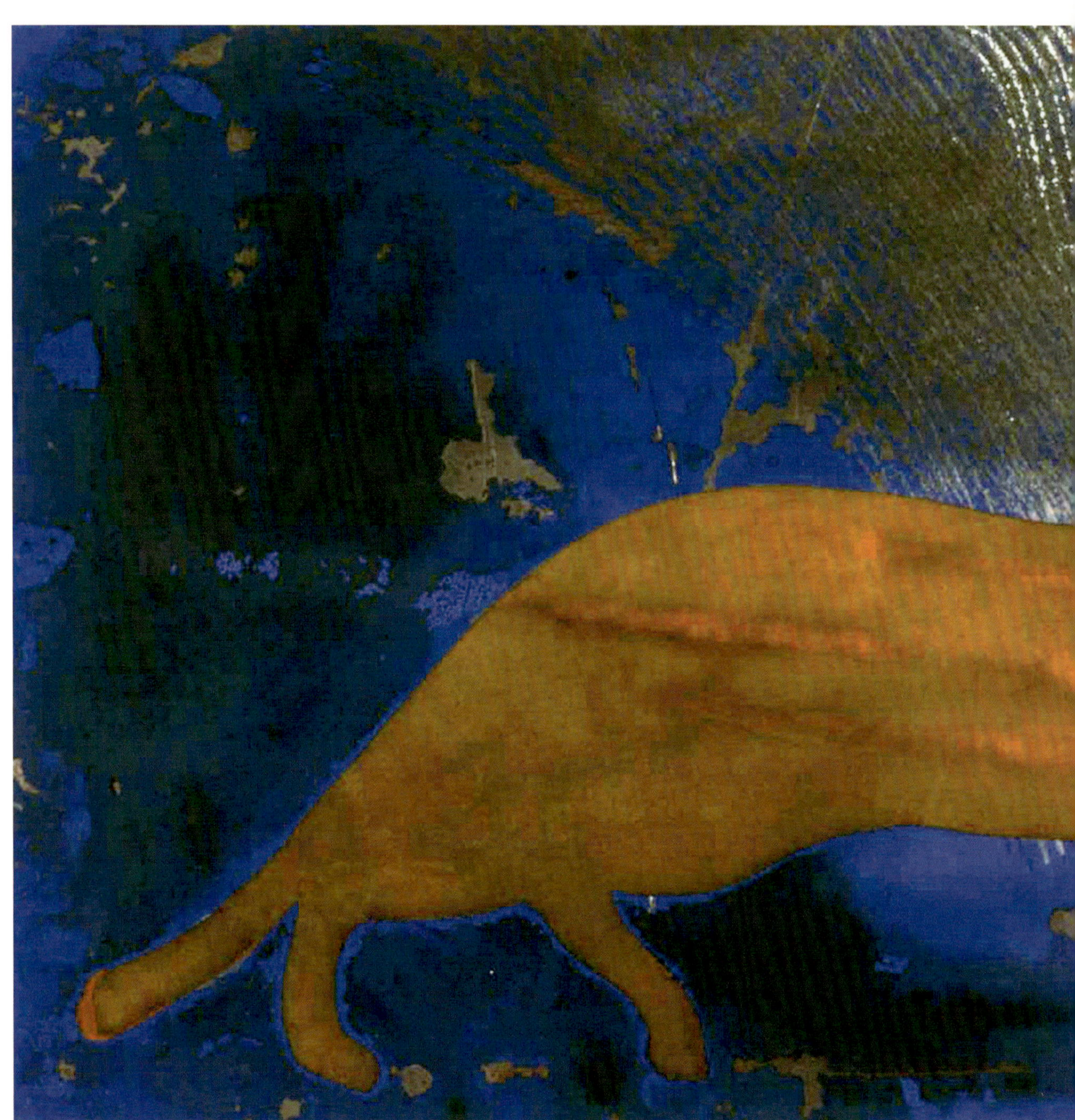

Katze mit Mond, 2005, fabric, acrylic on aluminium, 50 × 101 cm; Private collection, Cologne

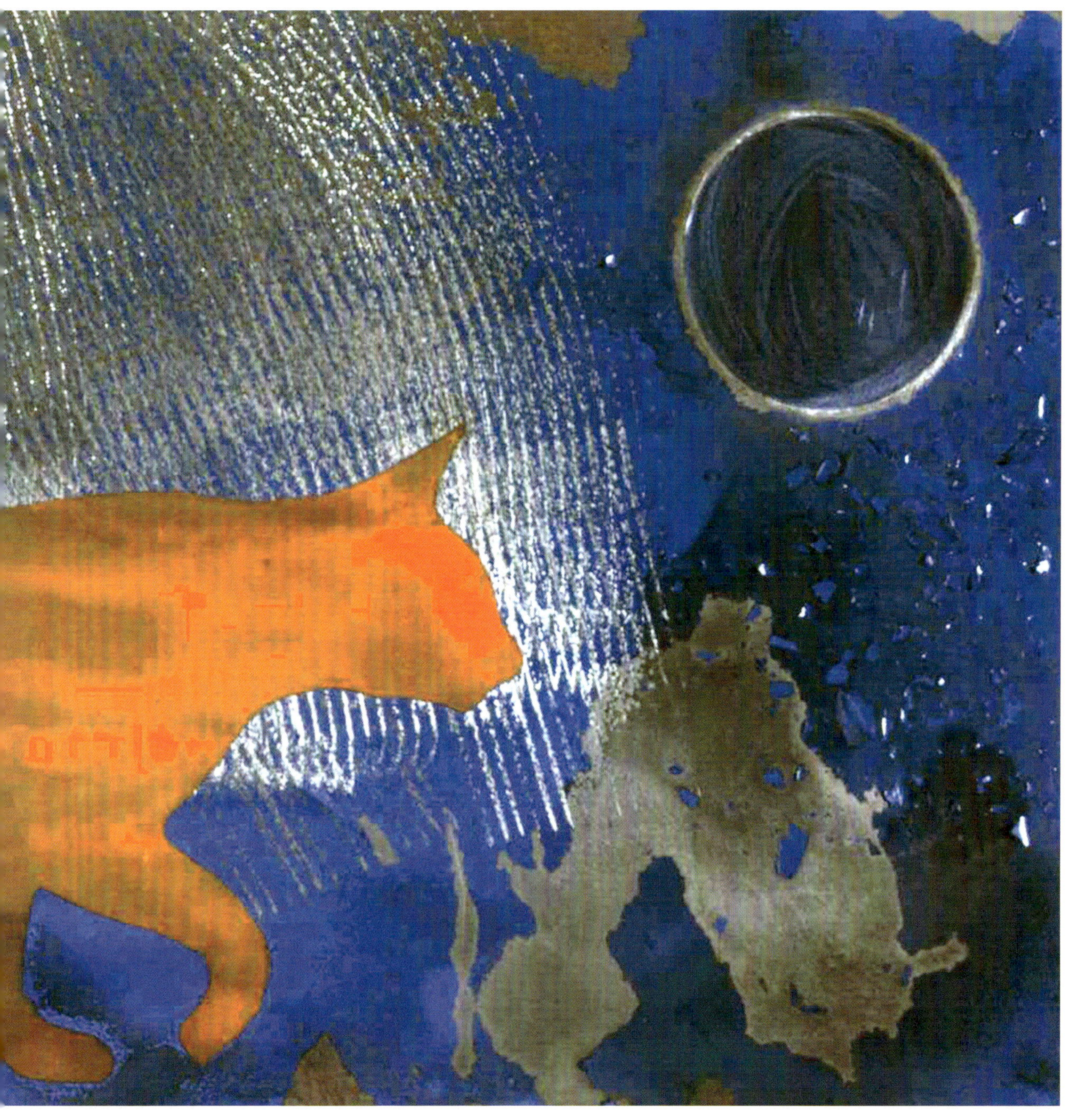

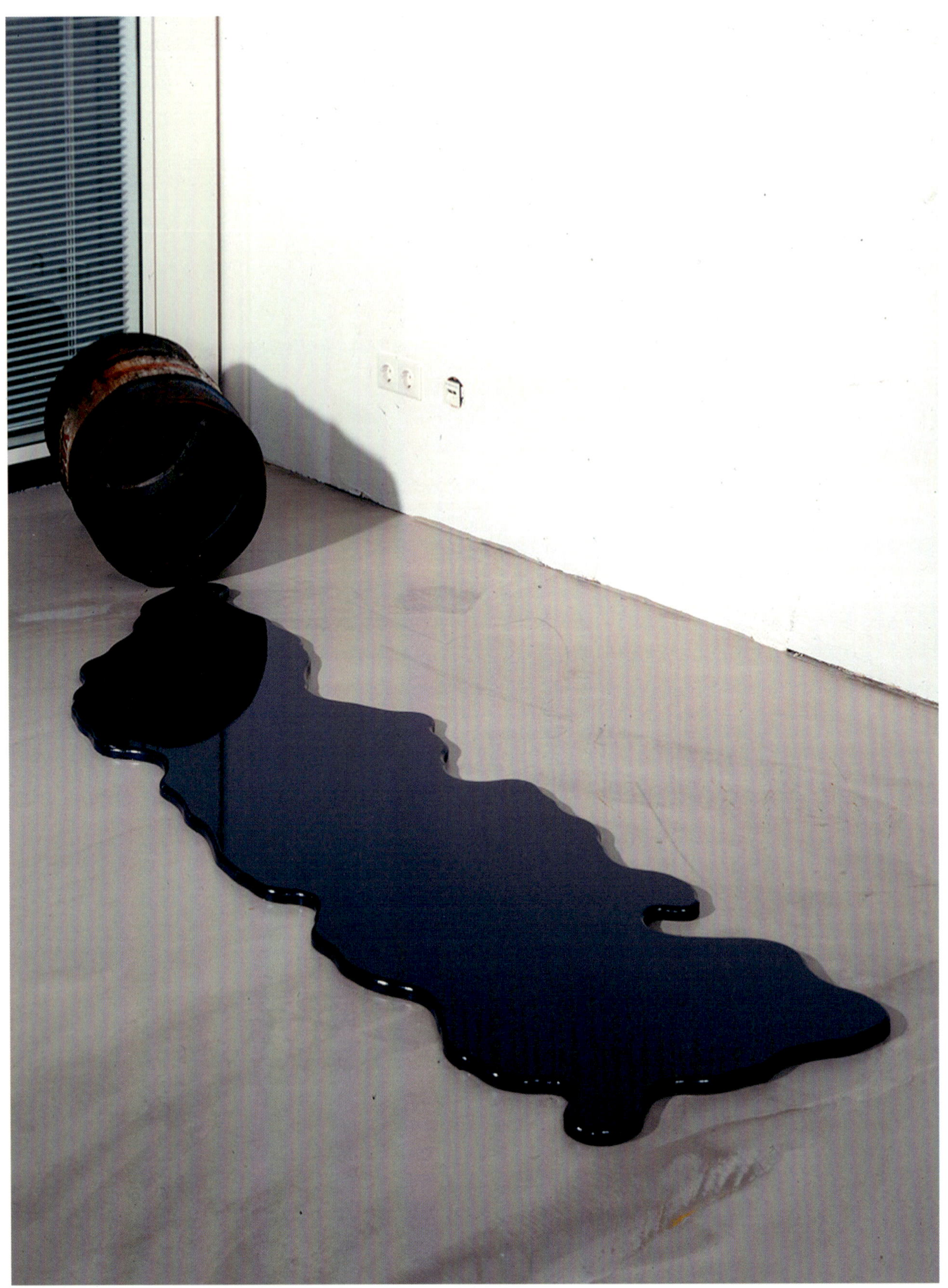

Fass 1, 2005, barrel, car finish, MDF, approx. 50 × 200 × 150 cm; Private collection, Cologne

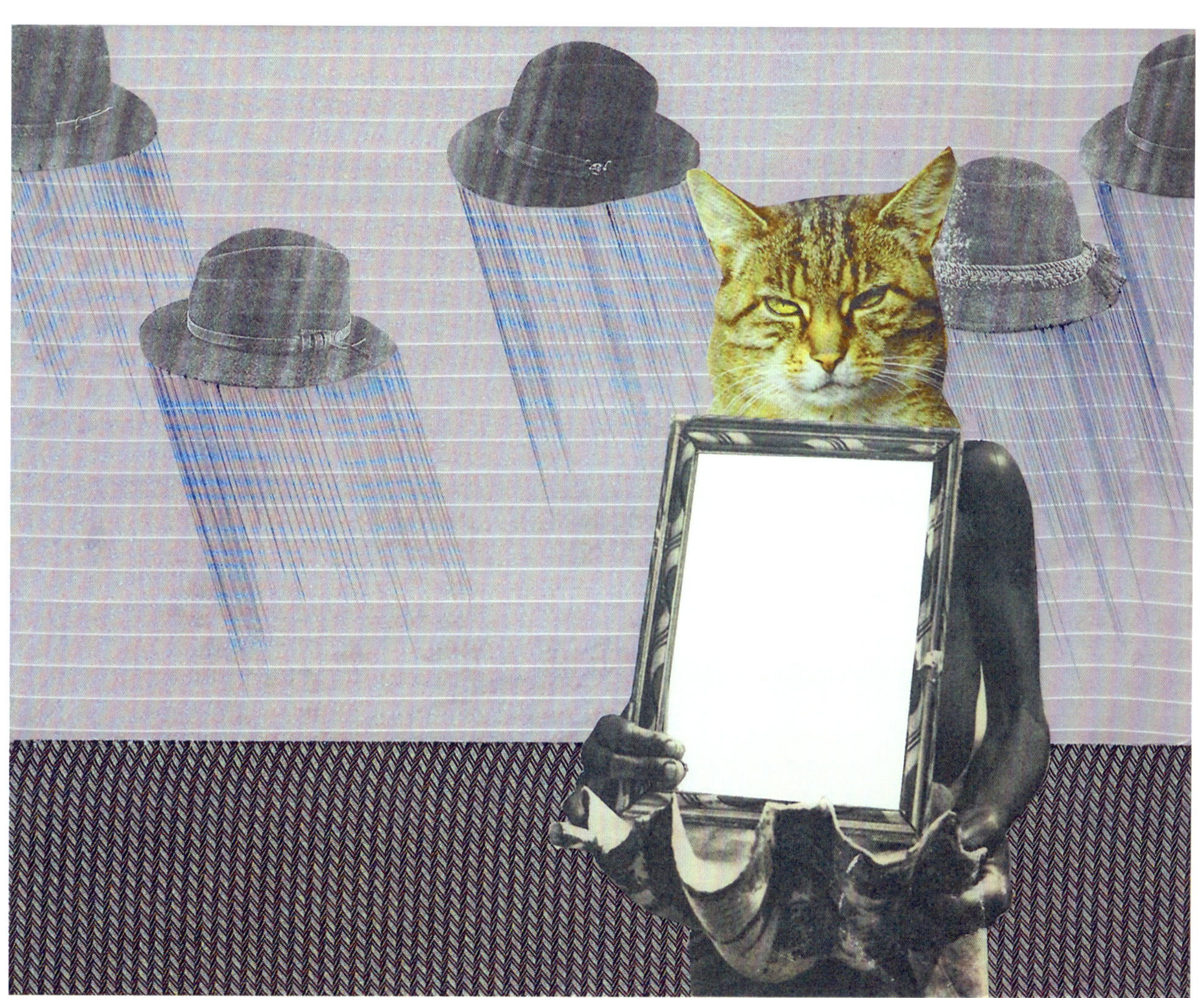

Auf dem Feld, 2006, fabric, paper on wood, 28 × 36 cm; Tanja Pol, Munich

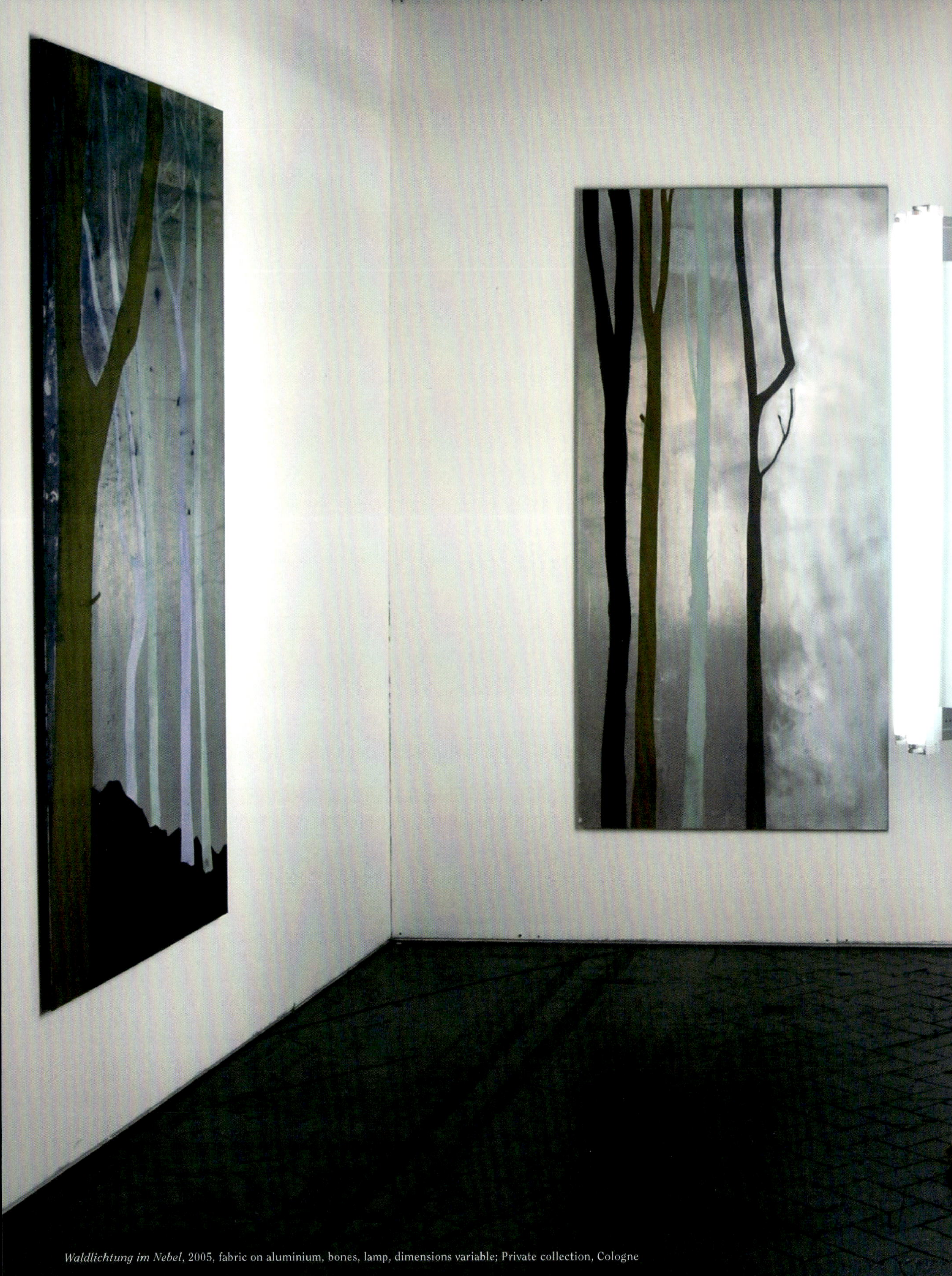

Waldlichtung im Nebel, 2005, fabric on aluminium, bones, lamp, dimensions variable; Private collection, Cologne

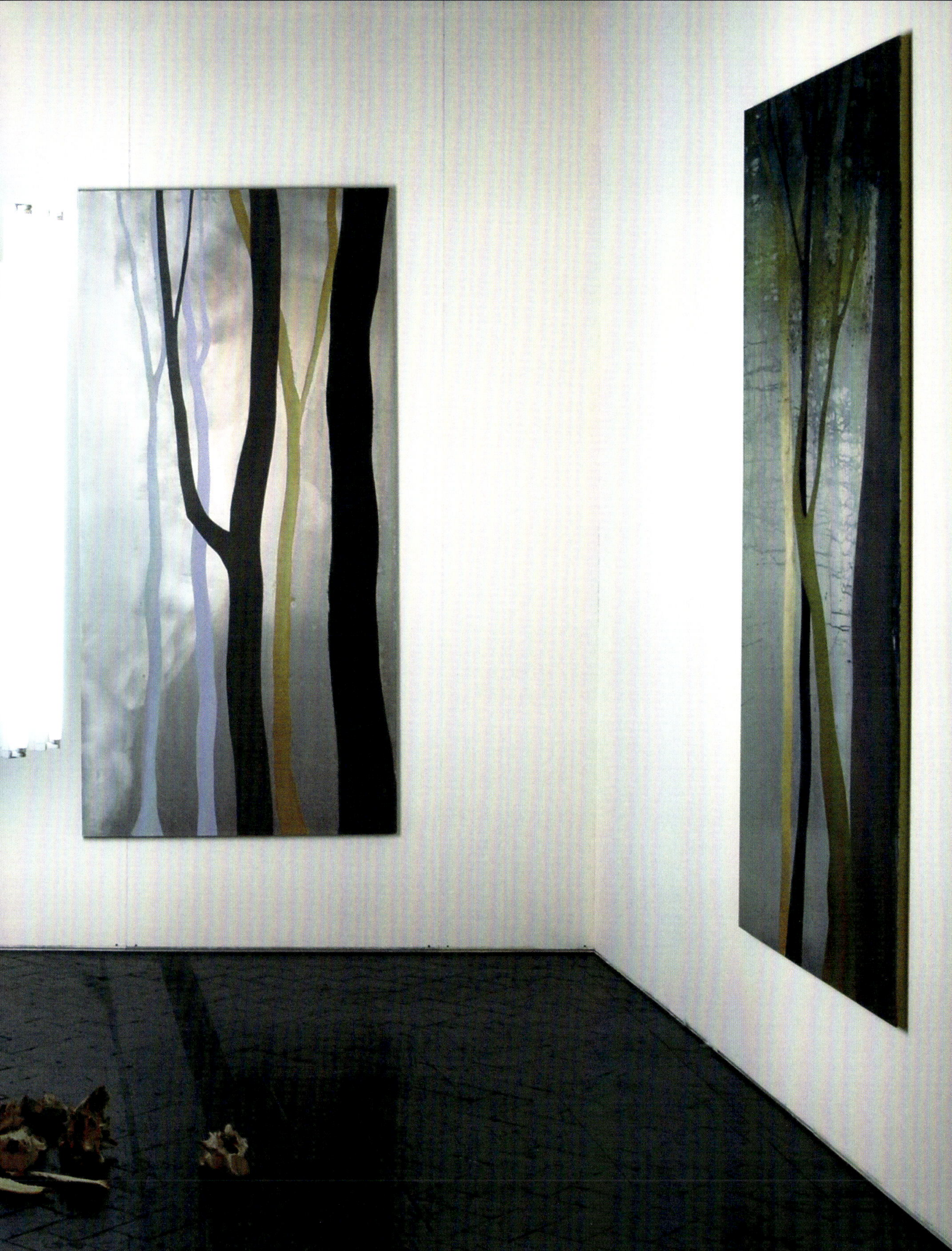

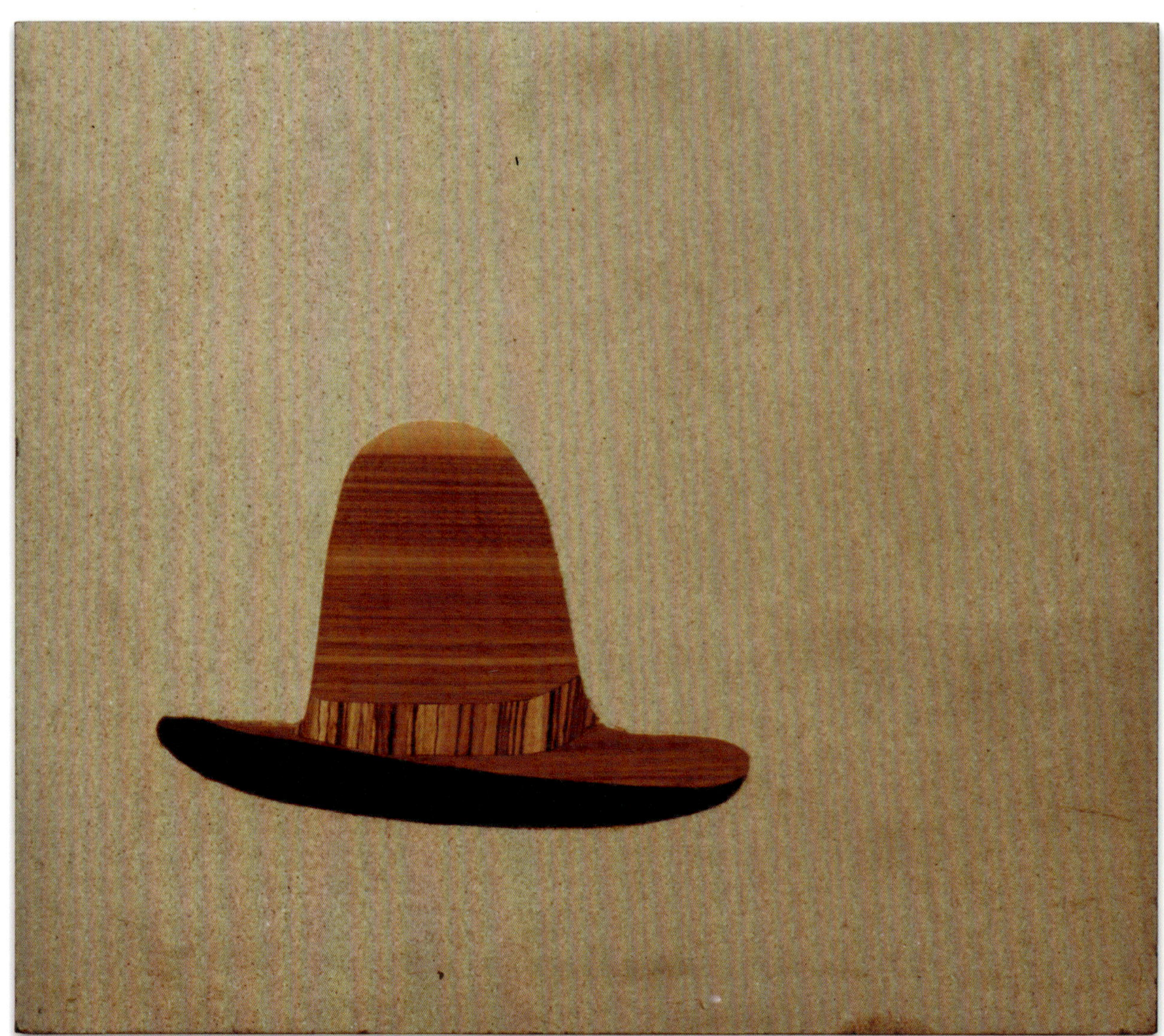

Goldhähnchens Ende: Hut, 2004, veneer on press board, 51 × 60 cm; Private collection, Cologne

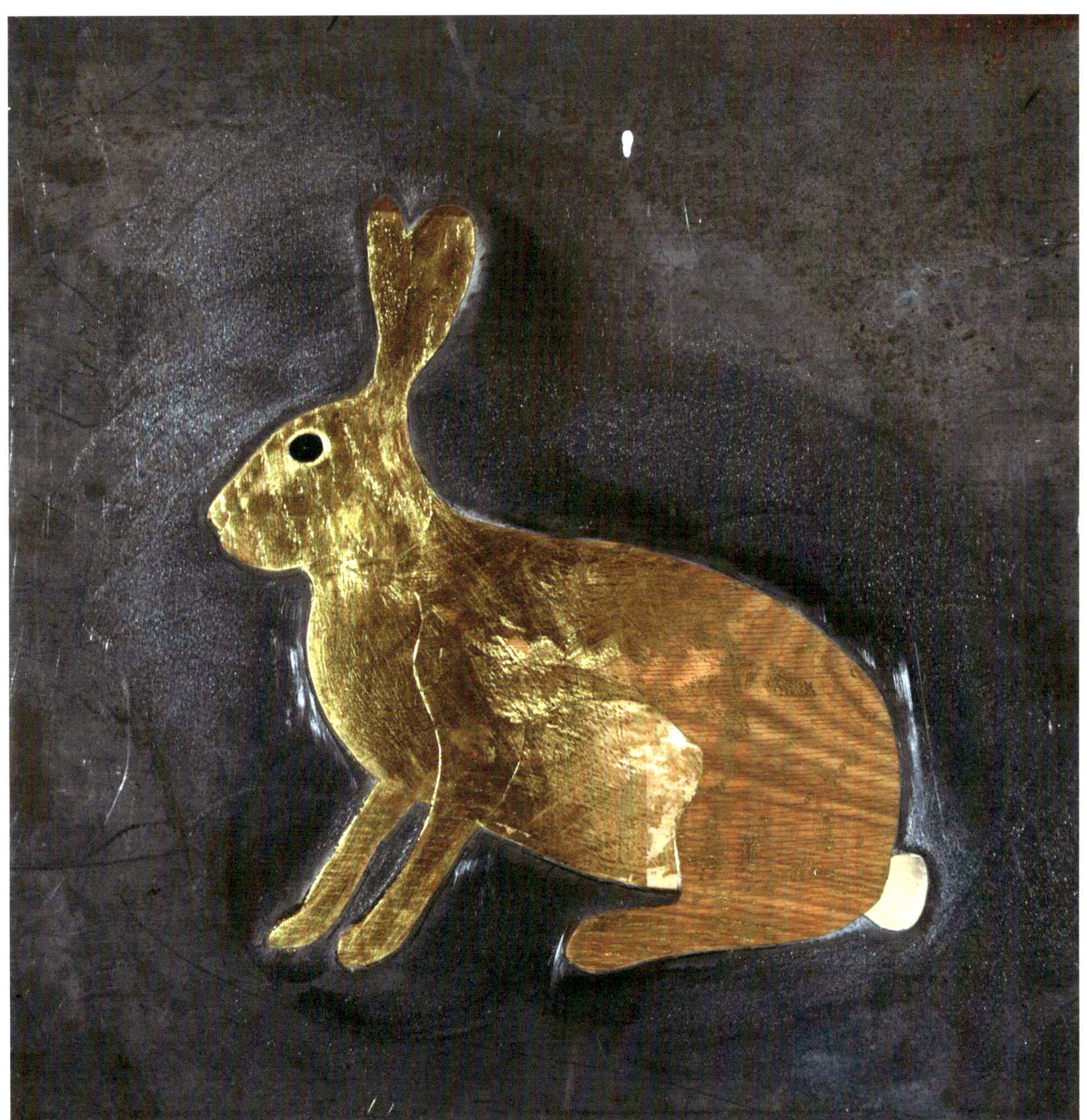

Hase, 2005, veneer, acrylic on aluminium, 50 × 50 cm; Private collection, Cologne

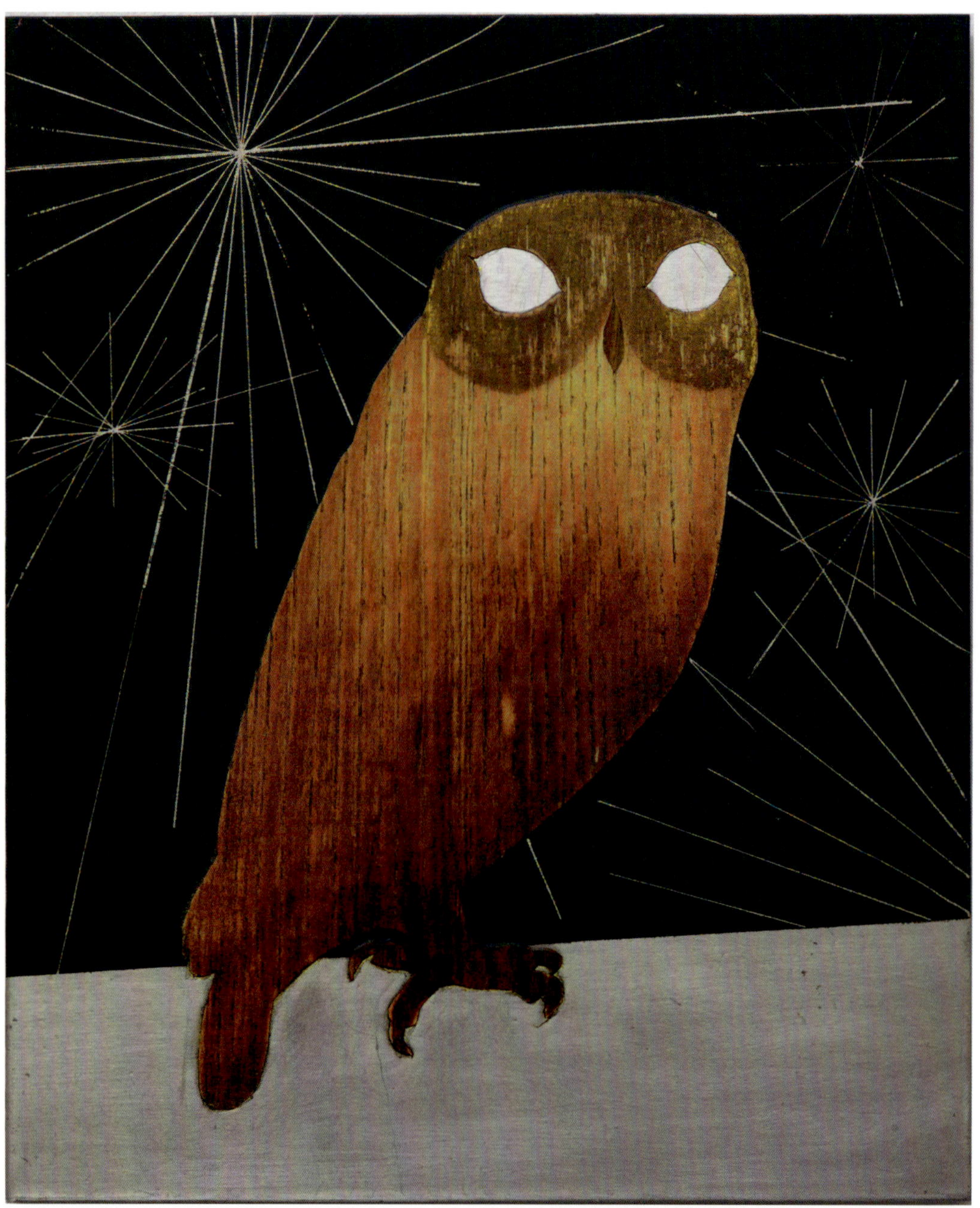

Frau Kauz, 2006, synthetic resin paint, veneer on aluminium, 36 × 30 cm; Private collection, Zurich

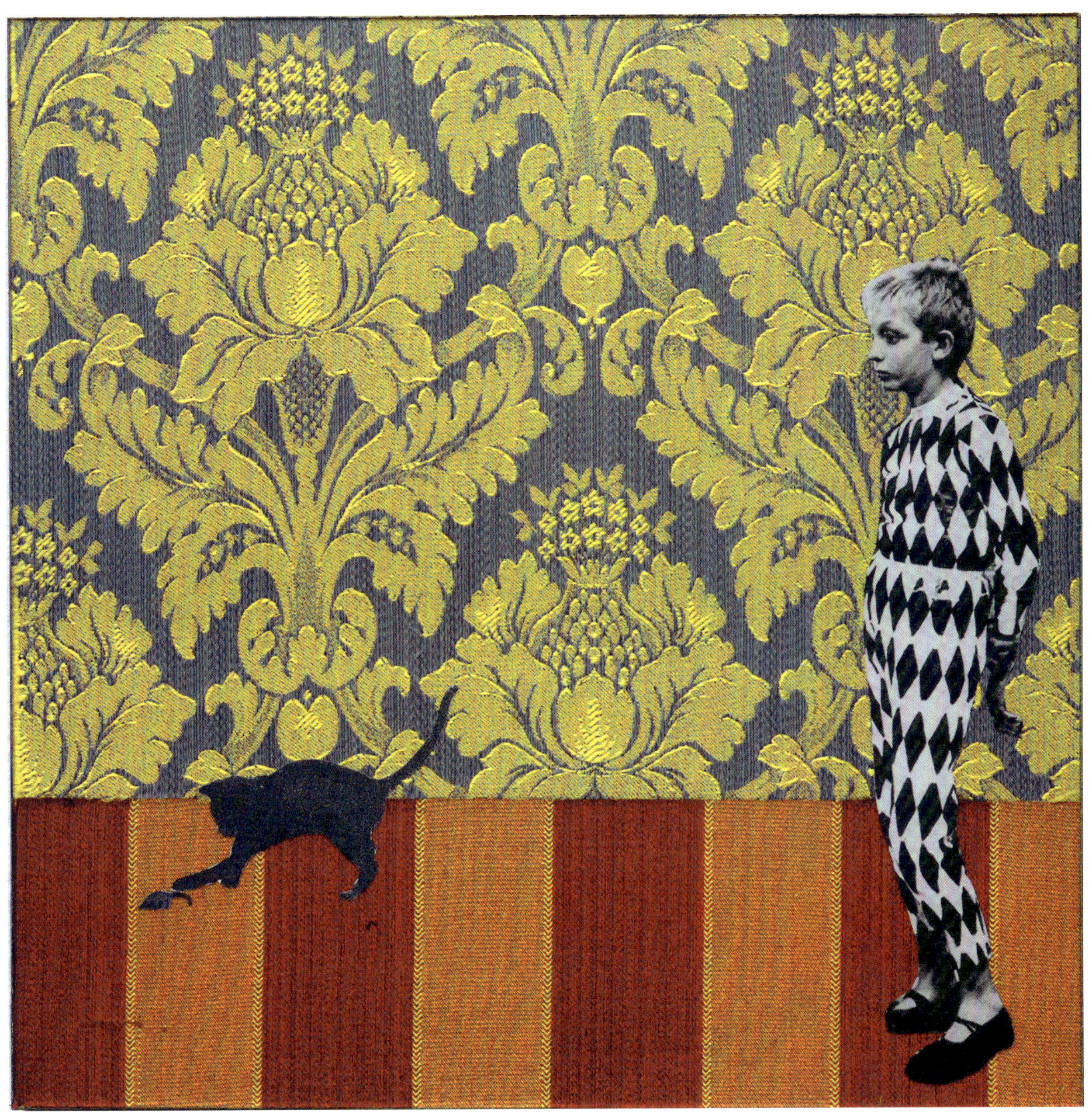

Spielzimmer, 2006, fabric, paper on MDF, 35 × 35 cm

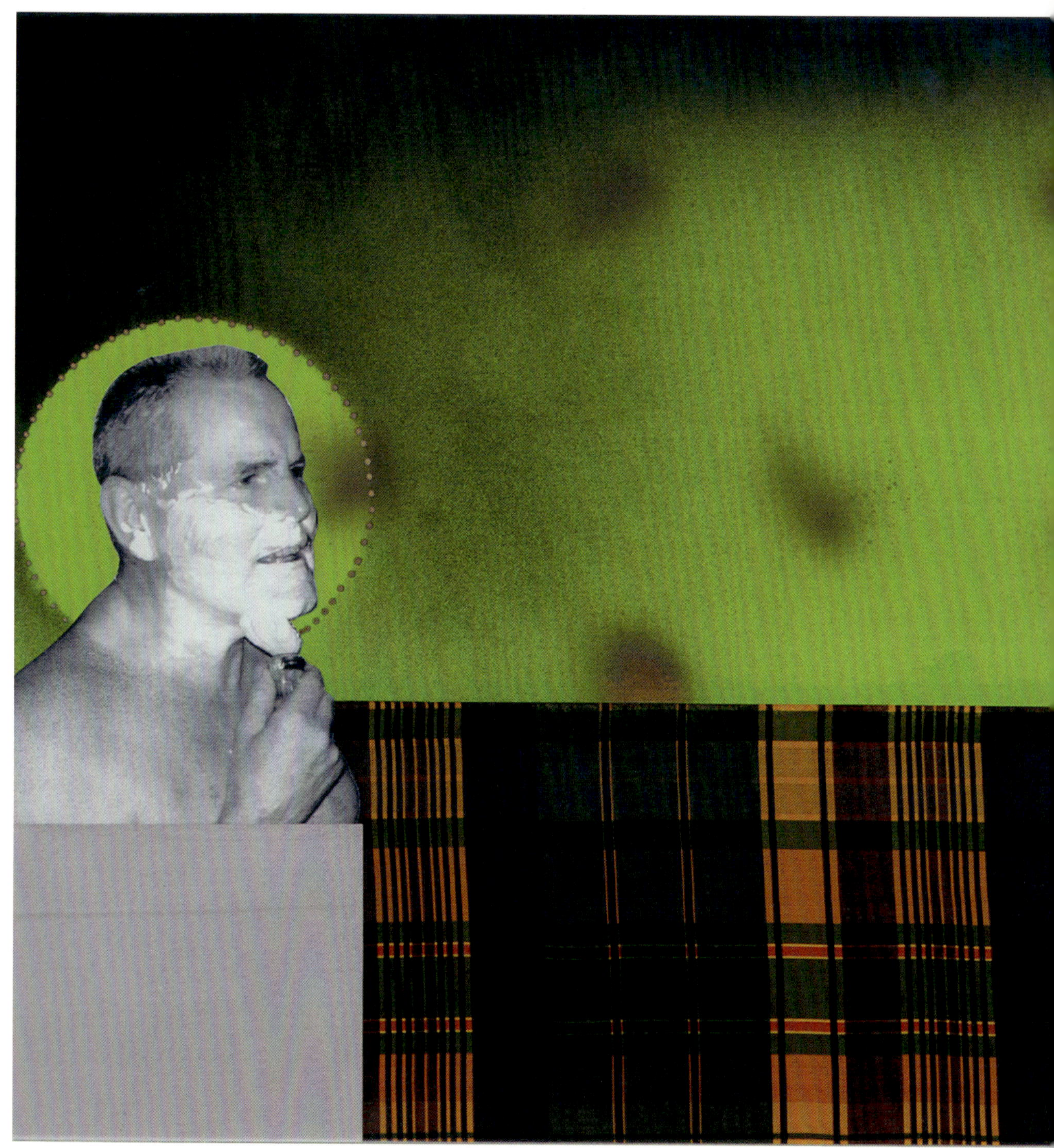

Steuerprüfung, 2006, wood, glass, fabric, paper, car lacquer, gold leaf, 46.3 × 88 cm; Private collection, Munich

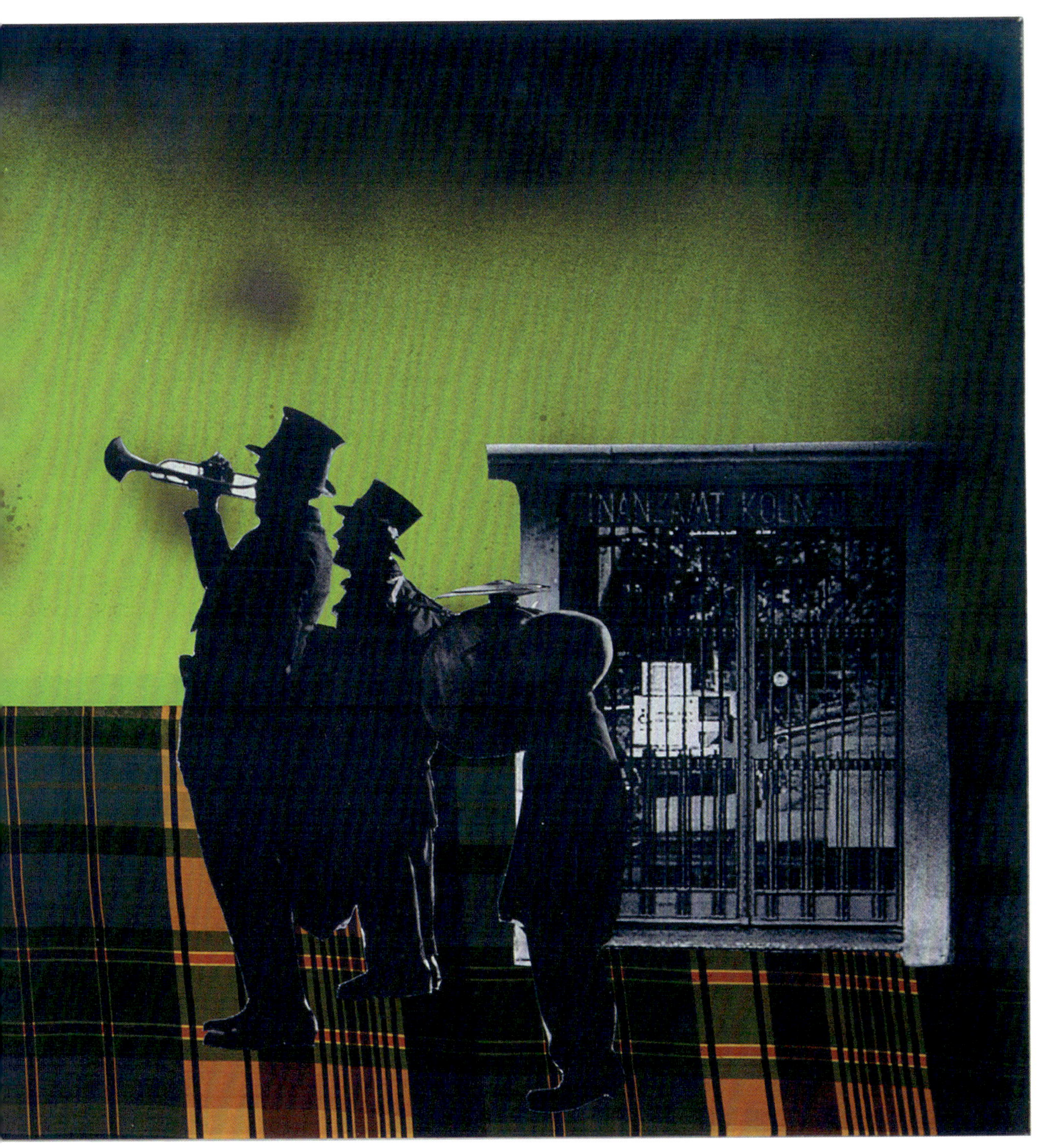
FINANZAMT KÖLN

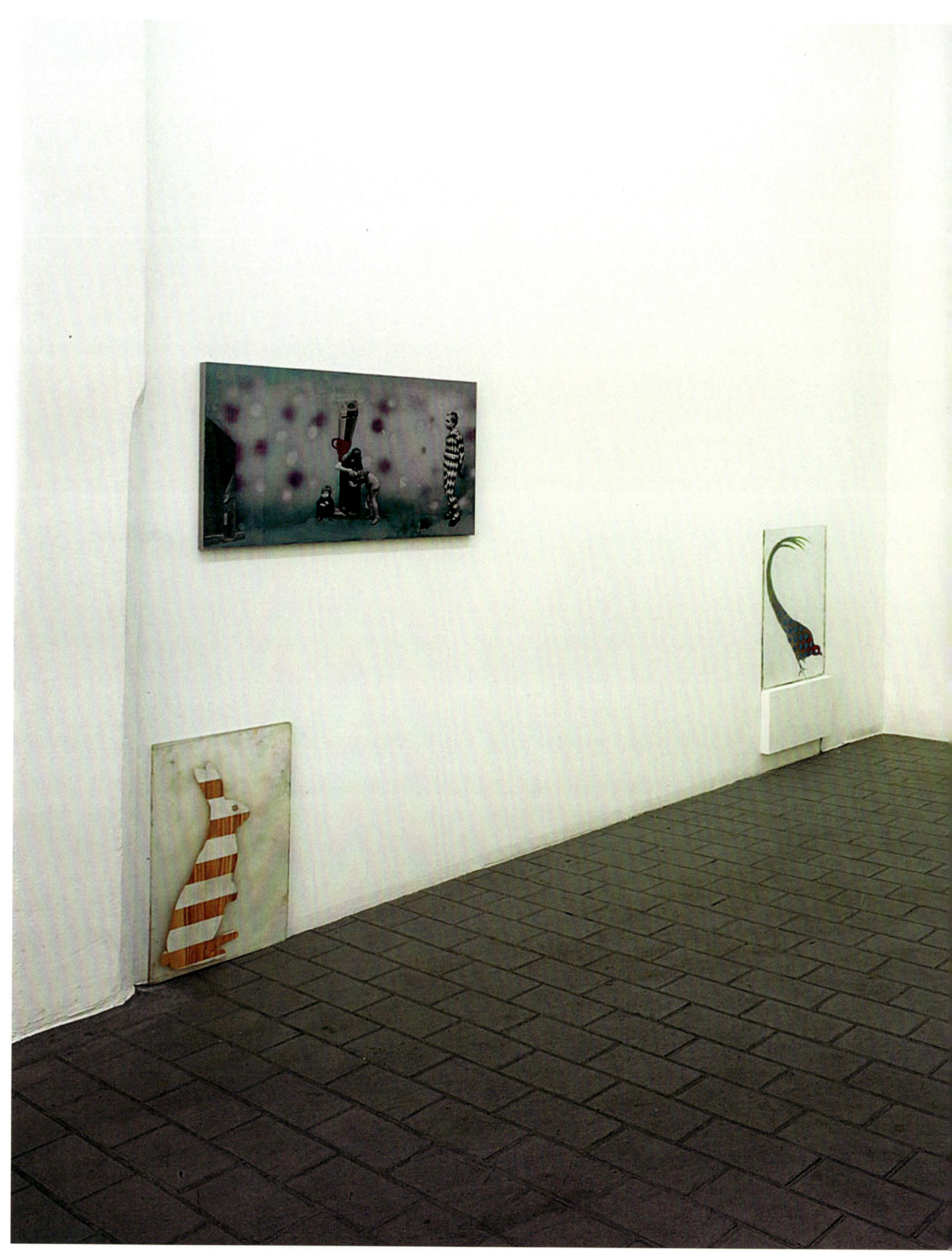

wie man wird, was man ist, 2006, installation view Sprüth Magers Projekte, Munich

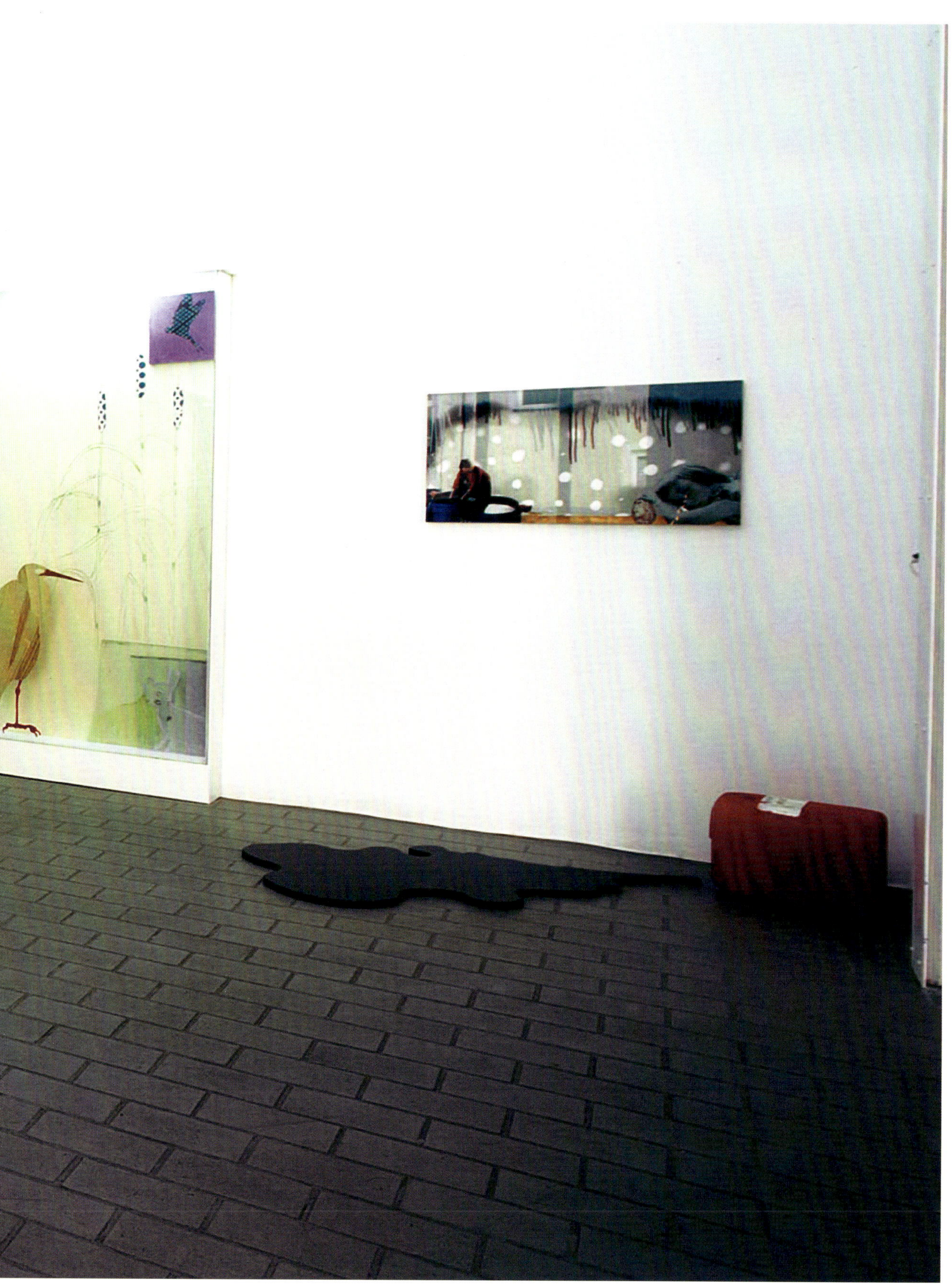

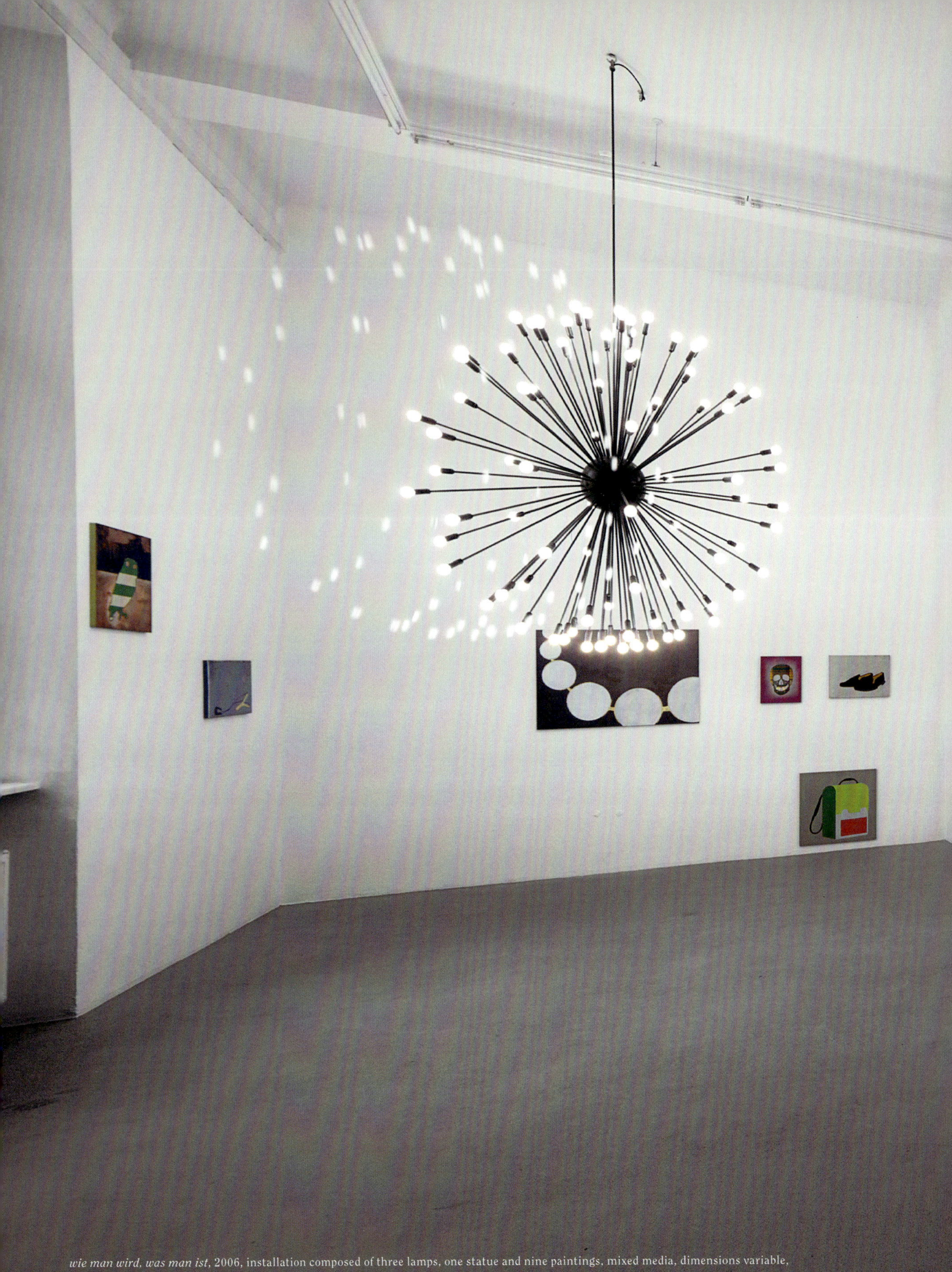

wie man wird, was man ist, 2006, installation composed of three lamps, one statue and nine paintings, mixed media, dimensions variable, installation view Sprüth Magers Projekte, Munich

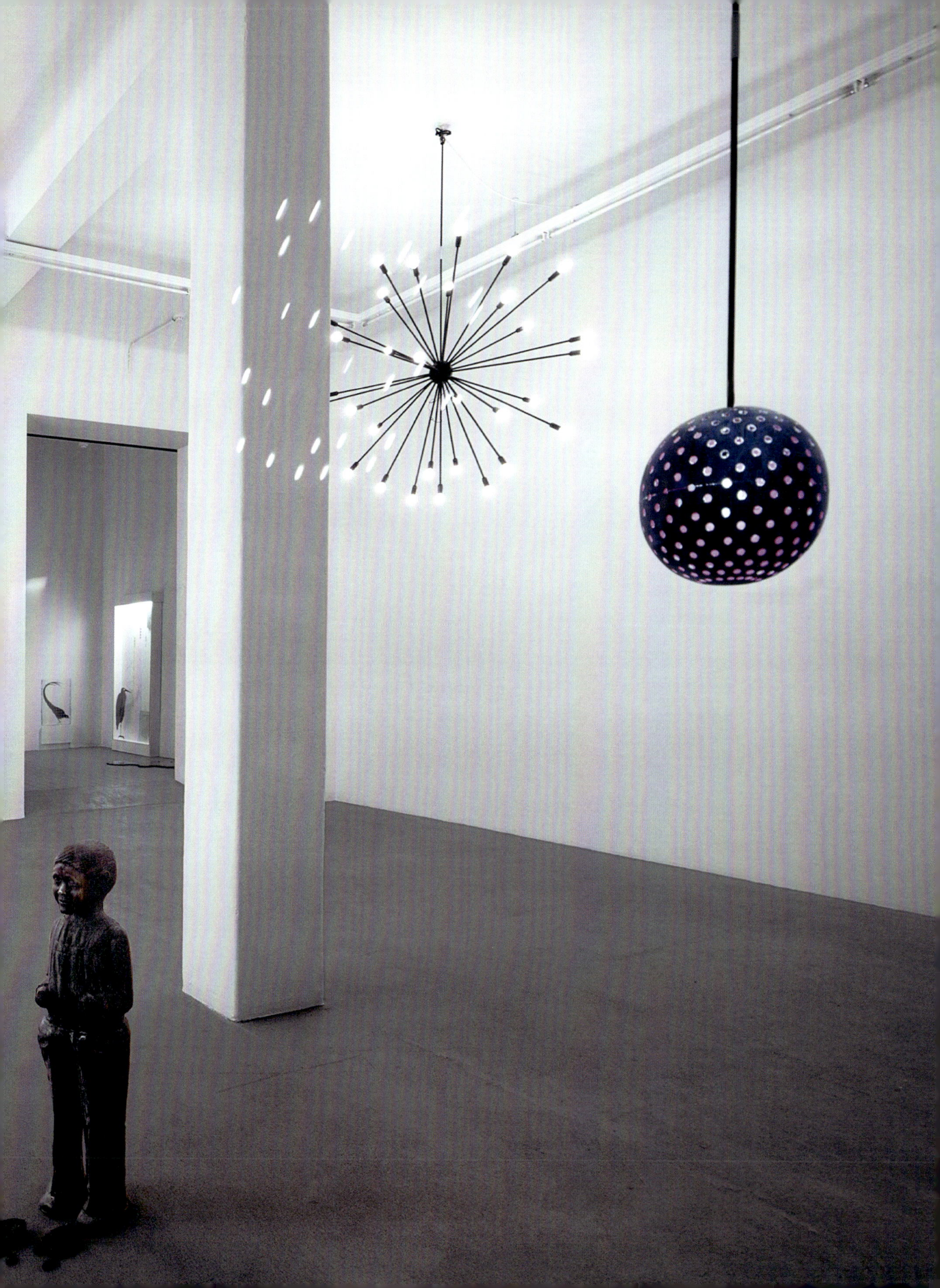

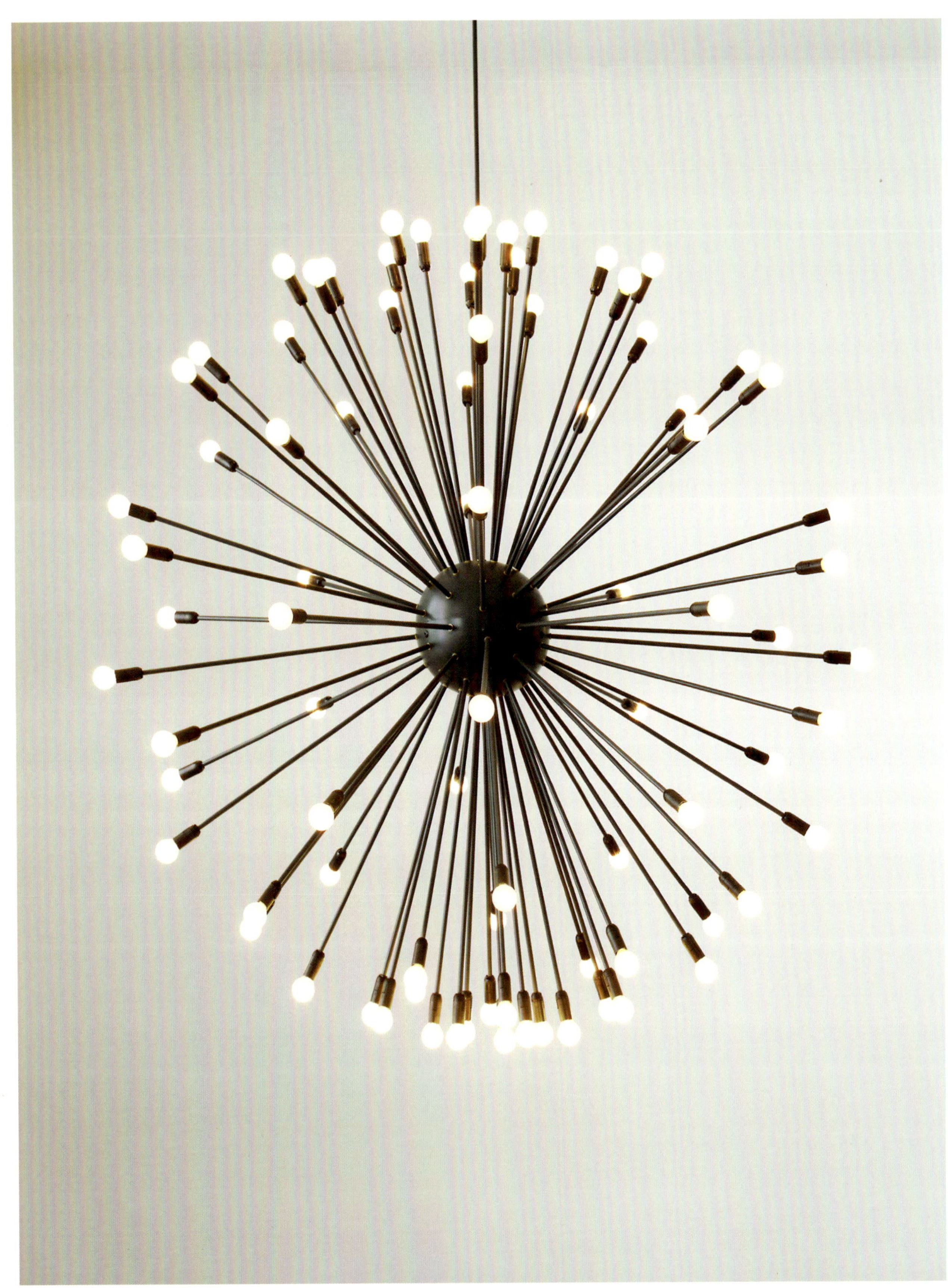

wie man wird, was man ist: Mutter, 2006, steel, electronics, diameter: 150 cm

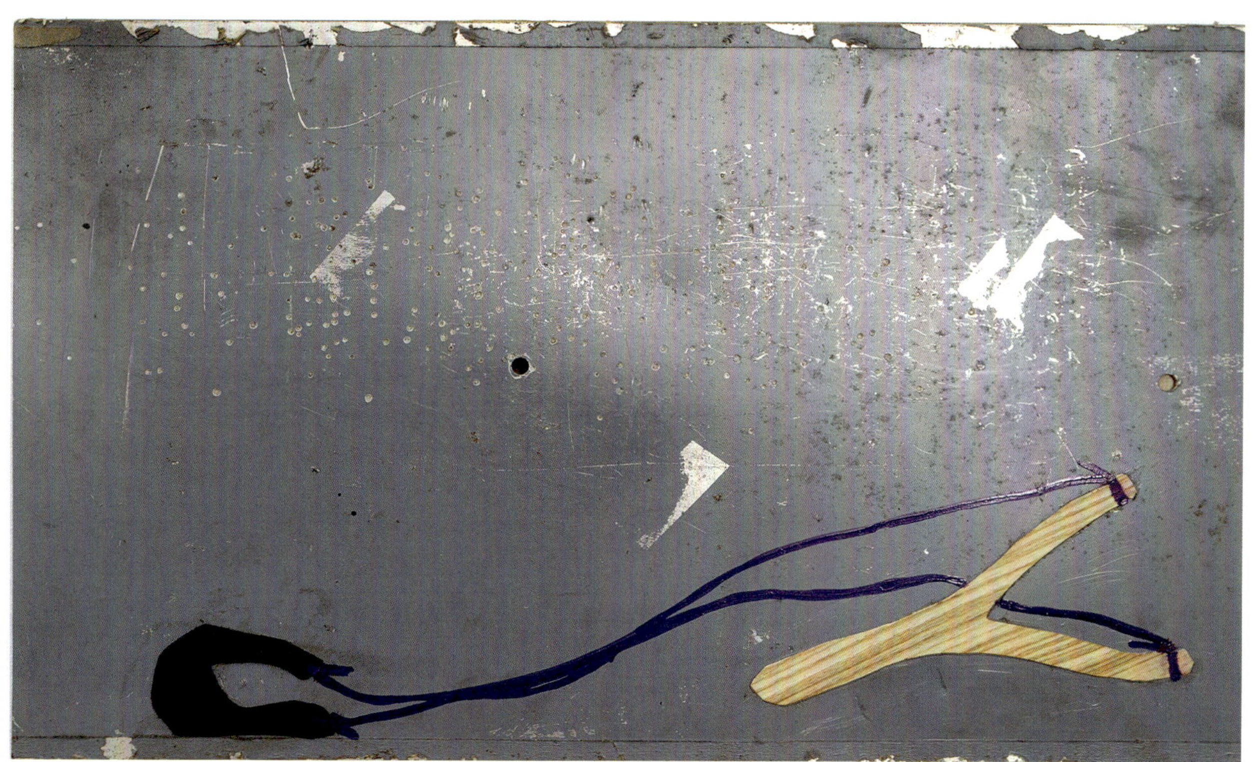

wie man wird, was man ist: Schleuder, 2006, chipboard, aluminium, lacquer, wood, 31 × 51 cm

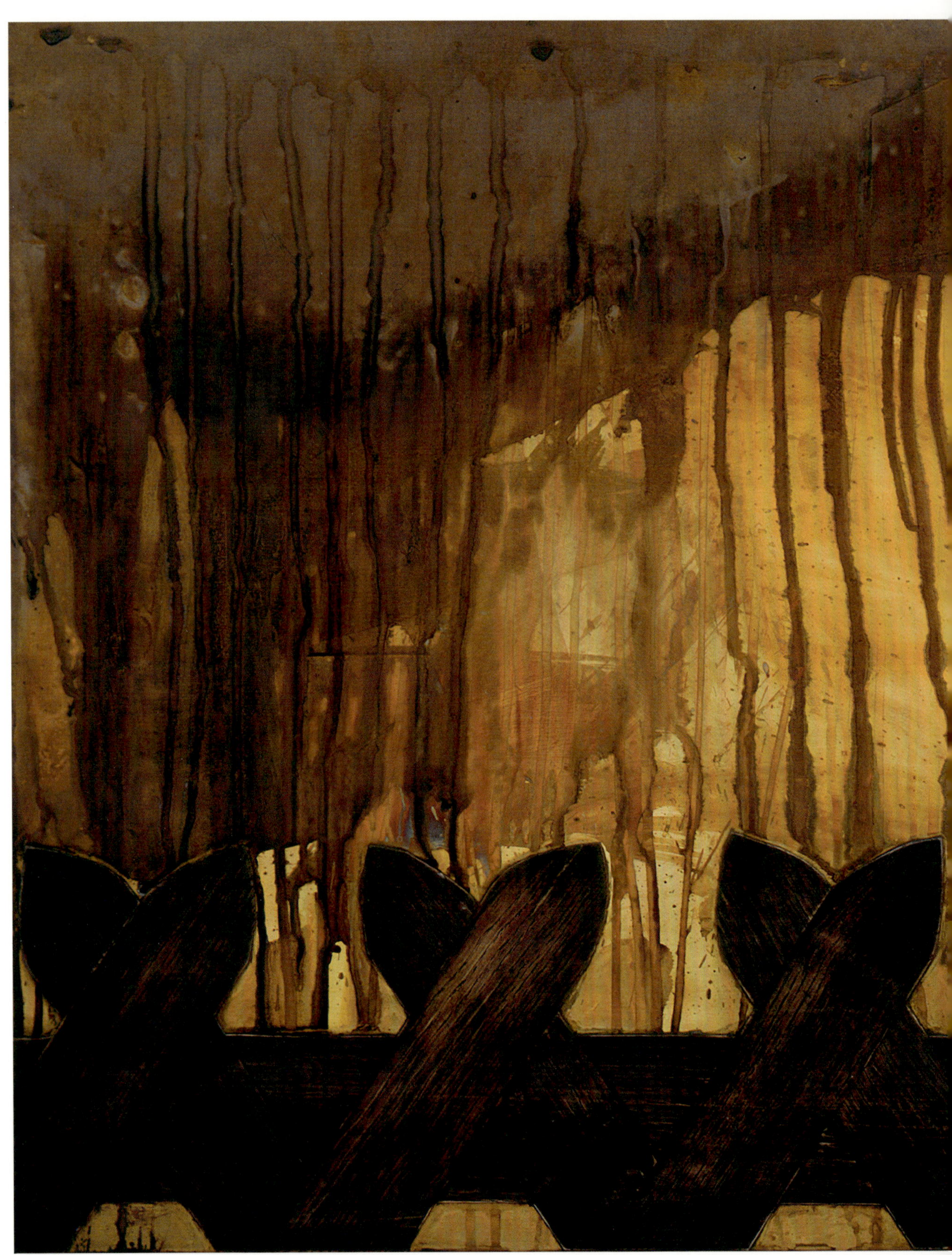

wie man wird, was man ist: Jägerzaun, 2006, etched brass, veneer, 60 × 95.5 cm

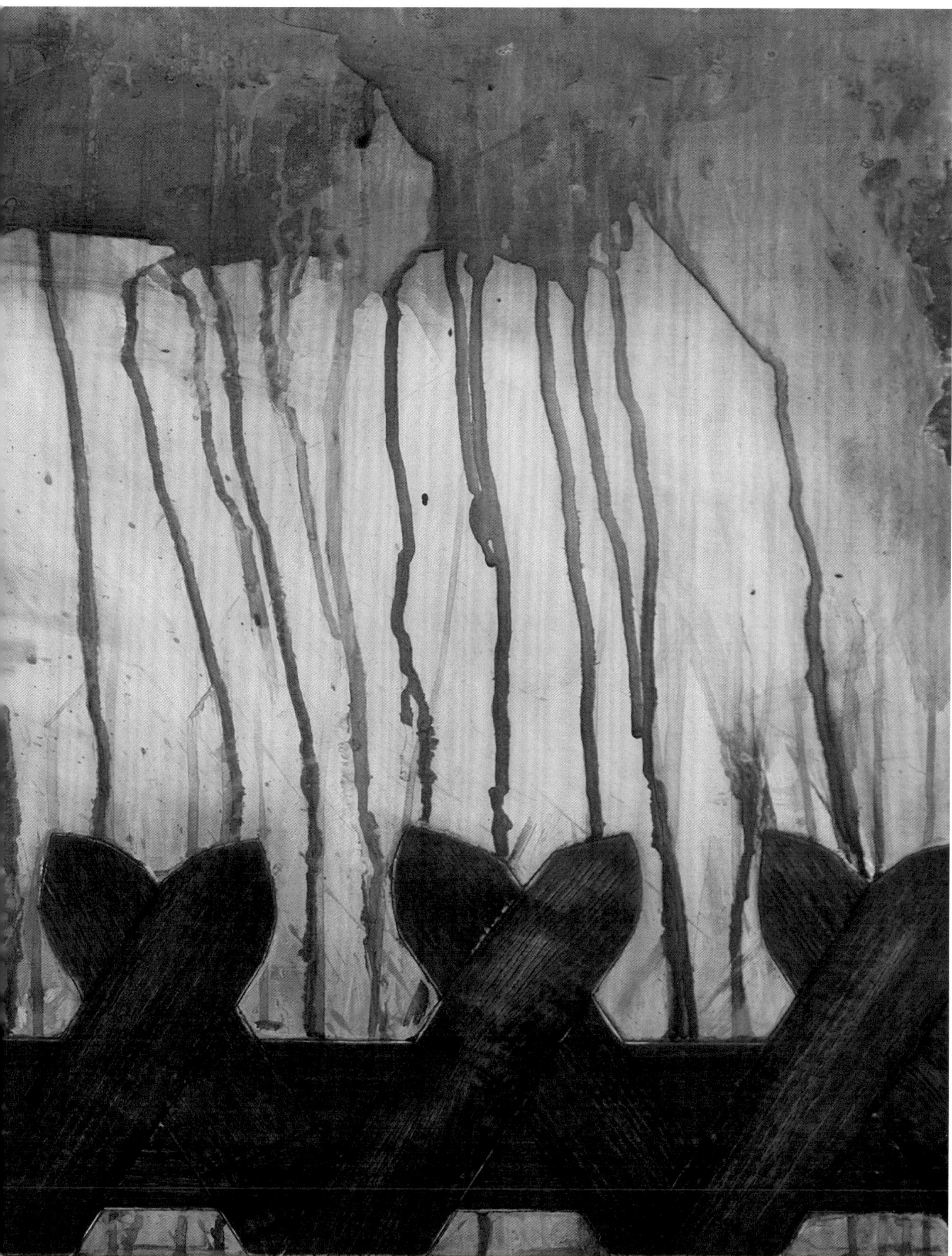

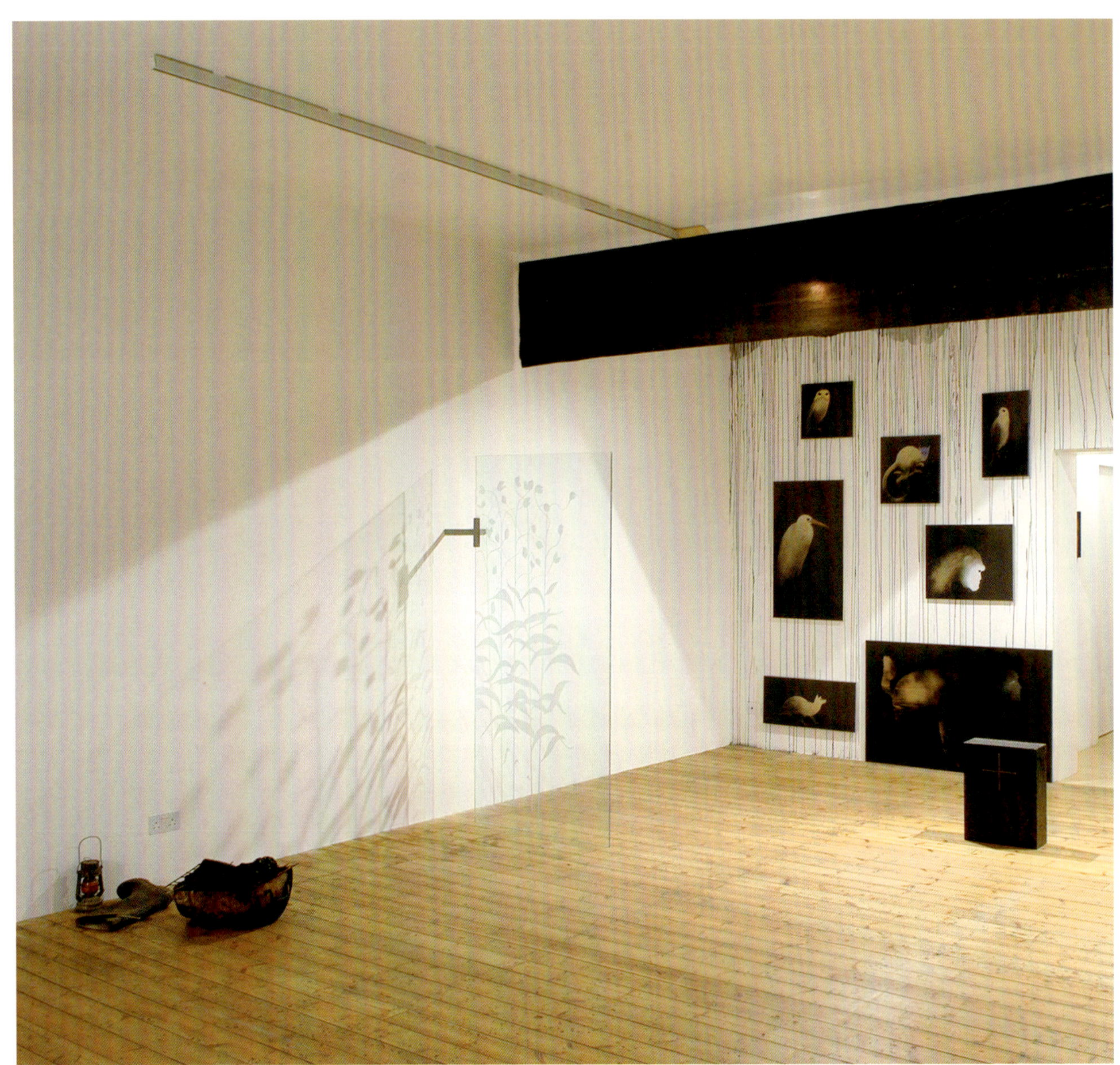

Expedition, 2006, installation composed of several sculptures, collages and video installation, mixed media, installation view westlondonprojects, London; Sender Collection

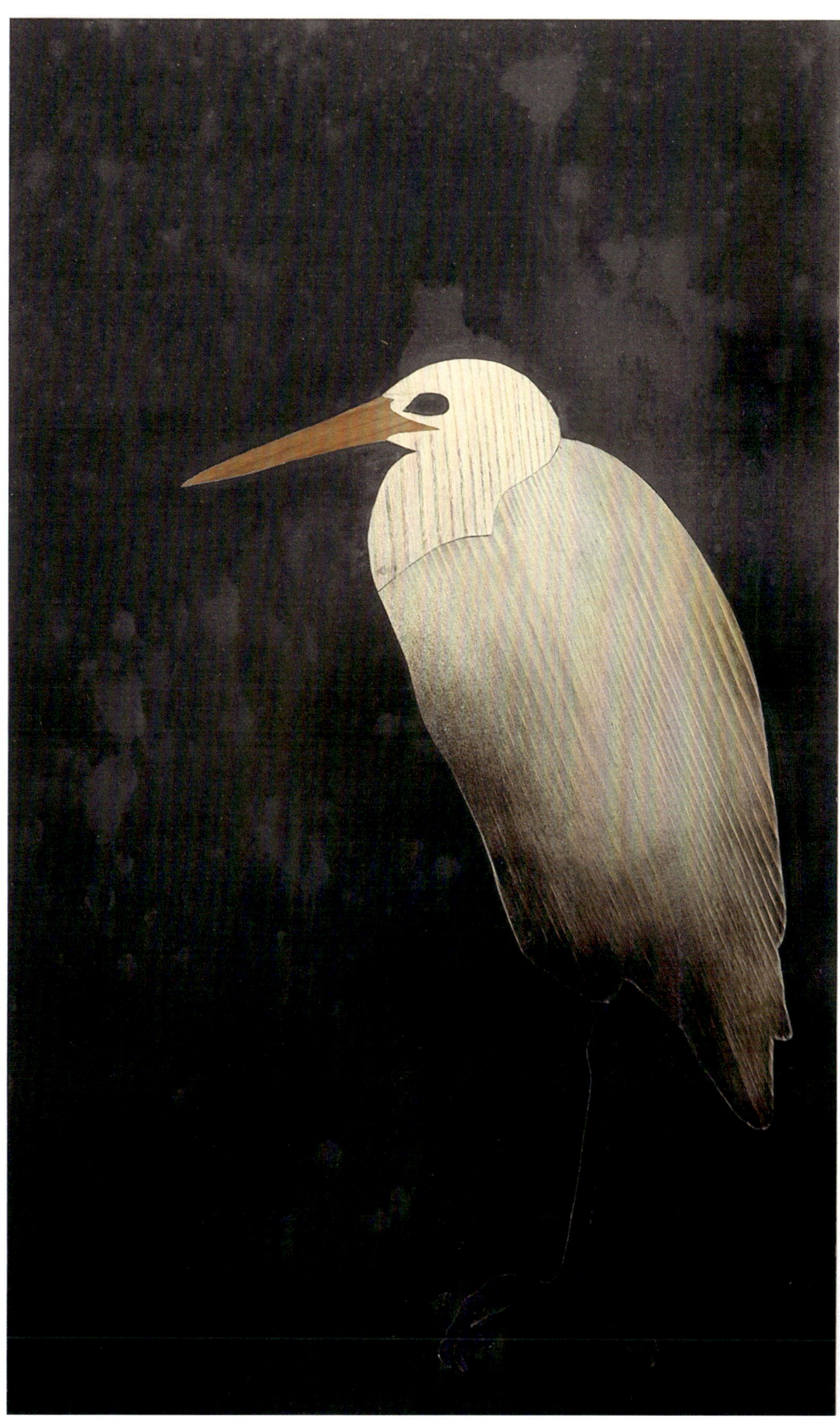

Expedition (Detail), 2006, veneer, acrylic on MDF; Sender Collection

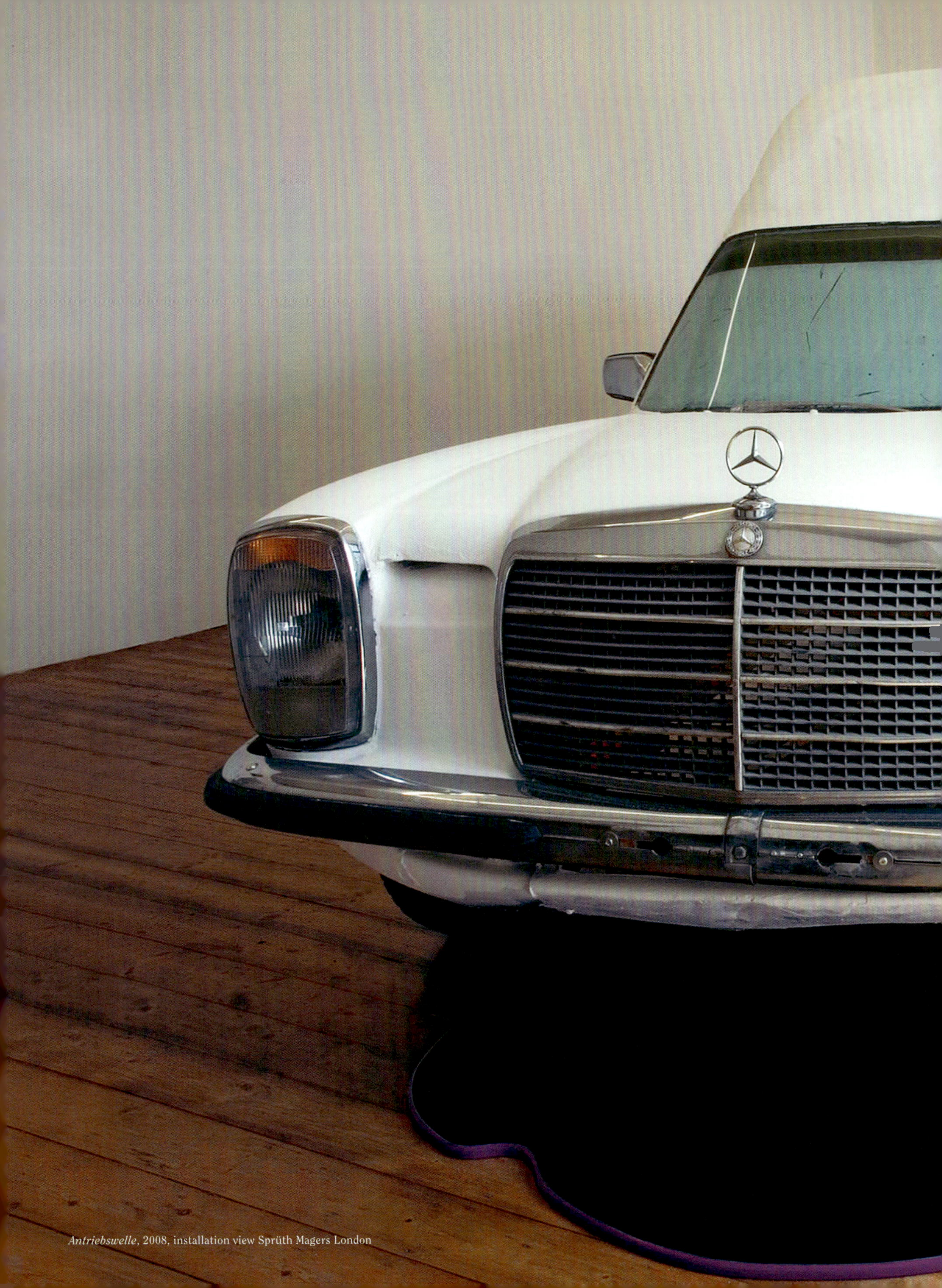

Antriebswelle, 2008, installation view Sprüth Magers London

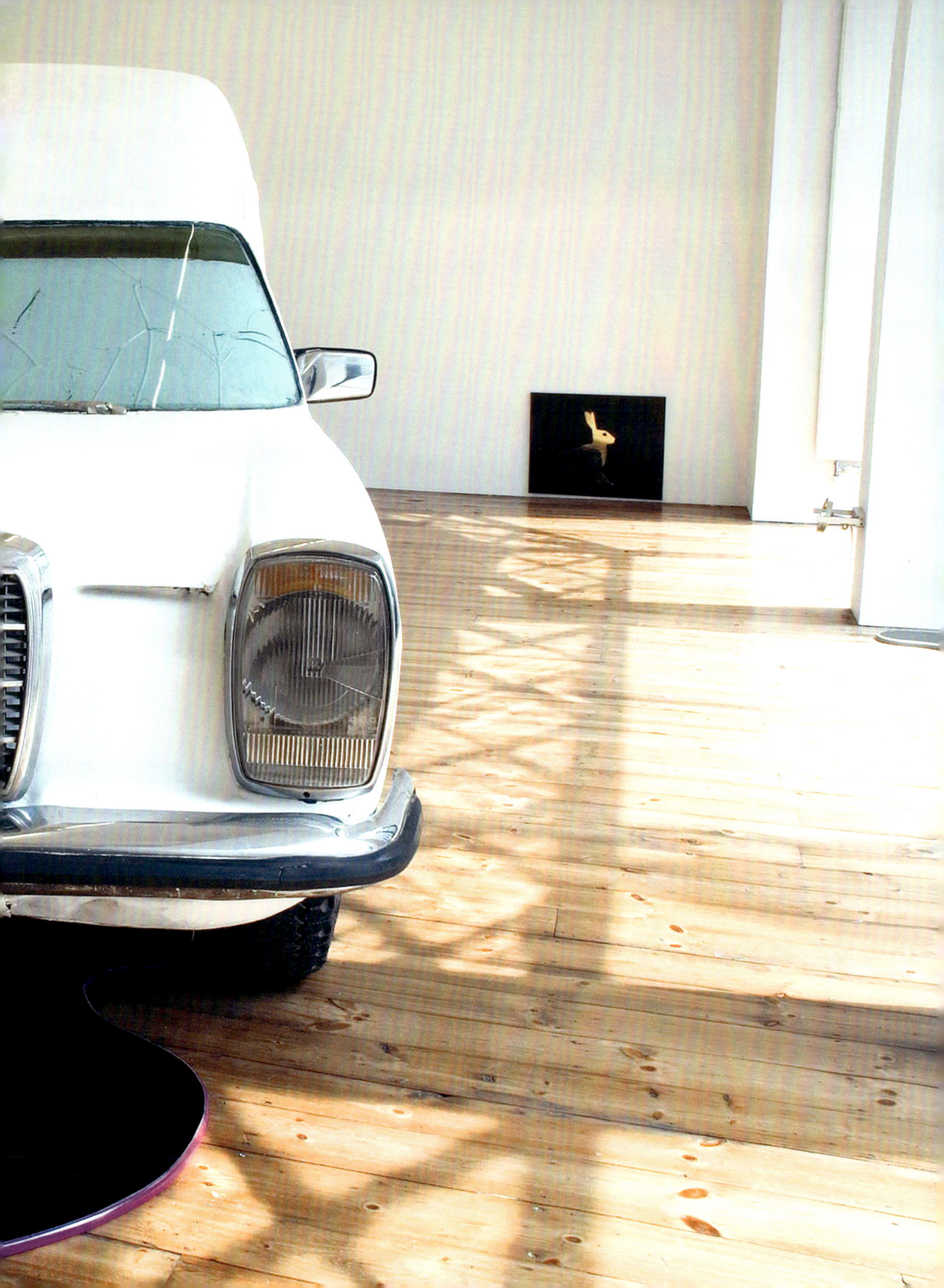

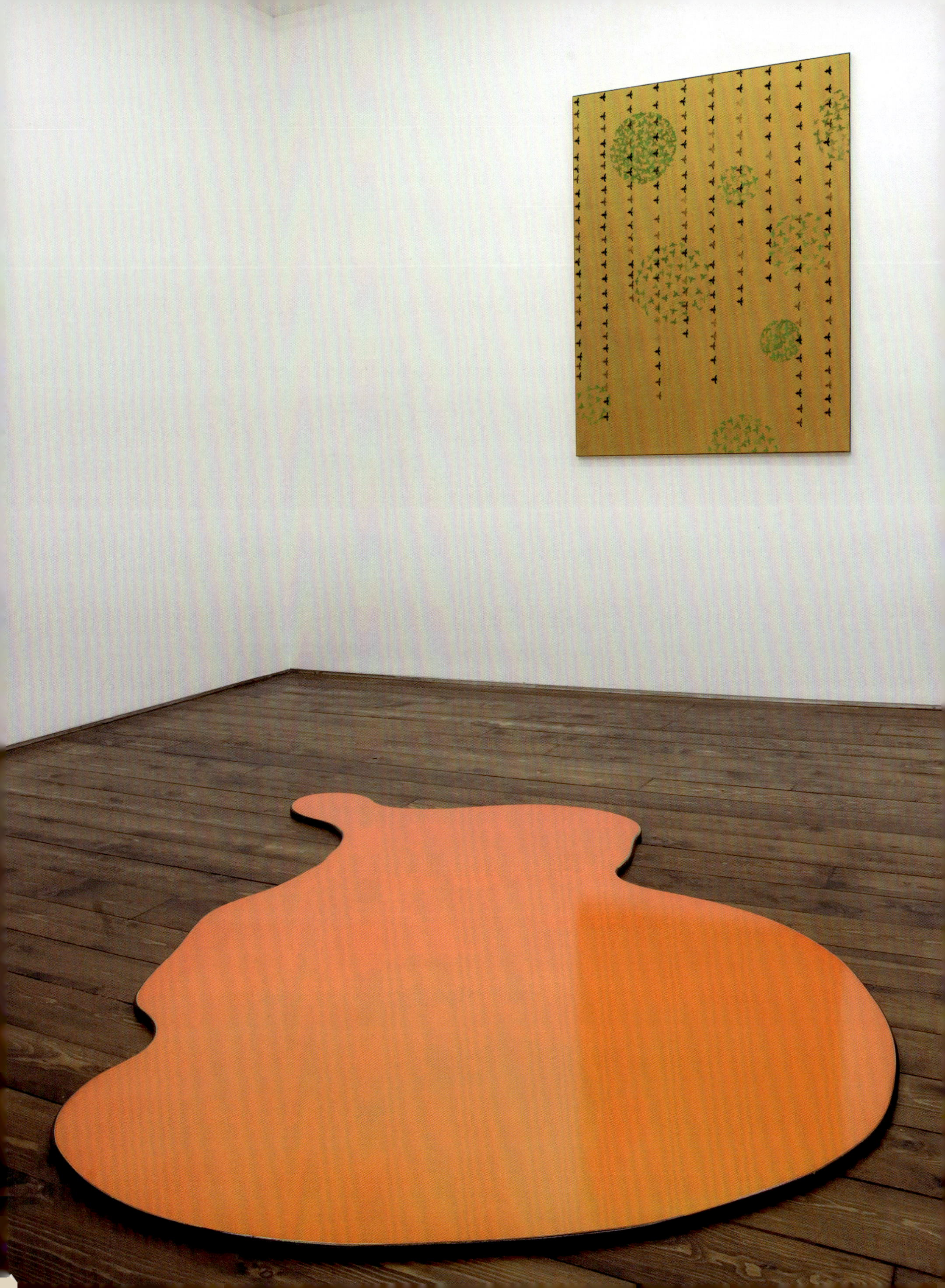

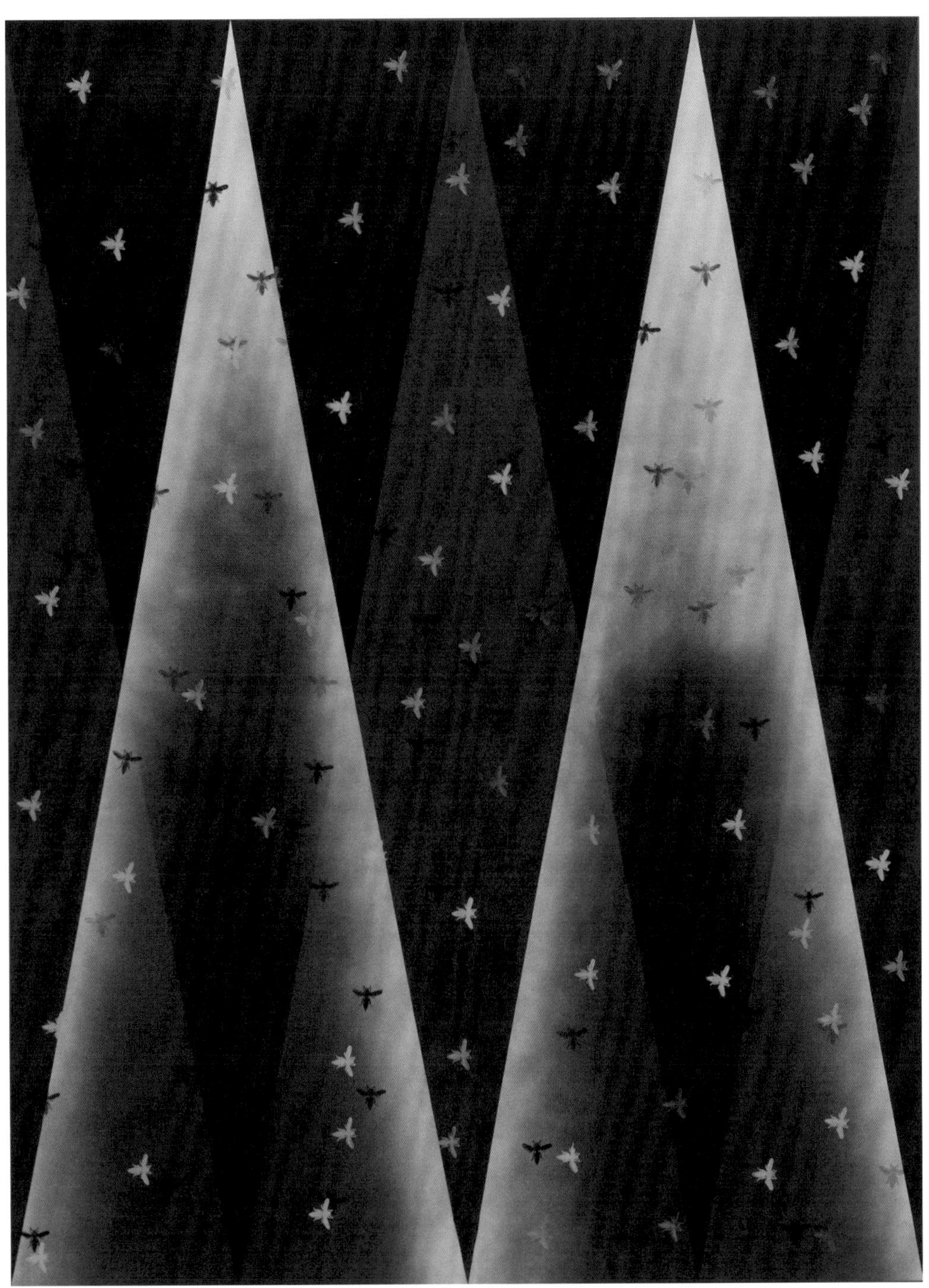

des bien 26, 2008, MDF, fabric, glass, acrylic, wood, silicone, 120 × 90.5 cm; Collection Pervan, Frankfurt
Facing Page: *Antriebswellenfleck 2*, 2008, MDF, car finish, 122 × 188 × 2 cm; Private collection, Belgium
des bien 33, 2008, MDF, glass, fabric, spray paint, silikon, 130 × 100 × 2.2 cm

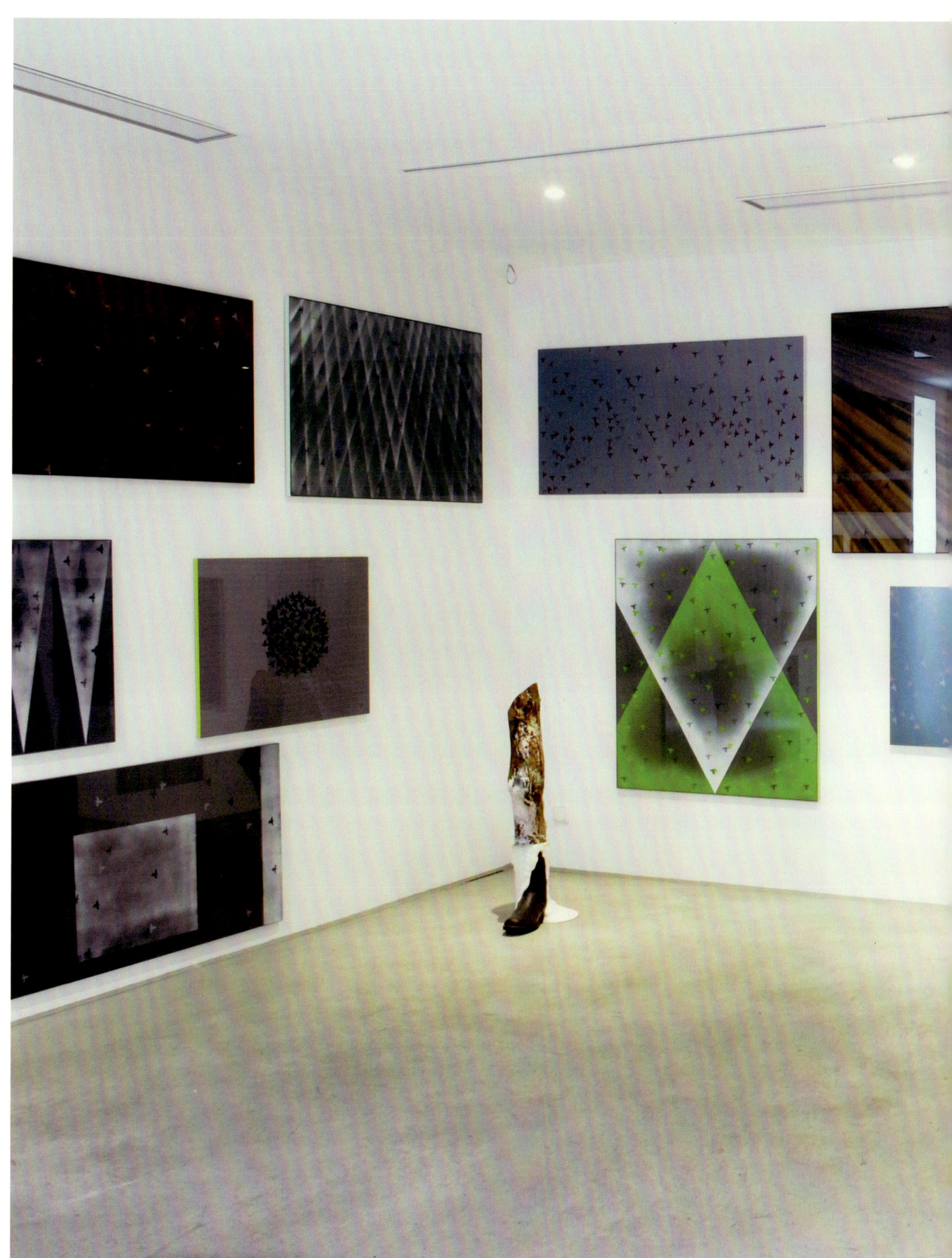

des bien ich, 2008, installation view Sprüth Magers Cologne

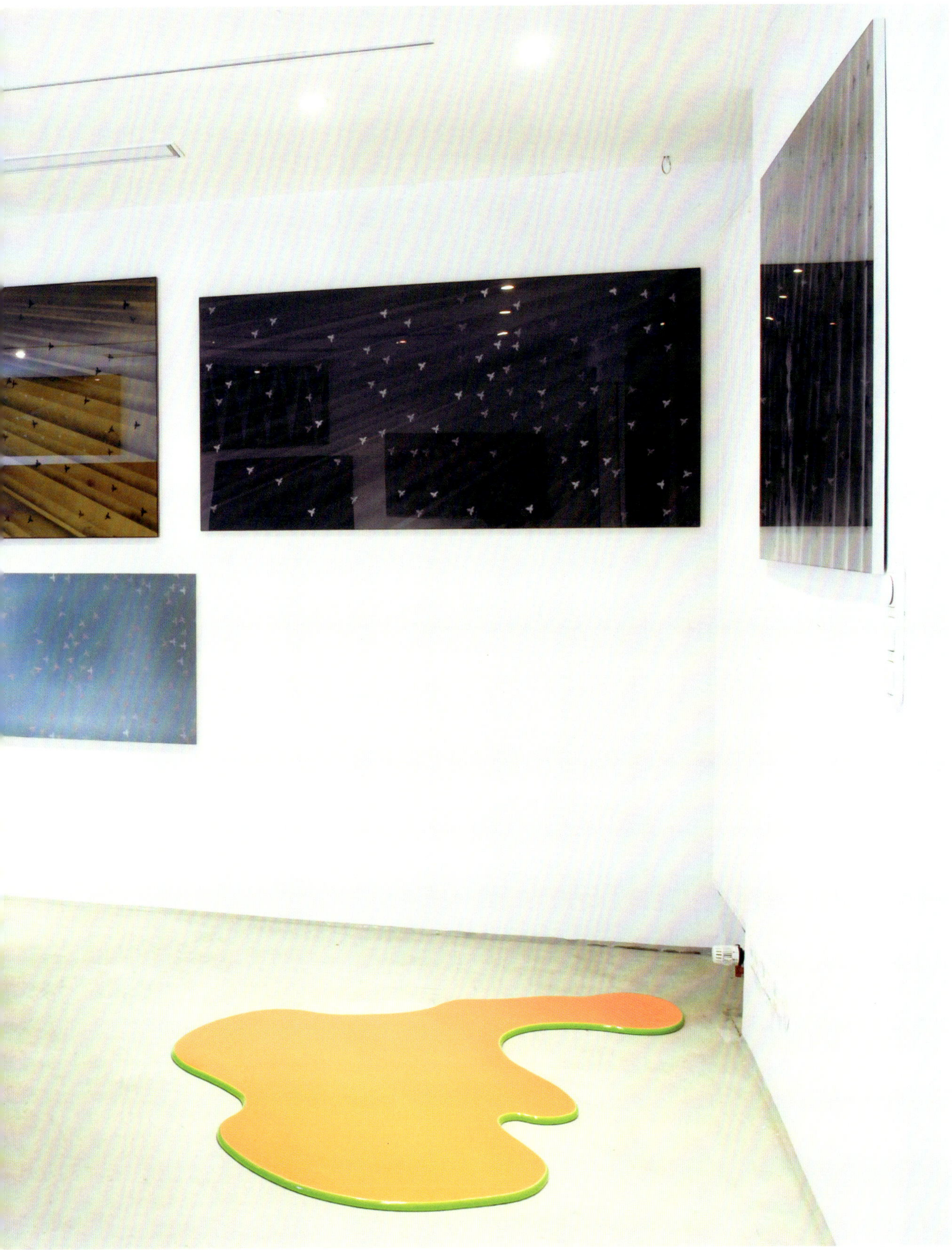

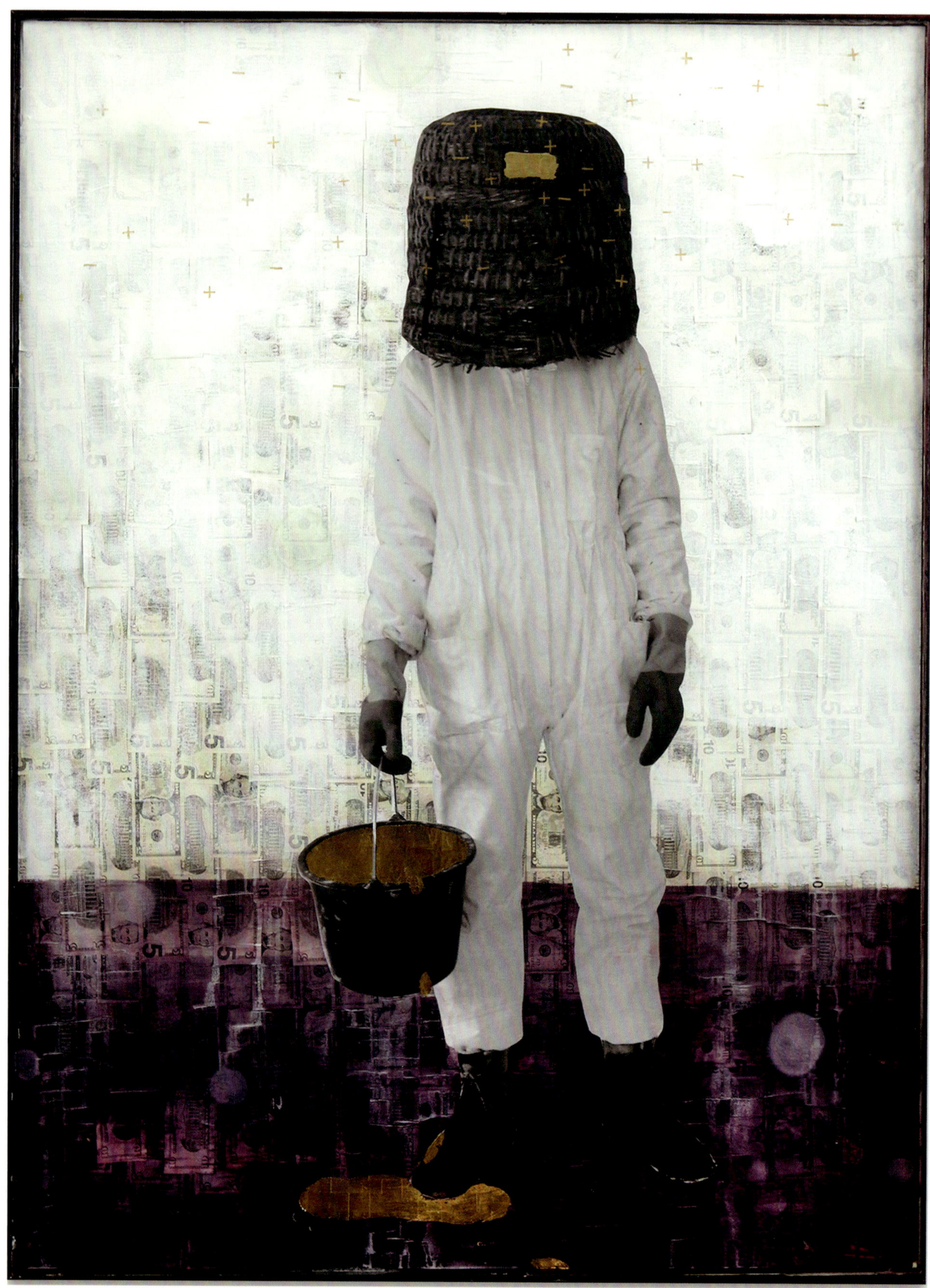

Bienenmann, 2009, paper, acrylic on wood, 162 × 122 × 3 cm; Private collection, New York

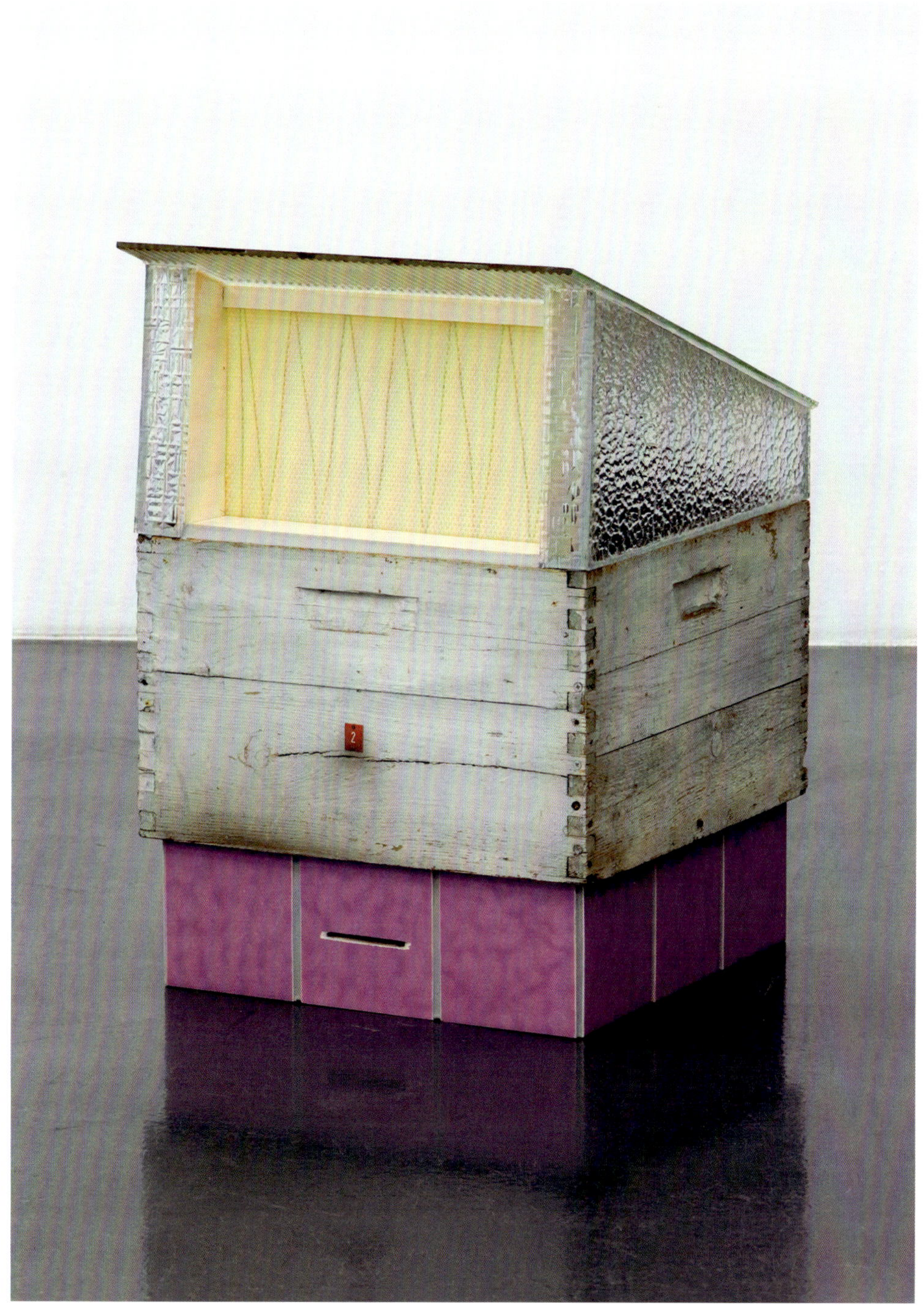

Begattungskästchen Ruck-Zuck, 2007, three parts, mixed media, dimensions variable; Goetz Collection

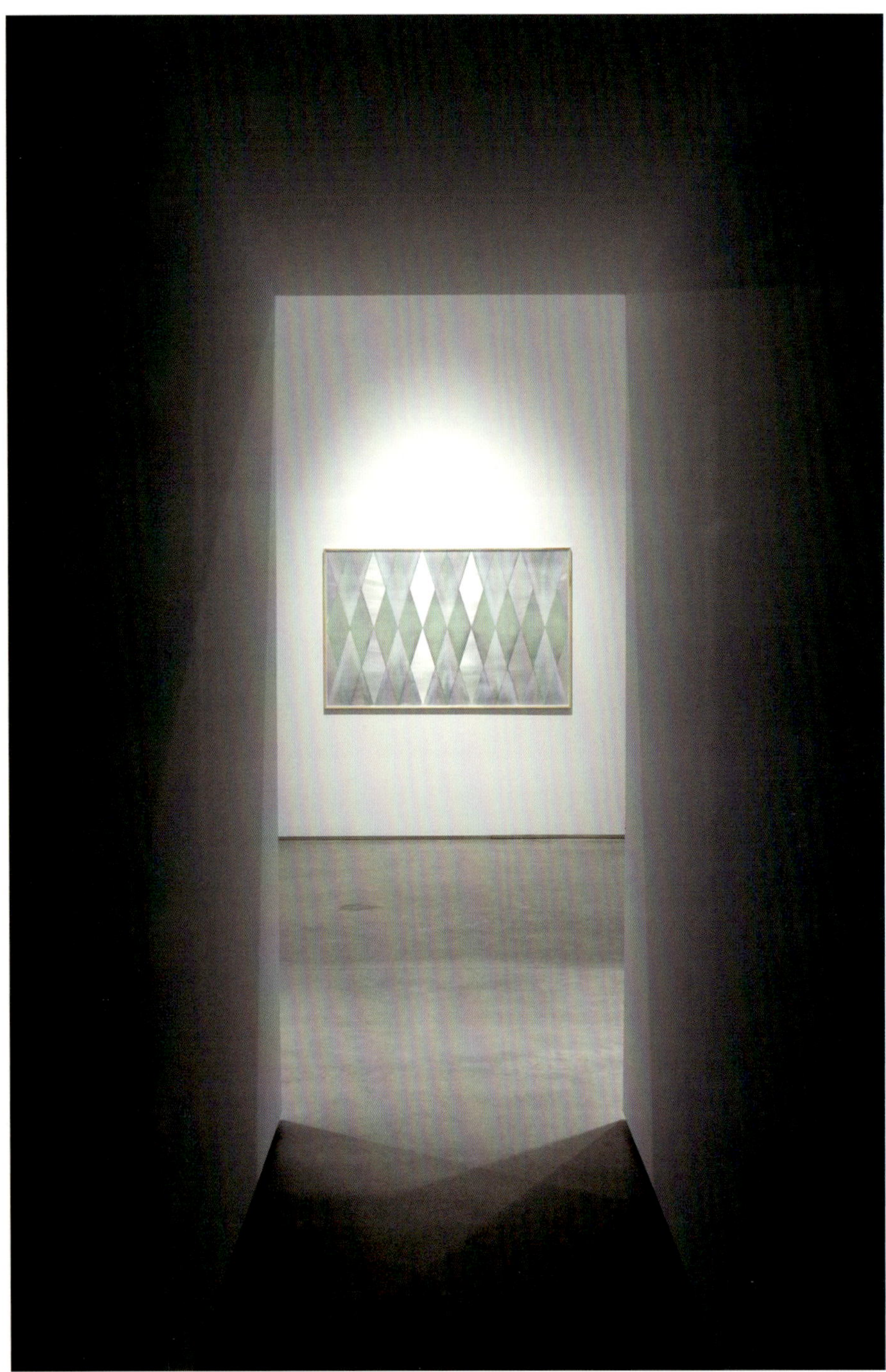

Volles Programm (Zicke Zacke), 2009, MDF, wood, glass, spraypaint, 102 × 162 cm

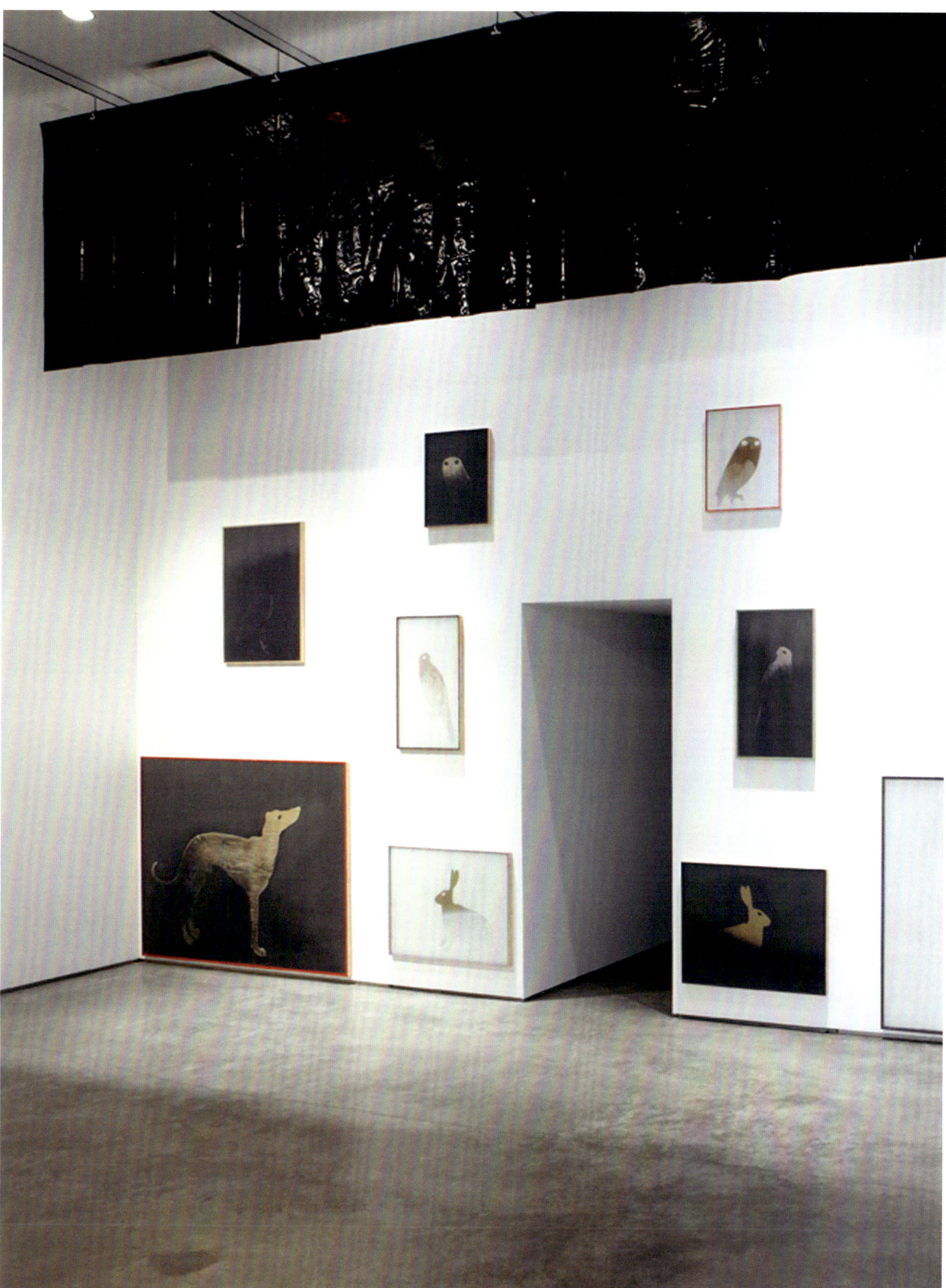

Volles Programm, 2009, installation view Marianne Boesky Gallery, New York

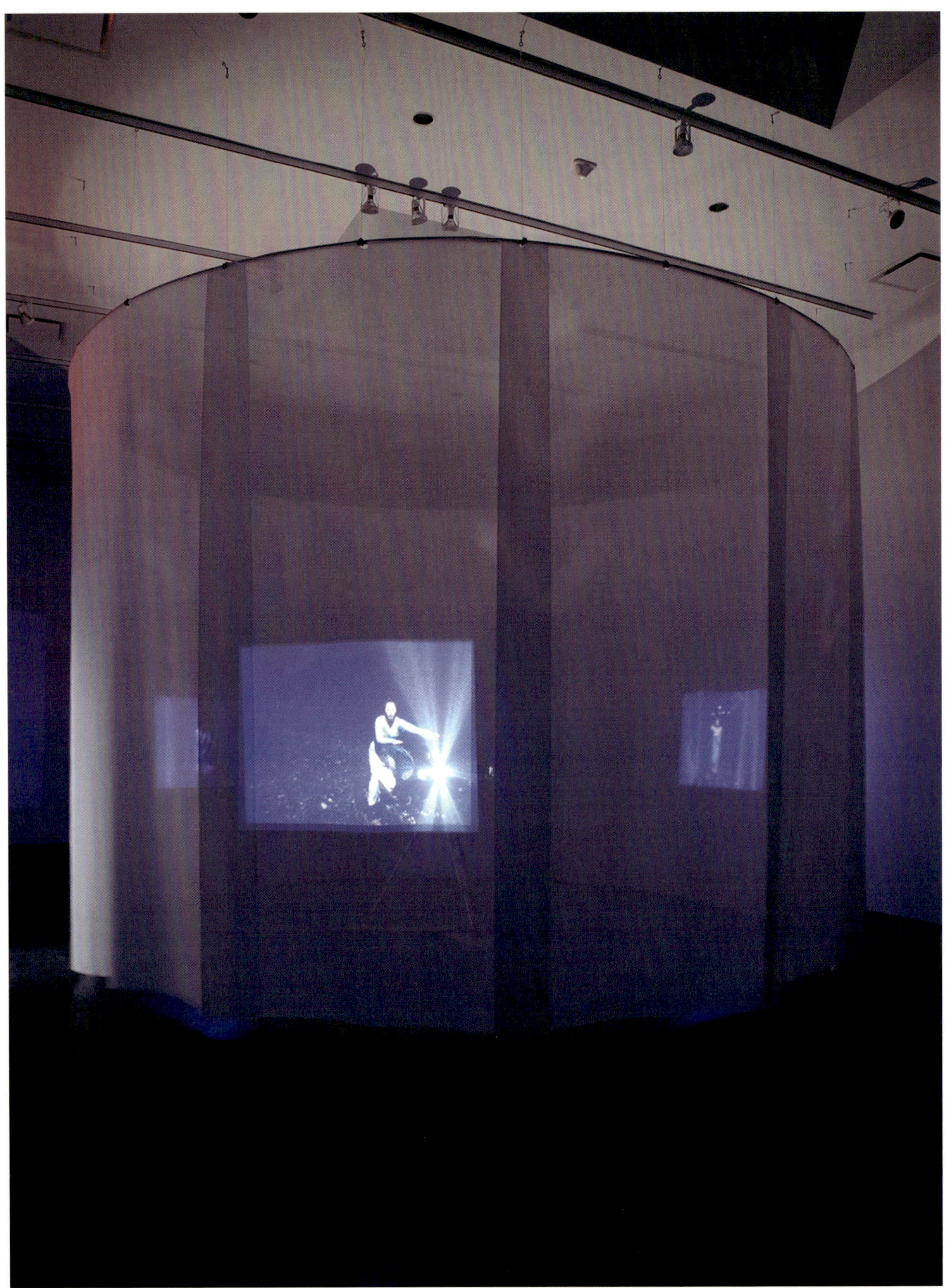

Volles Programm, 2009, video installation, Marianne Boesky Gallery, New York

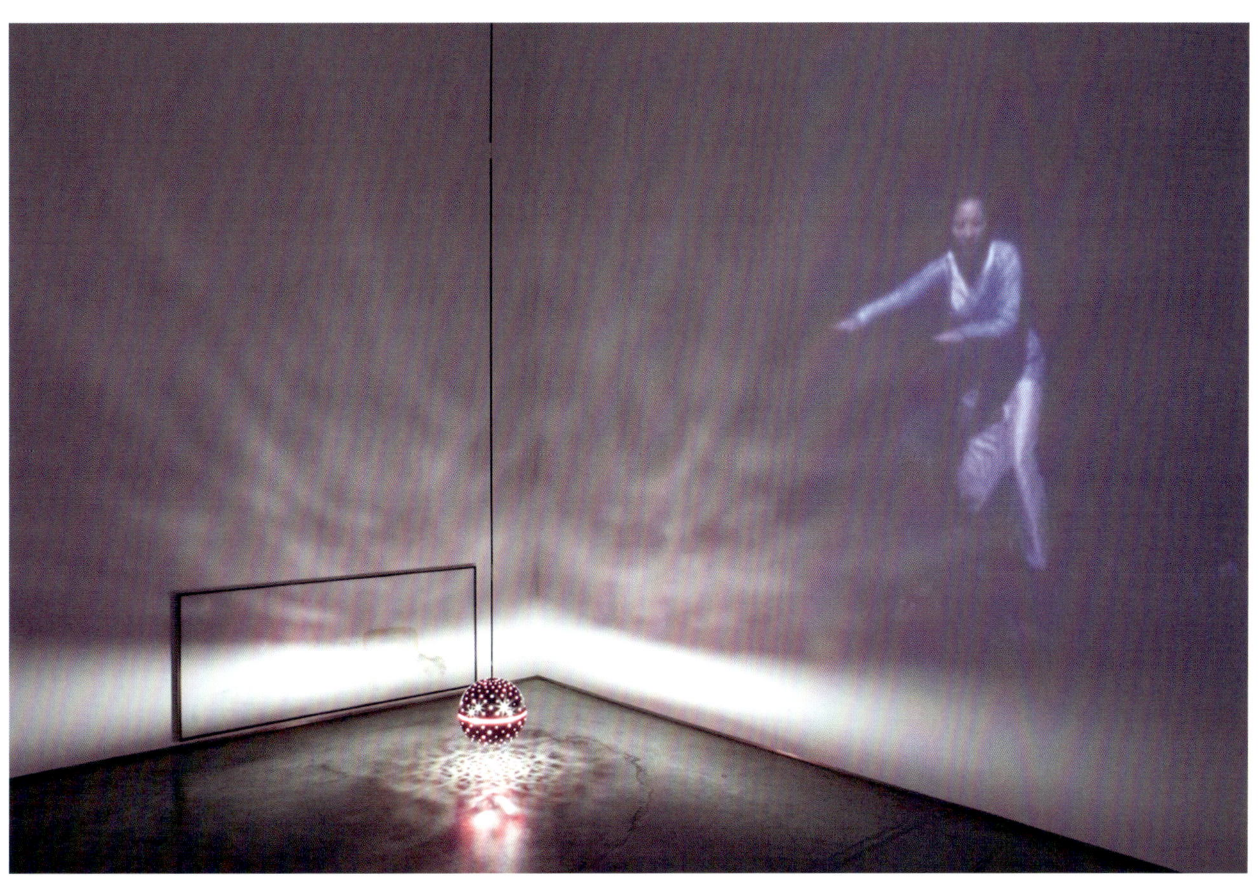

Volles Programm, 2009, installation view Marianne Boesky Gallery, New York

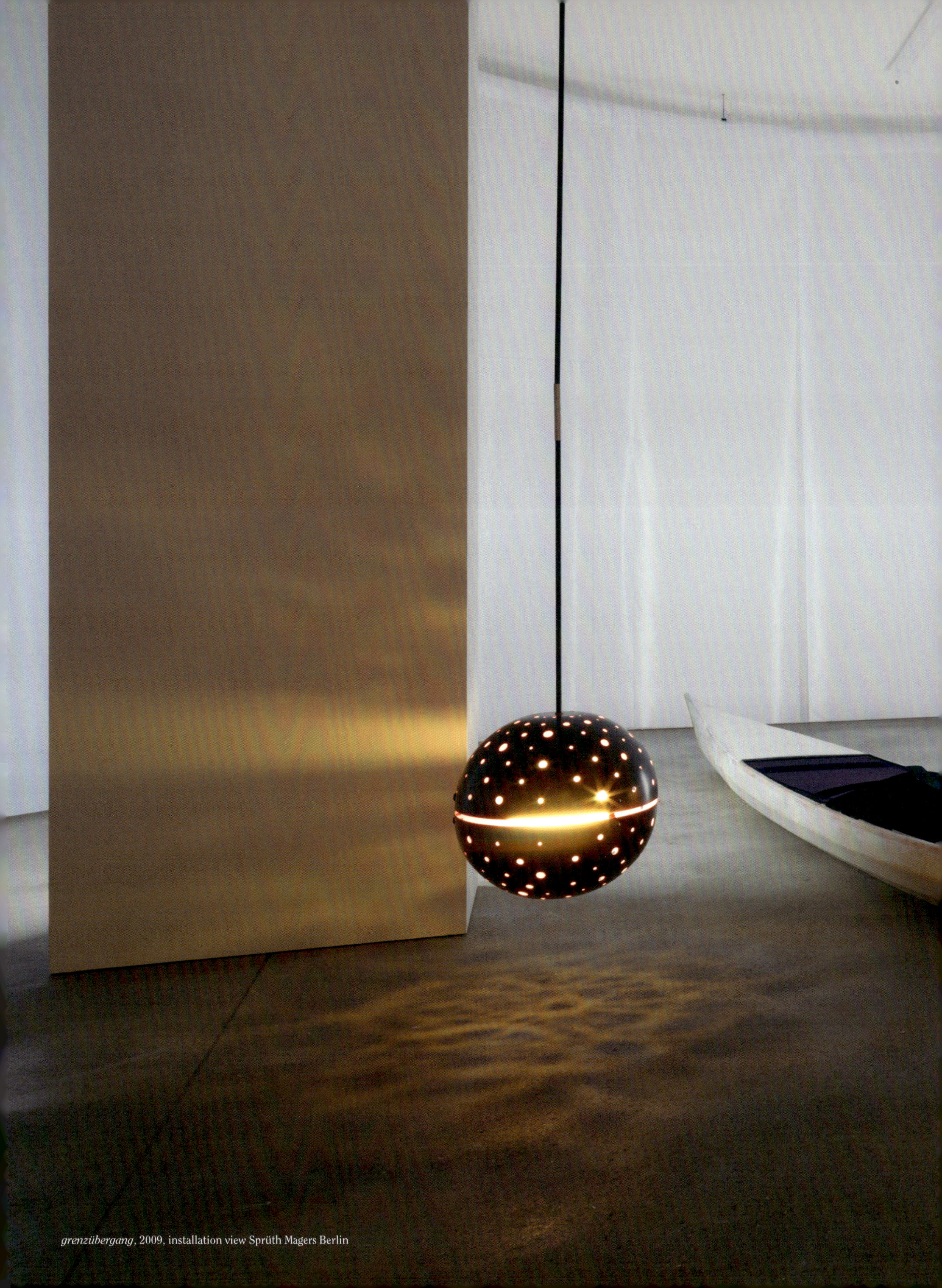

grenzübergang, 2009, installation view Sprüth Magers Berlin

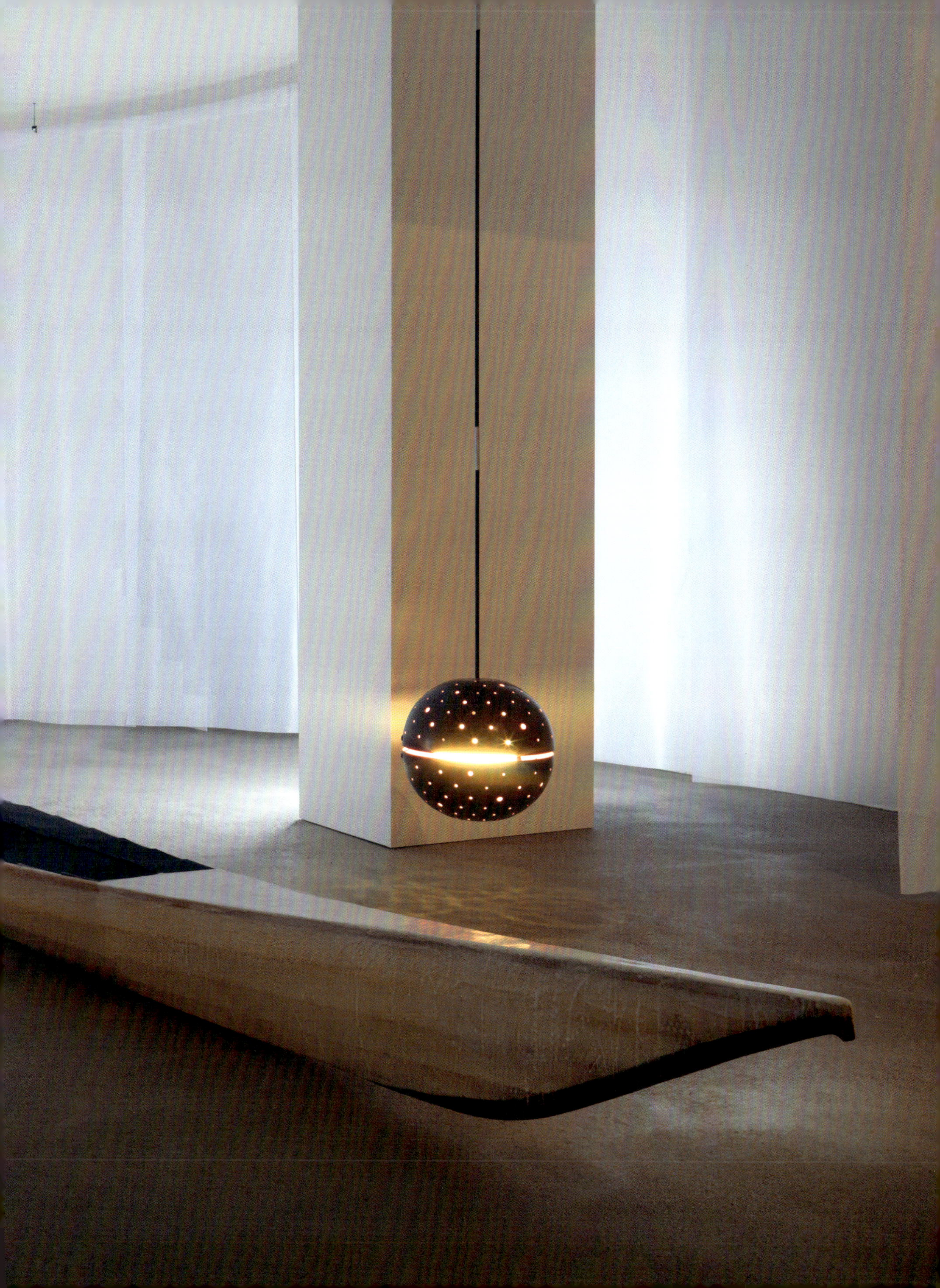

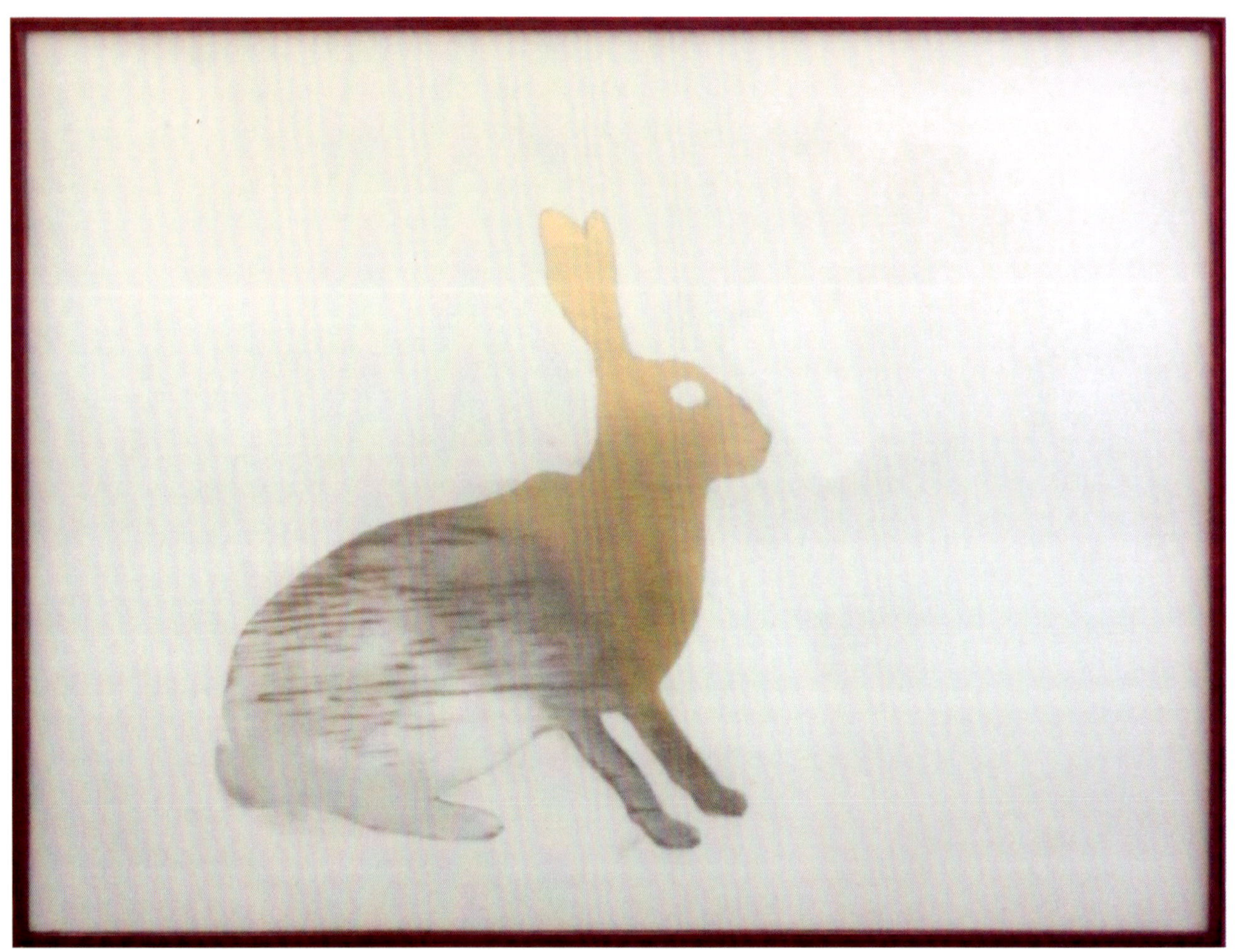

grenzübergang: Hase, 2009, aluminium, glass, wood, paint, 61 × 81 × 3 cm; Private collection, Munich

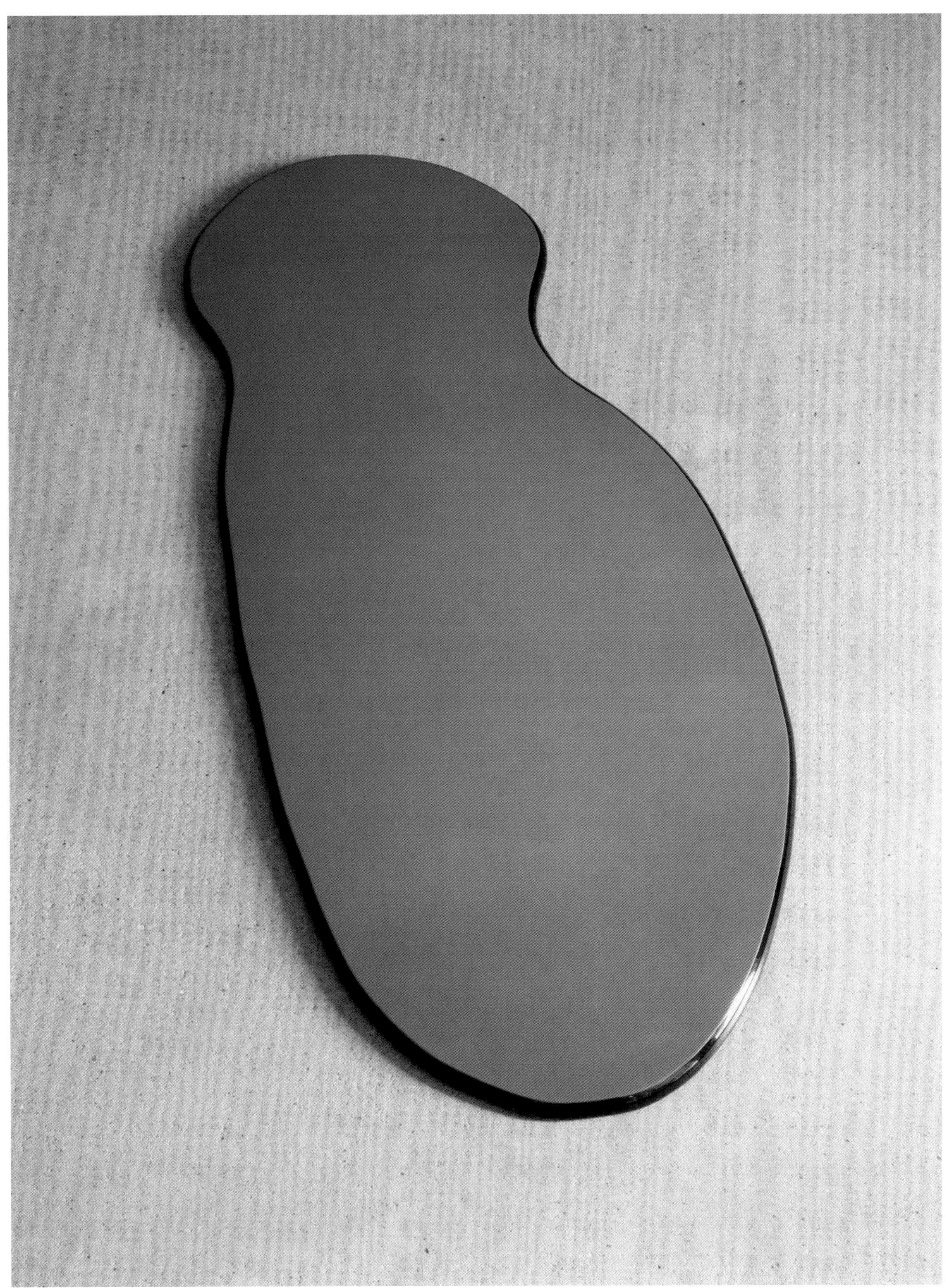

grenzübergang (Fleck, lila, schwarz), 2009, MDF, car finish, 95.5 × 42 cm

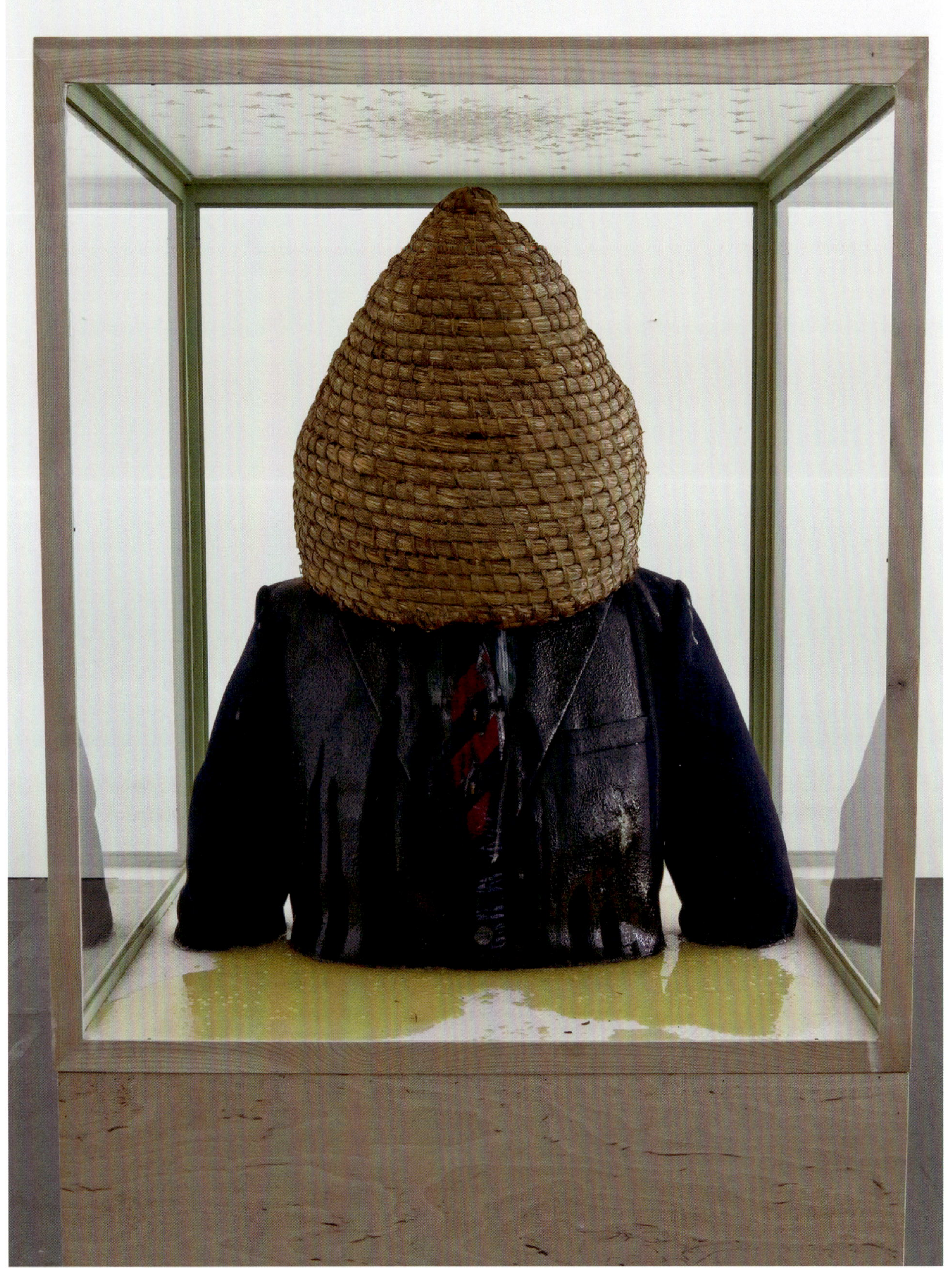

honeymanymän, 2010, wood, glass, fabric, beehive, epoxy, acrylic, 75 × 75 × 188 cm; Private collection

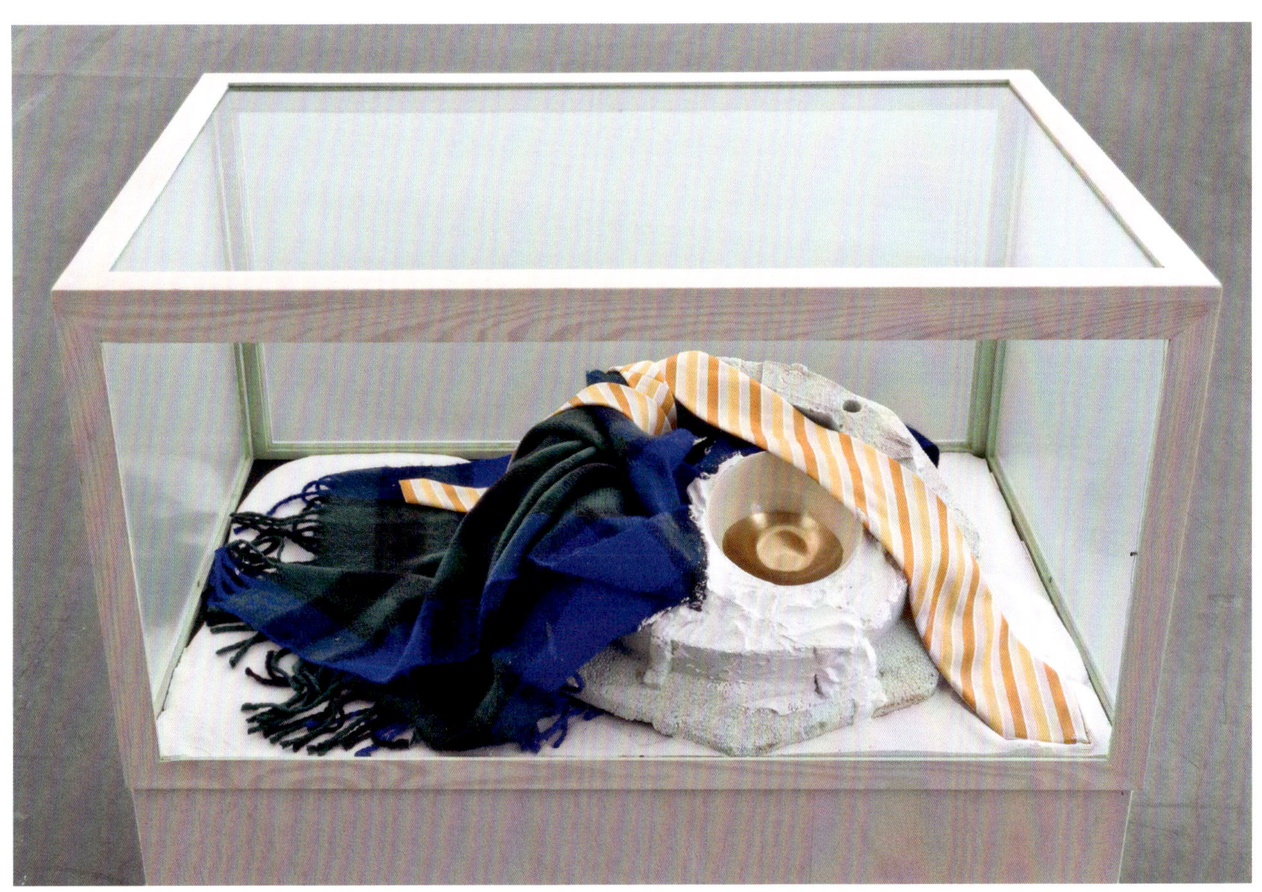

Wolldecke mit Schale, 2010, wood, glass, fabric, plaster, acrylic, chicken wire, 106 × 74.5 × 45 cm

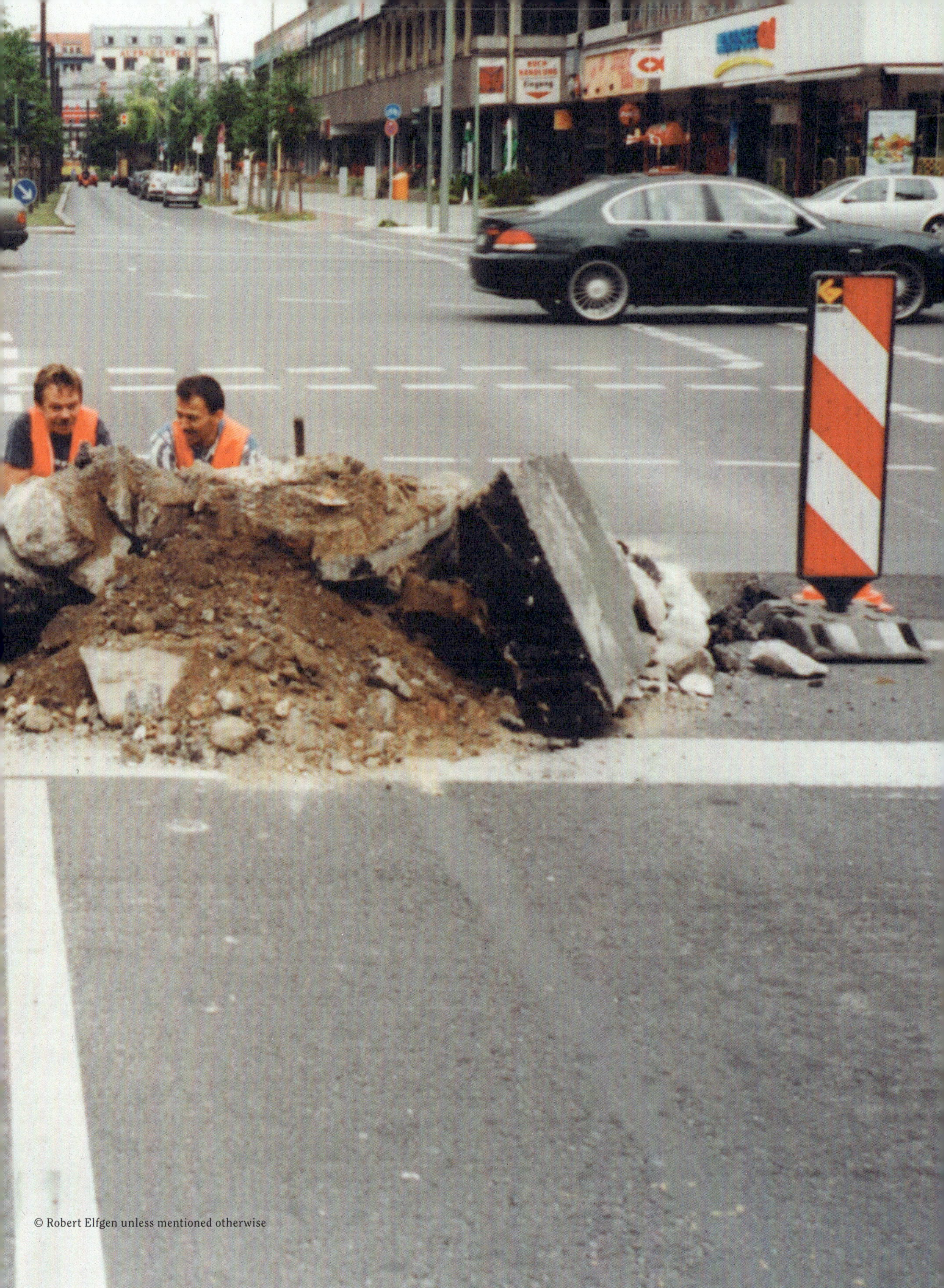
© Robert Elfgen unless mentioned otherwise

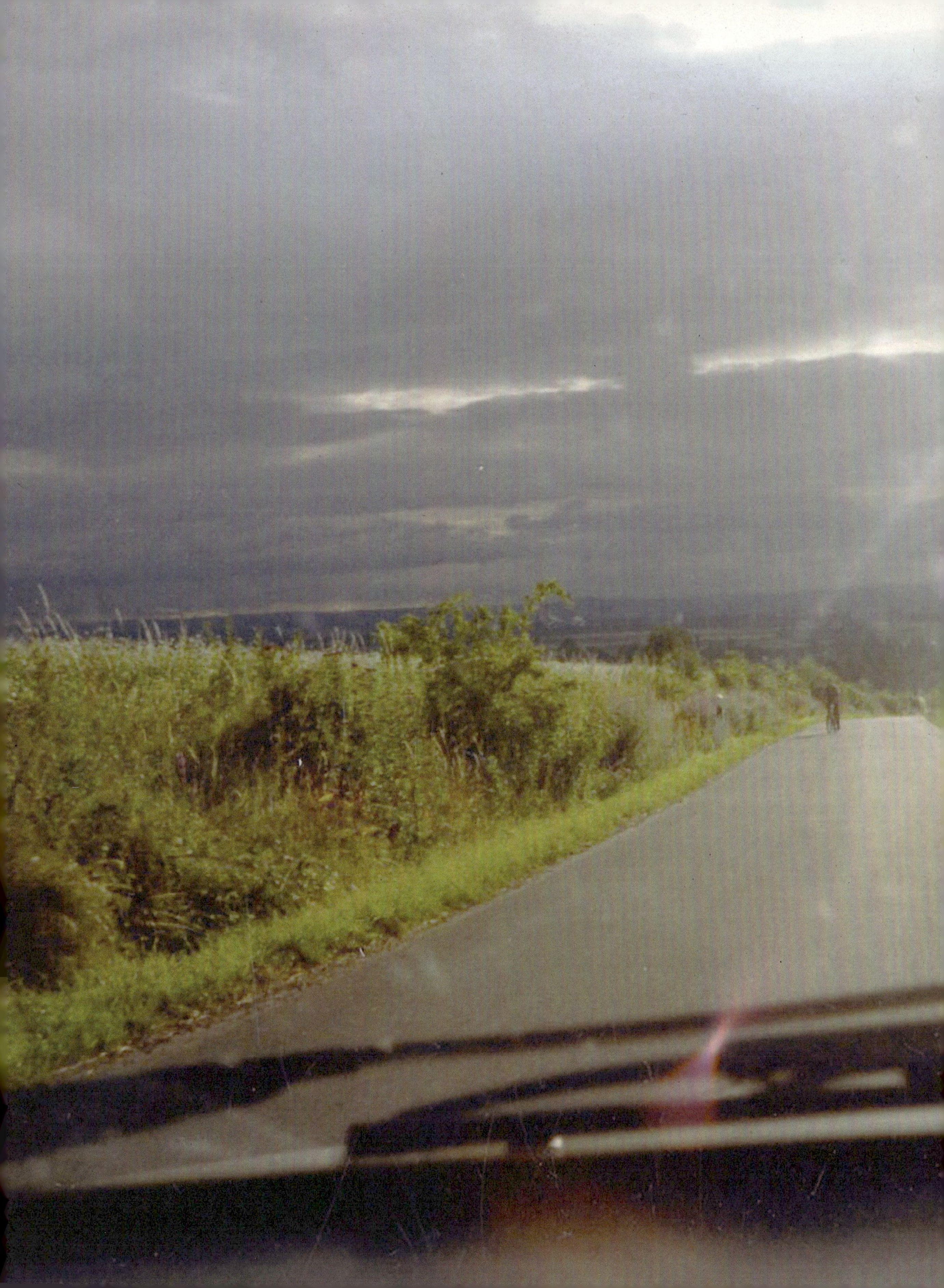

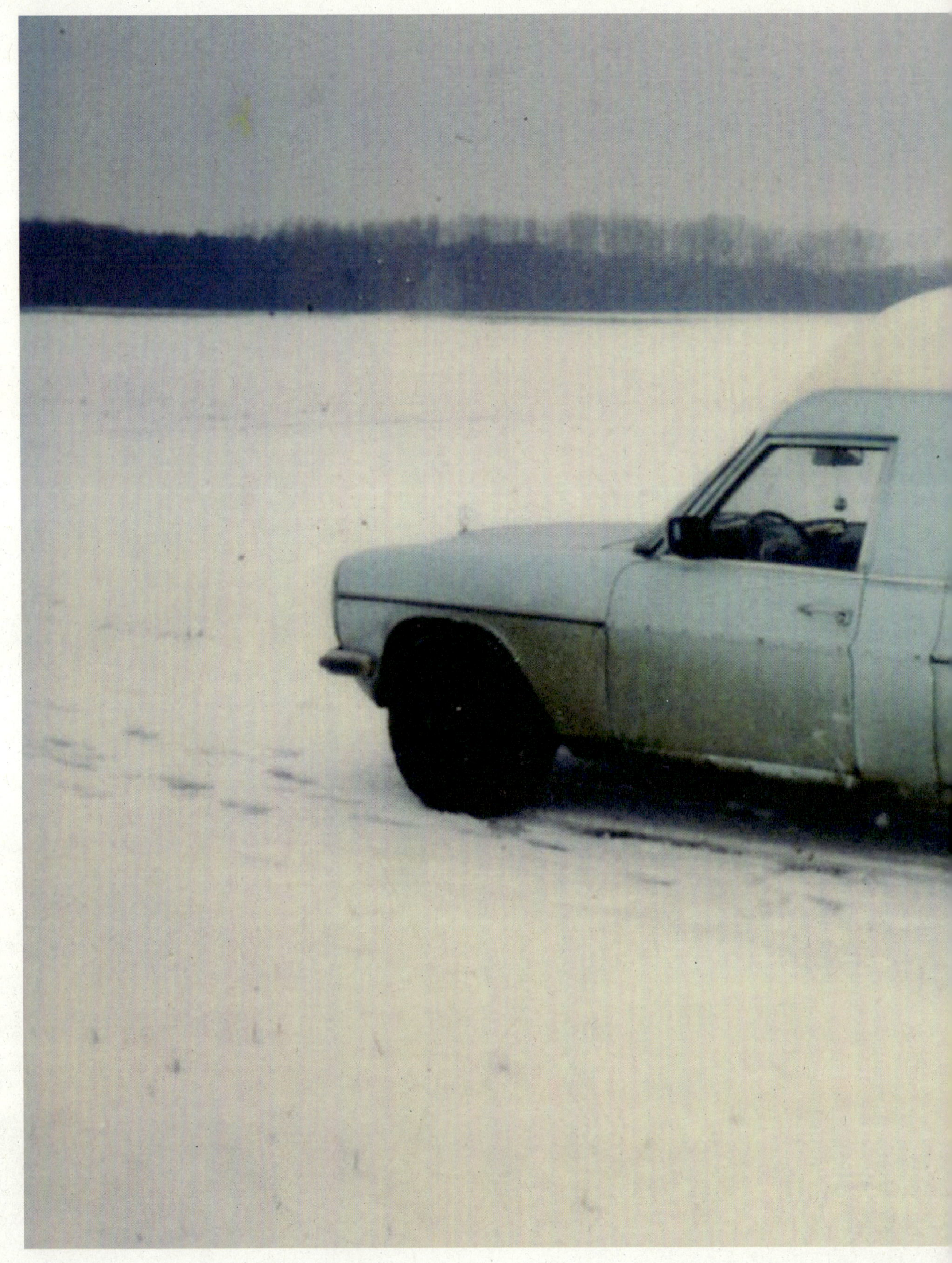

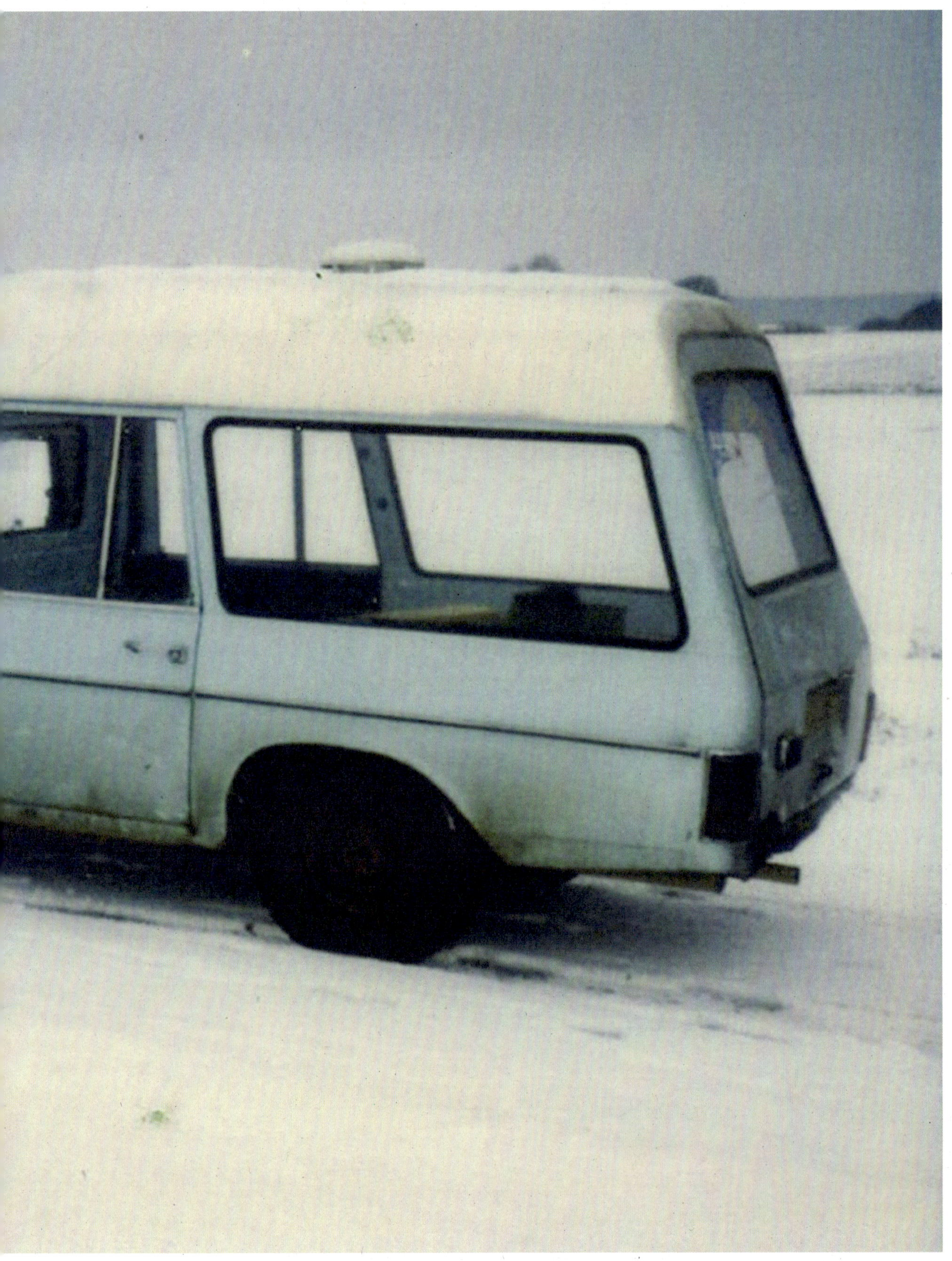

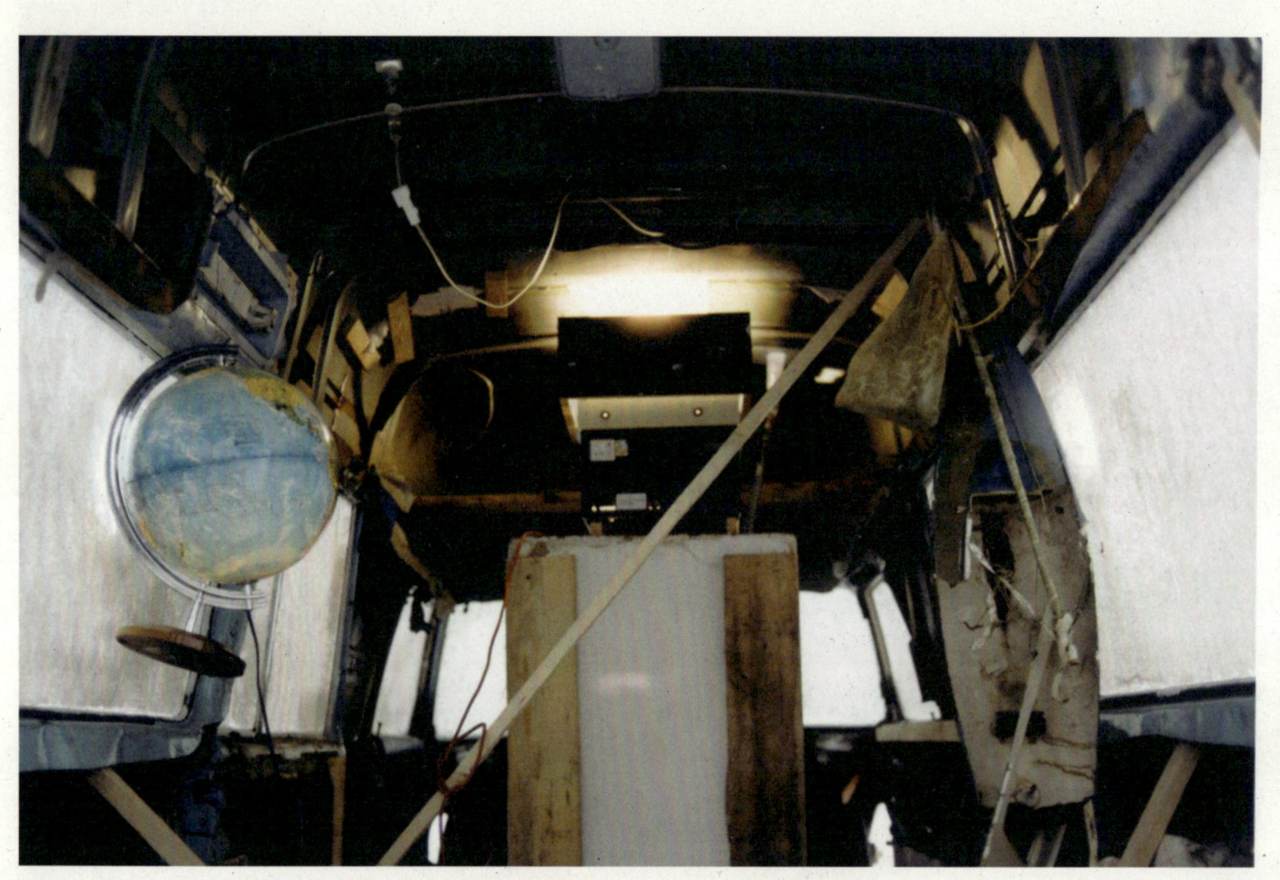

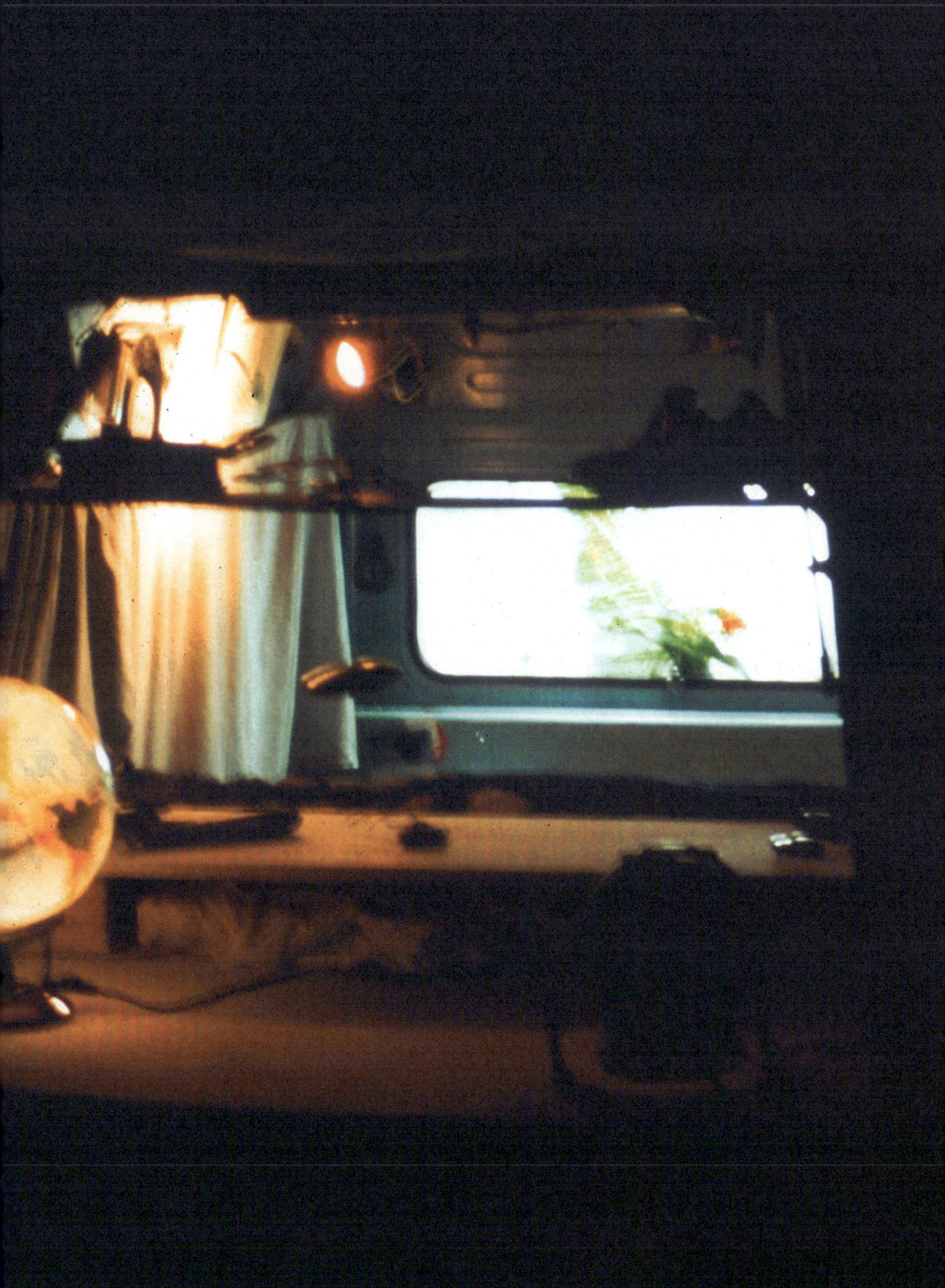

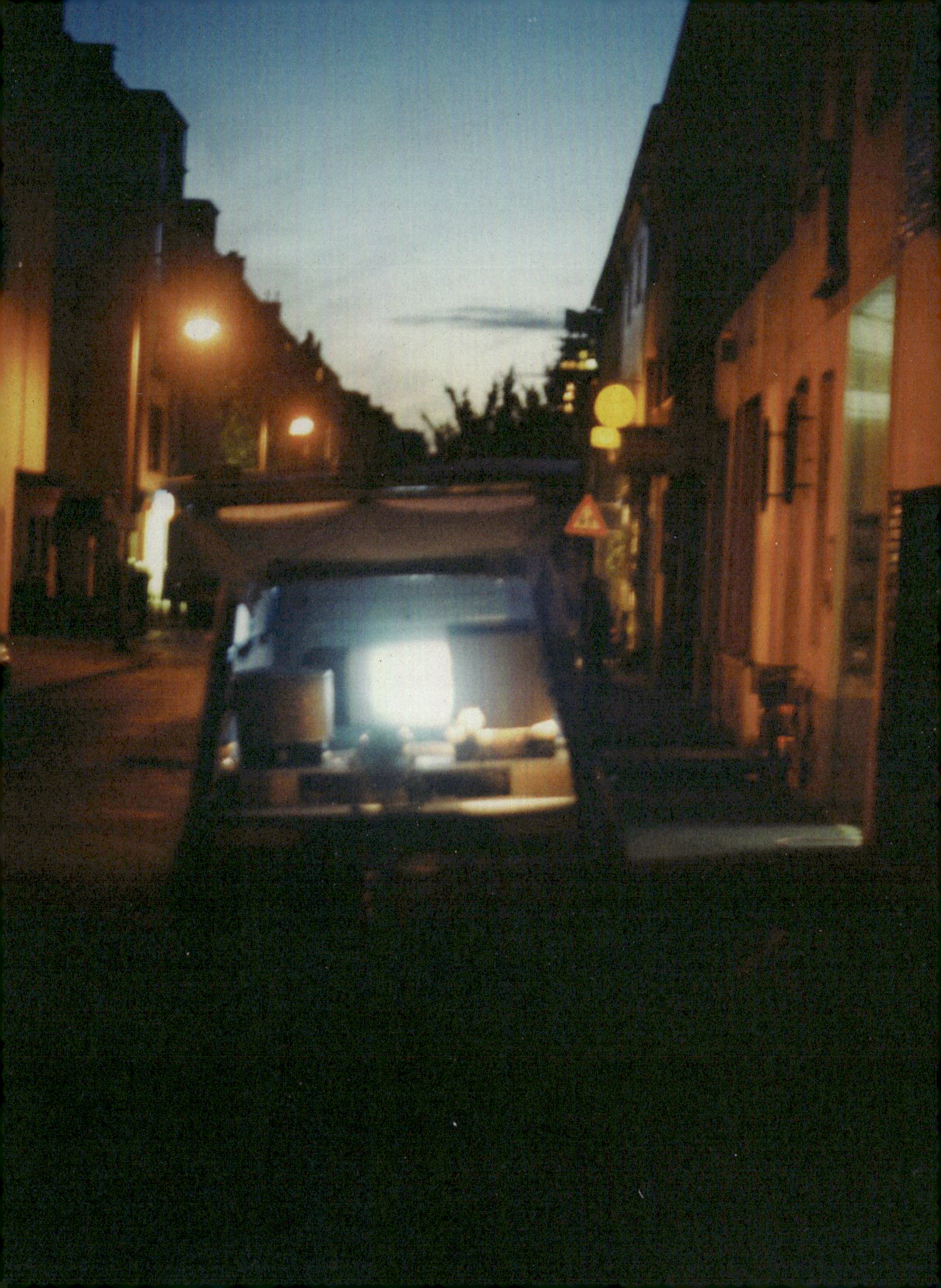

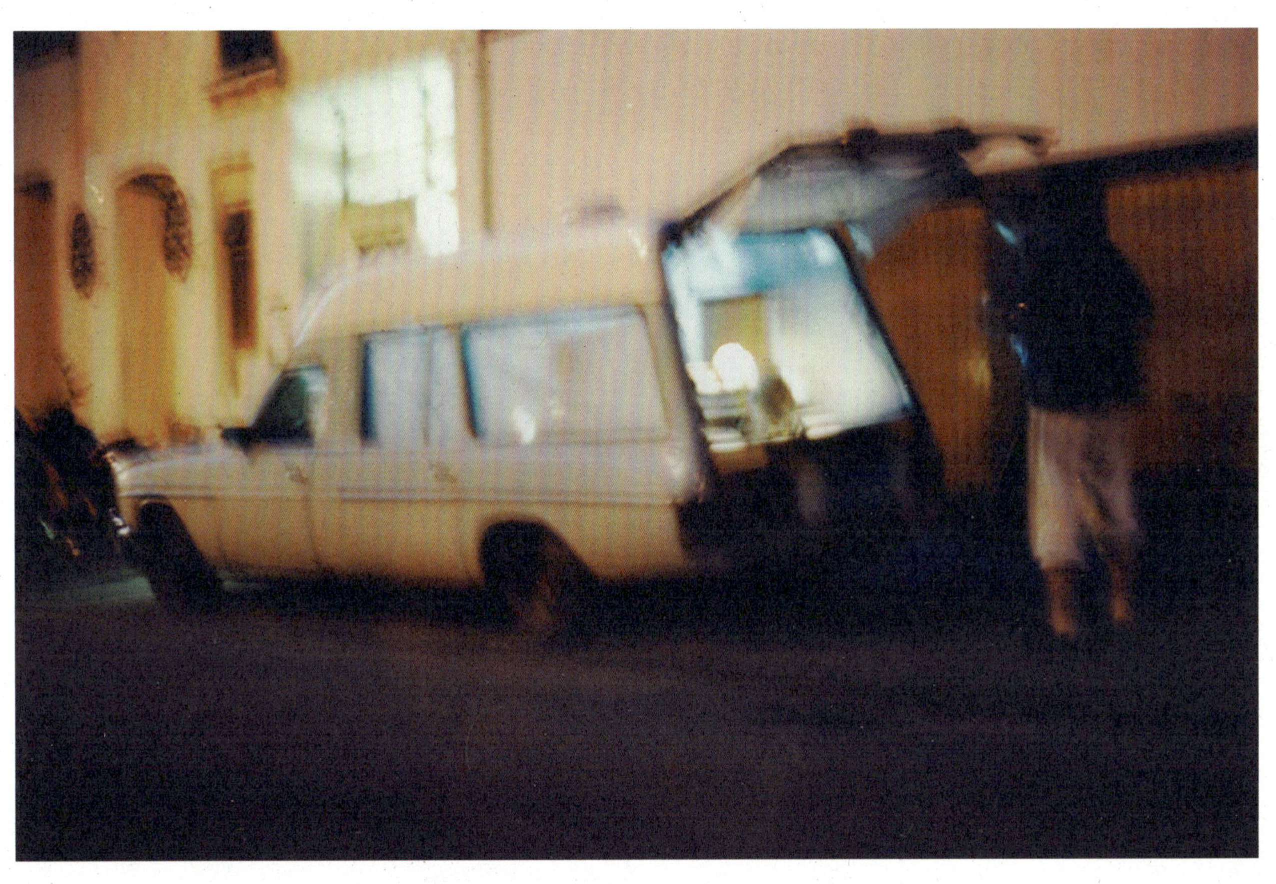

© Alexandra Sell

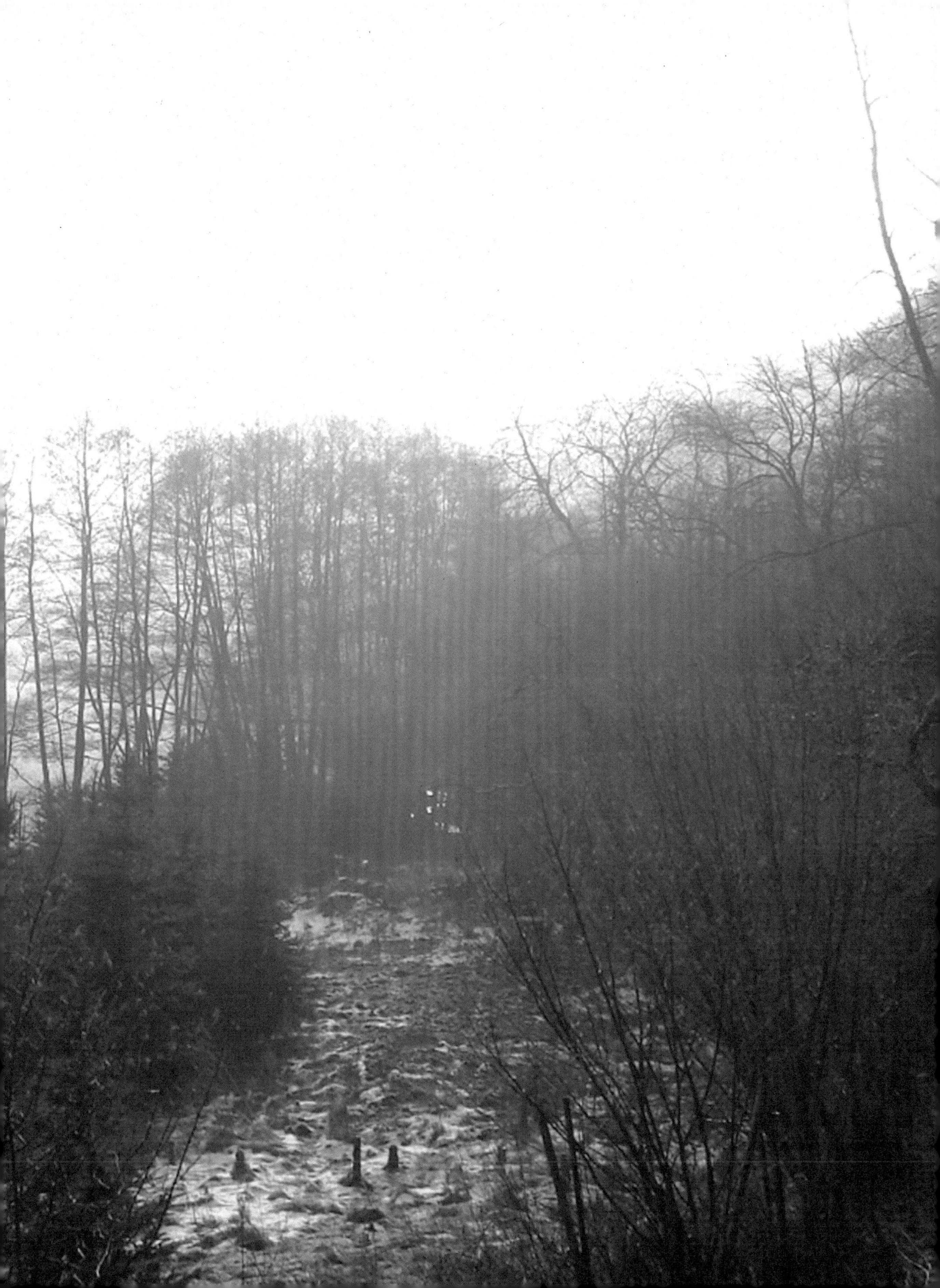

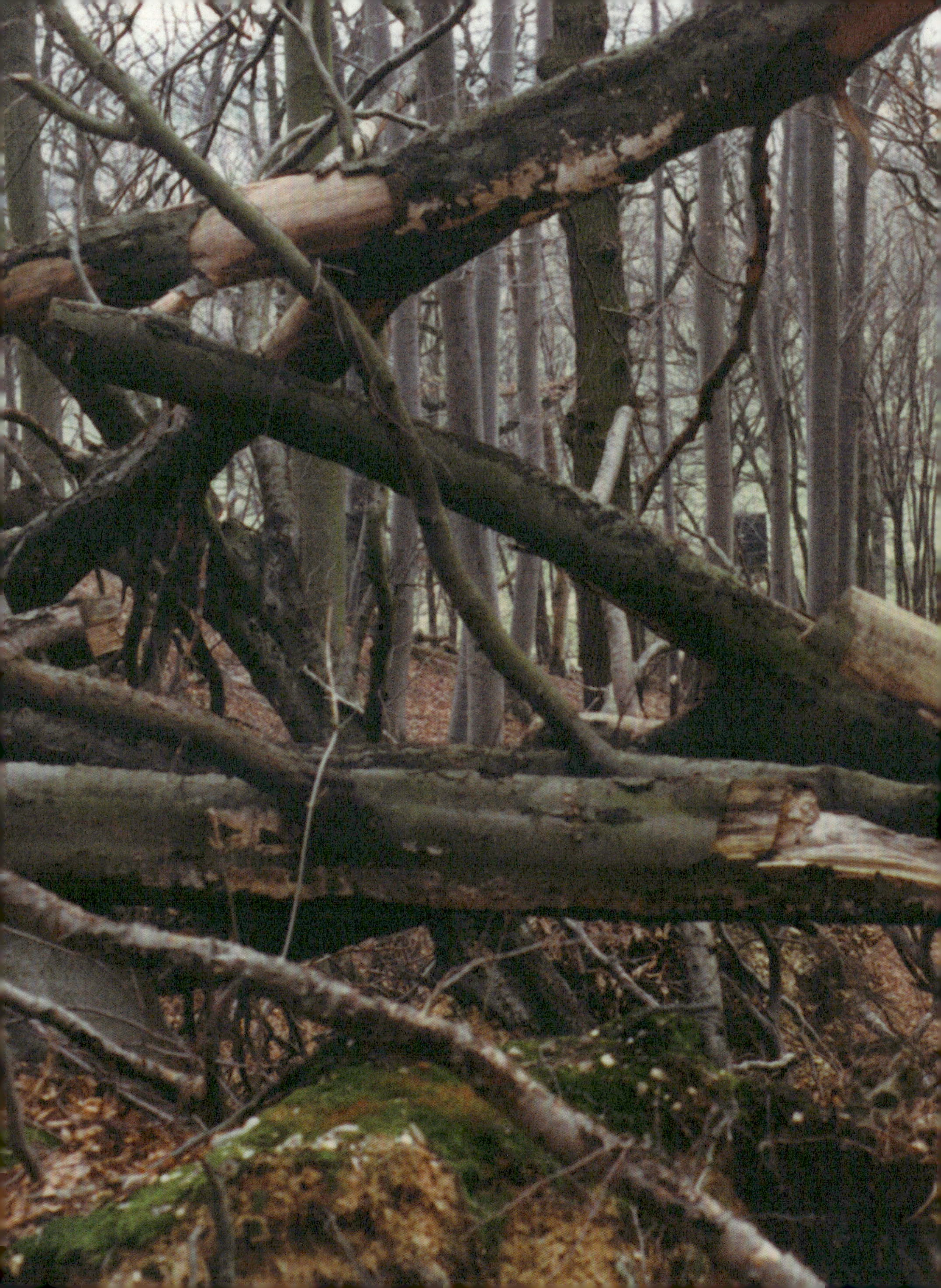

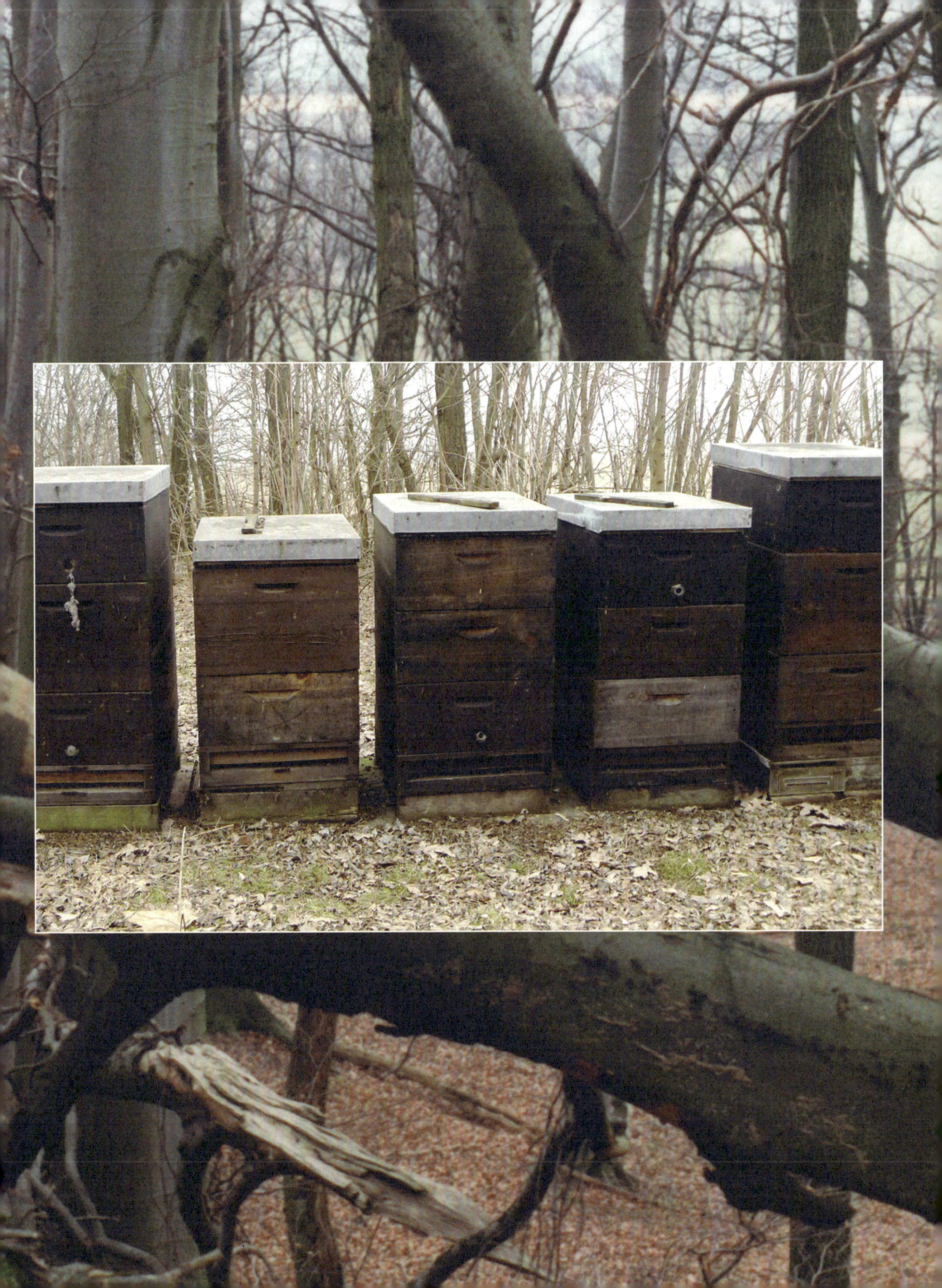

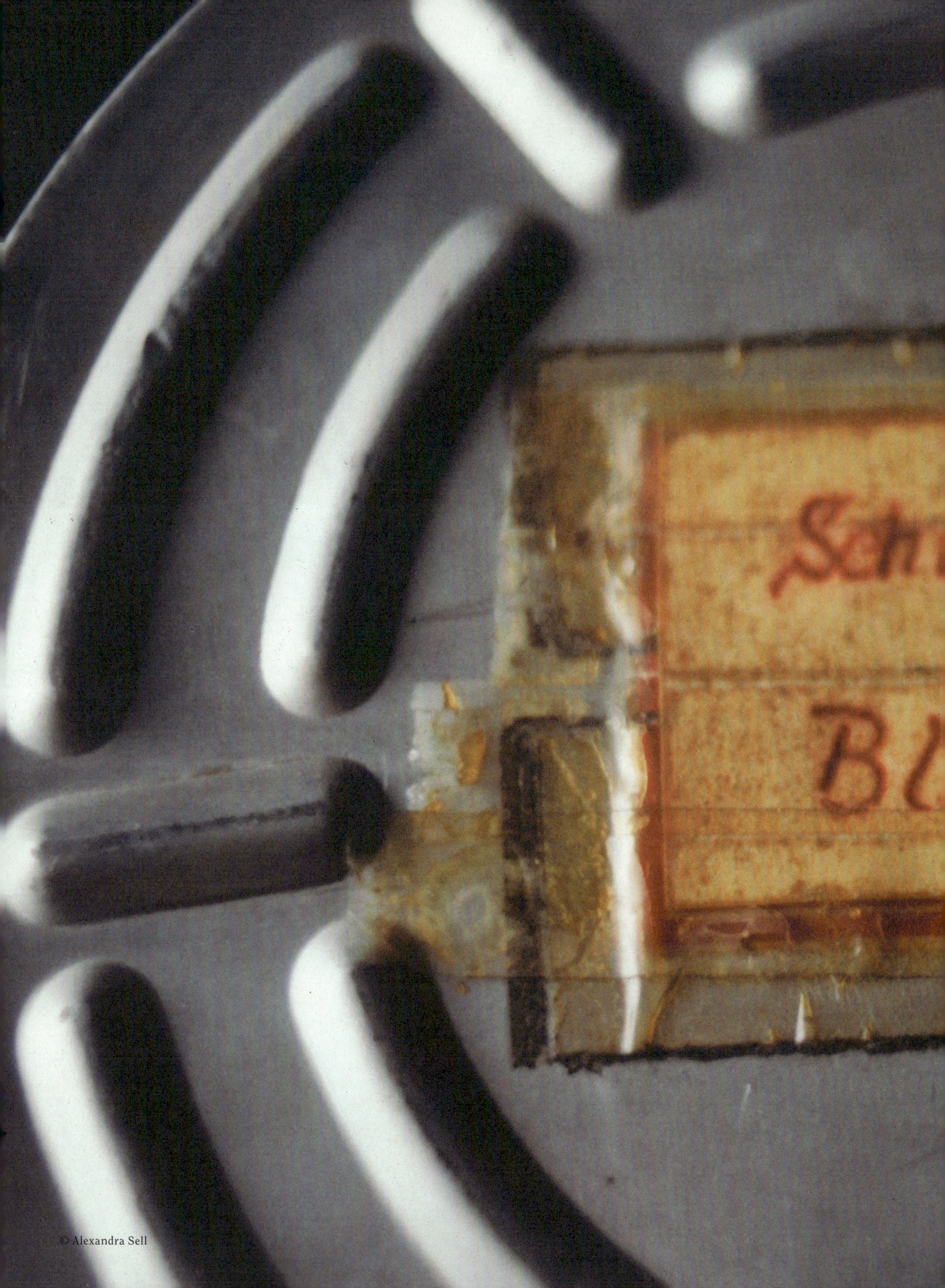

© Alexandra Sell

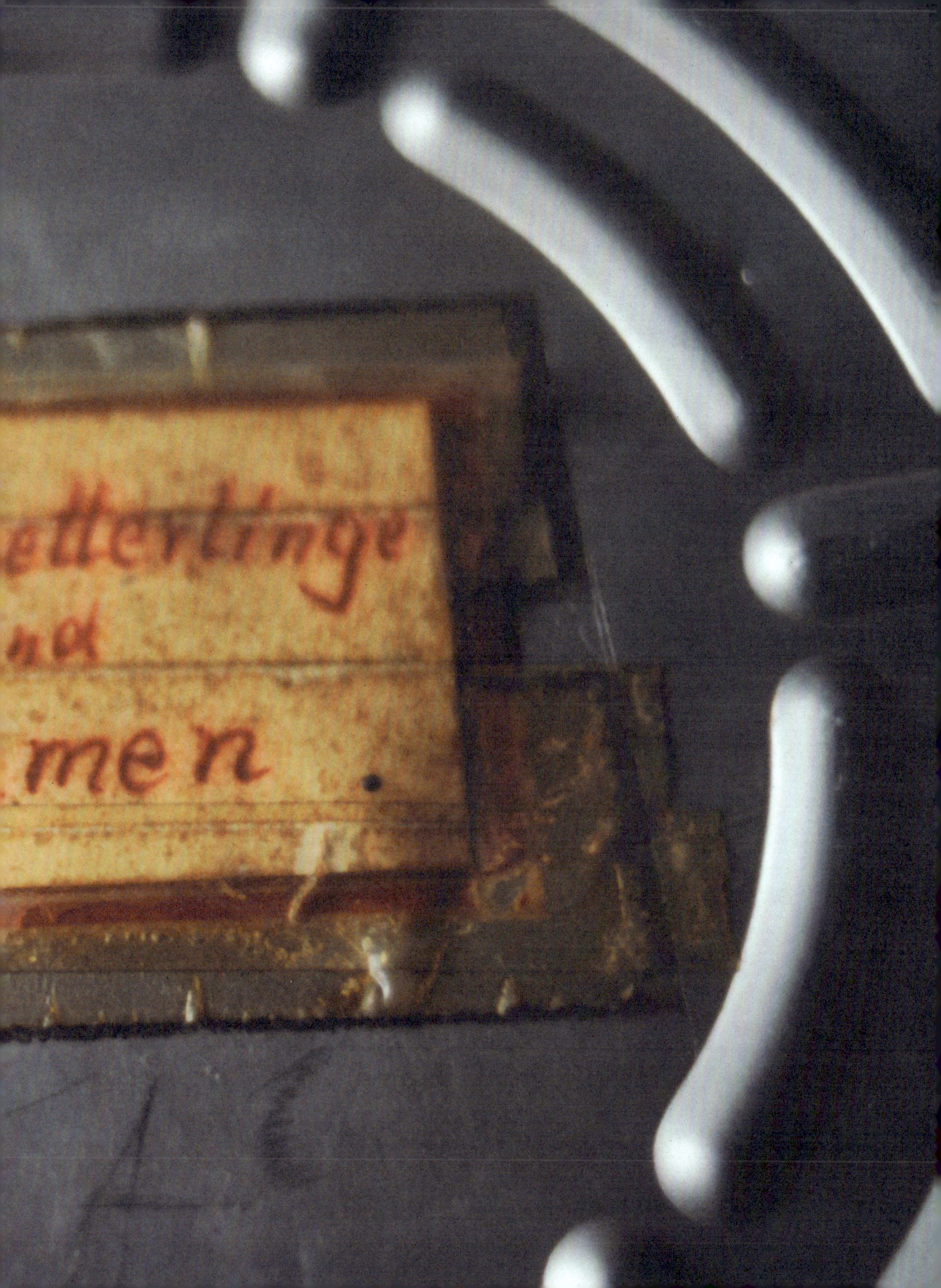
etterlinge
nd
men

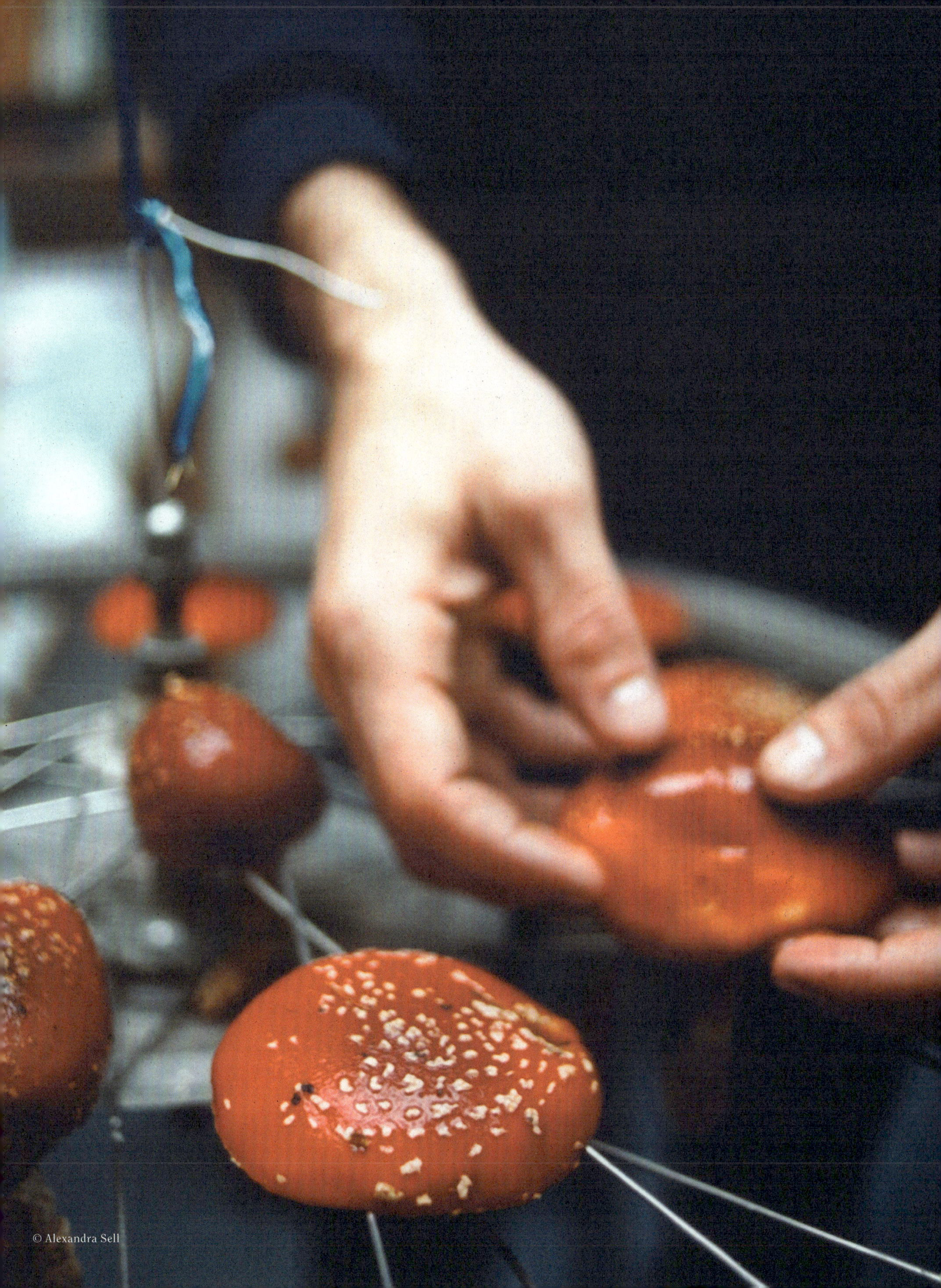
© Alexandra Sell

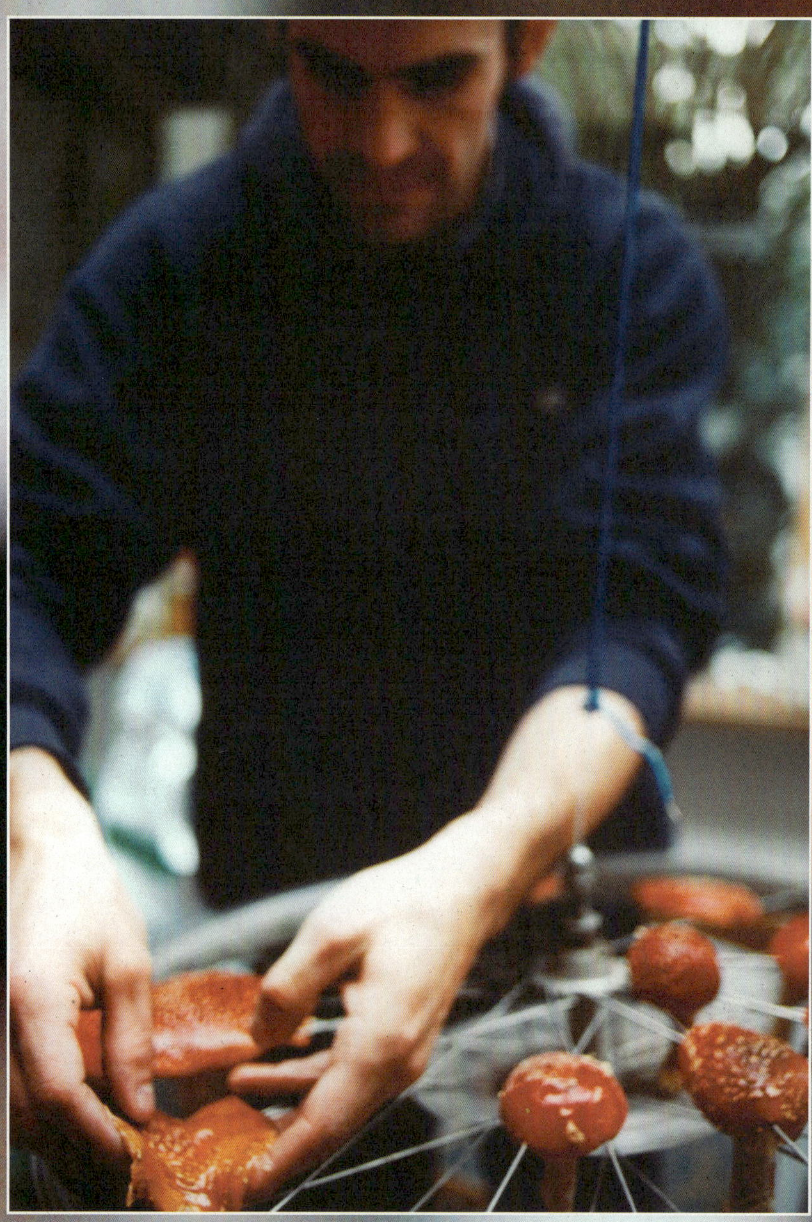

© Alexandra Sell

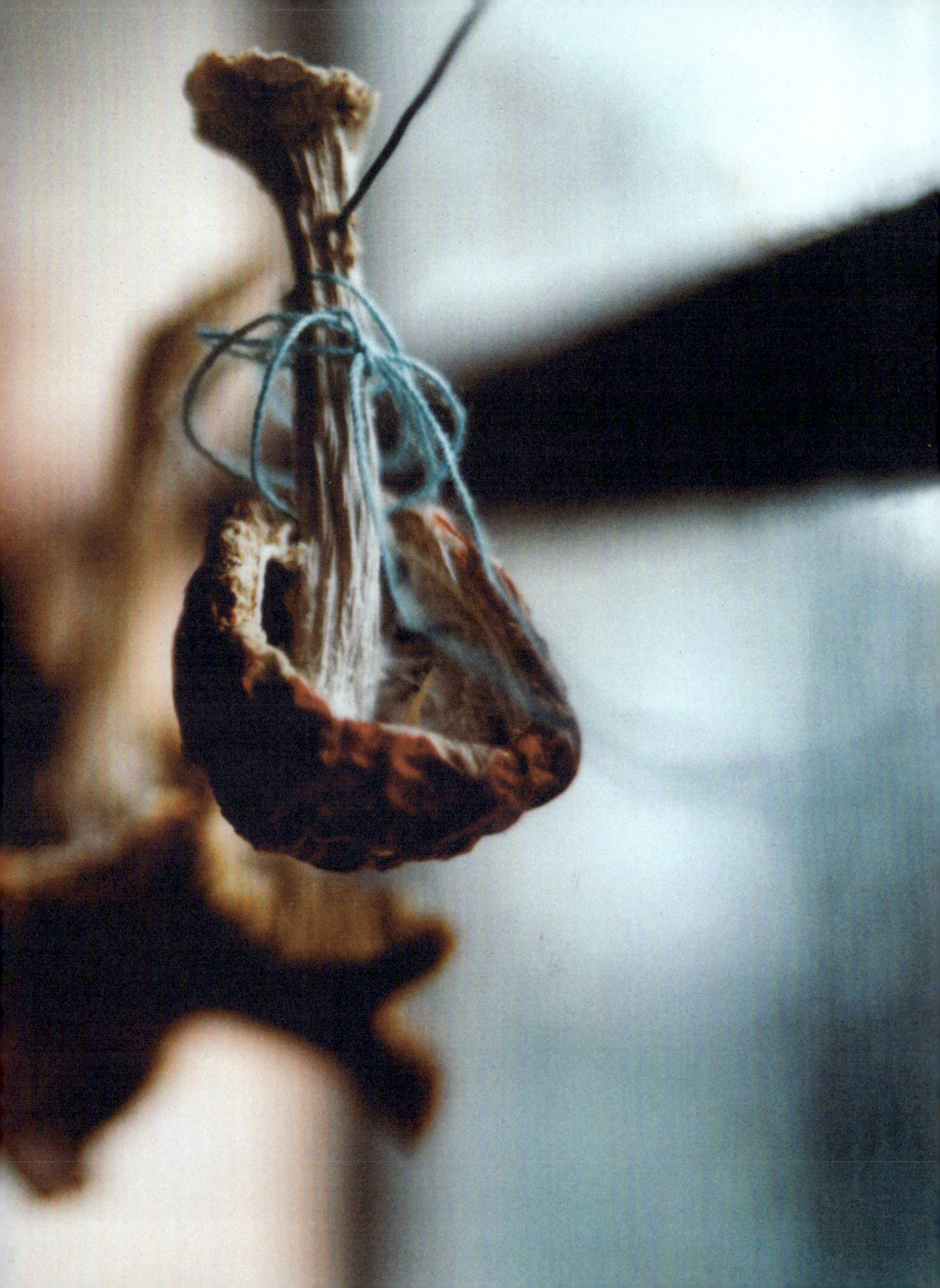

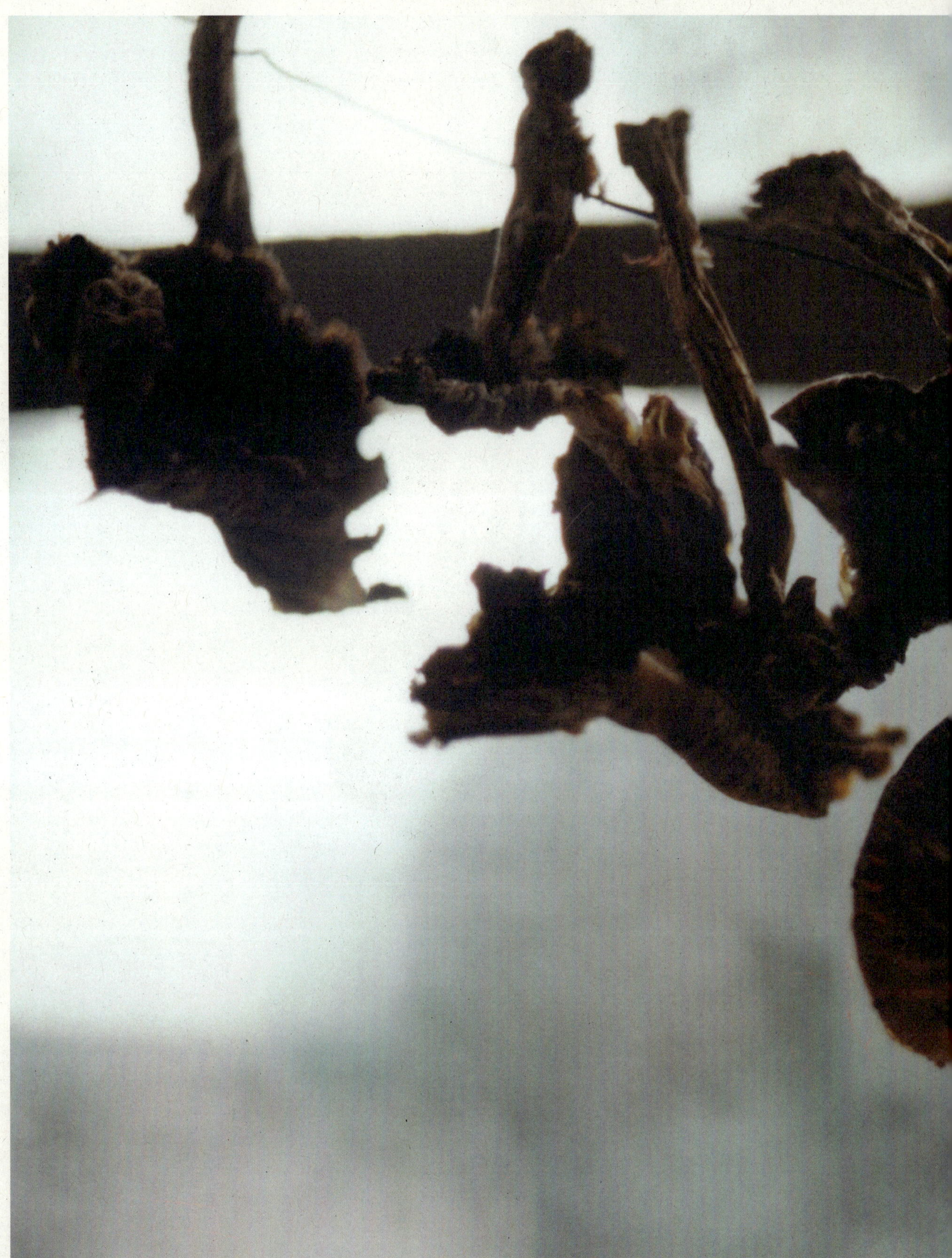

© Alexandra Sell

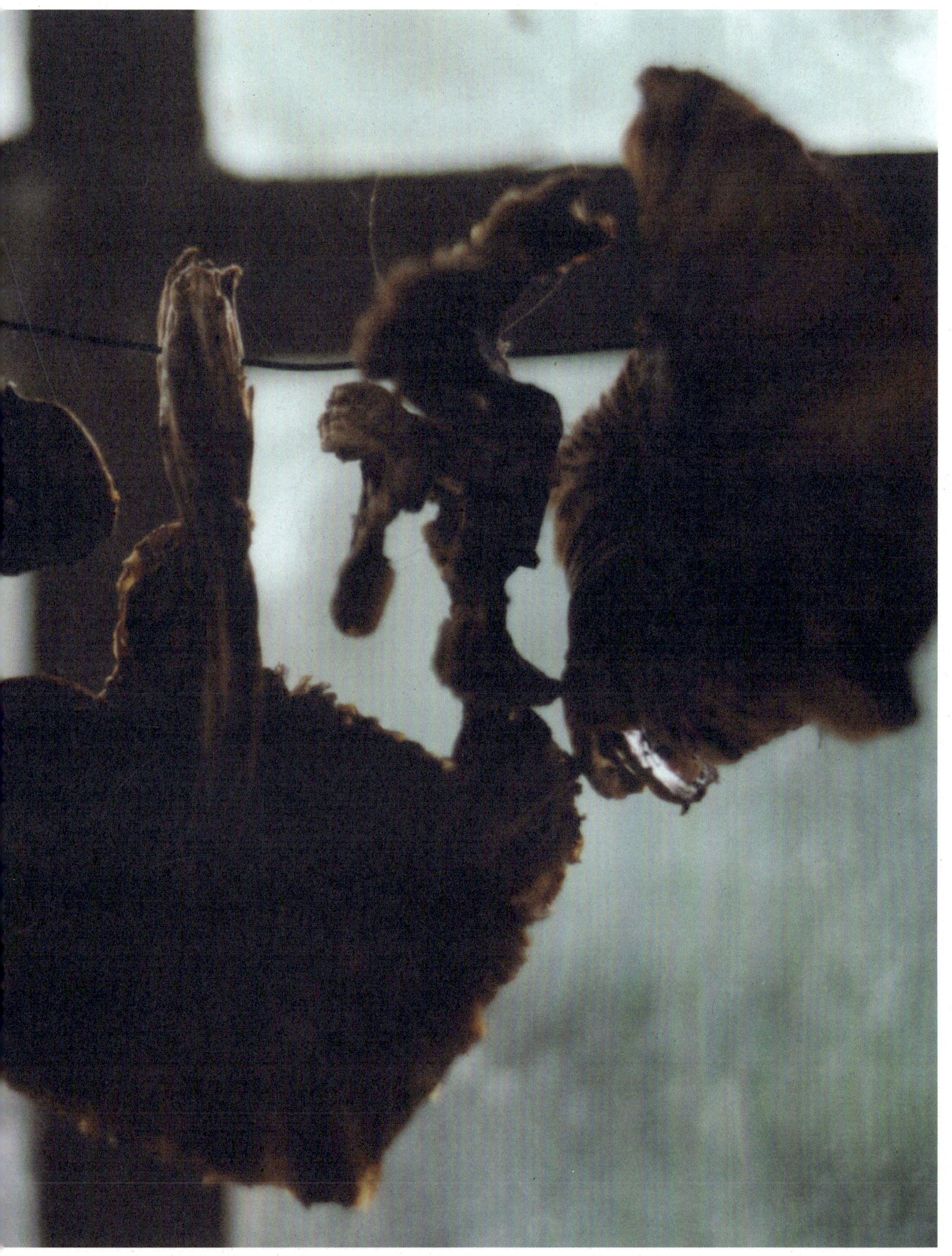

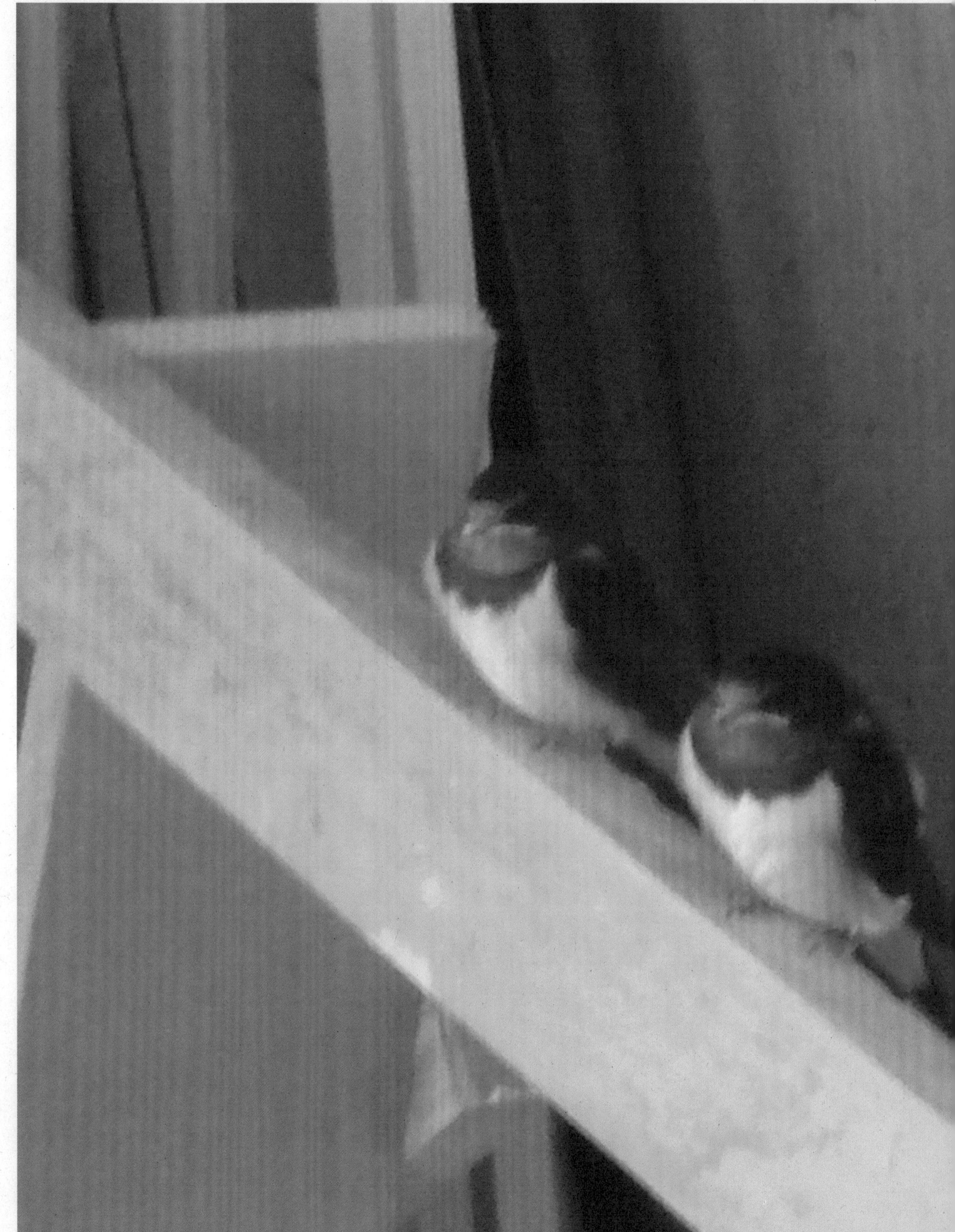

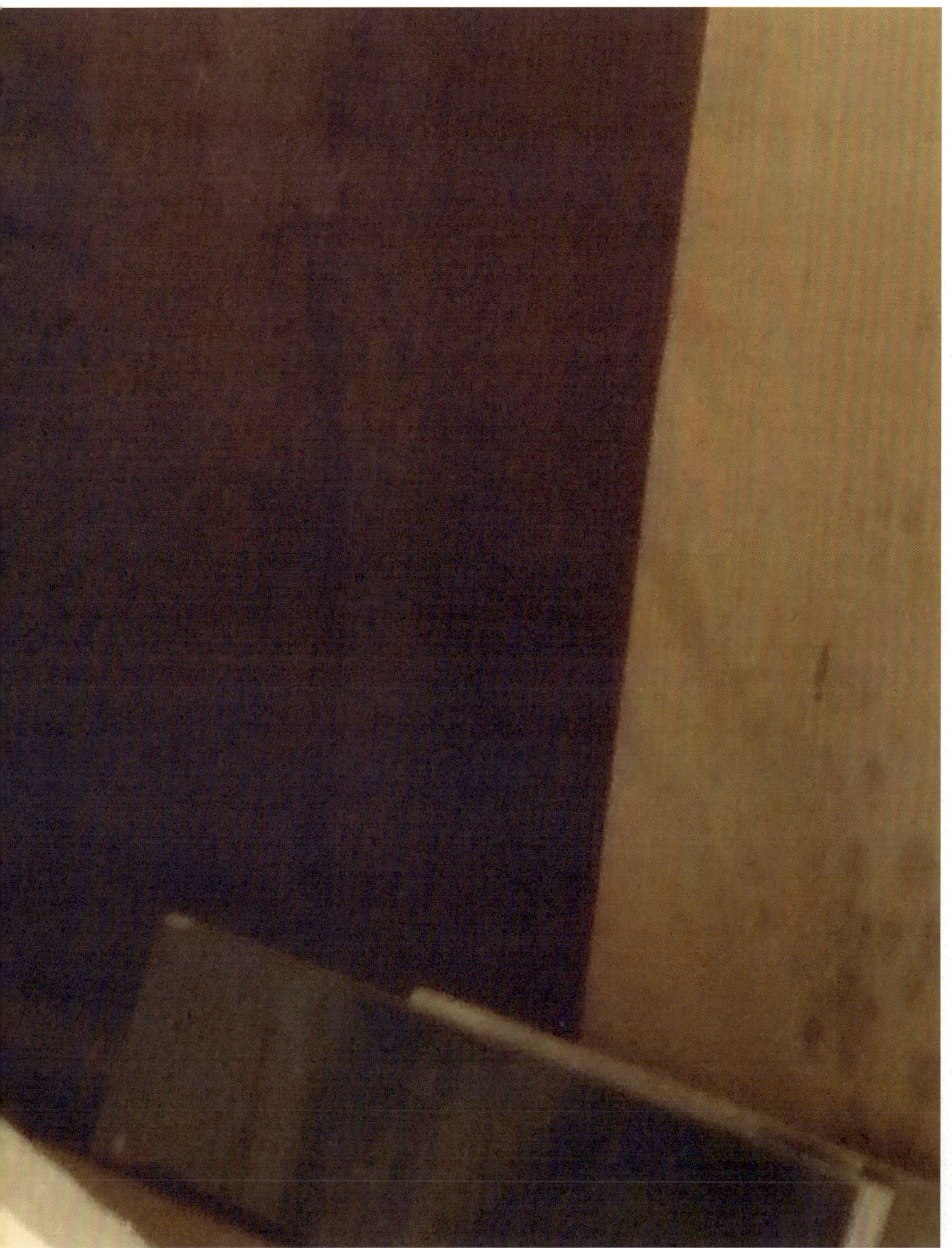

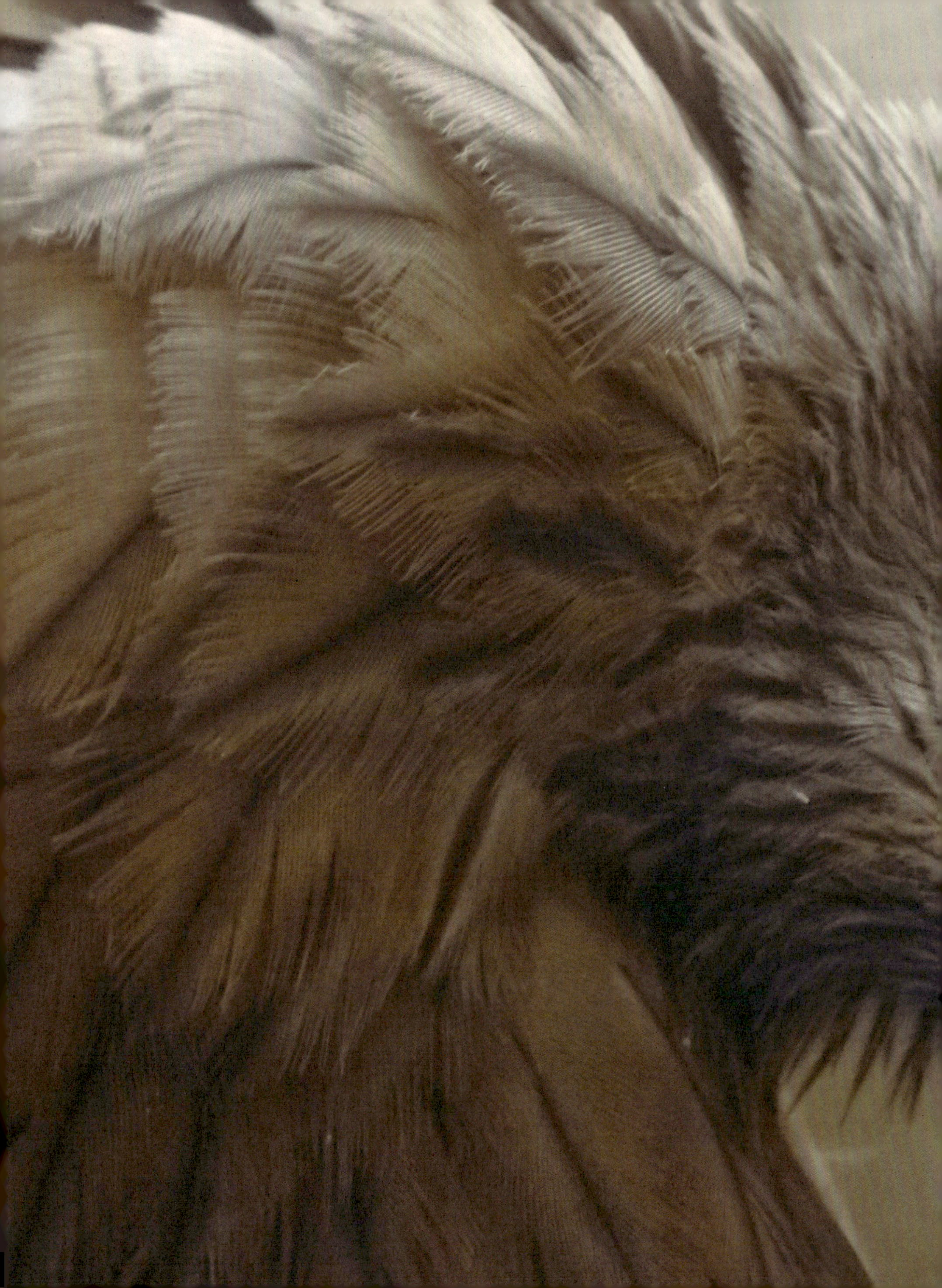

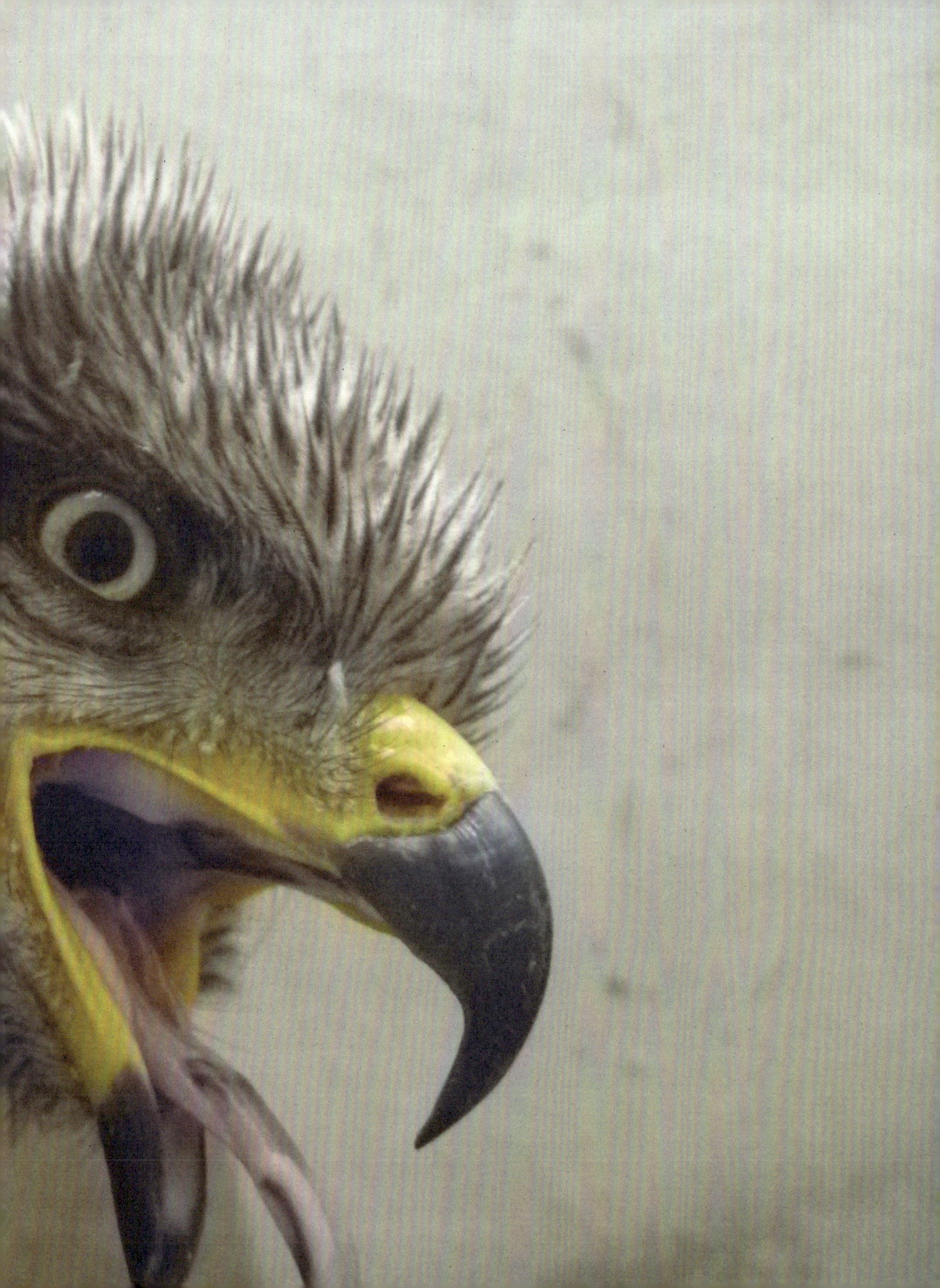

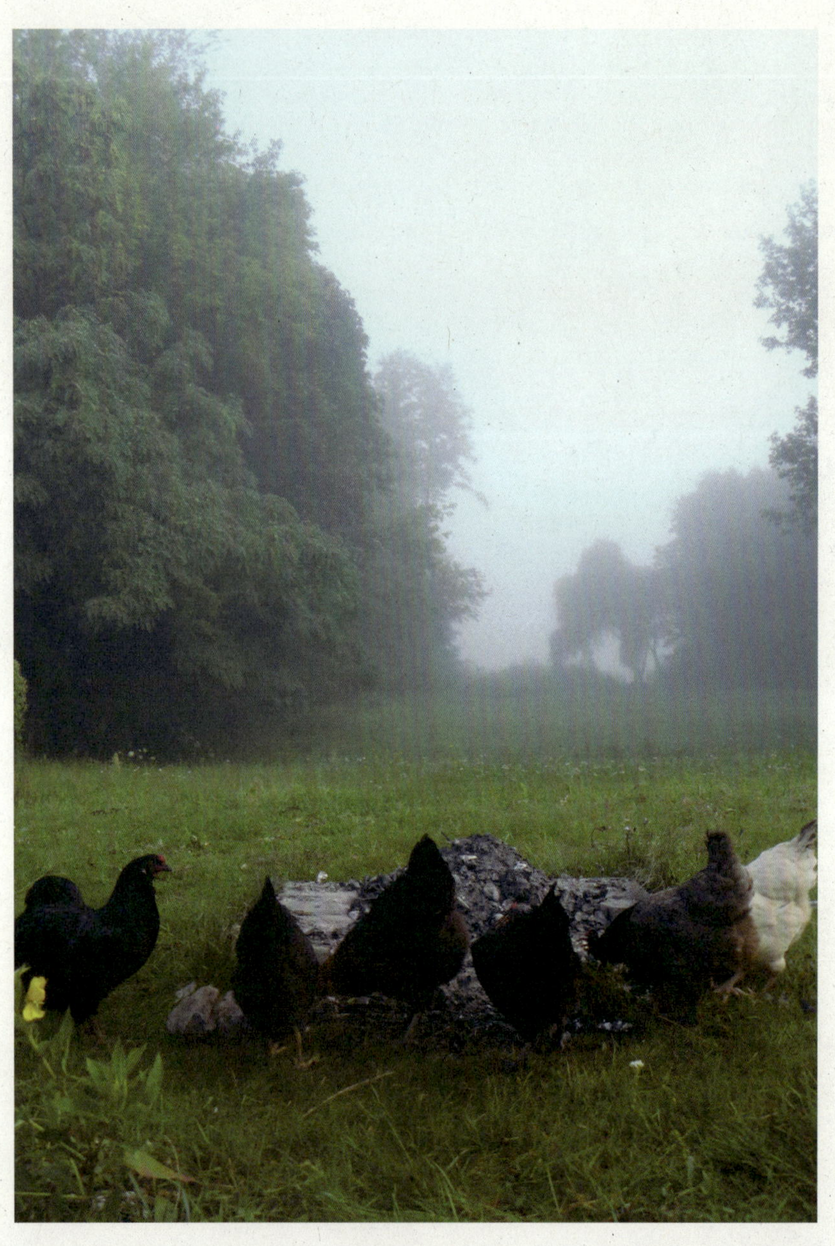

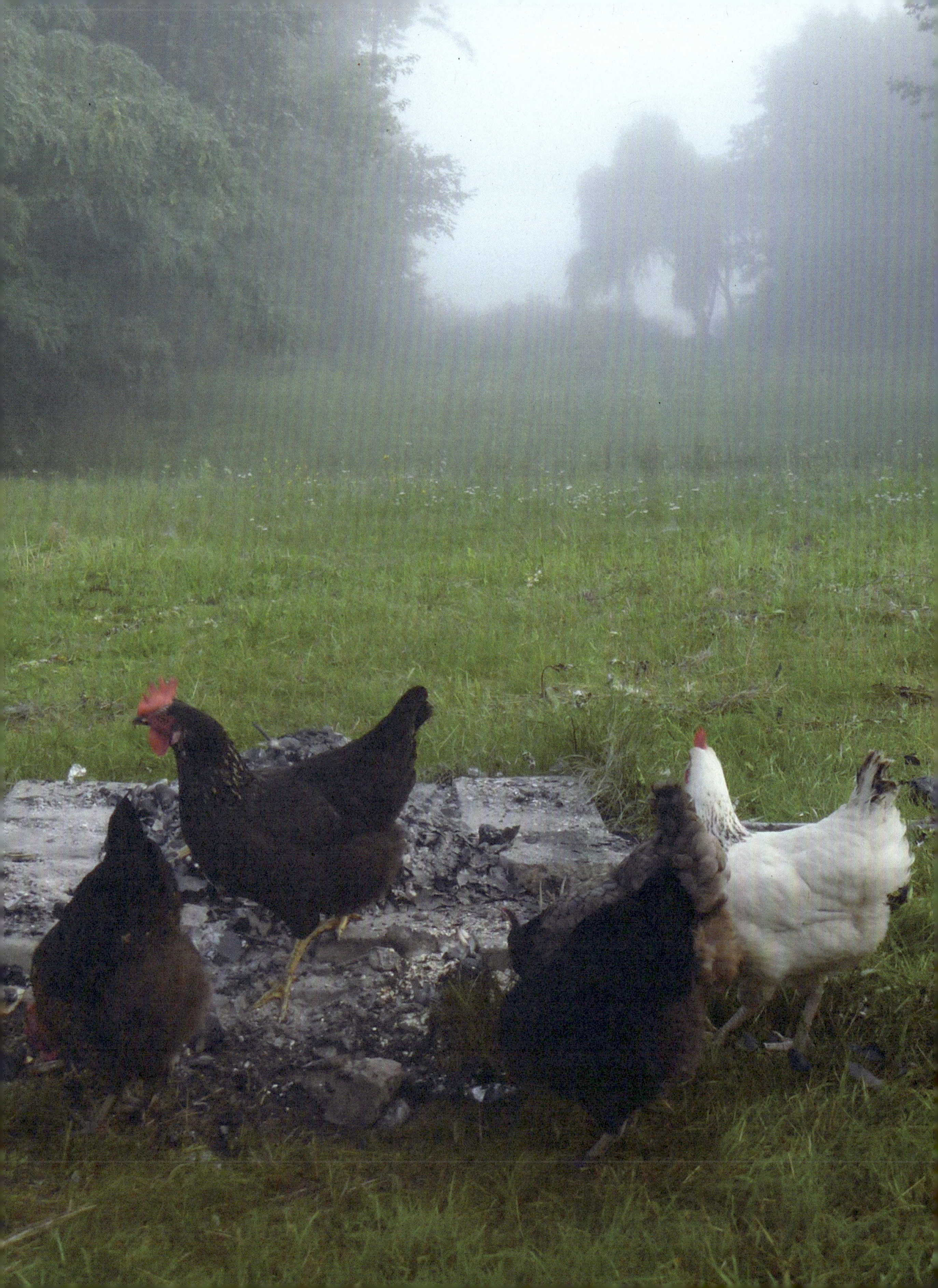

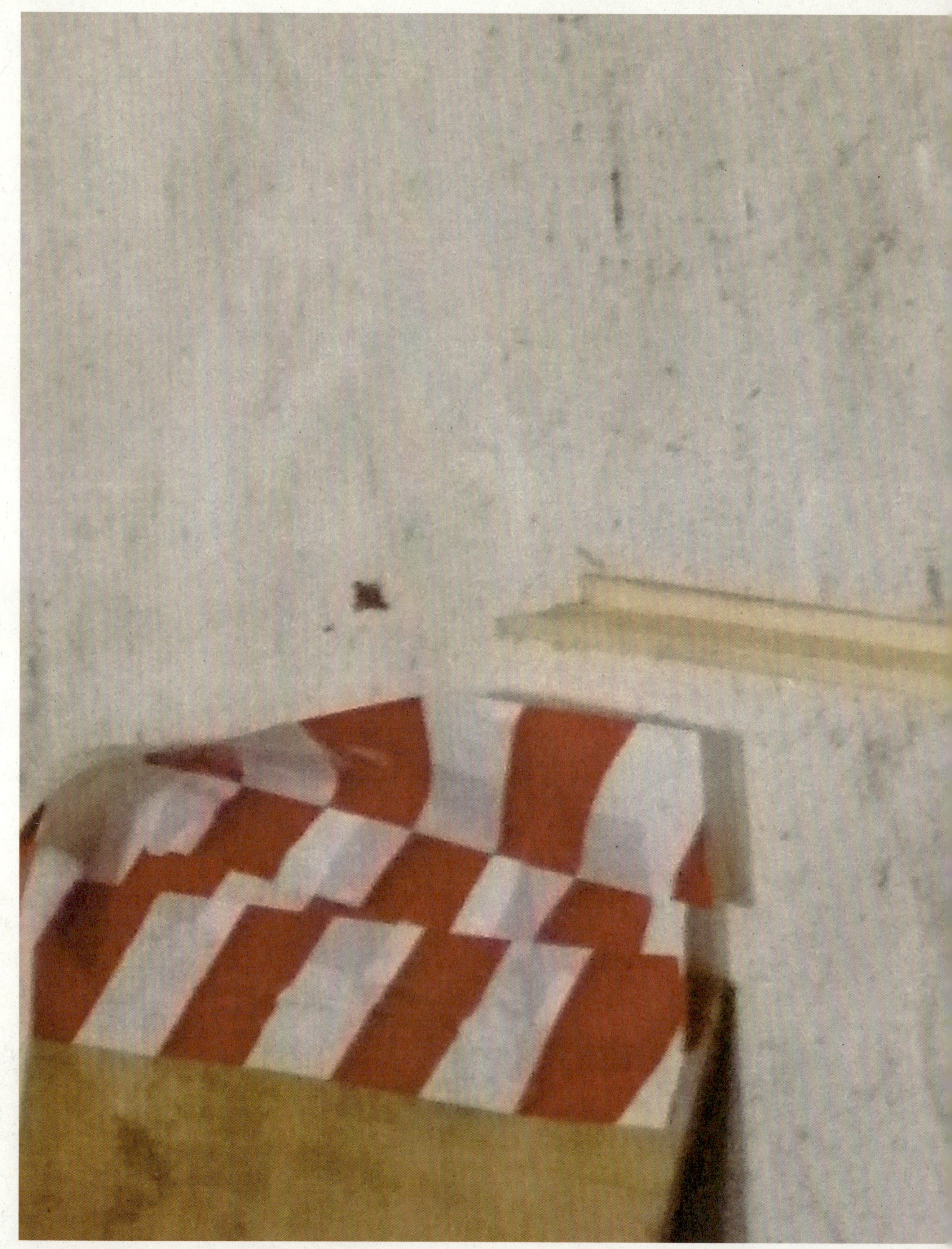

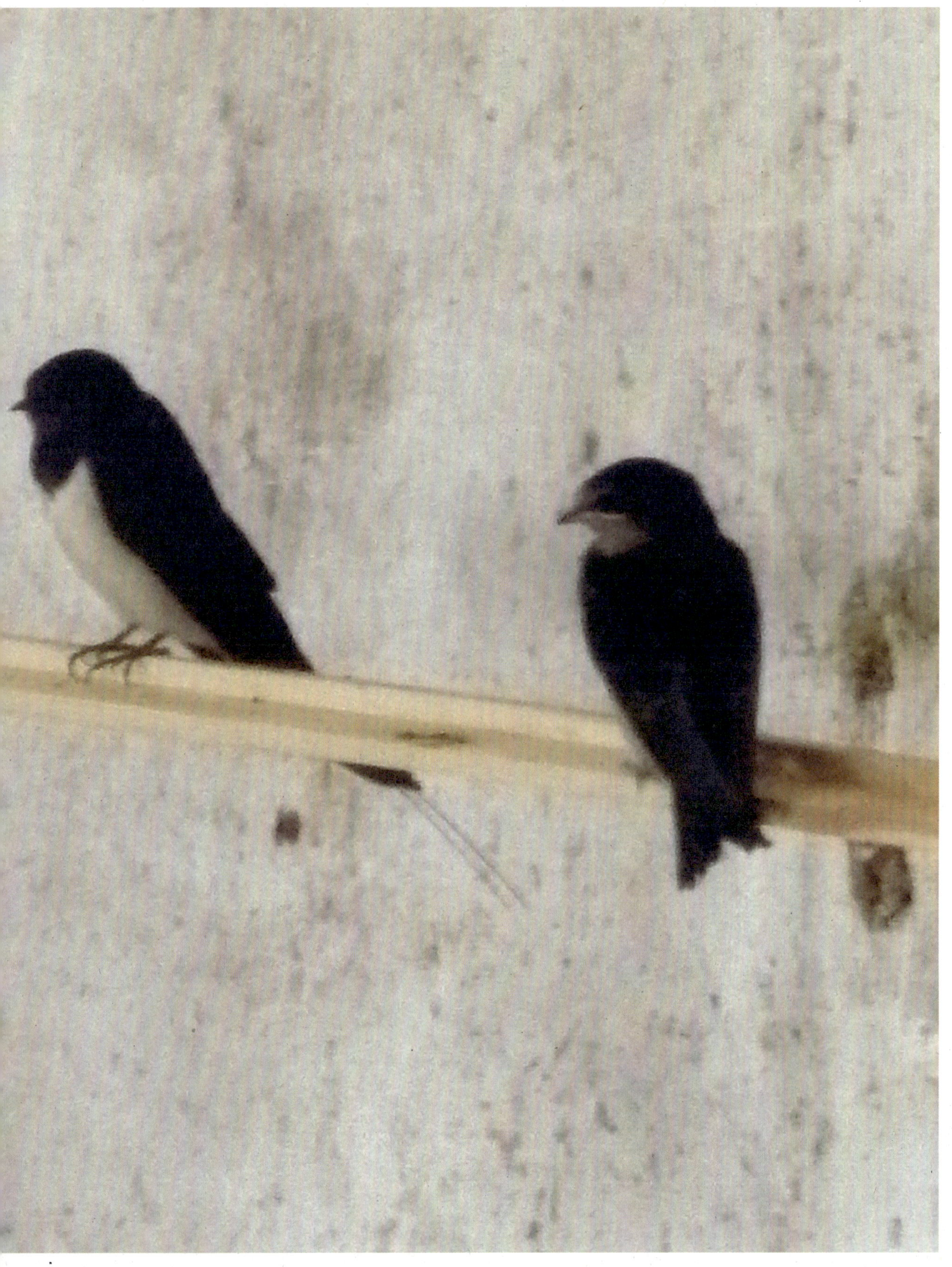

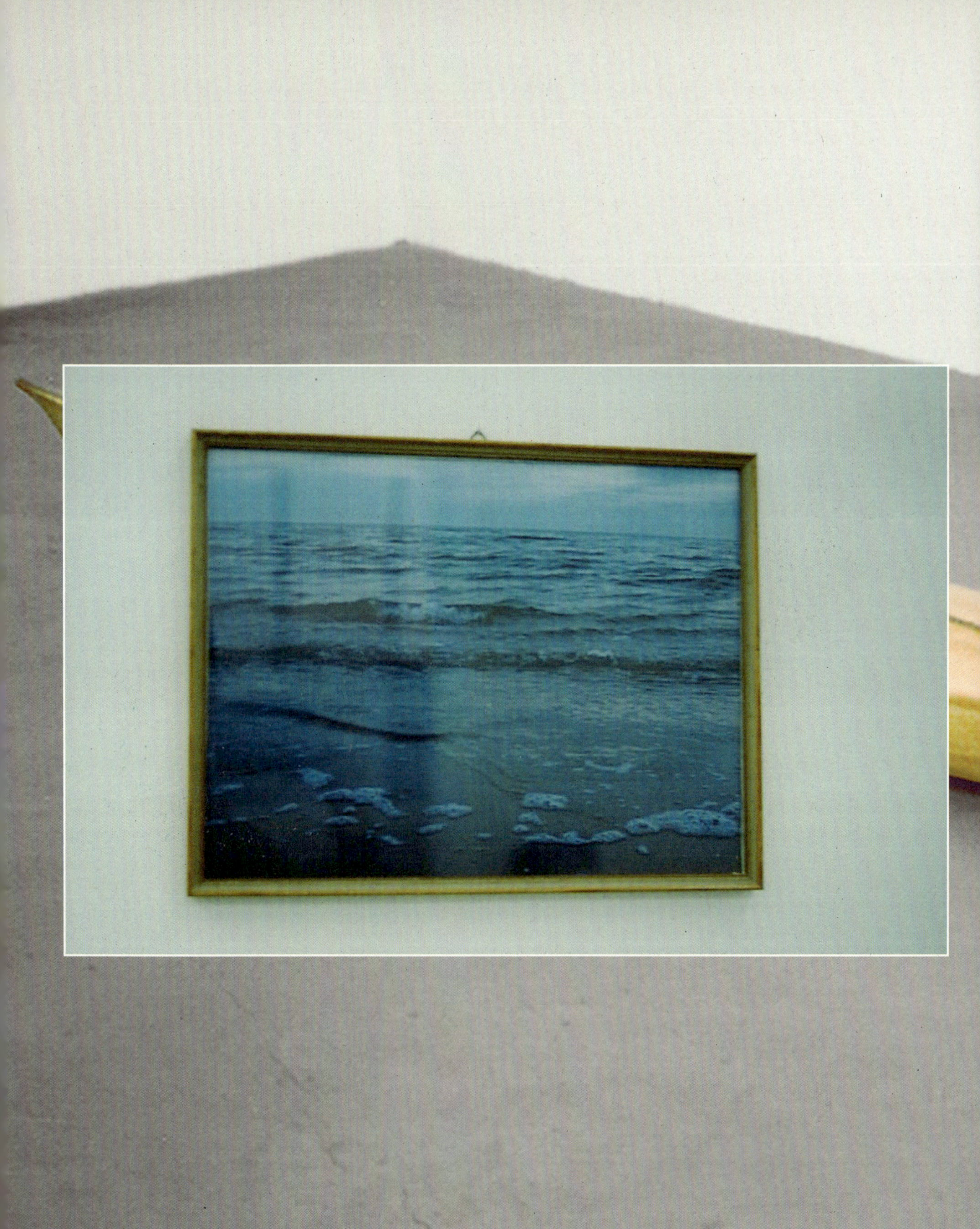

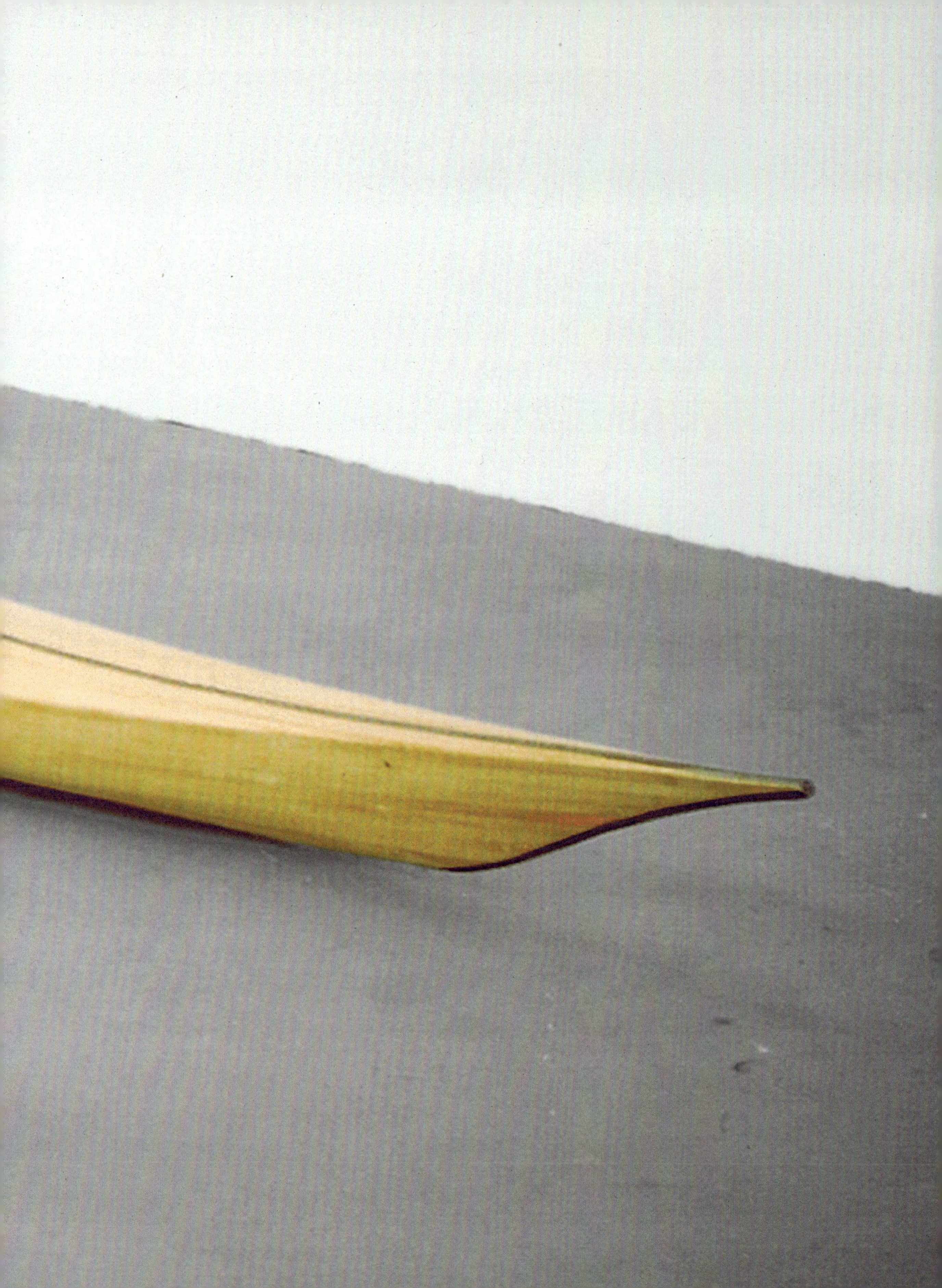

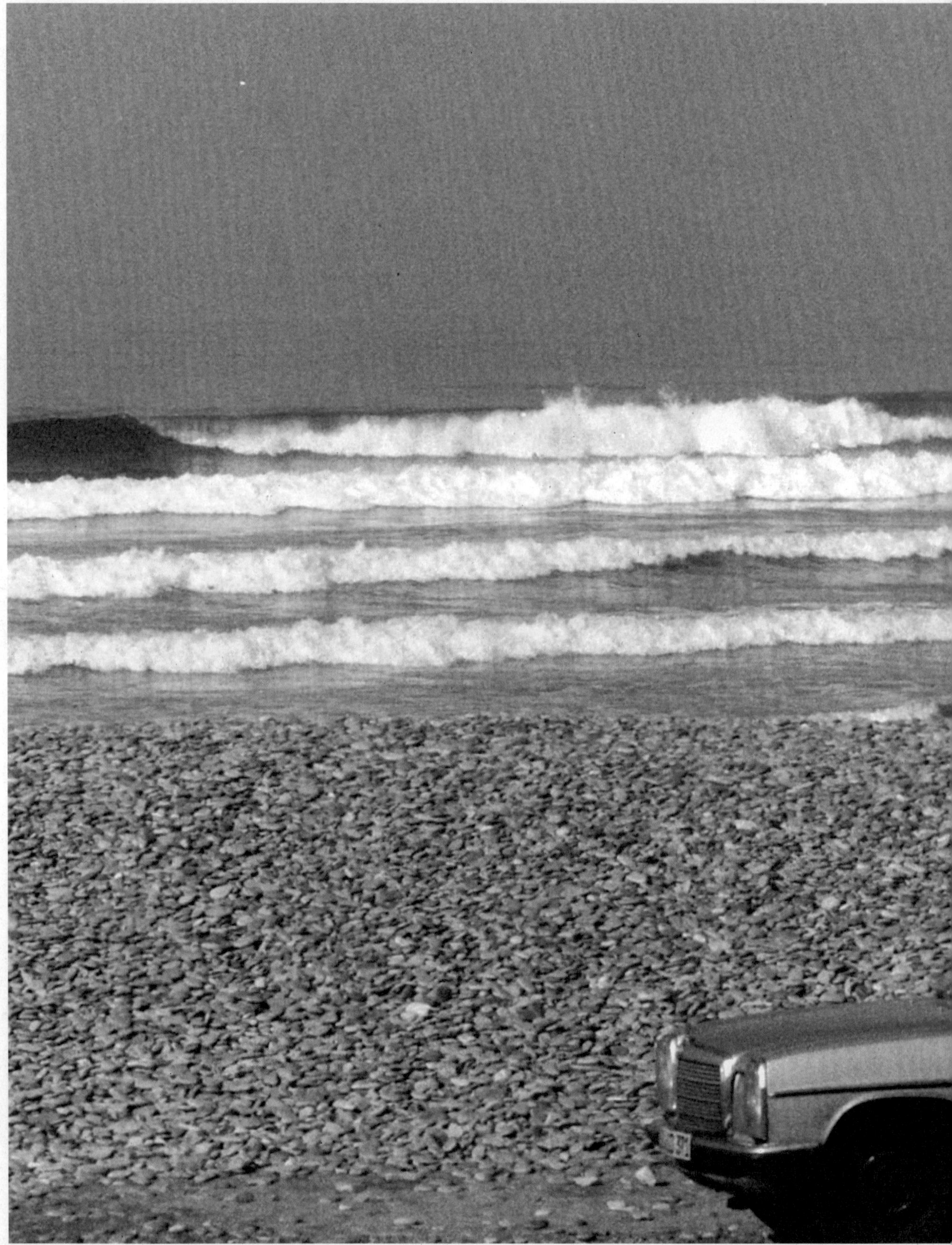

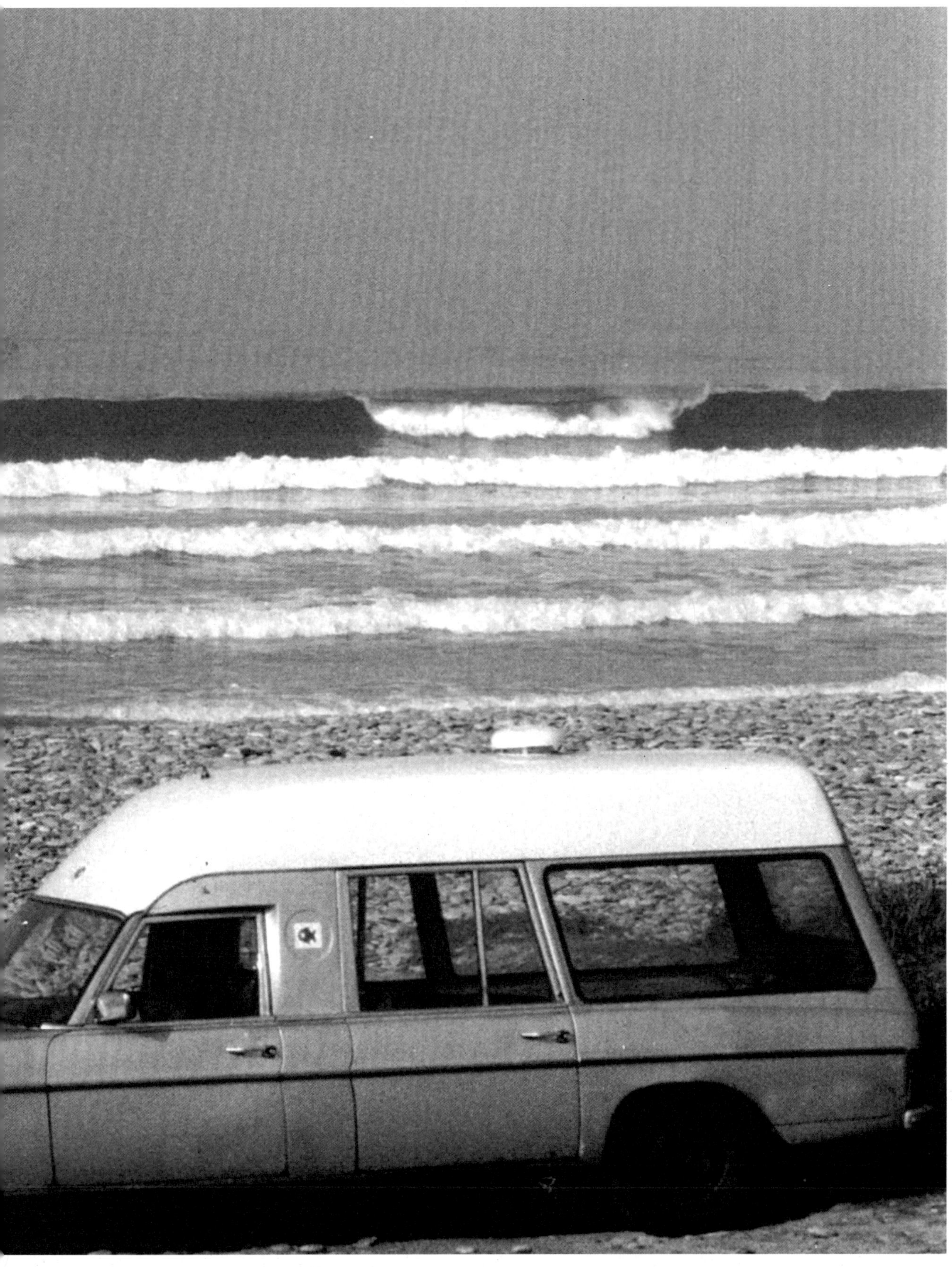

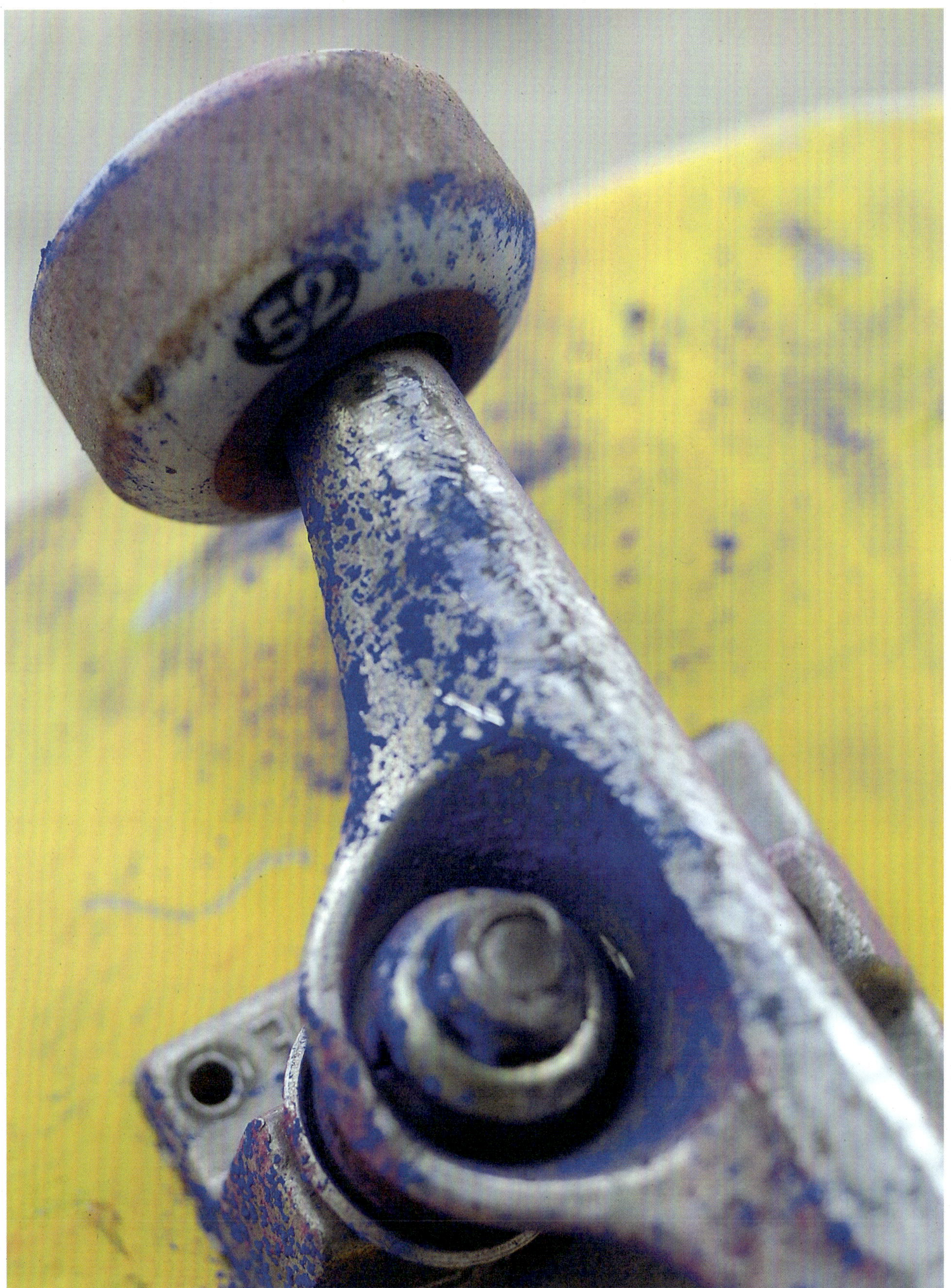

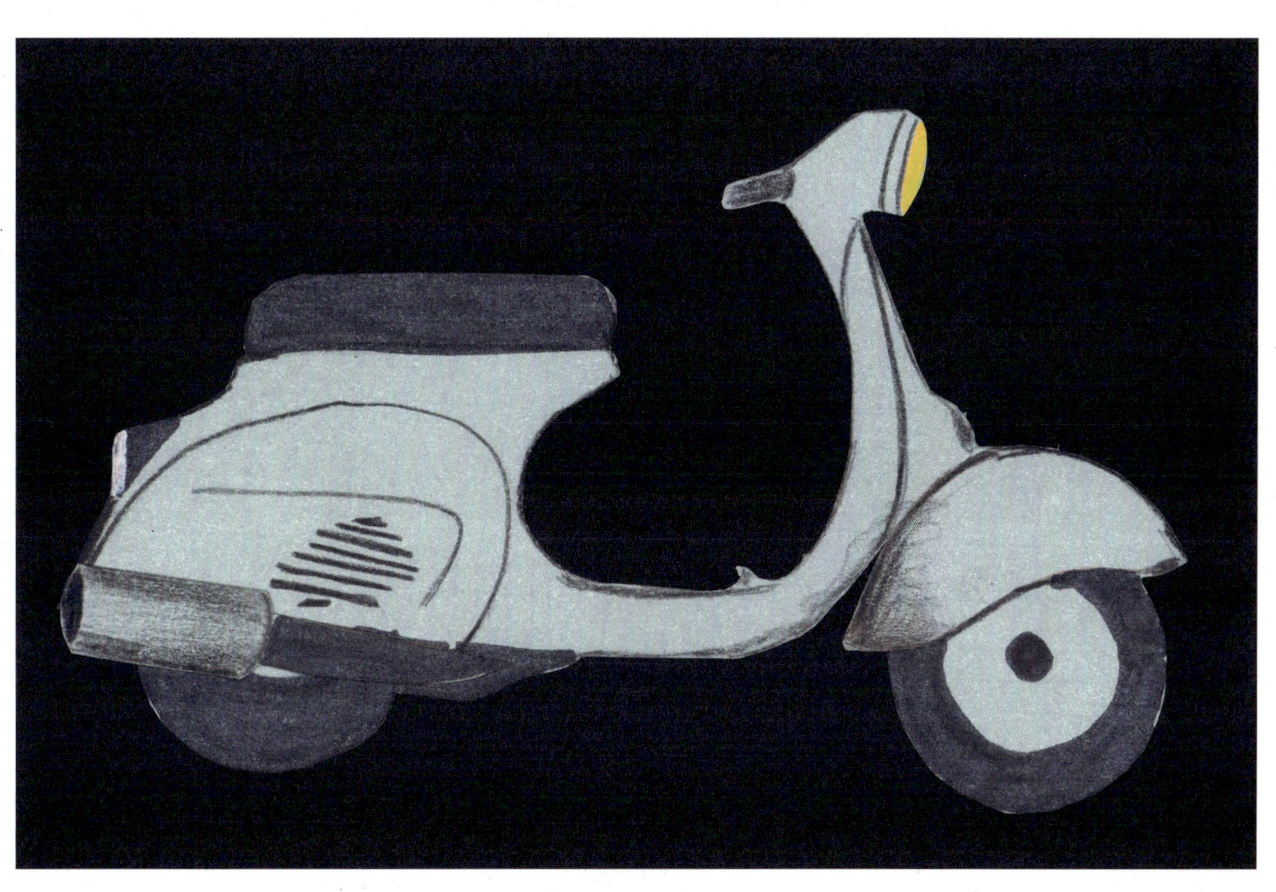

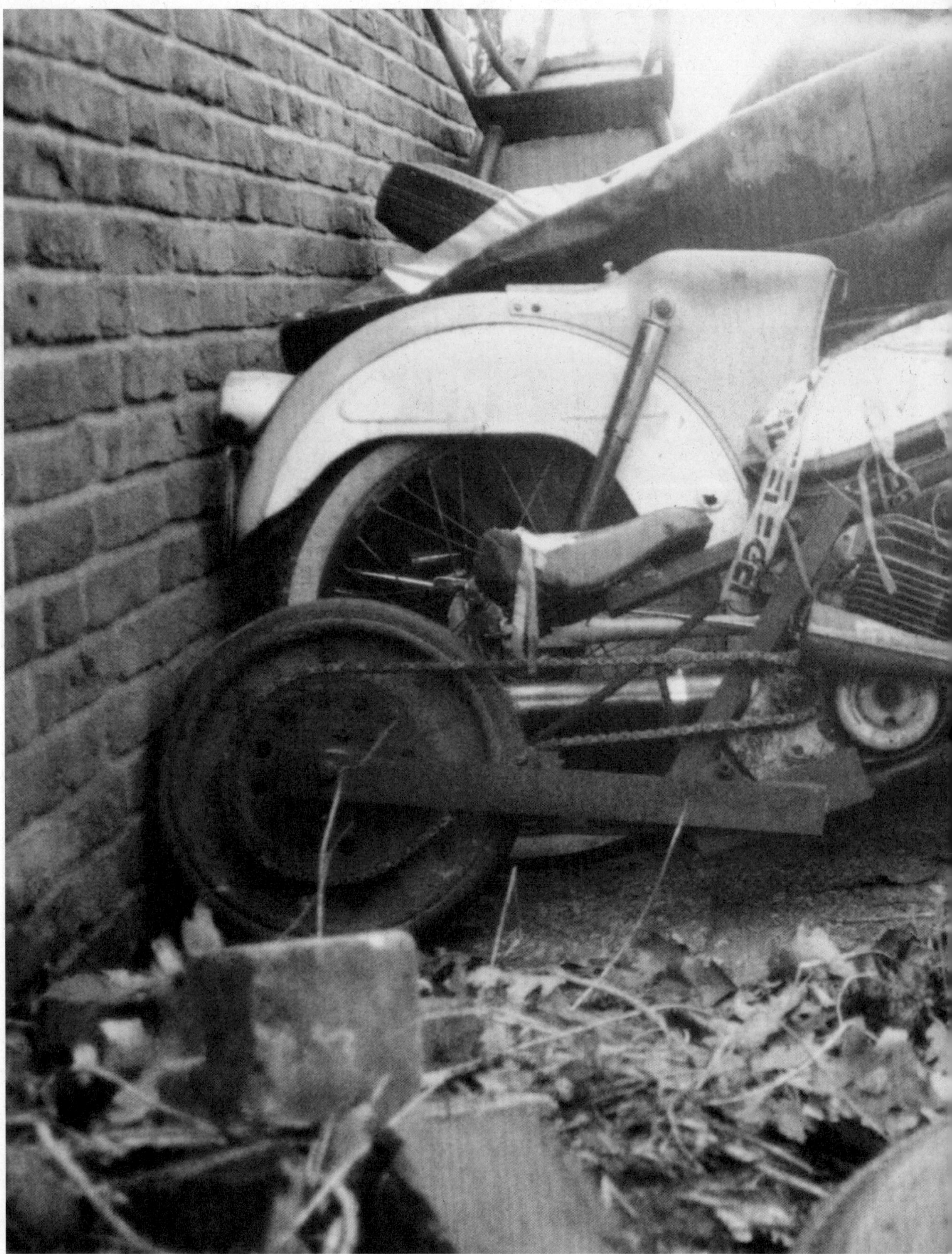

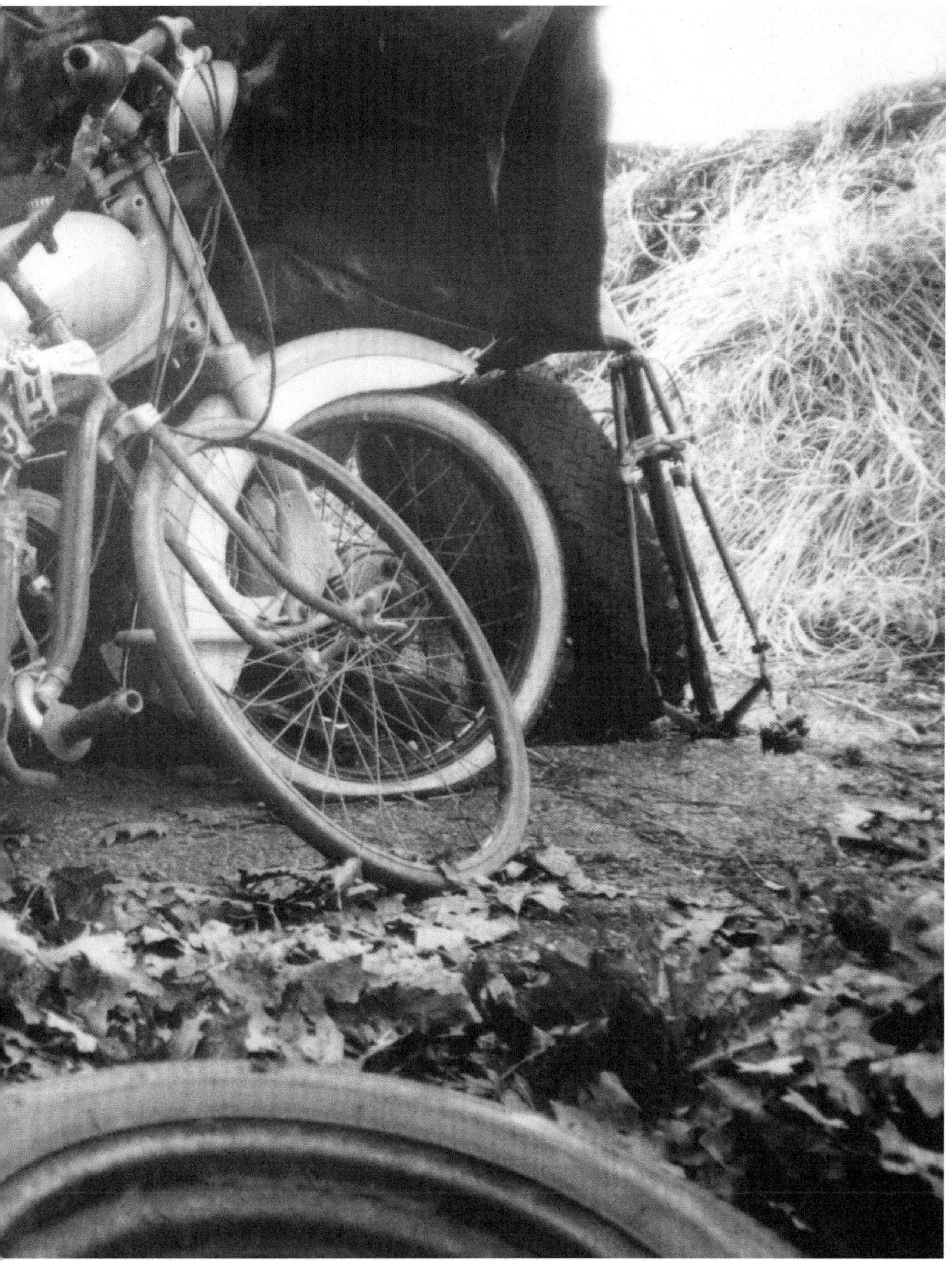

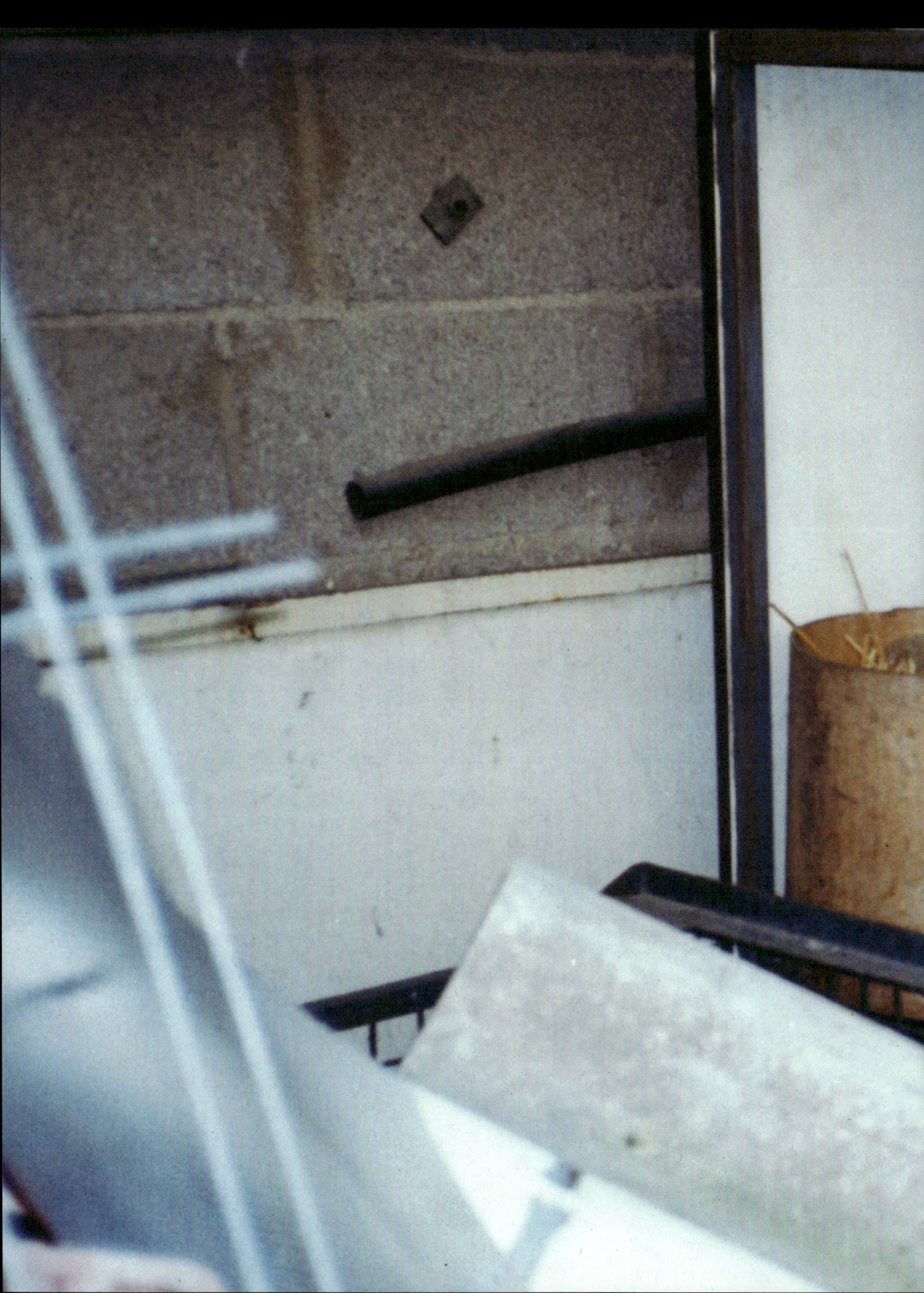

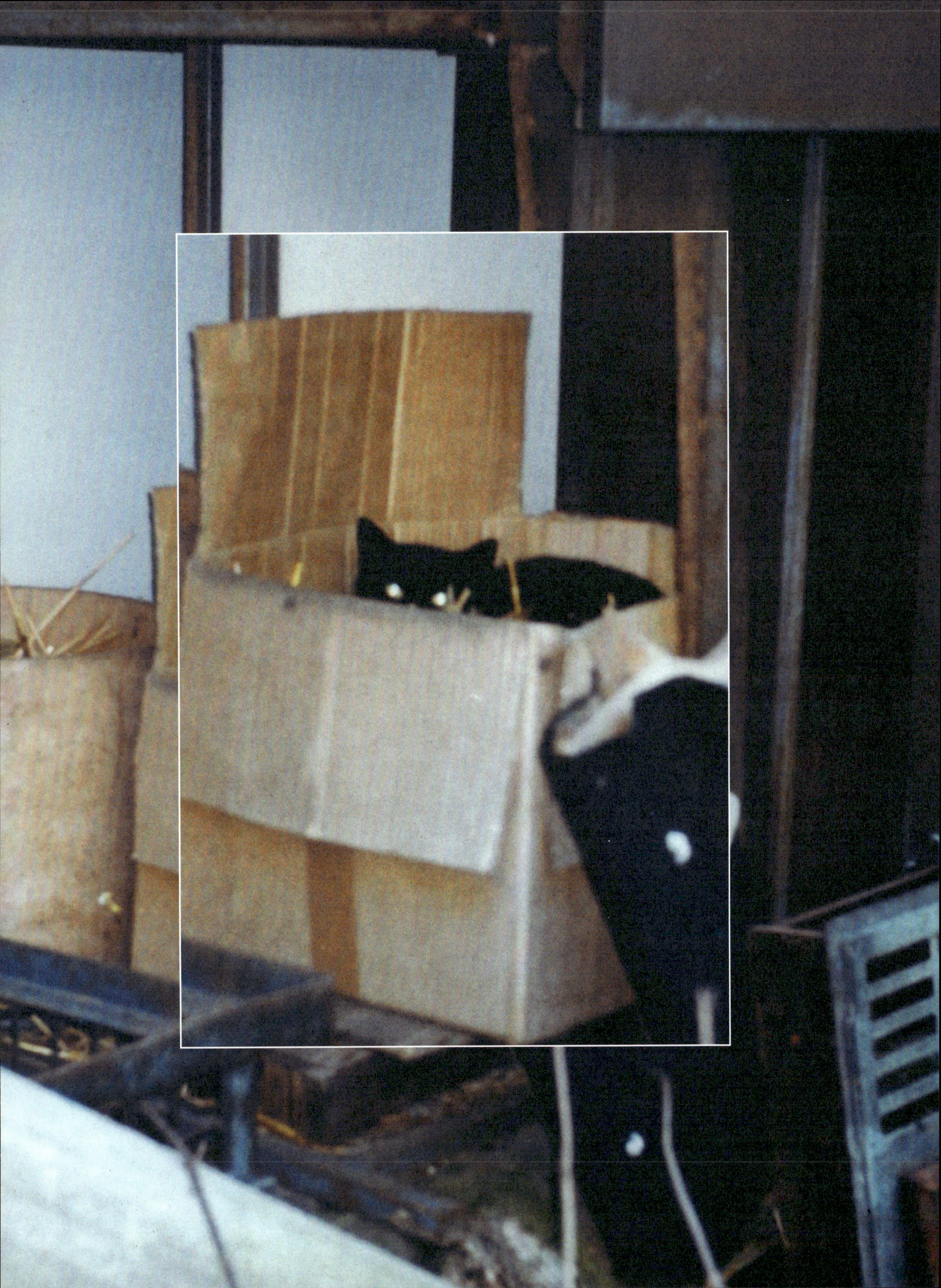

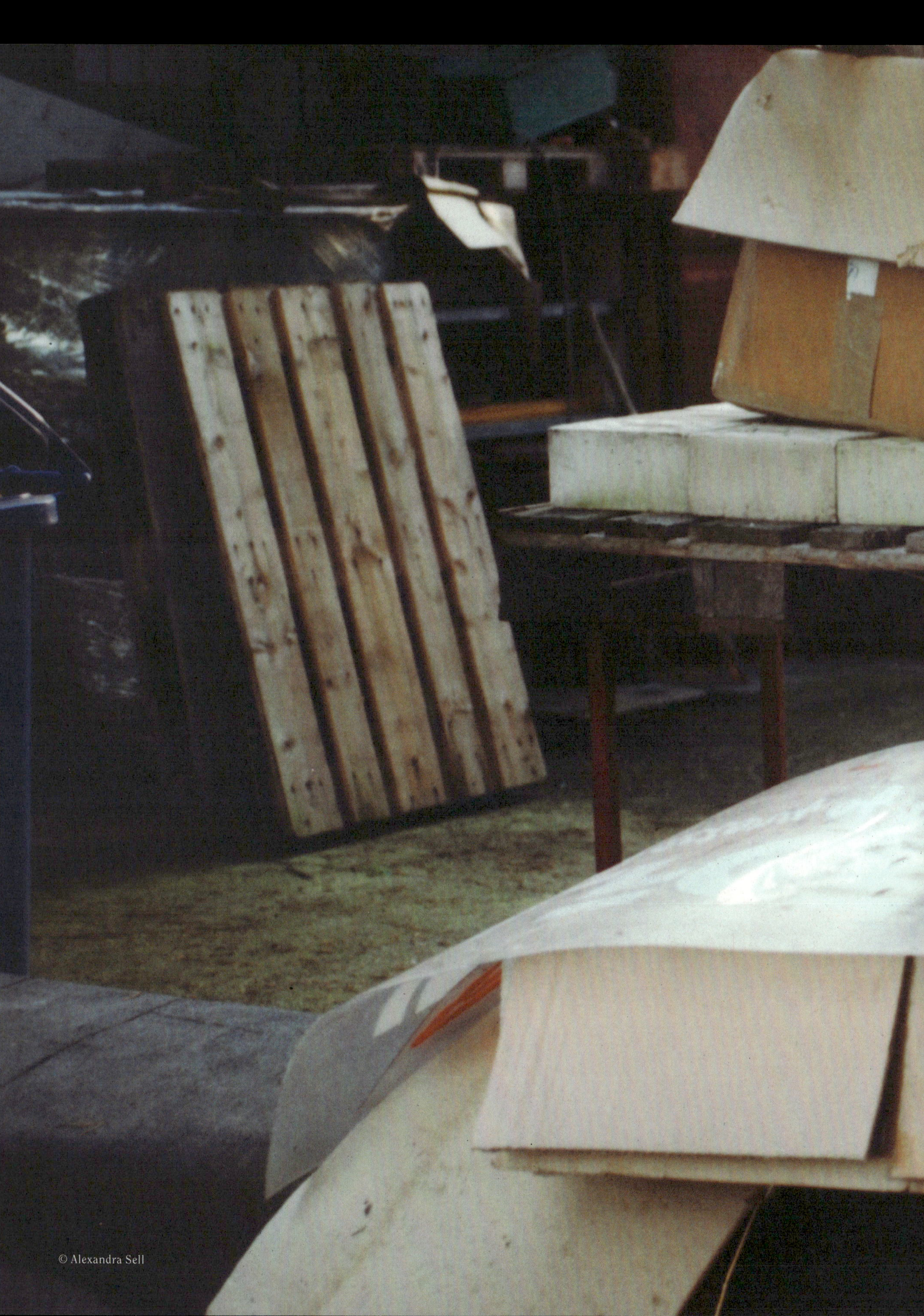

© Alexandra Sell

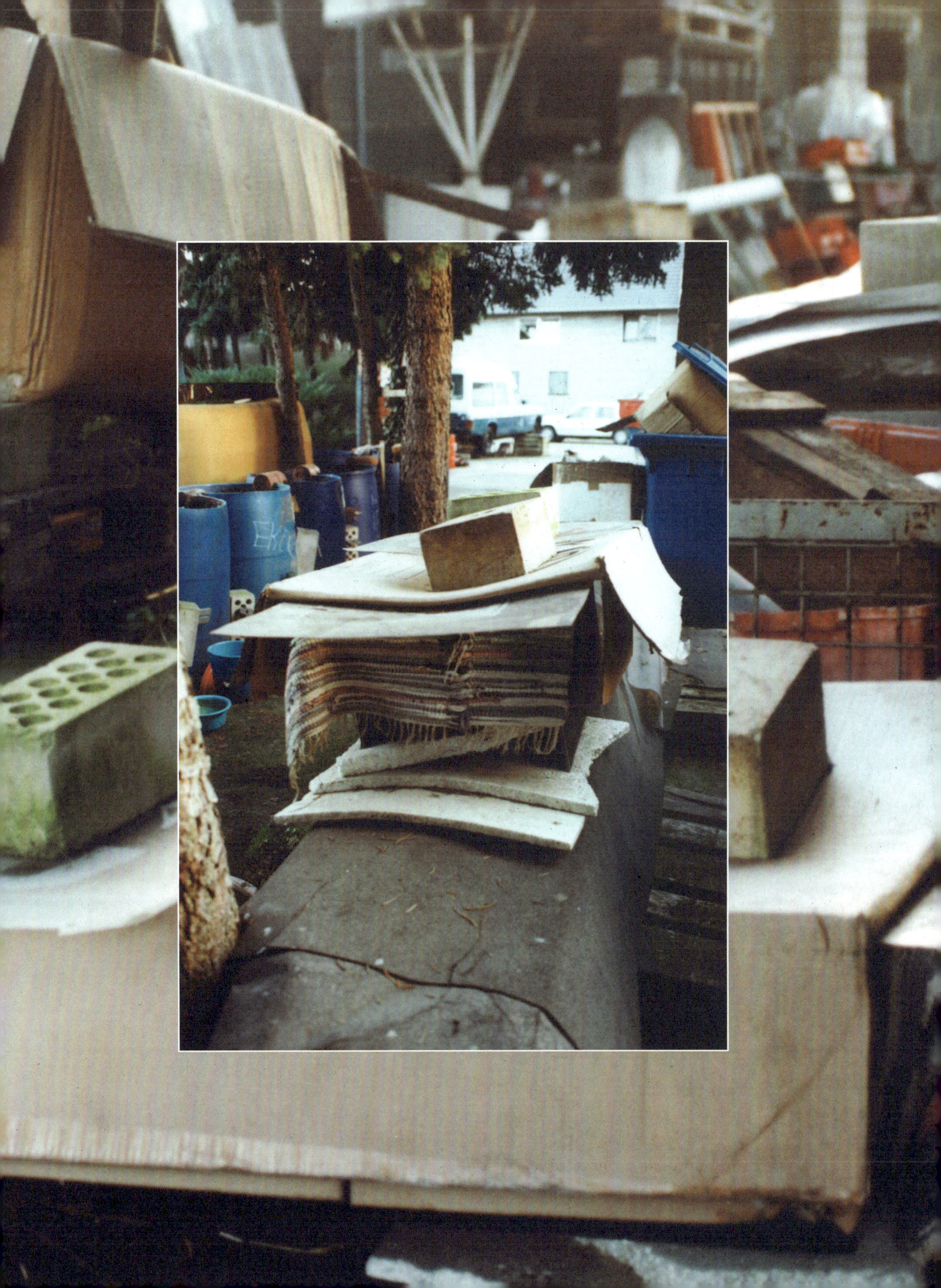

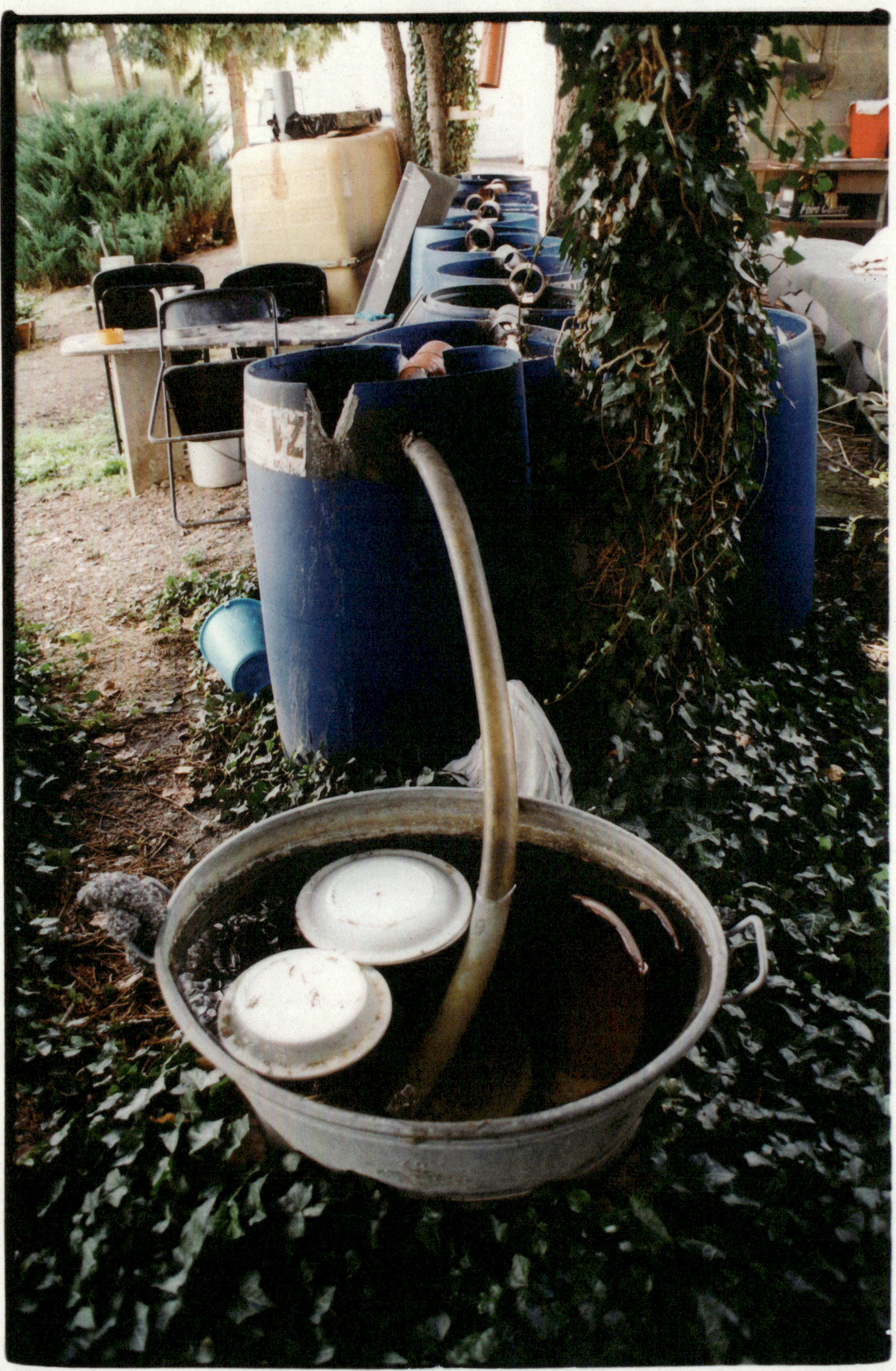

© Alexandra Sell

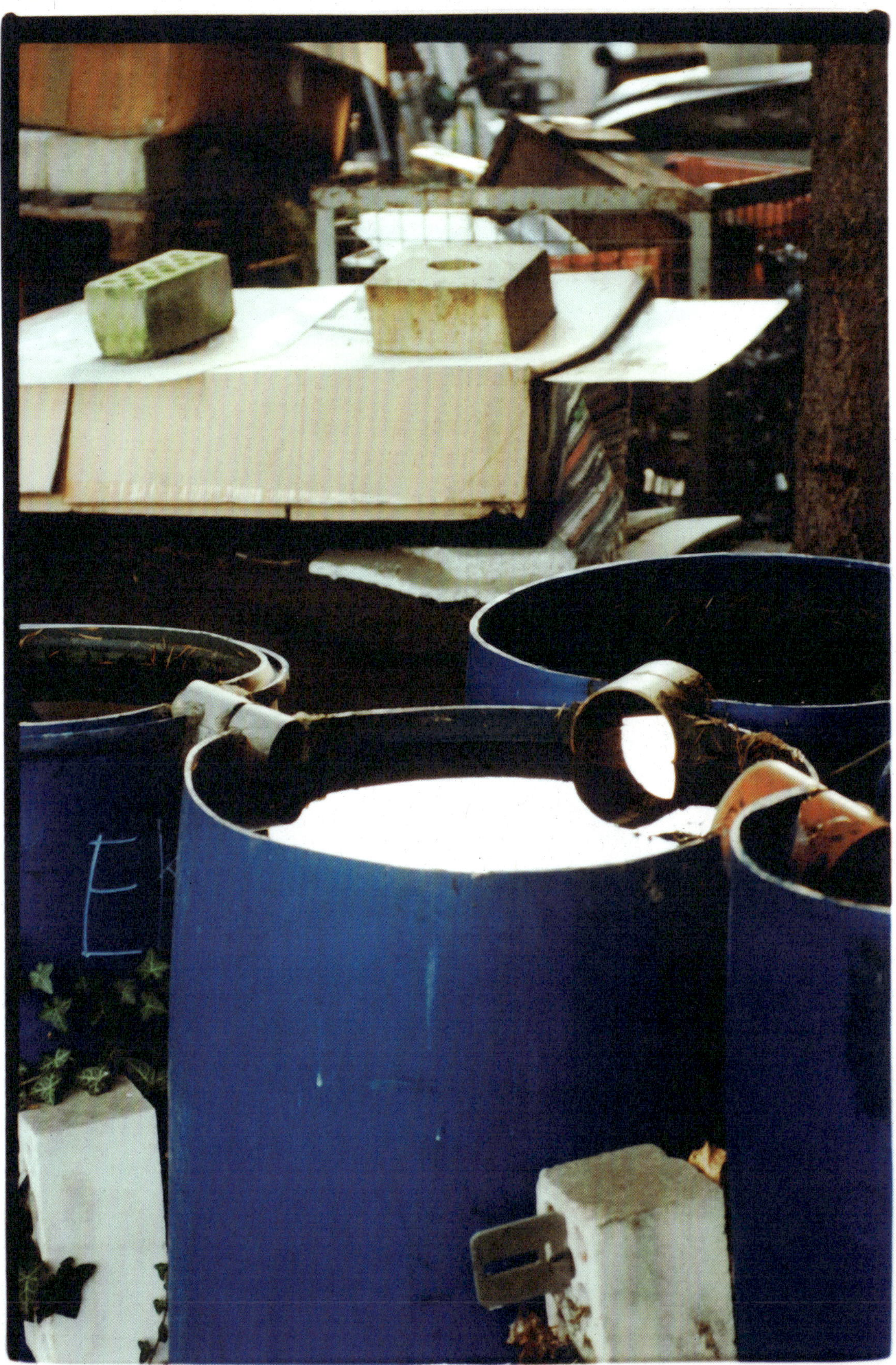

© Alexandra Sell

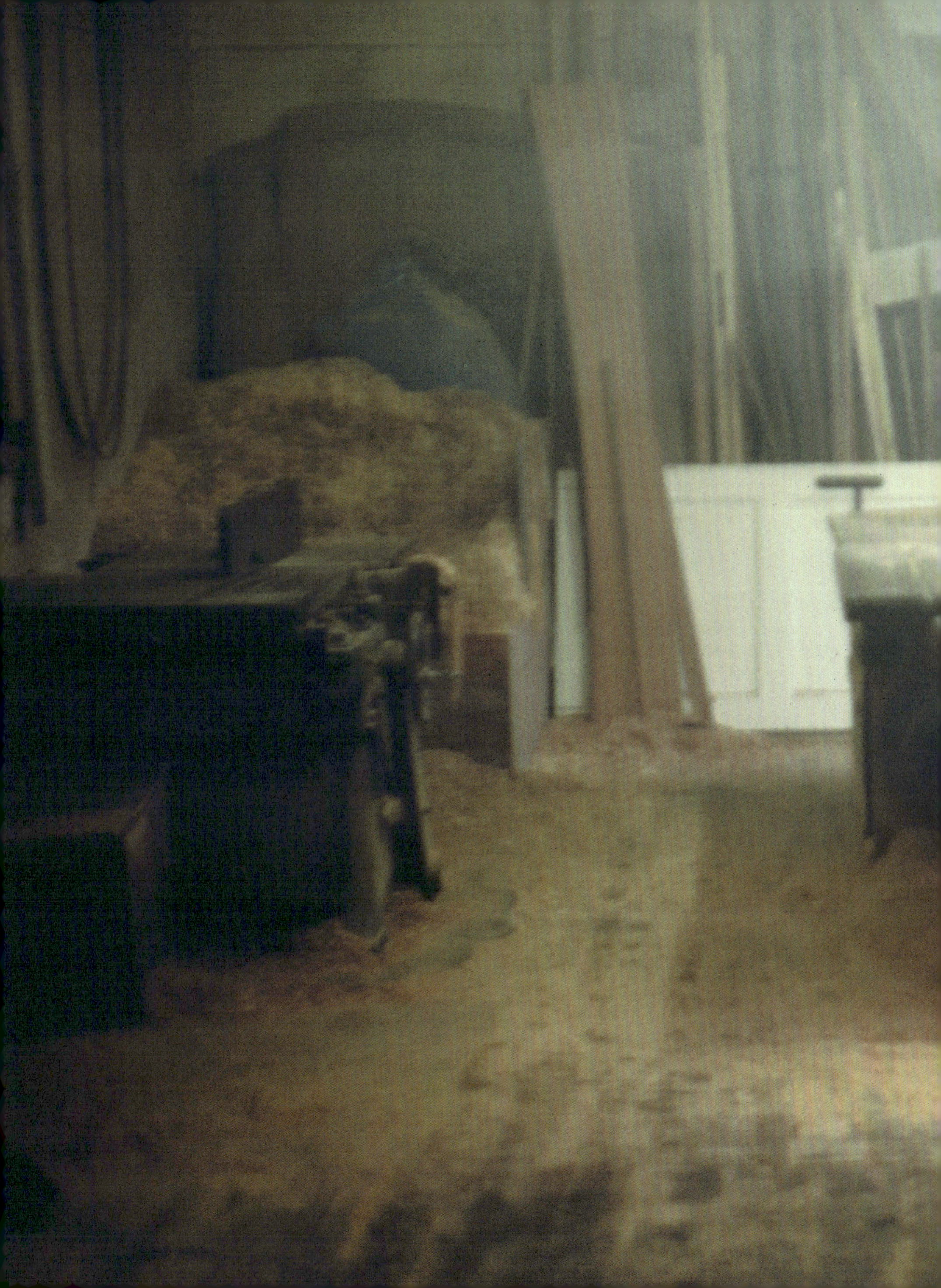

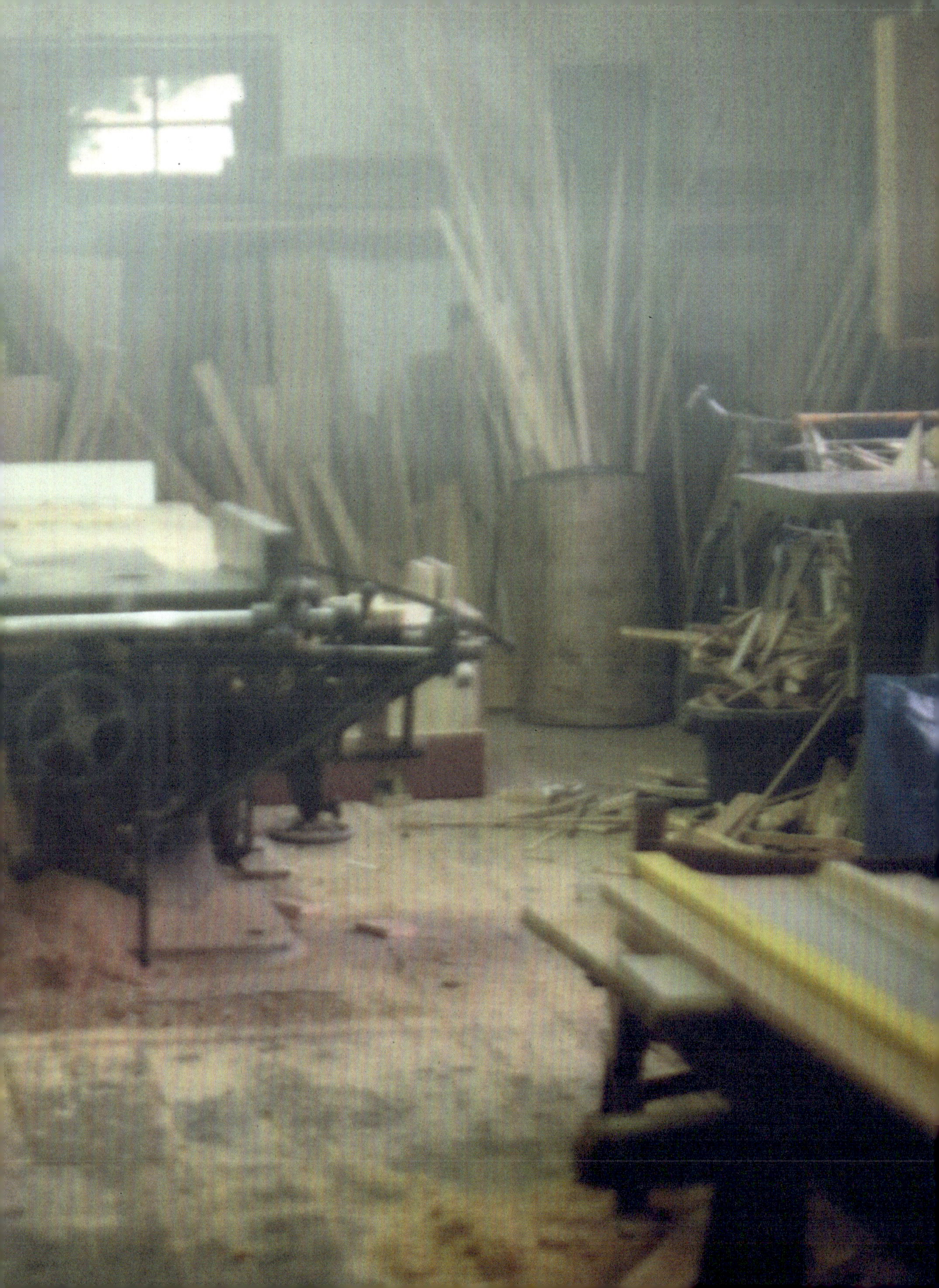

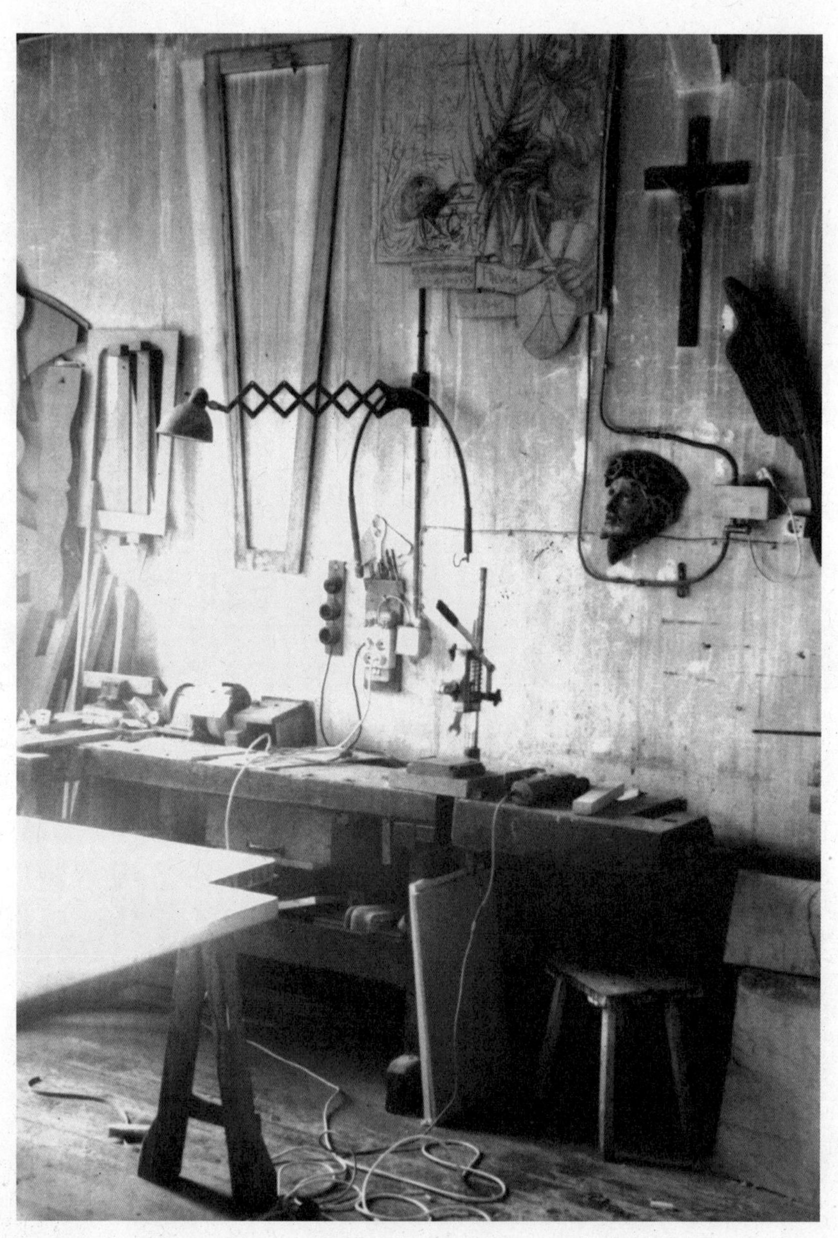

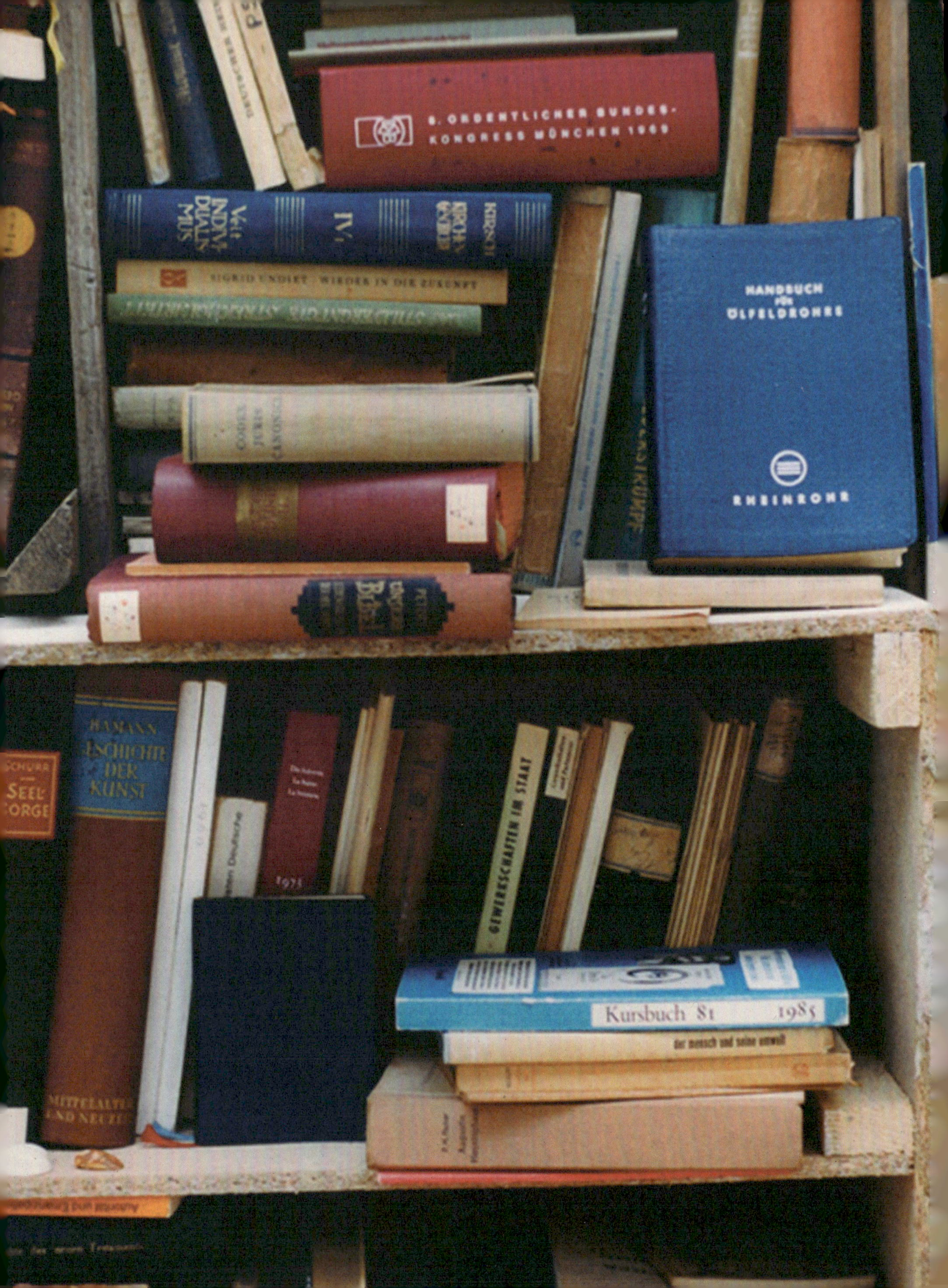

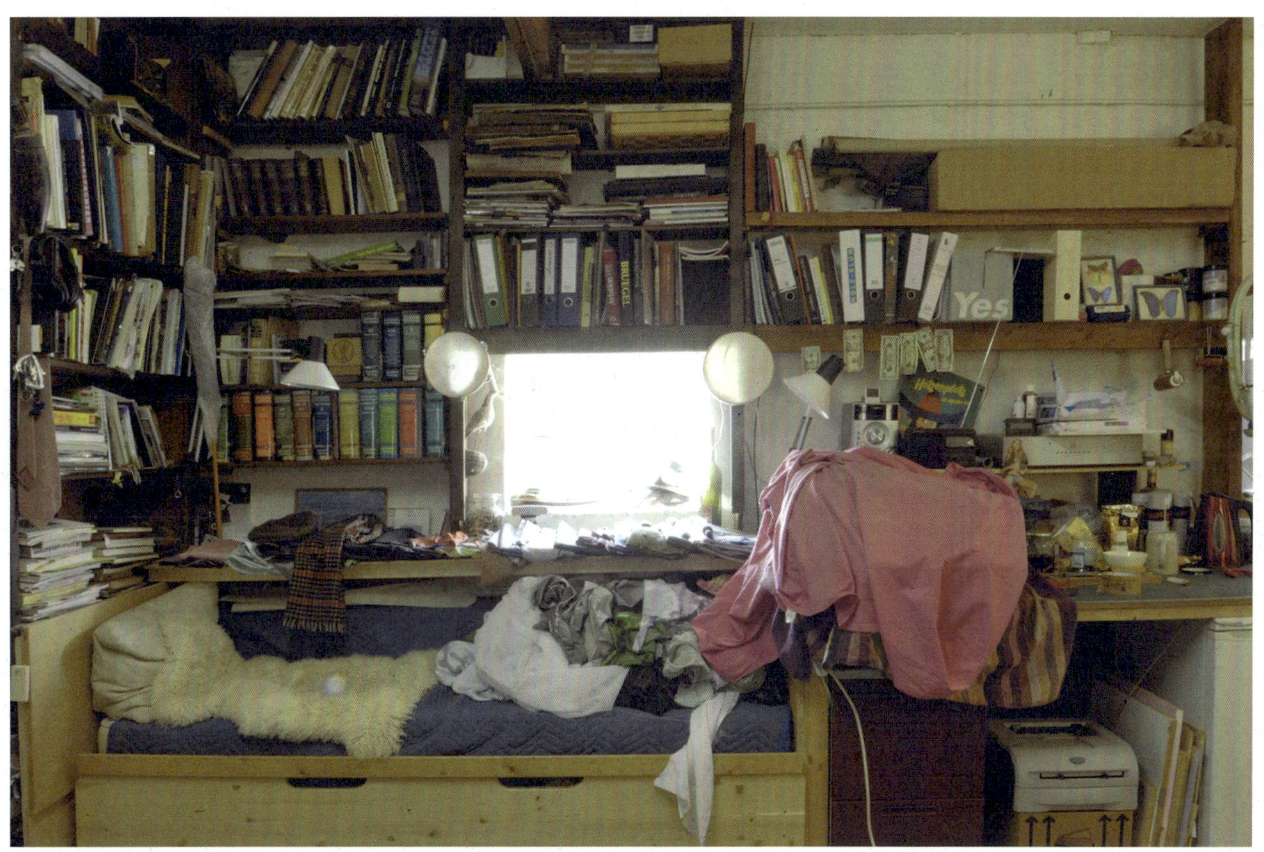

© Mareike Tocha

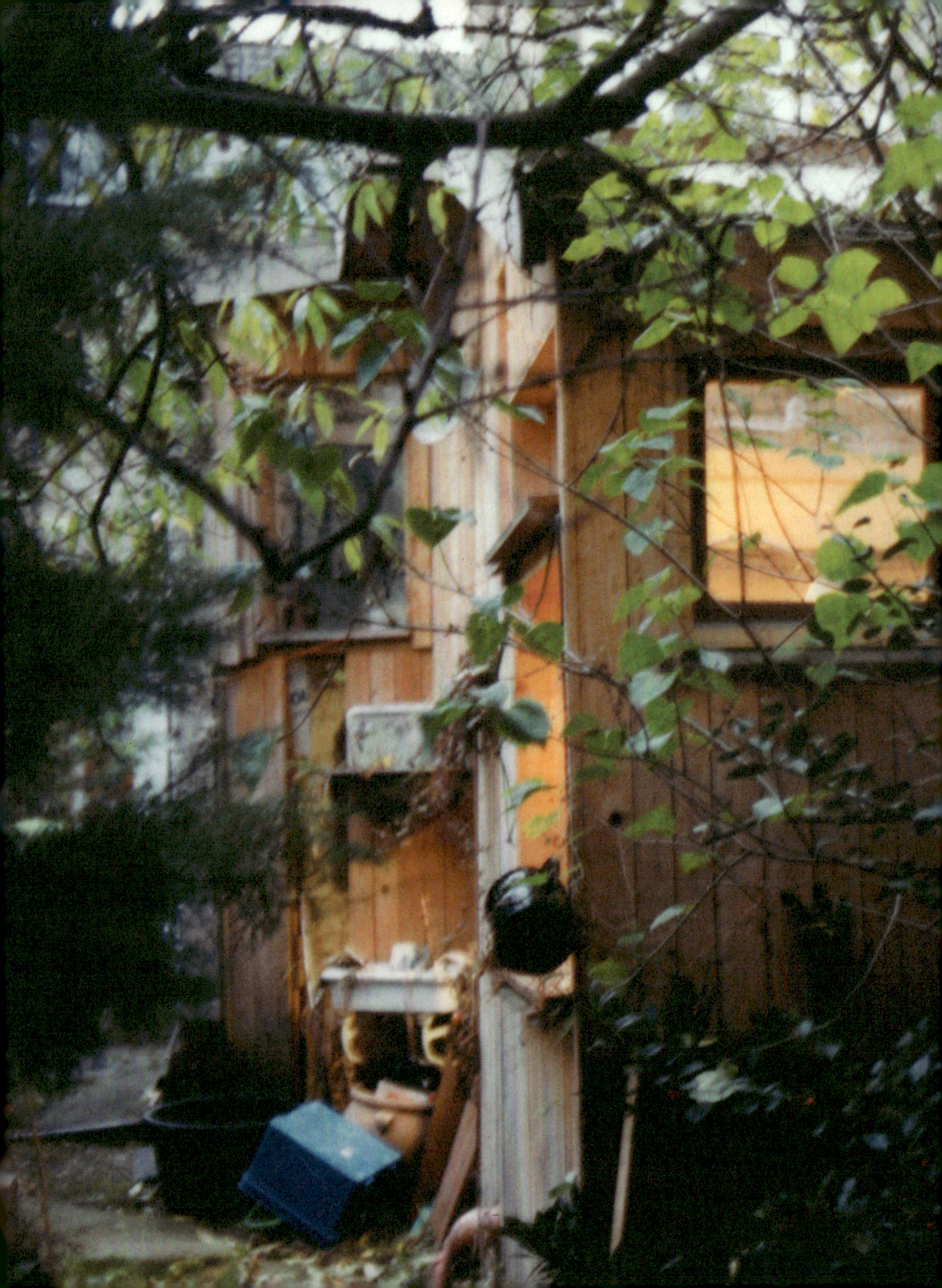

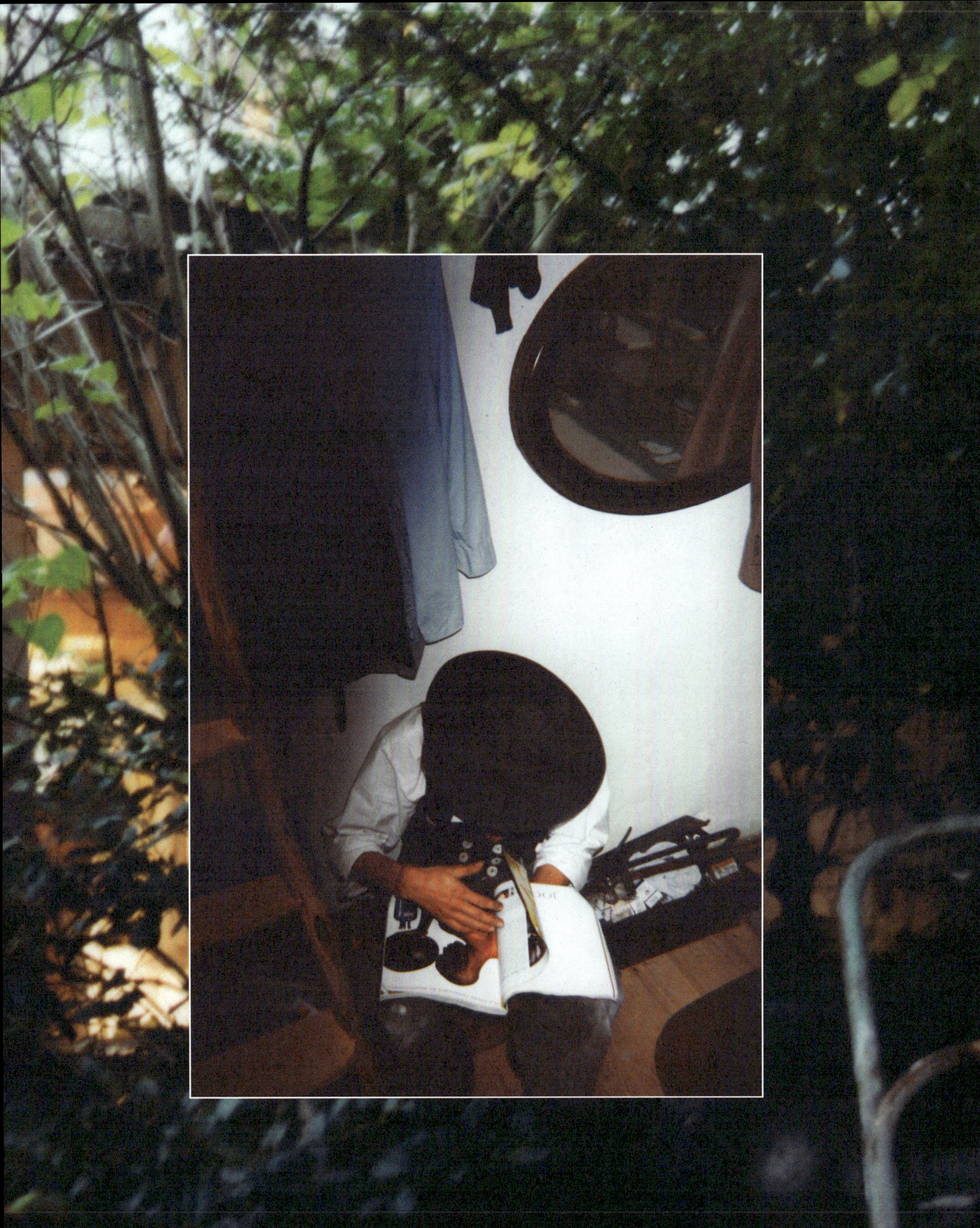

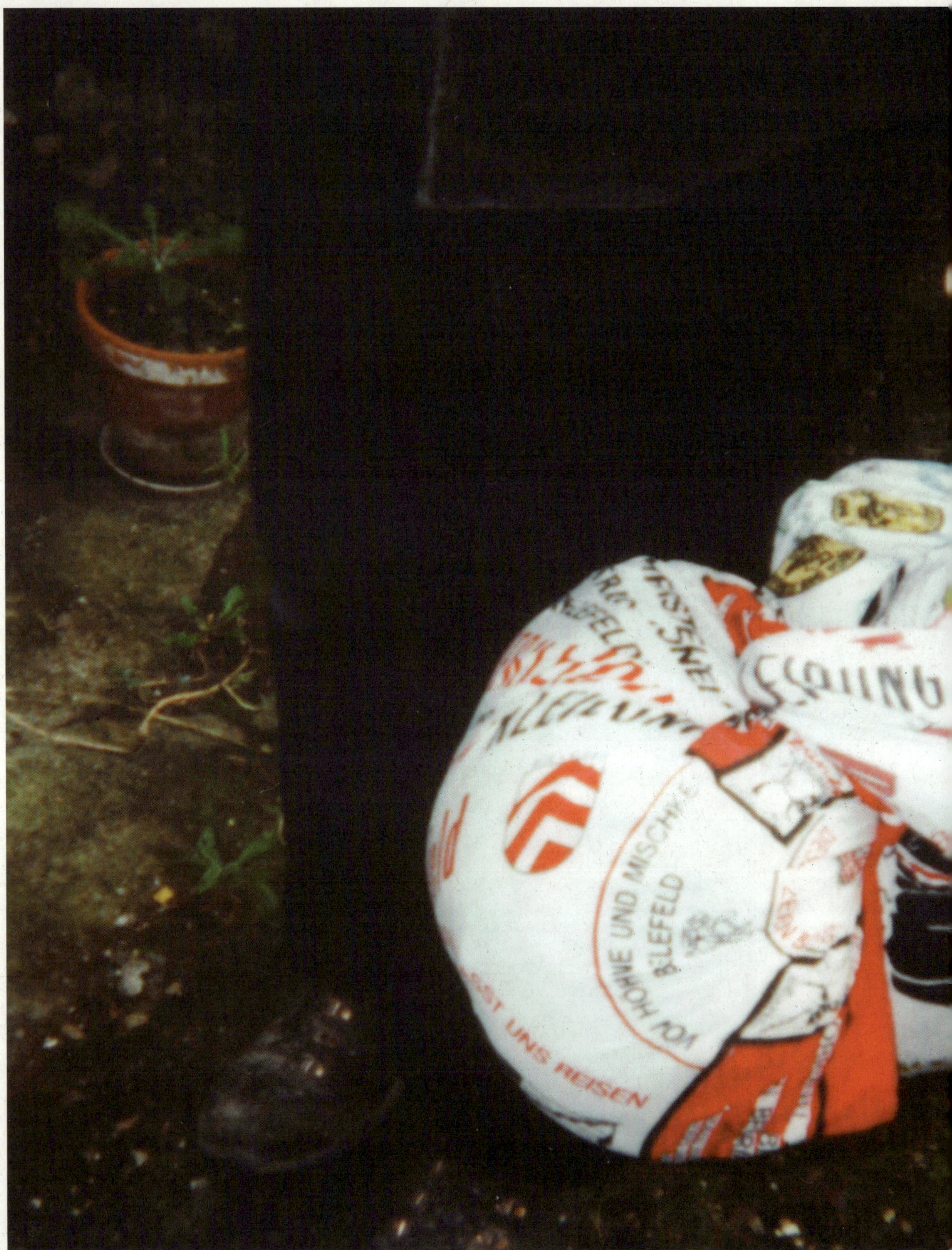
VON HOHNE UND MISCHKE
BIELEFELD
LÄSST UNS REISEN

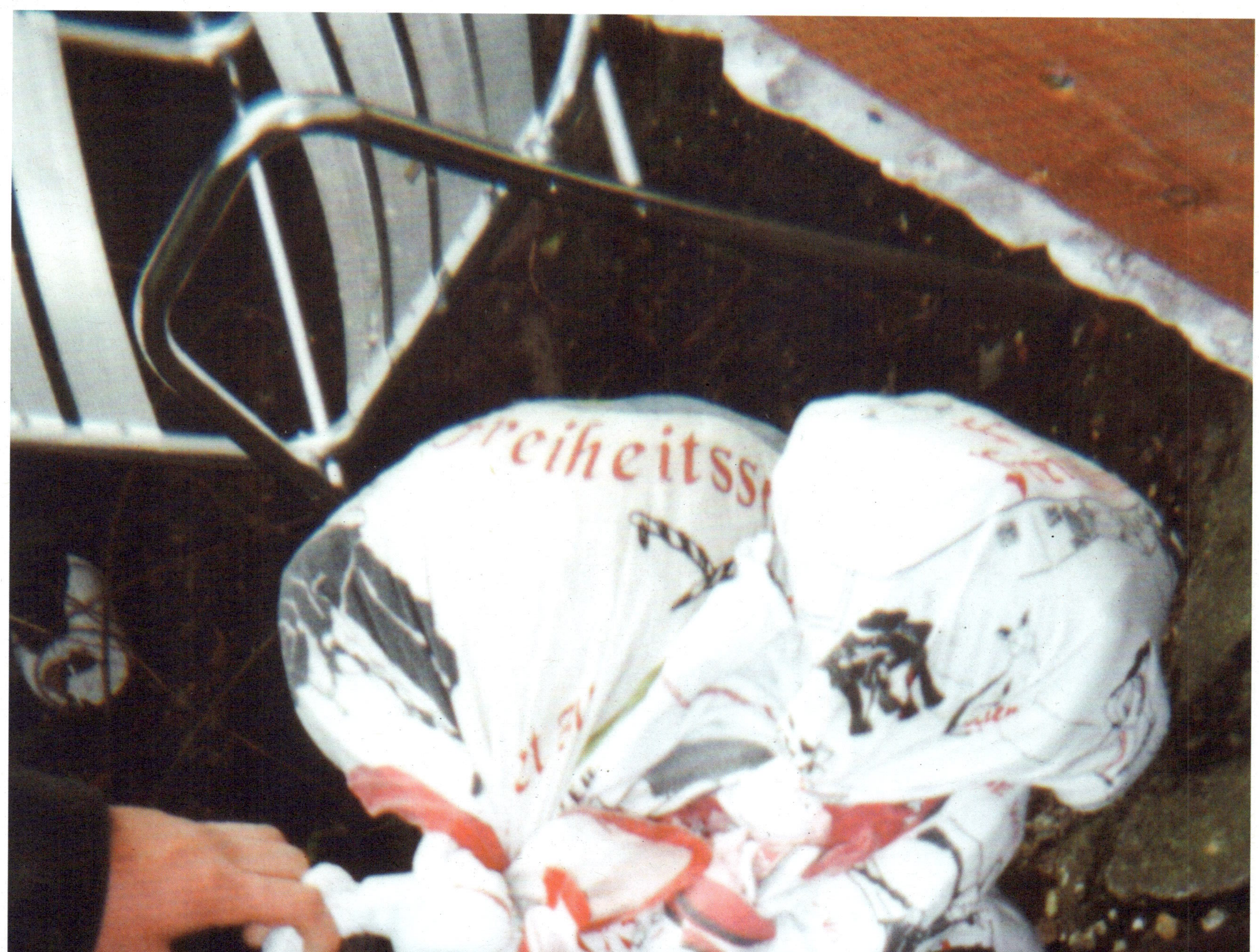
reiheitss

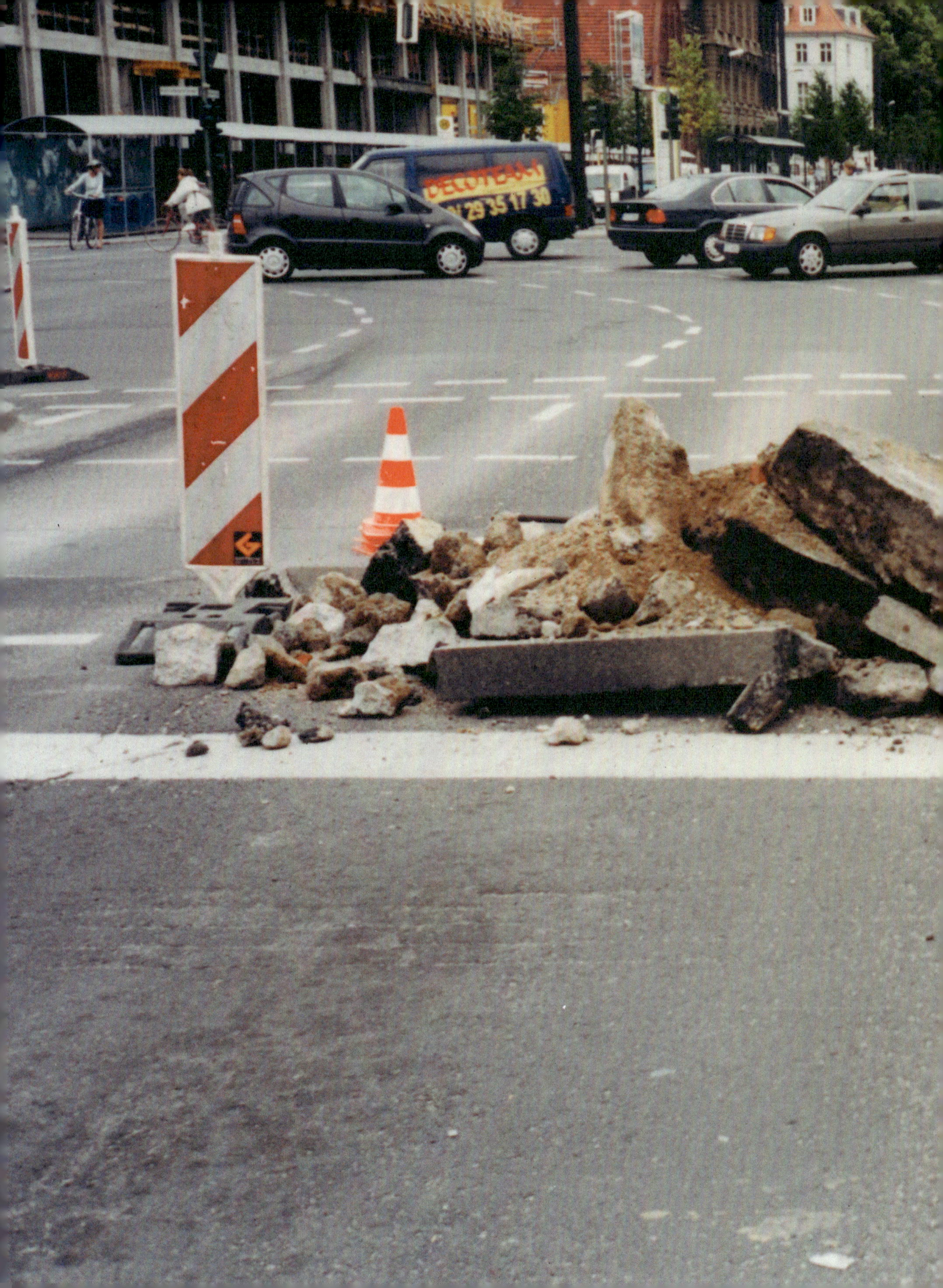

DECOTEAM
29 35 17 30

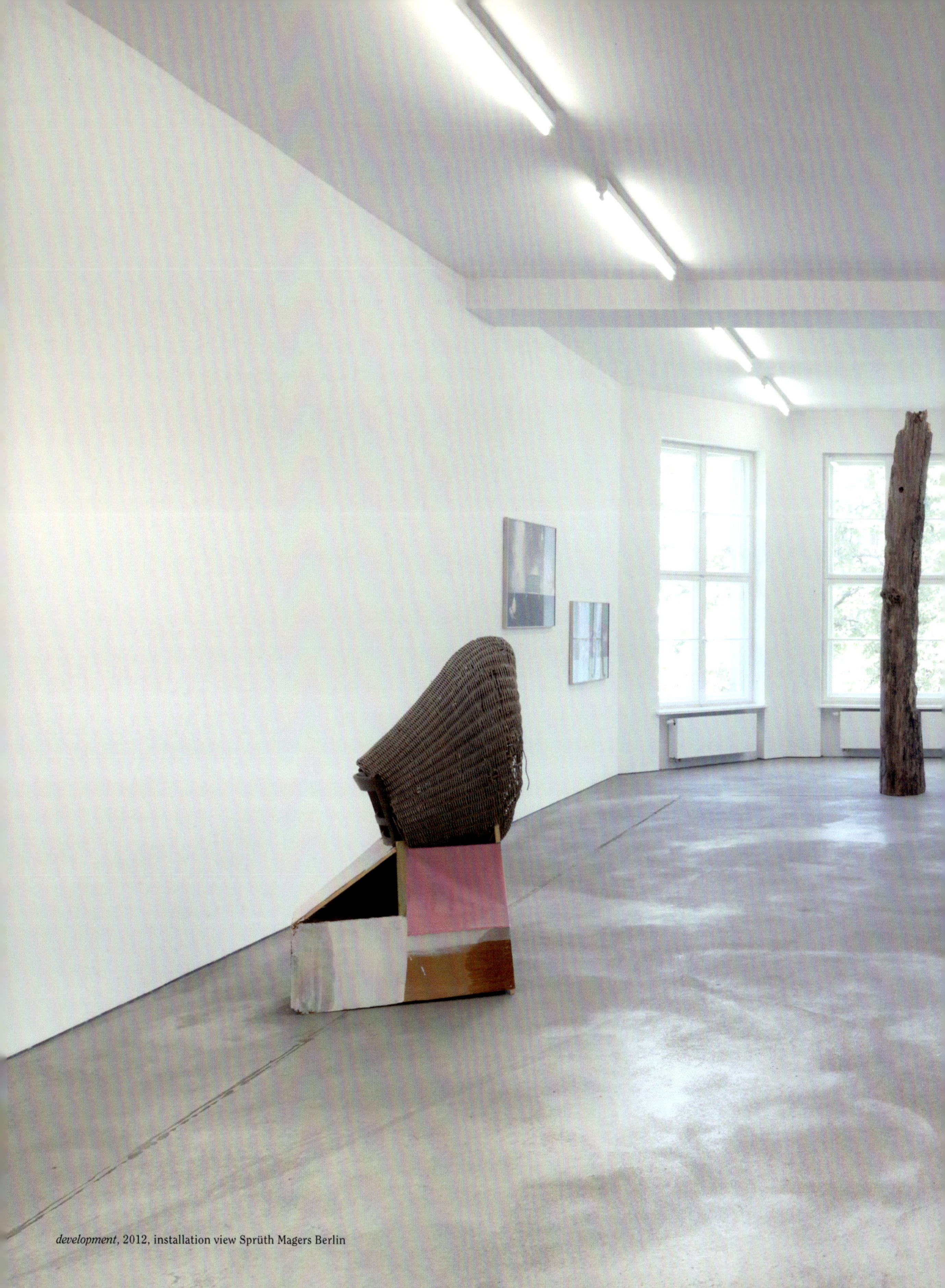

development, 2012, installation view Sprüth Magers Berlin

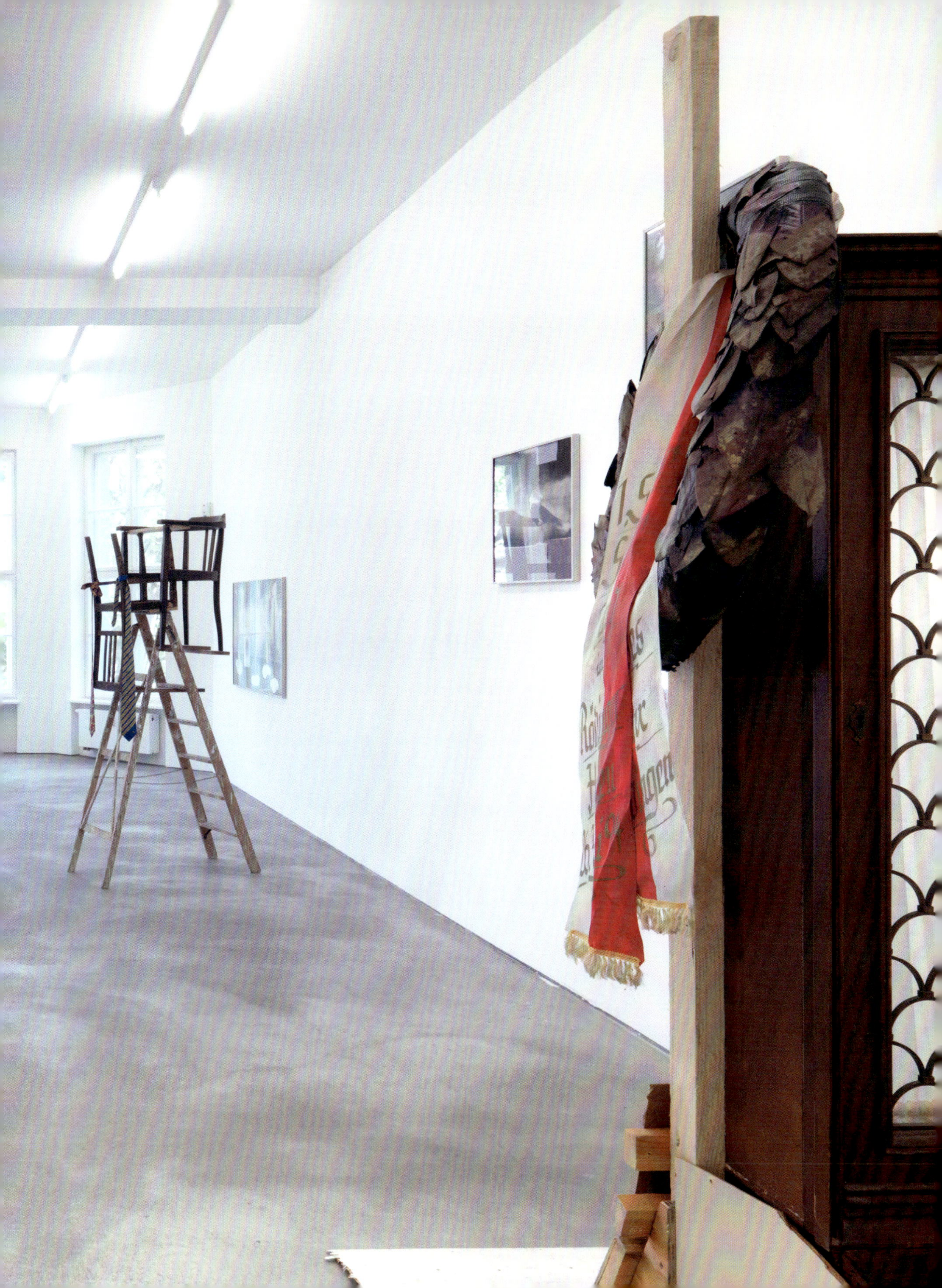

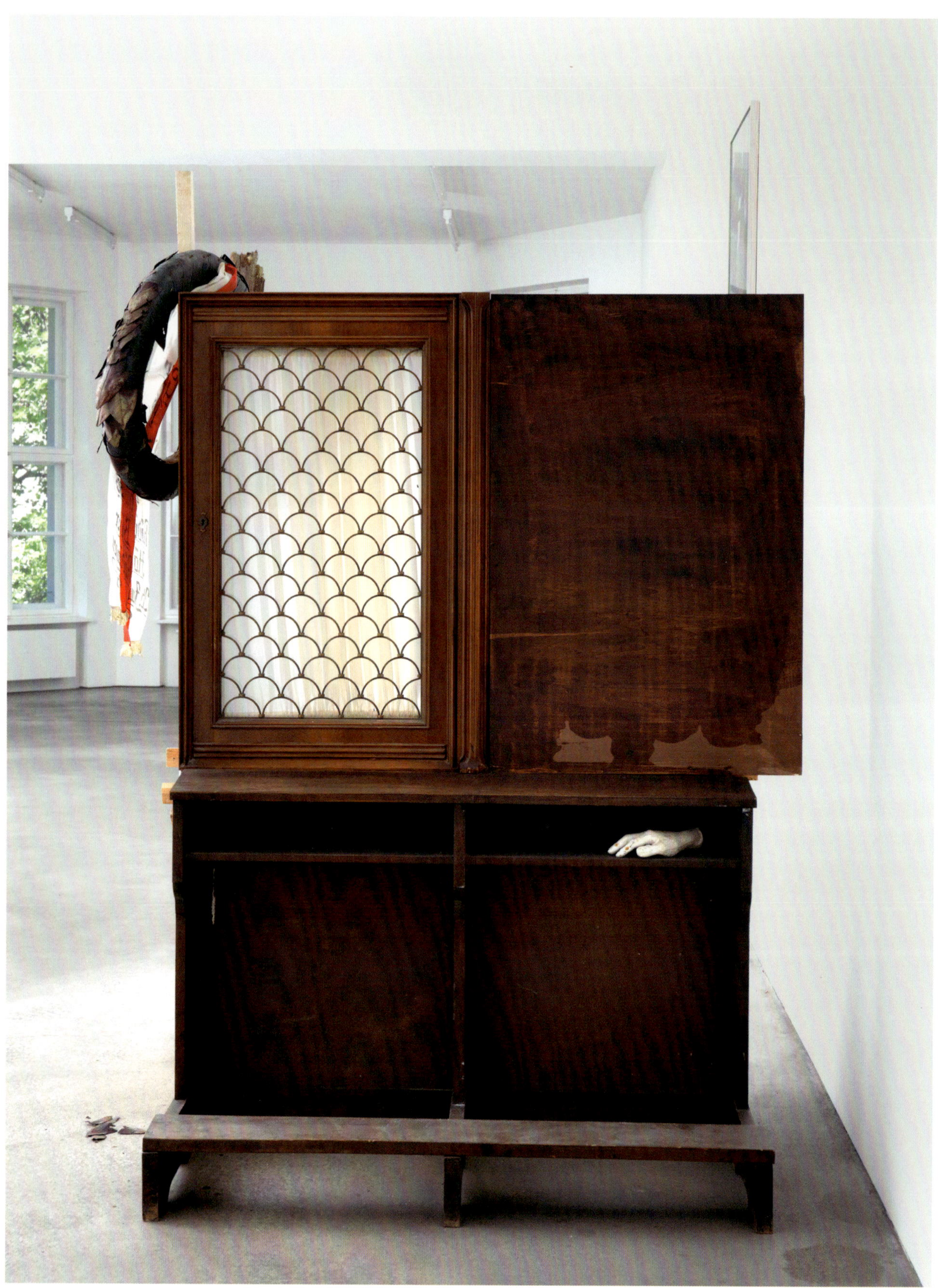

1 *seeblick*, 2012, confessional booth, ramp, victory wreath, 228 × 147 × 212 cm

DEVELOPMENT

Robert Elfgen bei Sprüth Magers Berlin, 2012

Text von Ruth Kißling

Die erste Arbeit, auf die der Betrachter in Robert Elfgens Ausstellung *development* direkt am Eingang des Ausstellungsraumes trifft, ist ein Beichtstuhl. Oder vielmehr nur eine Seite davon: diejenige, die mit Kniebank und vergittertem Fenster dem Gläubigen zugewiesen ist. Eine weiße Hand aus Gips liegt isoliert, beinahe drohend dort, wo sich sonst die Hände zum Gebet falten (Abb. 1).

Der Beichtstuhl verwehrt uns den Blick in den Raum und zwingt uns zum Innehalten. Fordert uns der Künstler auf, hier niederzuknien und unsere Sünden zu beichten? Müssen wir erst unser Gewissen erforschen, bevor wir uns der Kunst zuwenden dürfen? An wen soll sich unser Bekenntnis richten?

Auch der nächste Schritt bringt noch wenig Klarheit. Ein schon leicht ramponierter Siegerkranz krönt die Rudimente des Beichtstuhls, ein Spruchband kürt den Gewinner des „1. Sieger Schüler Rund in Rödingen Höllen 26. Juni 94" – aber wir erfahren nicht, um welche Art von Wettbewerb es sich hier handelt (Abb. 2).

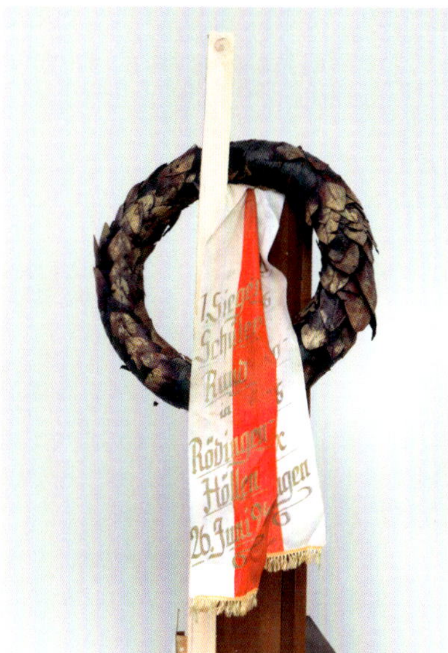

2 *seeblick* (Detail), 2012, confessional booth, ramp, victory wreath, 228 × 147 × 212 cm

DEVELOPMENT

Robert Elfgen at Sprüth Magers Berlin, 2012

Text by Ruth Kißling

The first work which the viewer encounters in Robert Elfgen's exhibition *development*, right at the entrance to the exhibition space, is a confessional box. Or rather, only side of it — the part with kneeler and grilled window which is assigned to the faithful. A white hand made of plaster lies in an almost menacing manner there where otherwise hands are folded in prayer (illus. 1).

The confessional box blocks our view of the exhibition space and compels us to pause and reflect. Is the artist issuing a summons for us to sink to our knees and confess our sins? Must we first examine our conscience before being allowed to turn our attention to art? To whom is our confession to be addressed?

The following step also brings little clarity. An already slightly displaced victory wreath crowns the remainders of the confessional box, and a banner designates the winner of the 'First Place, Pupils' Round in Rödingen Höllen, 26 June 94' –but we do not learn what type of competition is being referred to (illus. 2).

Die Rückseite des Beichtstuhls wartet jedoch mit einer Überraschung auf, die den Ernst des ersten Augenblicks vergessen macht: Statt dem Kabäuschen des Priesters besteht sie aus einer oft befahrenen Skateboardrampe. Diese lenkt endlich den Blick in den Raum, wo er frei zwischen den anderen Exponaten der Ausstellung hin und her wandern kann.

seeblick (2012), so der Titel der ersten Arbeit in *development*, ist eine Assemblage aus gebrauchten Fundstücken unterschiedlicher Herkunft und Funktion, die provisorisch mit MDF-Bruchstücken verbunden sind. Sie baut einen Kontrast auf zwischen dem Beichtstuhl als Ort der Selbstreflexion – als ein „Sich ins Verhältnis setzen" mit einem Glaubenssystem durch ein Ritual der religiös verinnerlichten Kommunikation – und der Skateboardrampe, die Vorstellungen der Jugendkultur von individualisiertem Lebensausdruck und Freiheit mit empathischem Bezug zur Umwelt einführt. Der Titel fügt dieser Zusammenstellung ein sprachliches Bild hinzu, das Naturbetrachtung und Landschaftsdarstellung aufruft, während die Worte des Kranzbandes eine absurde lautmalerische Verzierung des Ganzen bilden.

Unterschiedlichste Elemente treffen in *seeblick* aufeinander und machen die Arbeit zu einer Art „stabilem Ungleichgewicht"[1], aus dem eine innere

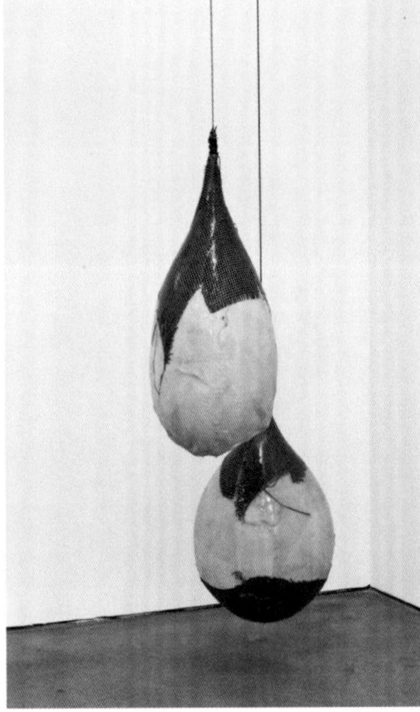
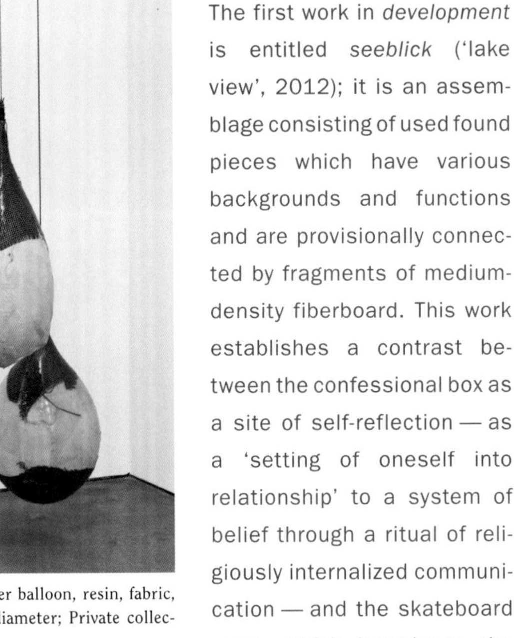

3 *Tropfen*, 2012, rubber balloon, resin, fabric, 160 cm high, 72 cm diameter; Private collection, Cologne

The back side of the confessional box, however, offers a surprise which causes the seriousness of the first moment to be forgotten: Instead of the cubicle of the priest, it consists of an evidently much–used skateboard ramp. This finally ushers the gaze into the space, where it can wander freely among the other objects on display in the exhibition.

The first work in *development* is entitled *seeblick* ('lake view', 2012); it is an assemblage consisting of used found pieces which have various backgrounds and functions and are provisionally connected by fragments of medium-density fiberboard. This work establishes a contrast between the confessional box as a site of self-reflection — as a 'setting of oneself into relationship' to a system of belief through a ritual of religiously internalized communication — and the skateboard ramp, which introduces the youth culture's ideas about individualized self-expression and freedom through an emphatic reference to the outer environment. The title adds to this combination a linguistic image which evokes the contemplation of nature and representation of landscape, while the words on the wreath's banner constitute an absurd, onomatopoeic embellishment of the whole.

Highly diverse elements come together in *seeblick* and transform the work into a sort of 'stable

Dynamik entsteht. Siegerkranz und Skateboardrampe illustrieren diese Dynamik mit dem Motiv des Wettbewerbs, der eine Entwicklung – development – initiiert und vorantreibt. Gleich zu Beginn der Ausstellung führt *seeblick* damit die inhaltlichen und formalen Leitmotive von Robert Elfgens Arbeiten ein. Sie kreisen um das dynamische und wechselhafte Verhältnis von Natur, Mensch und Gesellschaft. Dabei greift Elfgen immer wieder auf Vorhandenes zurück und kombiniert Gefundenes, Gebrauchtes und selbst Gebautes zu neuen Formfindungen. So bilden Assemblagen und Collagen – die Hybride der klassischen Kunstgattungen – das Inventar von *development*.

Elfgens Assemblagen bestehen aus Fundstücken aus dem alltäglichen Umfeld des Künstlers, die er zunächst absichtslos sammelt: Gegenstände des häuslichen Gebrauchs – Stühle, Trittleiter und Korbsessel, Objekte aus dem technisch-wissenschaftlichen Bereich wie Messballons (Abb. 3), oder die Skateboardrampe, ein aus Leidenschaft und zum Eigengebrauch gefertigtes Objekt. Der Beichtstuhl stammt aus der Auflösung eines katholischen Klosters, in dem Elfgen lange Zeit als Schreiner gearbeitet hat.
Diese Objets trouvés verbindet er mit billigen, leicht verfügbaren Materialien wie rohen Brettern, Pressspanplatten oder Stoffstücken und arbeitet sie mit organischen Materialien, Harz und Lehm, oder dickflüssigen Farben nach (Abb. 4).
Der Zusammenhalt der Objekte wirkt fragil, improvisiert und vor allem temporär. So, als könnten sie jederzeit in ihre ursprüngliche Funktion zurückkehren. Statt dauerhaft miteinander

disequilibrium'[1], which gives rise to an inner dynamism. The victory wreath and skateboard ramp illustrate this dynamism through the motif of competition, which initiates a 'development' and impels it onward. Thus right at the beginning of the exhibition, *seeblick* introduces the contentual and formal leitmotifs of Robert Elfgen's oeuvre. His works revolve around the dynamic and mutable relationship between nature, humankind, and society. He repeatedly takes up what is already present and combines found, used, and self-built objects into new formal inventions. Assemblages and collages — the hybrids of the classical artistic genres — accordingly constitute the inventory of *development*.

The assemblages consist of found objects from the everyday surroundings of the artist. He first collects them with no fixed intention: objects for domestic use such as chairs, stepladders, and wicker chairs; objects from the technical and scientific domain such as balloons for measurement (illus. 3); or, as in the case of the skateboard, an object made with all-consuming passion and destined for personal use. The confessional box comes from the closure of a Catholic monastery where Elfgen worked for a long time as a carpenter.
He attaches these objets trouvés to inexpensive, easily available materials such as rough boards, pressboards, or pieces of fabric, and he reworks them with organic materials such as resin and clay, or viscous paint (illus. 4).
The cohesion of the objects appears fragile, improvised, and above all temporary. It seems as if the objects could return to their original

zu verschmelzen, bleiben die Stellen des Aufeinandertreffens als markante Risse bestehen (Abb. 5).

Und gerade in diesen Rissen entfaltet sich die multiple Identität der Skulpturen: Sie oszillieren zwischen Vergangenheit und Gegenwart, zwischen Kunstwerk und Funktionsgegenstand, zwischen Ganzem und Detail. Elfgens Assemblagen spielen mit der Biografie ihrer Fundobjekte und aktivieren, wie ethnologische Artefakte, komplexe Aspekte der Vergangenheit in der Gegenwart. Im selben Moment rufen die Spuren des Zusammenfügens den zeitlichen Aspekt dieses Schaffensprozesses auf und verweisen damit auf die aktuelle Präsenz der Objekte.

„Jedes Element stellt eine Gesamtheit von konkreten und zugleich möglichen Beziehungen dar (…)"[2], so beschreibt Claude Lévi-Strauss in „Das wilde Denken" die Objekte, die der „Bricoleur" mittels ungewöhnlicher, abweichender Methoden aus vorhandenen Elementen erzeugt. Robert Elfgens Objekte lassen sich in diesem Sinne als „Bricolagen"[3] bezeichnen, die eine Vielzahl von Lesarten ermöglichen und Spuren seines assoziativen Vorgehens vermitteln. Darin klingen Parallelen zu Duchamps scheinbar intentionslosem Akt des Auswählens an, der ein Fundstück als

4 *Schmiergelder gut anlegen* (Detail), 2012, basket, chair, porcelain, cardboard, fabric, mud, acrylic, 147 × 85 × 90 cm

function at any time. Instead of blending permanently, the points of contact remain as distinctive fissures (illus. 5).

And precisely here lies the development of the multiple identity of the sculptures: They oscillate between past and present, between work of art and functional object, between whole and detail. Elfgen's assemblages play with the biography of their found objects and, like ethnological artifacts, activate complex aspects of the past. At the same moment, the traces of the joining highlight the temporal aspect of this creative process and thereby point towards the actual presence of the objects.

'Every element represents a totality of concrete and simultaneously possible relationships [...]'[2] — this is how Claude Lévi-Strauss in The Savage Mind describes the objects which the 'bricoleur' creates out of already-present elements through unusual, divergent methods. In this sense, Robert Elfgen's objects may be designated as 'bricolages'[3] which evoke a range of possible interpretations and convey the traces of his associative procedure. Parallels resonate here with Duchamp's seemingly intentionless act of selection, which defines a found object as a work of art,[4] but also with the systematic-experimental processes of Surrealism, such as

Kunstwerk definiert[4], aber auch die systematisch-experimentellen Verfahren des Surrealismus wie die Écriture automatique, die auf eine Annäherung an das Unbewusste abzielen.[5] Elfgens Vorgehen, zusammen mit der Umwertung des scheinbar Nutzlosen und der Verwendung natürlicher Materialien, hat eine lange Vorgeschichte.

Immer wieder wird im 20. Jahrhundert die Frage nach dem Verhältnis von Kunst und Realität durch Einfügen realer Gegenstände thematisiert: in den Gemälden von Picasso und Braque, in den Materialcollagen des Dadaismus und Surrealismus, in Robert Rauschenbergs Combines oder Werken der Pop Art und Arte Povera. Fundstücke, Objets trouvés, werden integrale Bestandteile und thematisieren die Möglichkeiten der Repräsentation von Realität wie auch das Verhältnis zum Betrachter.

Die Frage nach der Darstellbarkeit von Realität tritt bei Robert Elfgen in den Hintergrund. Er zählt vielmehr auf den Verweischarakter der Objets trouvés im Verhältnis zum Betrachter und spielt mit der assoziativen Aufladung der Dinge, die seine Assemblagen „verlebendigt" und in unsere Realität einbettet. Mittels der Versatzstücke weist er auf Erzählungen unserer Gegenwart hin.

5 *seeblick* (Detail), 2012, confessional booth, ramp, victory wreath, 228 × 147 × 212 cm

automatic writing, which aim at an approach to the unconscious.[5] Elfgen's procedure, especially together with the reevaluation of seemingly useless items and the utilization of natural materials, establishes further links to the traditions of art in the twentieth century.

Again and again, the issue of the relationship between art and reality is thematized by the introduction of real objects — in the paintings of Picasso and Braque, in the material collages of Dadaism and Surrealism, in Robert Rauschenberg's combines, or in the works of Pop Art and Arte Povera. Found objects, objets trouvés, become integral components and inquire into both the possibilities of representing reality and the relationship to the viewer.

In the case of Robert Elfgen's use of found objects, the question as to the representability of reality plays less of a role. Instead he counts on the referential character of the objets trouvés in relationship to the viewer and plays with that associative energy of things which 'animates' his assemblages and embeds them within our reality. By means of these set-pieces, he refers to narratives of our present era.

anzüglichkeit ('innuendo', 2012) (illus. 6) consists of an evidently used ladder on which two chairs

anzüglichkeit (2012) (Abb. 6) besteht aus einer gebrauchten Leiter, auf der zwei aufeinander gestapelte Stühle montiert sind. Zwei Krawatten sind beiläufig an zwei der vorderen Stuhlbeine geknotet. Es entsteht ein thronartiges Objekt, dessen Durchlässigkeit und Abnutzung seine Monumentalität gleichzeitig konterkarieren. Die Krawatten „animieren" das Objekt und verweisen auf den Menschen im sozialen Gefüge: Man denkt are stacked one upon the other. Two neckties are casually knotted on two of the front chair legs. There arises a throne-like object whose permeability and wear undermine its monumentality. The neckties 'animate' the object and refer to people in a social framework: One thinks of advancement and success, of power and its insignia, of the saying 'clothes make people', and has the impression of hearing a quiet criticism

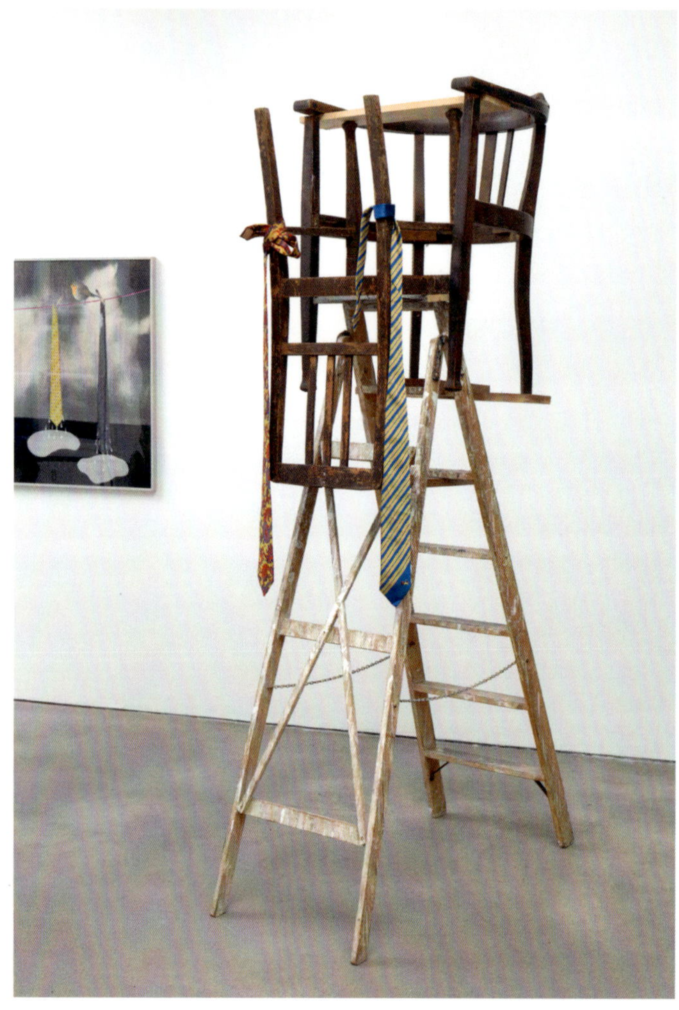

6 *anzüglichkeit*, 2012, ladder, chairs, ties, 210 × 53 × 110 cm

an Aufstieg und Erfolg, an Macht und ihre Insig-
nien, an „Kleider machen Leute" und meint eine
leise Kritik an der Scheinhaftigkeit und Erfolgs-
orientiertheit unserer Gesellschaft zu hören.

Auch im Ausstellungsraum entwickeln die Assemblagen einen sozialen Bezugsrahmen: Sie stehen
ohne Sockel direkt auf dem Boden und erschließen
sich als Ganzes erst durch die physische Bewegung des Betrachters im Raum. Die Fundstücke wie
Leiter und Stühle behalten auch in der Neukombi-
nation ihre am Menschen orientierten Maßstäbe
bei. Elfgens Objekte treten in eine direkte Kommunikation mit dem Betrachter und verwischen die
Grenze zwischen Lebens- und Kunstwirklichkeit.
Darum vollzieht sich ihre Wahrnehmung in einem
zirkulären Prozess von Sehen und Verstehen.[6]
development schließt den Betrachter auf unter-
schiedlichen Ebenen mit ein, obwohl die Geschlossenheit früherer situativer Installationen, die
sich auf spezifische Themen fokussierten und
damit räumlichen Allegorien, begehbaren Bildern, glichen, hier aufgegeben wurde.

Der visuelle Fixpunkt der Ausstellung ist die Arbeit
Brandenburg (2012) (Abb. 7), ein nackter, von
Insektenbefall und Blitzeinschlag gezeichneter
Baumstamm, den Elfgen im Wald gefunden hat.
Tote Insektenlarven und ein Spechtloch am obe-
ren Ende erinnern an seine vorigen Bewohner. Der
Stamm ist im Erker des Raumes aufgestellt und
stellt so eine Verbindung zur Natur vor dem Fens-
ter her. Als Naturrelikt, beinahe wie ein Mahnmal,
positioniert er die Artefakte der Ausstellung vor
der Folie natürlicher Schaffensprozesse. Von
Menschenhand unbearbeitet, steht dieses Objet

of the illusoriousness and success-orientation of
our society.

The assemblages establish a framework of
social reference in the exhibition space as well:
They stand without pedestals directly on the
floor and reveal themselves in their totality only
through the physical movement of the viewer
through the space. Found objects such as ladder
and chairs retain, also in the new combination,
their functionality and orientation to human
dimensions. Elfgen's objects enter into a direct
communication with the viewer and blur the
border between the realities of life and of art.
Their perception is accordingly accomplished in
a circular process of vision and comprehension.[6]
development includes the viewer on various
levels, although there is a renunciation of the
closed nature of earlier situational installations
which focused on specific themes and thereby
resembled spatial allegories, walk-in images.

The central focus of the exhibition is the work
Brandenburg (2012) (illus. 7), a bare tree trunk,
marked by insect attack and lightning stroke,
which Elfgen found in a forest. Dead insect
larvae and a woodpecker hole at the upper end
recall its previous inhabitants. The trunk is set
up at the bay window of the room and thereby
establishes a connection to nature. As a natural
object, it serves as a sort of memorial; it positions the artifacts of the exhibition against the
background of precesses of natural creation.
Untreated by human hands, this objet trouvé
stands for the transformational processes
and cycles of a nature which simultaneously

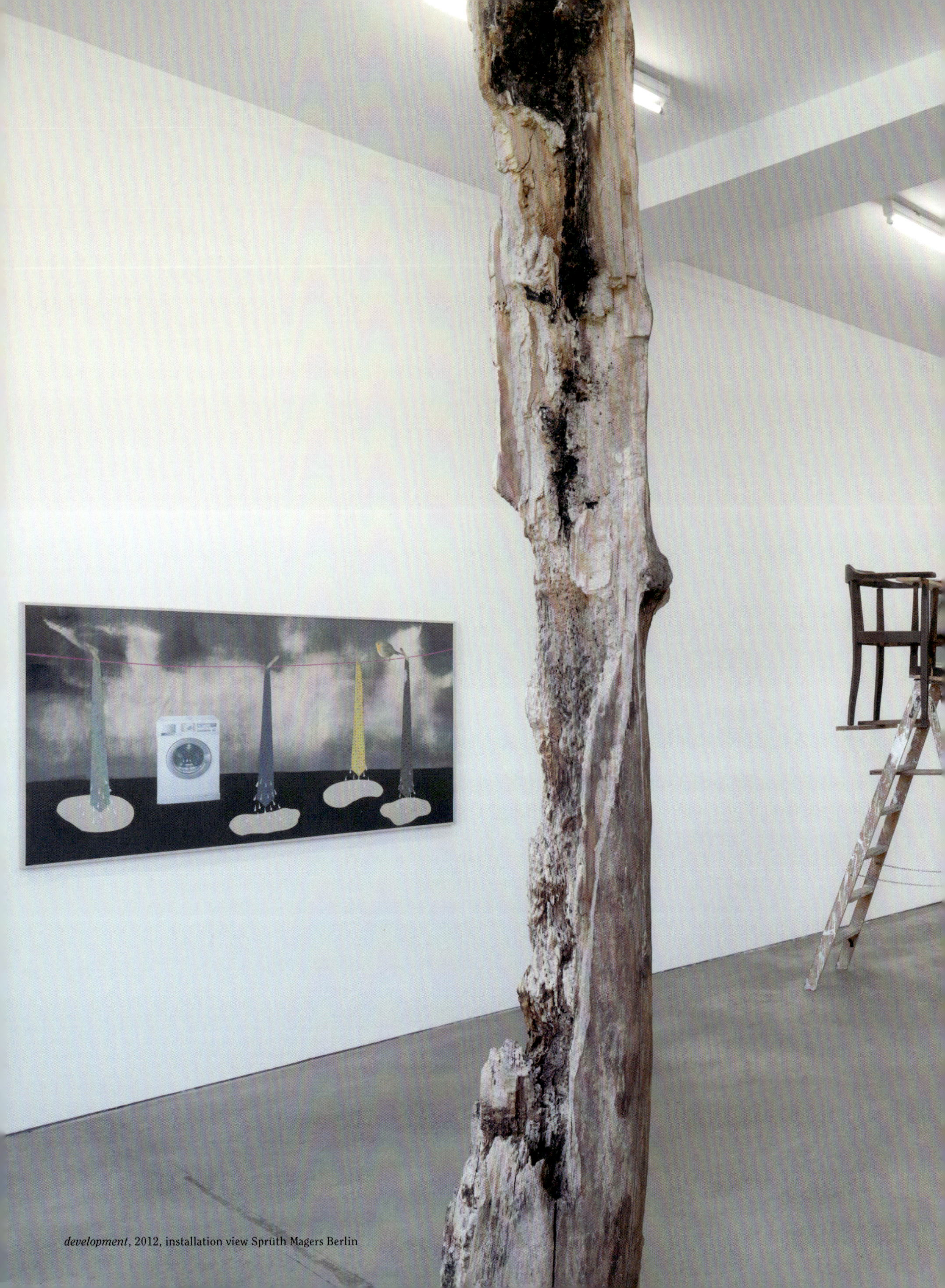

development, 2012, installation view Sprüth Magers Berlin

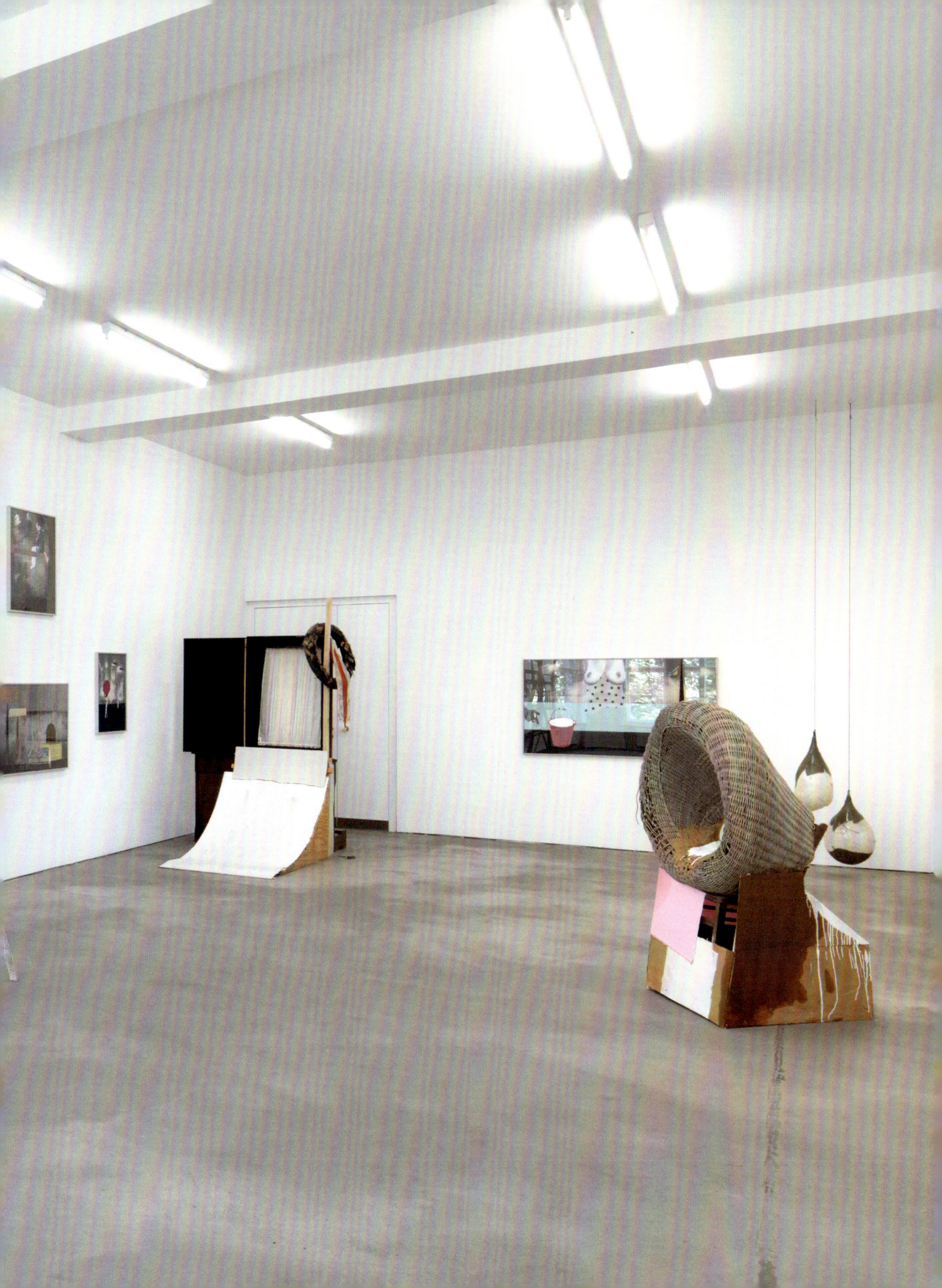

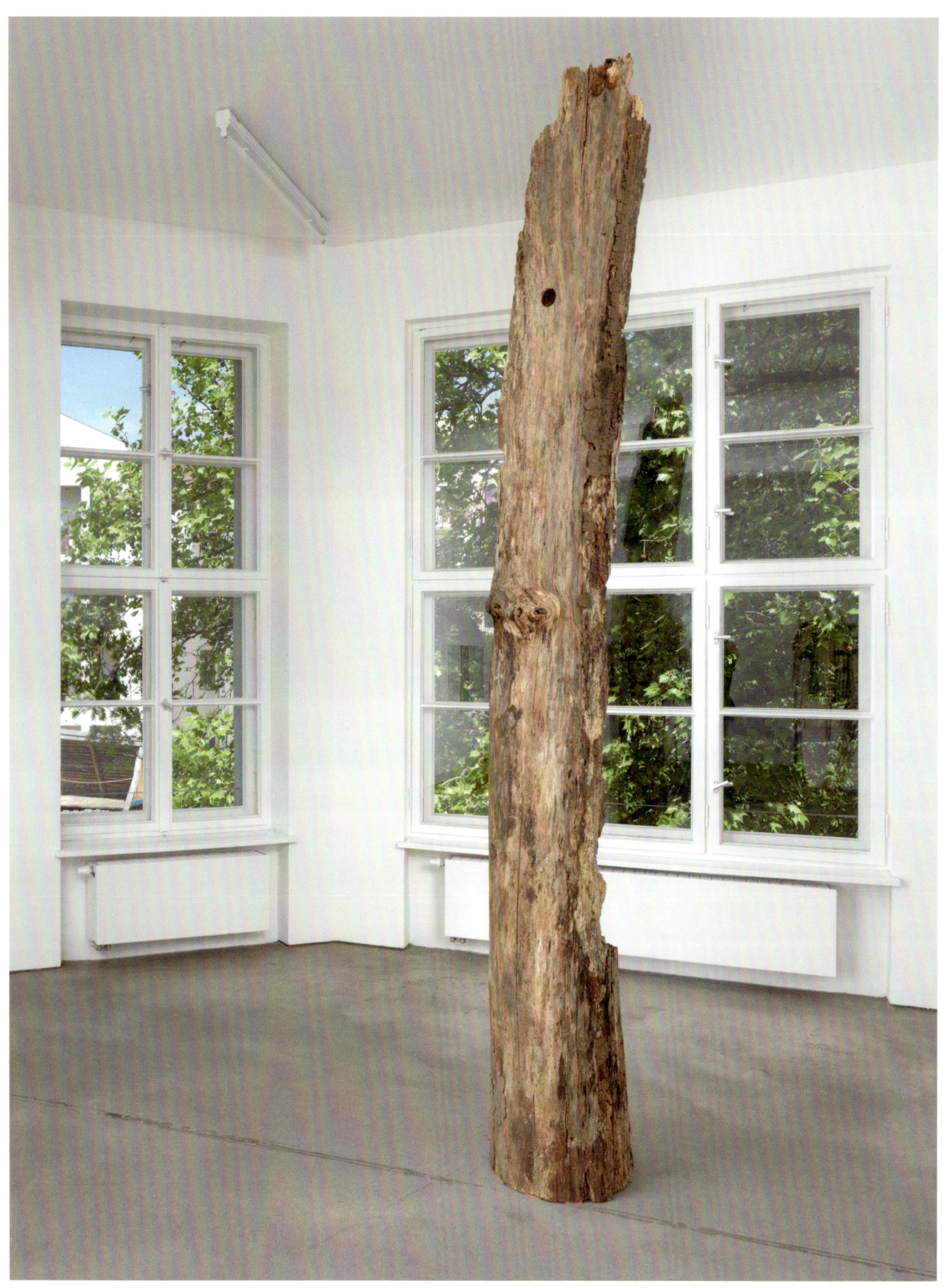

7 *Brandenburg*, 2012, tree trunk, 350 × 40 cm

trouvé für die Transformationsprozesse und Kreisläufe einer Natur, die nach ihren eigenen Gesetzmäßigkeiten in einem fort erzeugt und zerstört. Elfgens Arbeiten vermitteln ähnlich wie Caspar David Friedrichs *Der einsame Baum* (1822) (Abb. 8) die romantische Konfrontation des Menschen mit der Vergänglichkeit, die relativiert wird durch die Einbettung in einen in einen größeren, metaphysischen Raum.

Zirkuläre soziale Systeme und Transformationsprozesse hingegen klingen in einigen der neuen Collagen an. In *blaumeise* (2012) (Abb. 9) tropft Muttermilch aus dem Busen in einen Eimer und auf einen Teller, wo sie sich in eine silbern

creates and destroys in adherence to its own laws. Similarly to Caspar David Friedrich's *Der einsame Baum* ('The Solitary Tree') (1822) (illus. 8), Elfgen conveys the romantic confrontation of humankind with transience, which is relativized by being embedded within a vaster metaphysical context.

Circular social systems and transformational processes on the other hand are implicitly present in a few of the new collages. In *blaumeise* ('blue tit', 2012) (illus. 9), mother's milk drips in merry spurts from the breast into a bucket and onto a plate where it changes into a silvery, shimmering surface. A powerfulhand points

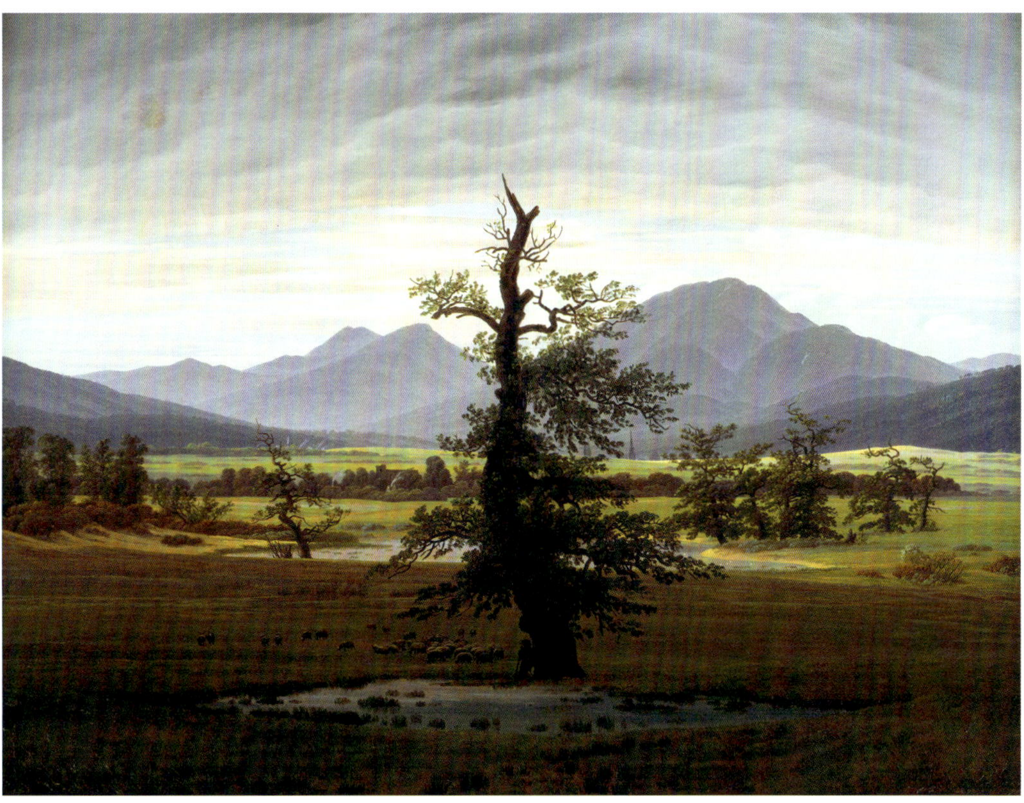

8 Caspar David Friedrich, *Der einsame Baum*, 1822, oil on canvas, 55 × 71 cm, Alte Nationalgalerie, Staatliche Museen zu Berlin

schimmernde Fläche verwandelt. Eine kräftige Hand weist auf den vollen Eimer, während über dem knapp gefüllten Teller nur eine schmale Krawatte schwebt, auf der ein Vogel sitzt. Die Tropfen scheinen energetische Qualität zu haben und eine Materialumwandlung vom Organischen, Nährenden zum Anorganischen, Bewert- und damit Veräußerbaren zu unterlaufen. Durch den Zeigegestus erhält die Komposition den Charakter einer allegorischen Handlungsanweisung.

Ähnlich führt die Collage *sträflicher leichtsinn* (2012) (Abb. 10) die fatalistische Haltung der heutigen Gesellschaft vor. Ein Mann sitzt auf einem hohen Ast mit dem Rücken zum Betrachter und beobachtet skeptisch die Tropfen, die aus einer vor ihm schwebenden Teekanne nach unten fallen. Eine Säge steckt hinter seinem Rücken tief in dem Ast, auf dem er sitzt. Bertolt Brechts Zeilen kommen in den Sinn:

to the full bucket, while above the scantily filled plate there hovers only a narrow necktie, upon which a bird is sitting. The drops seem to have an energetic quality and to undergo a material transformation from an organic and nourishing state into something anorganic which can be appraised and offered for sale. The pointing gesture imbues the composition with the character of an allegorical indication of action.

In a similar manner, the collage *sträflicher leichtsinn* ('culpable carelessness', 2012) (illus. 10) presents the fatalistic attitudes of contemporary society. A man is sitting on a high branch with his back to the viewer and skeptically observing the liquid leaking from a teapot hovering before him. Behind his back, a saw is stuck deep in the branch upon which he is sitting. Bertolt Brecht's lines come to mind:

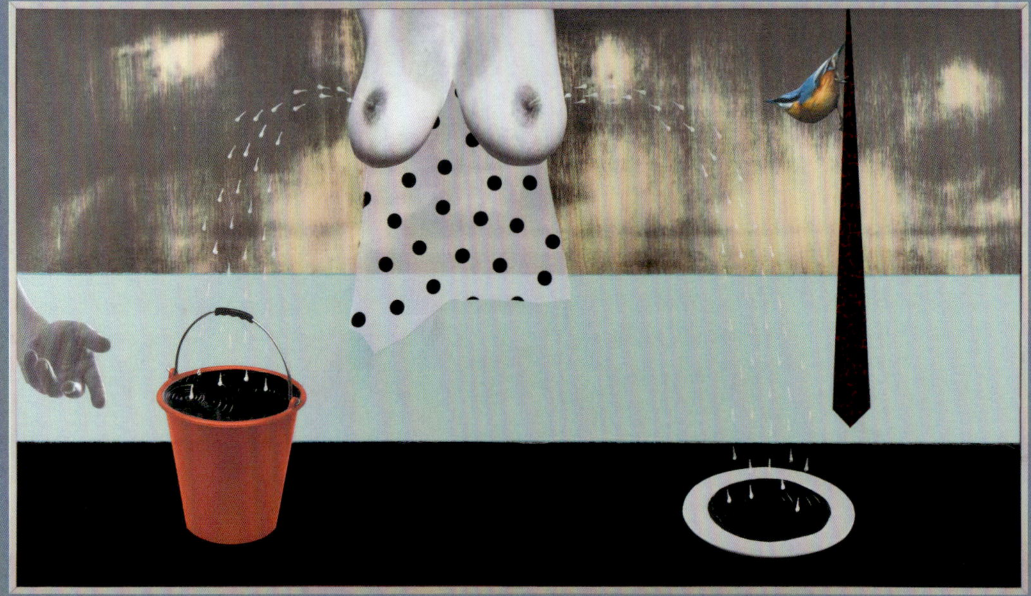

9 *blaumeise*, 2012, MDF, fabric, paper, stain, acrylic, wood, glass, 91 × 161.5 cm; Collection Reininghaus

„Sie sägten die Äste ab, auf denen sie saßen
Und schrieen sich zu ihre Erfahrungen,
Wie man schneller sägen könnte, und fuhren
Mit Krachen in die Tiefe, und die ihnen zusahen,
Schüttelten die Köpfe beim Sägen
Und sägten weiter."[7]

'They sawed away the branches on which they sat,
And cried out about their experiences
As to how to saw even faster, and dropped
Noisily into the depths, even as the onlookers
Shook their heads while sawing and
Continued to saw.'[7]

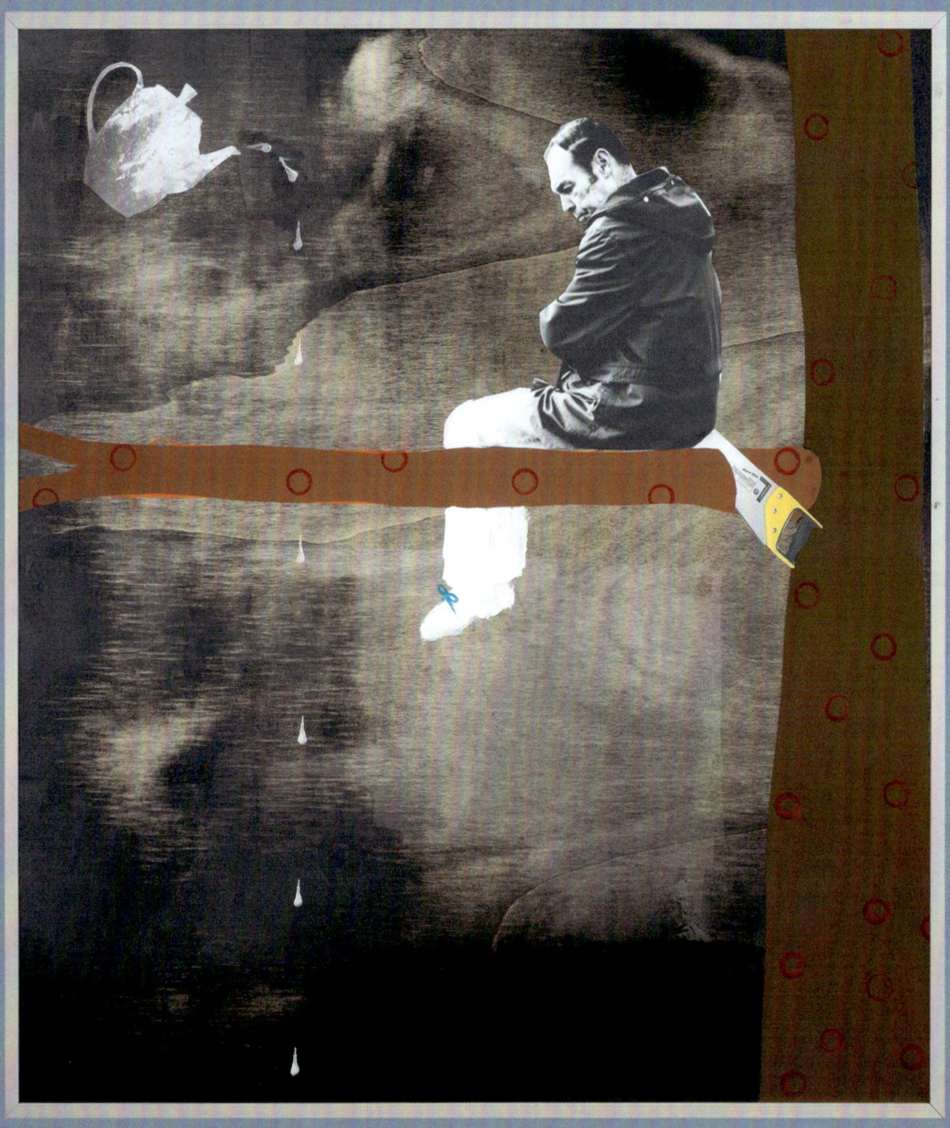

10 *sträflicher leichtsinn*, 2012, MDF, fabric, paper, stain, acrylic, wood, glass, 81.5 × 71.5 cm; Goetz Collection

Wie Brecht wirft Elfgen Fragen zur Nachhaltigkeit der zeitgenössischen Gesellschaft auf und bezieht uns in das Gefüge sozialer Kontrolle und Normen durch die Verdopplung des Blickes mit ein.

Robert Elfgen arbeitet bei seinen Collagen immer in formalen Serien. So folgen die in Zusammenhang mit *development* entstandenen Collagen alle einem ähnlichen kompositorischen Prinzip: Auf schwarz gebeiztem Untergrund kombiniert der Künstler stark vergrößerte Schwarzweiß- und Farbkopien mit Stoffen und Malerei. Glas und schmale Holzleisten, an der Innenseite farbig gefasst, rahmen die Materialcollagen ein. Sie erhalten dadurch eine beinahe objekthafte Dreidimensionalität, die den Eindruck vermittelt, wie durch ein Fenster in eine andere Welt zu blicken.[8] Breite Stoffstreifen bilden hier eine Miniaturbühne für intime Szenerien. Der zwischen hell und dunkel changierende Hintergrund löst diese Welt in einer diffusen und gleichzeitig transzendierenden Räumlichkeit auf, die an den Goldgrund mittelalterlicher Bildtafeln erinnert (Abb. 11). Die Collagen erweitern den realen Raum in einen imaginären Vorstellungsraum.

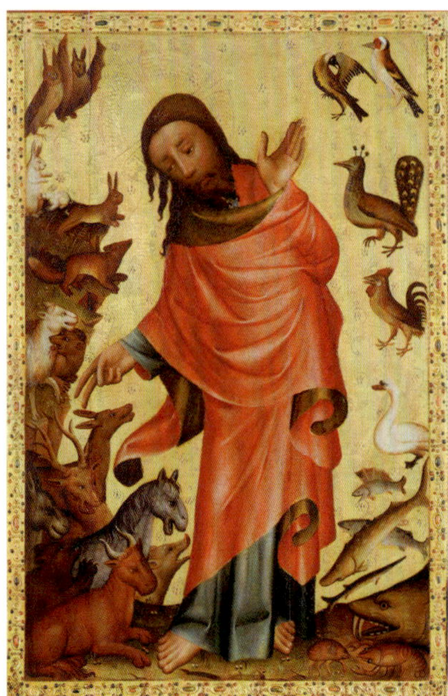

11 Meister Bertram, *Grabower Altar* (Detail: Creation of the animals), 1379–1383, tempera on wood, Hamburger Kunsthalle

Bertolt Brecht's critical commentary concerning social control and norms, as well as about the issue of efficiency and sustainability in modern capitalistic society, seems to have been the inspiration for this collage.

In his collages, Robert Elfgen always works in formal series. The collages created in the context of *development* are all accordingly based on a similar compositional principle: On a black-stained ground, the artist combines extremely enlarged copies in both black-and-white and color with fabrics and painting. Glass and narrow strips of wood, painted on the inside, frame the material collages, which thereby attain an almost objective three-dimensionality, giving rise to the impression of looking through a window into another world.[8] Wide strips of cloth form a miniature stage for intimate scenarios. The background oscillating between bright and dark dissolves this world into a diffuse and simultaneously transcendent spatiality which is reminiscent of the golden ground of medieval panel paintings (illus. 11). The collages expand the real space into a realm of the imagination.

Recurrent motifs of the collages are people whose faces are turned away, neckties and hats,

Wiederkehrende Motive der Collagen sind Menschen mit abgewandten Gesichtern, Krawatten und Hüte, Tiere, vor allem Vögel wie Meisen, Kleiber und Krähen, Tropfen und spiegelnde Pfützen. Elfgen erzählt kleine Geschichten, deren inkongruente Kombinationen eine einnehmende Magie entwickeln und von einem „frisson of otherworldliness"[9] begleitet werden. Sie erinnern an die Übersetzungen unbewusster Bilder in der Pittura Metafisica und des Surrealismus (Abb. 13).

animals — especially birds such as titmice, nuthatches, and crows —, drops and reflecting puddles. Elfgen tells short stories whose incongruous combinations develop an engaging magic and are accompanied by a 'frisson of otherworldliness'[9]. They recall the translations of unconscious images in Pittura Metafisica and in Surrealism (illus. 13).

The collage *im park am leckebusch* ('in the park at leckebusch') (illus. 12) shows a man in restful

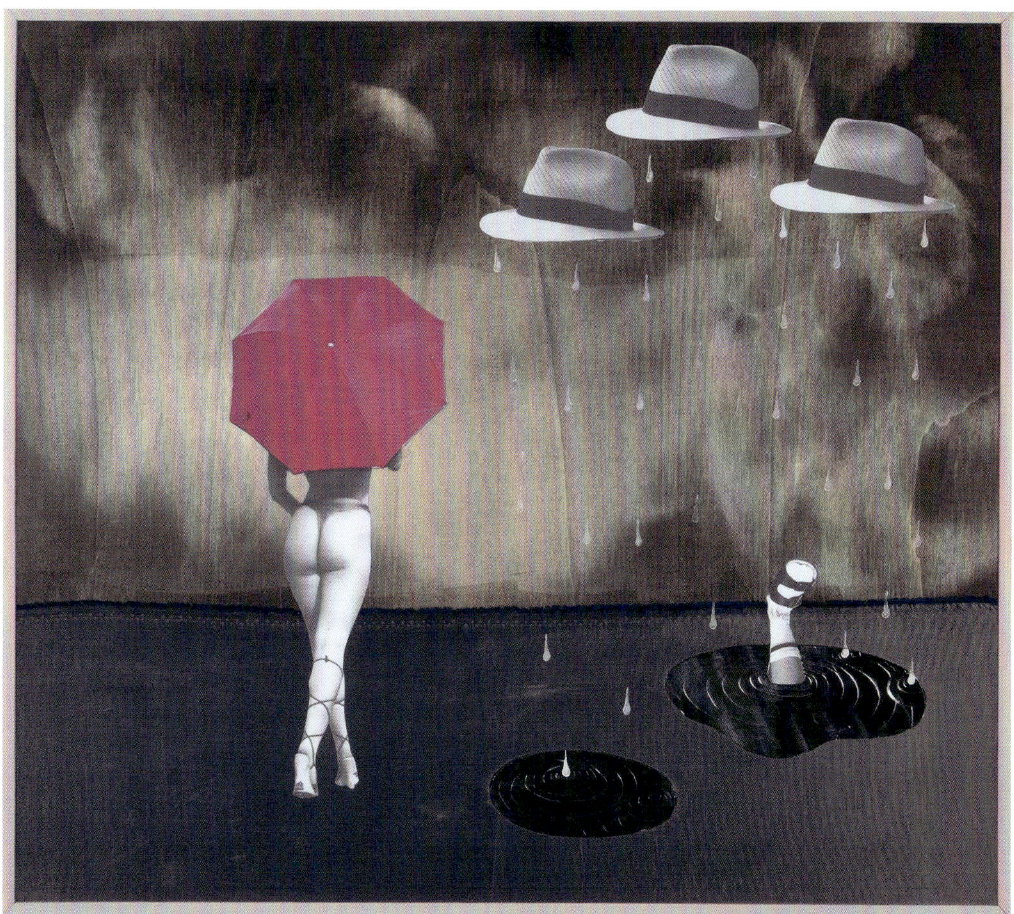

in den regen gehen, 2012, MDF, fabric, paper, stain, wood, glass, acrylic, 71.5 × 80.5 cm; Privat collection, Munich

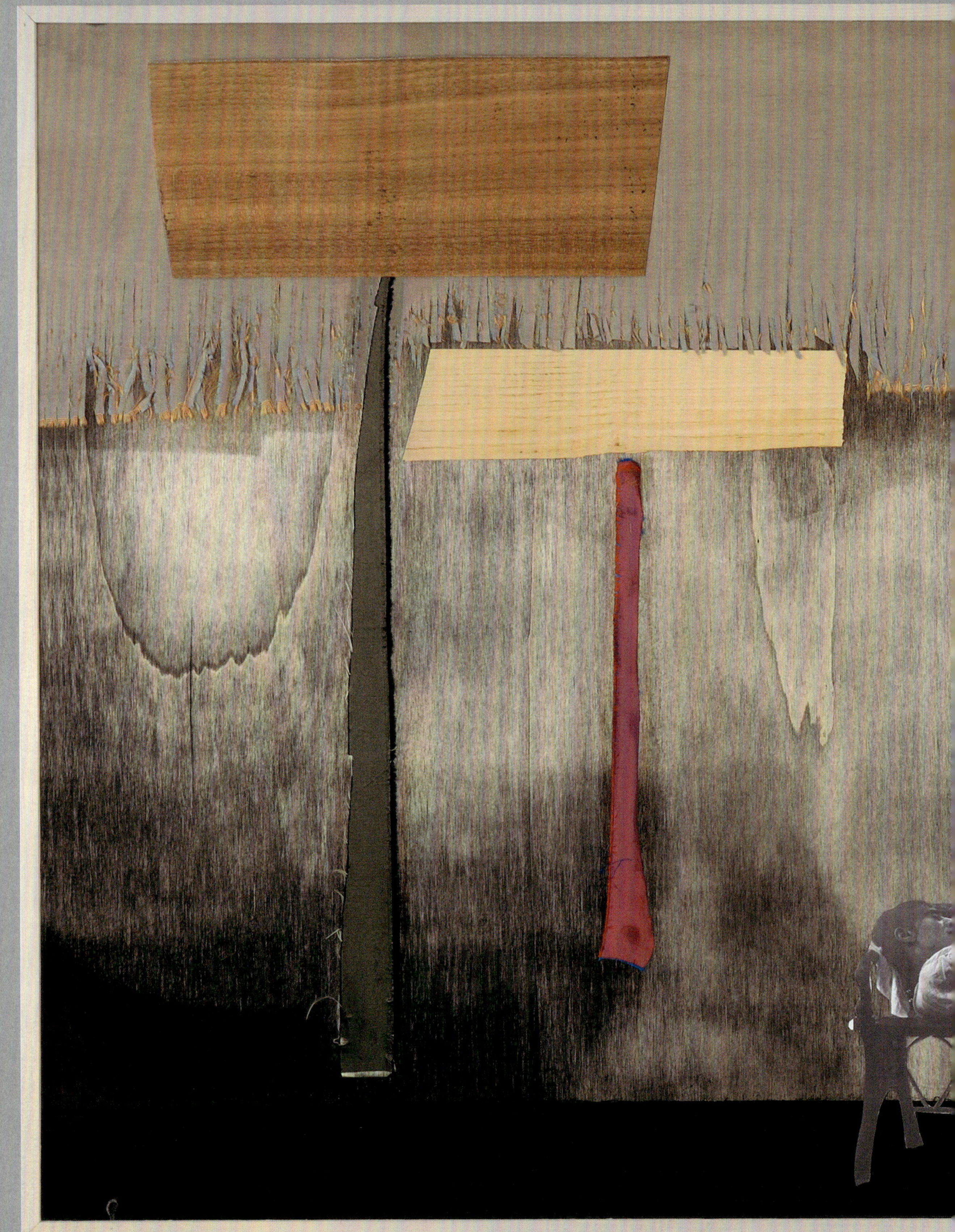

12 *im park am leckebusch*, 2012, MDF, fabric, paper, stain, acrylic, wood, glass, 71 × 140 cm

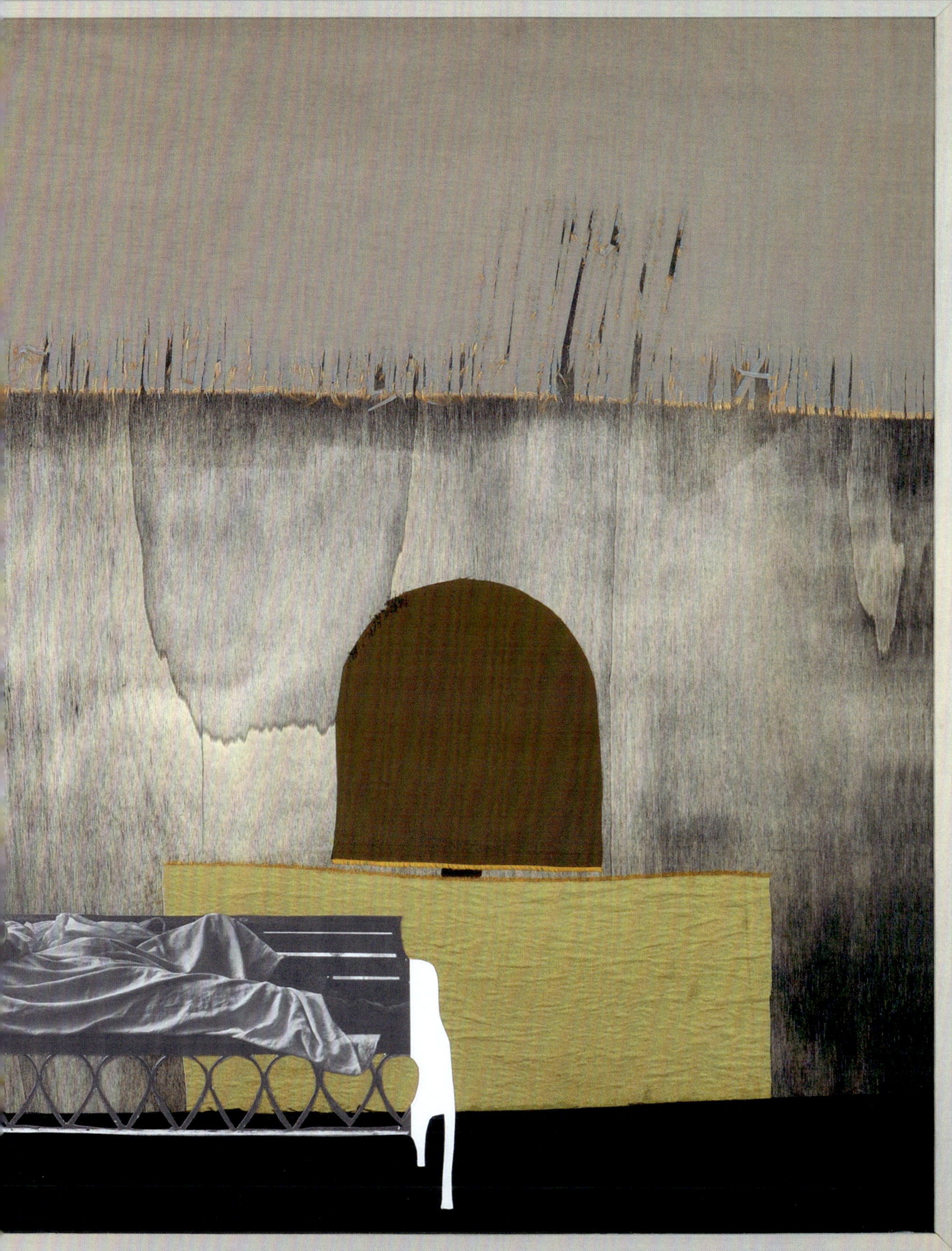

Die Collage *im park am leckebusch* (2012) (Abb. 12) zeigt einen Mann auf einer Parkbank in süßem Schlummer. Der Faltenwurf seines weißen Kittels verleiht ihm die Zeitlosigkeit antiker Statuen. Aus Stoff- und Furnierstücken entwirft Elfgen eine abstrahierte Landschaft, die am Horizont in einem Regenschauer aus ausgefranstem Stoff endet. Man meint, die Kühle und Ruhe dieses Augenblicks selbst zu spüren, in dem hier Natur, Landschaft und Mensch in traumhaftem Einklang zusammenkommen. Die Antikenreferenz der Figur ruft das Bild des „schlafenden Philosophen"[10] auf, das André Breton im ‚Surrealistischen Manifest' als Idealtypus entwirft und das den Traum als Quelle der Erkenntnis präsentiert.

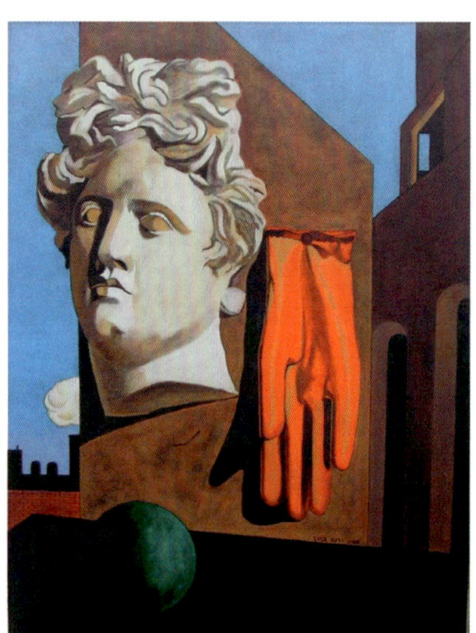

13 Giorgio de Chirico, *Le Chant d'Amour*, 1914, oil on canvas, 73 × 59.1 cm, The Museum of Modern Art, New York

slumber upon a park bench. The folds of his white frock endow him with the timelessness of ancient statues. Out of pieces of cloth and inlay, Elfgen creates an abstracted landscape which comes to an end at the horizon in a rain shower of tattered fabric. One has the impression of actually feeling the coolness and quiet of this moment when nature, landscape, and human being come together in dreamlike unity. The figure's reference to Antiquity summons up the image of the sleeping philosopher[10] which presents the dream as a source for attaining knowledge.

Elfgen finds his motifs on the Internet by entering such terms as 'man on branch' or 'poodle' in a search engine, and then making a selection from the abundance of displayed images. He processes them with printer and scanner until they have the appropriate size and texture. In some cases, they are subsequently overpainted or complemented with single-colored paper. This is a search for images whose prototype is connected to a poetical significance for him and causes the overall composition to arise associatively.

Elfgen findet seine Motive im Internet, indem er Begriffe wie „Mann auf Ast" oder „Pudel" eingibt und aus der Vielzahl der angezeigten Bilder auswählt. Mittels Drucker und Scanner bearbeitet er diese, bis sie die richtige Größe und Textur haben. Teilweise werden sie im Anschluss übermalt oder mit einfarbigem Papier ergänzt. Es ist ein Suchen nach Bildern, deren Prototyp für ihn mit poetischer Bedeutung verbunden ist und assoziativ eine Gesamtkomposition entstehen lässt.[11]

Auch die Titel seiner Werke wählt Elfgen nach dem Zufallsprinzip, im Falle der aktuellen

Elfgen also chooses the titles of his work according to a random principle, in the case of these current works from such sources as a handbook on repairing automobiles.[12] Words become

Arbeiten unter anderem aus einem Handbuch für Autoreparatur.[12] Worte werden zu zufälligen, bildhaften Fundstücken und ergänzen die Werke um eine sprachliche Ebene.

Die „Elemente dieser existierenden Welt", die wiedererkennbaren Motive, sind der Anker für die Annäherung an die Collagen und ihre Lesbarkeit. Dekontextualisiert und neu kombiniert in nicht eindeutigen Bildern initiieren sie einen intimen, inkludierenden Betrachtungsakt, der auf die individuelle Assoziation des Betrachters baut. Wie in den Assemblagen spielt auch bei den Collagen die offene formale Struktur eine zentrale Rolle: Der physische Prozess des Gemacht-werdens – das Ausschneiden der Motive und das Zurechtzupfen der Stoffe – macht die Collagen zu Objekten unserer unmittelbaren Realität. Die Rahmung hinter Glas vereinheitlicht die Oberfläche nur scheinbar – auch hier bleibt der Riss, die Inkongruenz des Materials und der Motive stets präsent.

Während die Assemblagen eine physische Anbindung an die Realität behalten, werden die Collagen zu visuellen Interpretationen des Alltäglichen. Thomas Hirschhorn spricht von seinen Collagen als einer „neuen Welt", die eine eigene Realität besitzt: „It's [the collage] a true, real entire interpretation, an interpretation that wants to create something new. Doing collages means creating a new world with elements of this existing world."[13]

Die gebrochene Homogenität der Collagen und Assemblagen verbildlicht in dieser „neuen Welt" die zeitgenössische Erfahrung, in der Fragmentierung, Hybridisierung, Appropriation und

coincidental, illustrative objets trouvés and extend the works onto a linguistic level.

The 'elements of this existing world', the recognizable motifs, serve as an anchor for approaching the collages and their legibility. Decontextualized and recombined into ambiguous images, they give rise to an intimate, inclusive act of contemplation which builds upon the individual associations of the viewer. As with the assemblages, in the collages the open, formal structure plays a fundamental role: The physical process of being made —the cutting-out of the motifs and the tugging of the fabrics into proper shape — turns the collages into objects of our immediate reality. The framing behind glass only seems to unify the surface — here as well the rupture, the incongruity betweenthe material and the motifs, remains constantly present.

Whereas the assemblages retain a physical connection to reality, the collages become visual interpretations of everyday life. Thomas Hirschhorn speaks of his collages as if about a 'new world' possessing its own reality: 'It's (the collage) a true, real, entire interpretation, an interpretation that wants to create something new. Doing collages means creating a new world with elements of this existing world.'[13]

The broken homogeneity of the collages and assemblages illustrates in this 'new world' the contemporary experience in which fragmentations, hybridization, appropriation, and simultaneity have come to constitute normality, and to which the coherent, illusionistic work can no longer do justice.[14]

Simultaneität Normalität geworden sind und der das kohärent illusionistische Werk nicht mehr gerecht werden kann.[14]

Elfgen verfolgt mit der Dekontextualisierung und Neuordnung der Motive allerdings keinen bildkritischen Ansatz. Es geht ihm nicht um einen Skeptizismus gegenüber dem Bild an sich. Vielmehr erhalten seine Motive, zufällig ausgewählt aus einer unüberschaubaren Masse von Bildern und neu zusammengesetzt, allgemeingültigen, allegorischen Charakter, der sich vor den abstrakten Hintergründen verstärkt. In Walter Benjamins Darstellung der Entstehung der Allegorie finden wir Elfgens Arbeiten gespiegelt:

With his decontextualization and rearrangement of the motifs, however, Elfgen does not pursue a critical approach with regard to the image. He is not concerned with a skepticism towards the image in itself. Instead his motifs, randomly selected from an almost limitless mass of images and then recombined, acquire a generalized, allegorical character which is enhanced by the abstract backgrounds. In Walter Benjamin's description of the emergence of allegory, we find a mirroring of Elfgen's works: 'That which is affected by the allegorical intention is separated out from the interconnections of life; it is struck dead and preserved simultaneously. Allegory

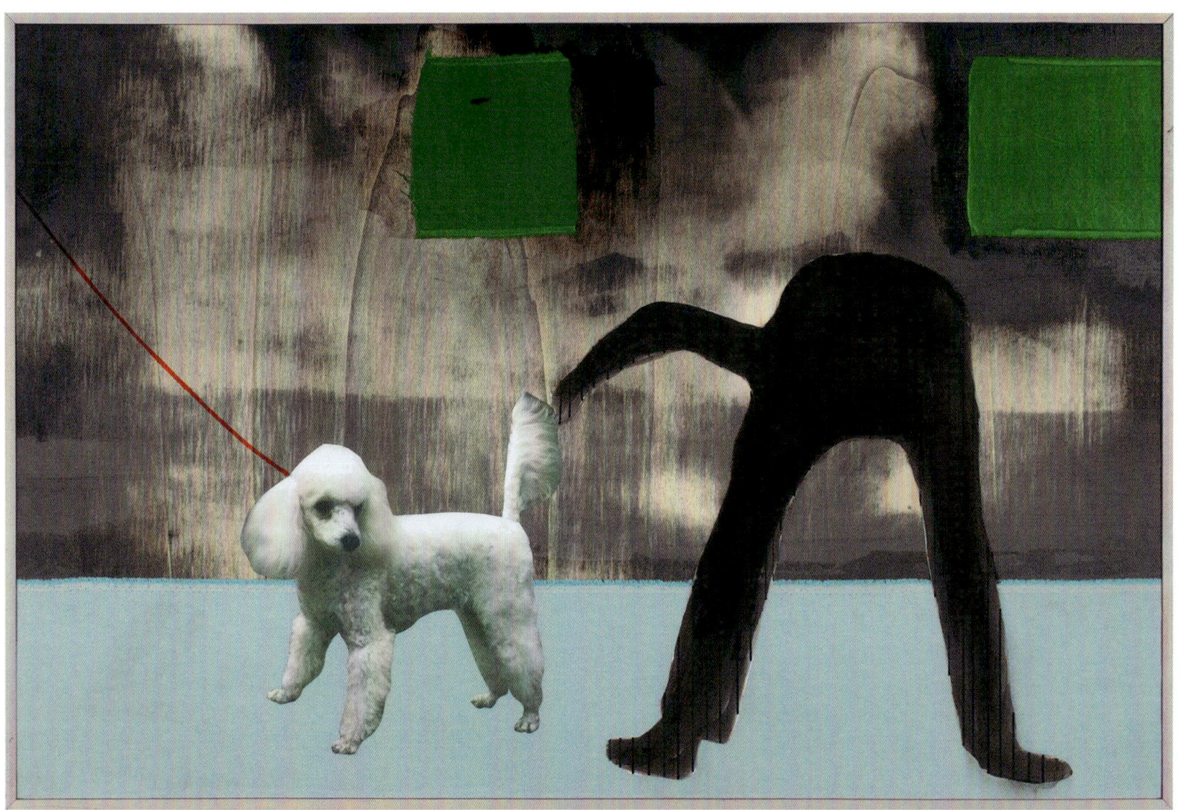

auf der suche nach dem sinn, 2012, MDF, fabric, paper, stain, acrylic, wood, glass, 71 × 107 × 4 cm

„Das von der allegorischen Intention Betroffene wird aus den Zusammenhängen des Lebens ausgesondert: es wird erschlagen und konserviert zugleich. Die Allegorie hält an den Trümmern fest. Sie bietet das Bild der erstarrten Unruhe."[15] Robert Elfgen vertraut auf eine fortgesetzte symbolische Kraft von Bildern, die in unserem kulturellen Gedächtnis verankert sind. Basierend auf biografischen Geschichten und Erfahrungen verhandelt er immer wieder die Frage, wie der Mensch in der Welt steht. Sein Augenmerk gilt den Systemen und Ritualen, die das Individuum in eine Gesellschaft eingliedern. Dem Unbehagen am zeitgenössischen Status quo setzt Elfgen die romantische Idee eines Mythos entgegen, den eine Gemeinschaft braucht[16]: „Dem mythenlosen

holds onto the ruins. It offers an image of frozen agitation.'[15]

Elfgen puts his faith in an ongoing symbolical power of images which are anchored in our cultural and biographical memory. On the basis of biographical stories and experience, Elfgen repeatedly addresses the question as to how humankind is situated in the world. He concerns himself with systems and rituals which integrate the individual into a society. He confronts the discomfiture with regard to the contemporary status quo with the romantic idea of a myth which is required by a community.[16] 'The mythless individual of modernism lacks the power of abbreviation, of limiting the horizon such as is performed by myth. Myth is the matrix

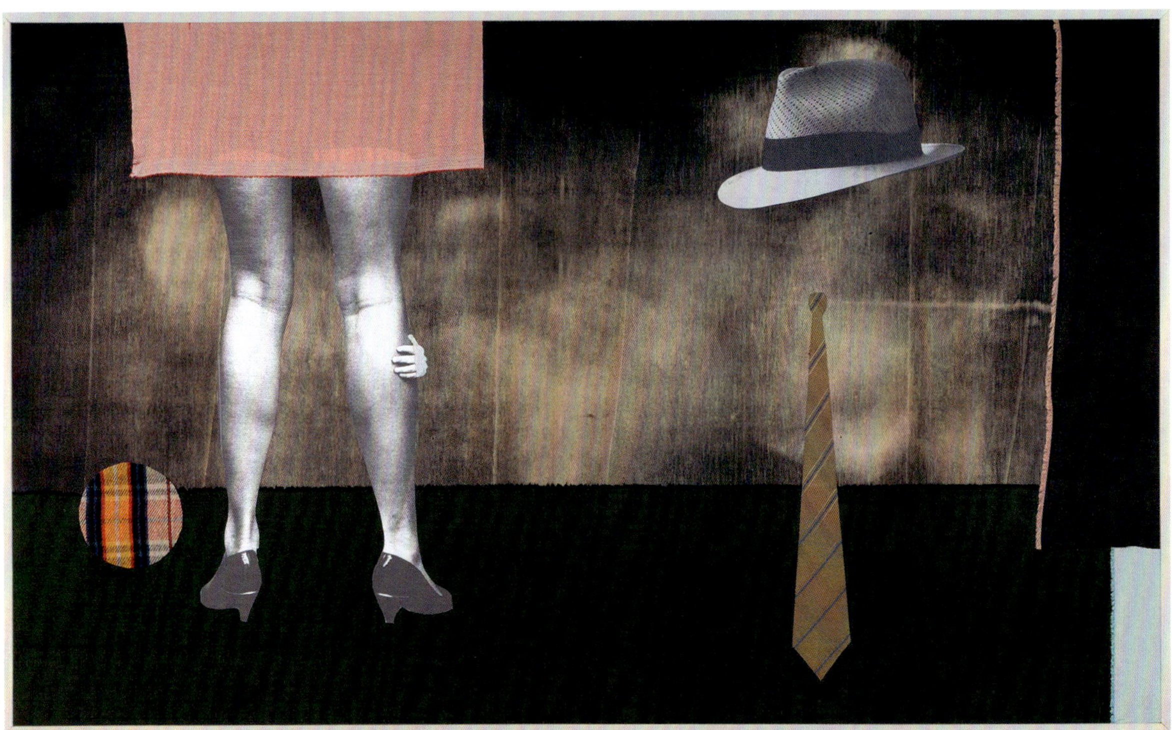

prenzlauerberg, 2012, MDF, fabric, paper, stain, acrylic, wood, glass, 81 × 135 cm

Menschen der Moderne fehlt die Kraft der Abbreviatur, der Horizontbegrenzung, die der Mythos leistet. Der Mythos ist die Matrix des Weltbildes – er stellt ein Bild von der Welt und umstellt die Welt mit Bildern"[17]. Elfgen erzeugt solche Bilder, indem er sich die „Wissenschaft des Konkreten"[18], das Wissen, das sich aus der Anschauung der sinnlich erfahrbaren Welt vermittelt, zueigen macht und in seine Werke übersetzt, um damit Hinweise auf tradierte Erzählungen zu geben.

Anders als frühere Installationen Elfgens ist *development* ein „Sich-entwickeln", ein Umherschweifen, ein Erfahren von Andeutungen und ein Spiel mit Assoziationen, ohne sich eindeutig festzulegen. Es ist ein Kommunikationsraum und gerade der Beichtstuhl zu Beginn der Ausstellung weist darauf hin. Er markiert eine Grenze zwischen äußerer Realität und Innerlichkeit, zwischen Realem und Imaginärem. Hier ist diese Grenze fließend, denn in die neu erschaffene Bildwelt mit ihren engen Bezügen zur realen Außenwelt schließt Robert Elfgen uns mit ein.

of the world view — it conveys an image of the world and converts the world through images'[17]. Elfgen creates these sorts of images by internalizing the 'science of the concrete'[18], the knowledge conveyed by the contemplation of a world that can be experienced by the senses, and transferring it into his works, in order to make references to traditional narrations.

In contrast to Elfgen's earlier installations, *development* constitutes a 'self-developing', a wandering about, an experiencing of allusions, and a playing with associations without committing oneself to a single, unambiguous perspective. This is a space of communication and the confessional box at the beginning of the exhibition provides an indication of this aspect. It marks a border between outer reality and personal inwardness, between the real and the imaginary. This border is fluid, for Elfgen encloses us within this newly created visual world which makes immediate reference to our real, outer world.

1. Josef H. Reichholf, Stabile Ungleichgewichte. Die Ökologie der Zukunft, Frankfurt am Main 2008. Reichholf geht davon aus, dass Ungleichgewichte in der Natur die natürliche Evolution, aber ebenso auch die wirtschaftlichen und sozialen Entwicklungen vorantreiben. Diese Auffassung steht im Gegensatz zu der statischen Vorstellung von Ökologie, die auf die Erhaltung bzw. Wiederherstellung eines Gleichgewichts abzielt.

2. Claude Lévi-Strauss, Das wilde Denken, Frankfurt am Main 1968 [frz. 1962], S. 31.

3. Die Bezeichnung von Robert Elfgens Arbeiten als ‚Bricolage' unternimmt erstmals Thomas W. Kuhn in seiner Rezension der Ausstellung. „Robert Elfgen: des bien ich", in: Kunstforum International, Bd. 192, 2008, S. 312.

4. „Er hat ihn AUSGEWÄHLT. Er hat einen gewöhnlichen Artikel genommen und so aufgestellt, dass seine nützliche Bedeutung hinter dem neuen Titel und unter dem neuen Gesichtspunkt verschwand – er hat einen neuen Gedanken für diesen Artikel geschaffen." Vermutlich Duchamp, Roché, Wood, (Hrsg.), „The Richard Mutt Case", in: The Blind Man, Nr. 2, Mai 1917, nicht paginiert.

5. Patrick Waldberg, Der Surrealismus, Köln 1981, S. 10.

6. Krauss spricht in Zusammenhang mit Readymades von einem zirkulären Wahrnehmungsprozess, der von diesen transformierten und transformierenden Objekten ausgelöst wird. Rosalind E. Krauss, Passages in Modern Sculpture, Cambridge 1977, S. 78.

7. Jan Kopf (Hrsg.), Bertolt Brecht. Die Gedichte, Frankfurt am Main 2008, 1. Auflg., S. 1094.

8. Lambert Wiesing, Artifizielle Präsenz. Studien zur Philosophie des Bildes, Frankfurt am Main 2005, S. 99 ff.

9. Laura Hoptman, in: Richard Flood, Laura Hoptman, Massimiliano Gioni (Hrsg.): Collage: The unmonumental picture, Ausst.–Kat. New Museum, New York, London 2007, S. 10.

10. „Wann werden wir schlafende Logiker, schlafende Philosophen haben?", André Breton, „Manifest des Surrealismus" (1924), in: Waldberg (1981), S. 92.

1. Josef H. Reichholf, Stabile Ungleichgleichgewichte. Die Ökologie der Zukunft, Frankfurt am Main 2008. Reichholf posits that imbalances in nature serve as a stimulus, not only to natural evolution, but also to economic and social developments. This perspective stands in opposition to the static concept of ecology, which aims at the preservation or restoration of an equilibrium.

2. Claude Lévi-Strauss, Das wilde Denken, Frankfurt am Main 1968 [french 1962], p. 31.

3. It was Thomas W. Kuhn who, in his review of the exhibition des bien ich, first used the term 'bricolage' in reference to Robert Elfgen's works, in Kunstforum International, vol. 192, 2008, p. 312.

4. 'He SELECTED it. He took a familiar article and presented it in such a way that its practical significance disappeared behind the new title and from the new point of view — he created a new concept for this article.' Probably Duchamp, Roché, Wood (eds.), 'The Richard Mutt Case', in The Blind Man, no. 2, May 1917, n. p.

5. Patrick Waldberg, Der Surrealismus, Cologne 1981, p. 10.

6. Rosalind E. Krauss, Passages in Modern Sculpture, MIT 1977, p. 78. With respect to readymades, Krauss speaks of a circular perceptual process which is set in motion by these transformed and transforming objects.

7. Jan Kopf (ed.), Bertolt Brecht. Die Gedichte, Frankfurt am Main 2008, 1st ed., p. 1094.

8. Lambert Wiesing, Artifizielle Präsenz. Studien zur Philosophie des Bildes, Frankfurt am Main 2005, pp. 99 ff.

9. Laura Hoptman, in Richard Flood, Laura Hoptman, Massimiliano Gioni (eds.) Collage: The unmonumental picture, ex. cat. New Museum, New York, London 2007, p. 10.

10. 'When will we have sleeping logicians, sleeping philosophers?', André Breton, 'Manifest des Surrealismus' (1924), in Waldberg (1981), p. 92.

11. '...and immediately I had no other thought than to incorporate it (translator's note: the ‚Picture of a Cut Man') into my material for poetic construction. I had

11. „und sogleich hatte ich keinen anderen Gedanken, als es (das „Bild vom zerschnittenen Mann", AdV) meinem Material für poetische Konstruktion einzuverleiben. Ich hatte ihm kaum dieses Interesse zugestanden, als es auch schon von einer ununterbrochenen Reihe von Sätzen abgelöst wurde, die mich kaum weniger überraschten (...)." – so beschreibt André Breton das Vermögen solcher poetischer Bilder. zit. nach Waldberg, S. 95.

12. Dieter Korp, Jetzt helfe ich mir selbst. Mercedes-Benz, Bd. 24, Auflg. Nr. 118 197, Stuttgart.

13. Thomas Hirschhorn, in: Flood, Hoptman, Gioni (Hrsg.), 2007, S. 44.

14. Sally O'Reilly, in: Blanche Craig (Hrsg.), Collage. Assembling contemporary art, London 2008, S.11.

15. Walter Benjamin, Illuminationen. Ausgewählte Schriften 1, Frankfurt am Main 1977, S. 235–236.

16. Vgl. Rüdiger Safranski, Romantik. Eine deutsche Affäre, Wien 2007, S. 152 ff.

17. Norbert Bolz, Eine kurze Geschichte des Scheins, München 1991.

18. Lévi-Strauss (1968), S. 29.

scarcely acknowledged this interest to him when it was already superseded by an uninterrupted series of sentences that scarcely surprised me any less [...].' This is how André Breton describes the inherent capability of this sort of poetic image. Breton, André, Surrealist Manifesto, quoted according to Waldberg, p. 95.

12. Dieter Korp, Jetzt helfe ich mir selbst. Mercedes-Benz, vol. 24, ed. no. 118 197, Stuttgart.

13. Thomas Hirschhorn, in: Flood, Gioni, Hoptman (eds.), 2007, p. 44.

14. Sally O'Reilly, in: Blanche Craig (ed.), Collage. Assembling contemporary art, London, 2008, p. 11.

15. Walter Benjamin, Illuminationen. Ausgewählte Schriften 1, Frankfurt am Main 1977, pp. 235–236.

16. Cf. Rüdiger Safranski, Romantik. Eine deutsche Affäre, Vienna 2007, p. 152 ff.

17. Norbert Bolz, Eine kurze Geschichte des Scheins, Munich 1991.

18. Lévi-Strauss (1968), p. 29.

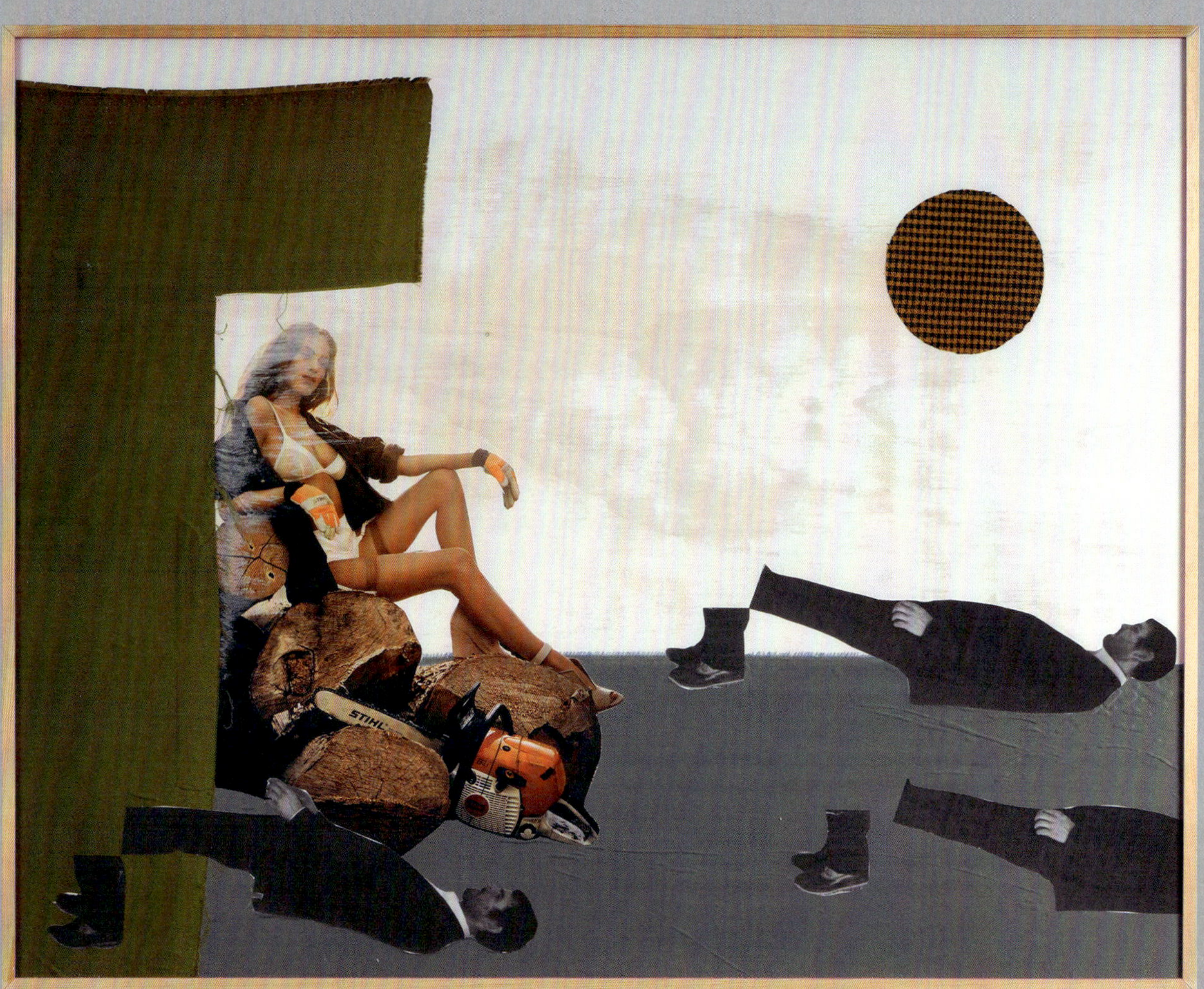

neulich im wald, 2012, MDF, fabric, paper, stain, acrylic, wood, glass, 67 × 85.5 cm

ROBERT ELFGEN

geboren/born 1972 in Wesseling am Rhein,
Deutschland/Germany
lebt und arbeitet in Köln und Berlin/
lives and works in Cologne and Berlin

Ausbildung/Education

1997 – 2001
Hochschule für Bildende Künste Braunschweig
(John M. Armleder), Braunschweig
2001 – 2004
Studienstipendium/grant of Cusanuswerk Bonn,
Bonn
2001
Kunstakademie Düsseldorf (Rosemarie Trockel),
Düsseldorf
2004
Meisterschüler (Rosemarie Trockel)
Atelierstipendium/grant of Kölnischer Kunstverein
und/and Imhoff-Stiftung, Köln/Cologne
Peter-Mertes-Stipendium, Bonner Kunstverein, Bonn
2007
Arbeitsstipendium der/grant of Stiftung
Kunstfonds
Förderpreis des Landes NRW für junge
Künstlerinnen und Künstler
2009
Grafikpreis des Landes NRW

Einzelausstellungen (Auswahl)/
Solo exhibitions (Selection)

2012
development, Sprüth Magers, Berlin (Kat./Cat.)
2009
Volles Programm, Marianne Boesky Gallery,
New York
grenzübergang, Sprüth Magers, Berlin

2008
Antriebswelle, Sprüth Magers, London
des bien ich, Sprüth Magers, Köln/Cologne
Förderpreisausstellung für Bildende Kunst
des Landes Nordrhein-Westfalen
(mit/with Manuel Graf), Reichsabtei
Aachen-Kornelimunster, Aachen
2007
Elfgen-Technik versenden und empfangen,
Samsa, Berlin
2006
wie man wird, was man ist,
Sprüth Magers Projekte, München/Munich
Expedition, westlondonprojects, London
2005
1+1=3 Elfgen Technik, Peter-Mertes-Stipendium,
Bonner Kunstverein, Bonn (Kat./Cat.)
2003
Raumtaucher, Simultanhalle,
Köln/Cologne (Kat./Cat.)
Raumtaucher, Screening,
Hafenlichtspiele Düsseldorf,
Düsseldorf
1999
Kulturzentrum Antwerpen, Antwerpen/Antwerp

Gruppenausstellungen (Auswahl)/
Group exhibitions (Selection)

2012
Rheinland, Galería Helga de Alvear, Madrid
Plaisirs du Jardin (mit/with Michail Pirgelis,
Stephanie Stein), Museum Morsbroich,
Leverkusen
2011
Kunst-Stoff. Textilien in der Kunst seit 1960,
Städtische Galerie Karlsruhe, Karlsruhe
Morgen, Provinz Editionen, Bochum
Scoopers, Screening Image Movementat
Oslo10, Basel
Winter in America, Tanja Pol Galerie,
München/Munich

2010

DIE FUGE – Portrait II, Floreria Flor-art,
Buenos Aires

2009

*Ausgezeichnet! – Der Grafikpreis des Landes
NRW 2009*, Reichsabtei Aachen-Kornelimünster,
Aachen

2008

*Paul Thek. Werkschau im Kontext
zeitgenössischer Kunst*, (Gemeinschaftsarbeit mit/
cooperation with Kai Althoff),
Sammlung Falckenberg, Hamburg

2007

*Paul Thek. Werkschau im Kontext zeitgenössischer
Kunst*, (Gemeinschaftsarbeit mit/cooperation
with Kai Althoff), ZKM | Zentrum für Kunst
und Medientechnologie, Karlsruhe
Atelierstipendiaten des Kölnischen Kunstvereins,
Die Brücke, Köln/Cologne
Sicht Weisen – Kunst auf der Talachse, Kunst
im öffentlichen Raum Wuppertal, Wuppertal

2006

Wo warst du! All Ambra, Tiroler Künstlerschaft,
Innsbruck
Kunst-Aktion zur jungen Nacht 2006, Aktion
mit/with Helge Tscharn am Friesenplatz,
kunst:dialoge am Museum Ludwig,
Köln/Cologne
Lieber Friedrich, Kunstverein Kassel, Kassel

2005

Regarding Düsseldorf – Junge Kunst in Düsseldorf,
701 e.V., Düsseldorf
Der Kunst ihre Räume, Bonner Kunstverein, Bonn
Servus, UNION, Köln/Cologne
Köln-Quartett 05, Fuhrwerkswaage
Kunstraum Köln, Köln/Cologne
7, Sprüth Magers Lee, London
RE-ESCAPE....))))))), Galerie im Regierungsviertel,
Berlin

2004

Supra Caput Esse, (mit/with Kai Althoff, Abel Auer,

Armin Krämer), Corvi-Mora, London
Akademierundgang, Deutsche Bank Düsseldorf,
Düsseldorf
Djordjadze/Elfgen/Scheepers,
Sprüth Magers Projekte, München/Munich
Auf dem Berlich, Köln/Cologne
Run-Spaces International, Simultanhalle,
Köln/Cologne
Rheinschau, Köln/Cologne
Für die Konstruktion des Unmöglichen,
European Kunsthalle, Köln/Cologne

2003

Immer die beiden Anderen, Neue Bügelei,
Wuppertal

2002

Lehrer/Schüler: Klasse Rosemarie Trockel,
Kunstverein Gelsenkirchen, Gelsenkirchen

2001

Cusanus-Stipendiaten, Pasinger Fabrik,
München/Munich

2000

Fahrvergnügen, Klasse John M. Armleder,
American Fine Arts Co., New York
Generation Gold, Haus Schwarzenberg, Berlin

1999

Lovely Music Project, Klasse John M. Armleder,
Kunstverein Braunschweig, Braunschweig

IMPRESSUM/COLOPHON

Herausgeber/Editor
Sprüth Magers Berlin London
Tanja Pol Galerie, Munich
Marianne Boesky Gallery, New York

Redaktion/Editing
Ruth Kißling

Konzeption/Concept
Robert Elfgen, Ruth Kißling,
Swantje Hoffmann

Gestaltung/Design
Swantje Hoffmann

Texte/Texts
Lilian Haberer, Ruth Kißling

Übersetzung/Translation
George Frederick Takis

Lektorat/Copy Editing
DISTANZ Verlag

Korrektorat/Proof Reading
Esther Dörring

Lithografie/Image Editing
Jochen Arentzen, Swantje Hoffmann

Produktion/Production Management
Swantje Hoffmann

Reproduktionen/Reproductions
© Sprüth Magers Berlin London; © Robert Elfgen;
© Alexandra Sell; © Kunstmuseum Basel, S./p. 17;
© bpk/Hamburger Kunsthalle/Elke Walford,
S./pp.: 21, 176; © bpk/Nationalgalerie, Staatliche
Museen zu Berlin/Jörg P. Anders, S./p.: 173;
© bpk/Kupferstichkabinett, Staatliche Museen zu
Berlin/Jörg P. Anders, S./p.: 38; © The Museum of
Modern Art, New York/Scala, Florence, S./p.: 180

Gesamtherstellung/Production
Primeline

Fotonachweis/Picture Credits
Jochen Arentzen, S./pp.: 88, 90–91;
Andy Keate, S./pp.: 27–33; Bernhard Schaub,
S./pp.: 3, 34–37, 64–69; Mareike Tocha,
S./pp.: Cover, 174–175, 177–179, 182–183,
187; Wilfried Pezzi, S./pp.: 24–25;
Stephen White, S./pp.: 74–76; Jens Ziehe,
S./pp.: 86–87, 160–164, 166–168, 170–172

Cover
ich und der lauf, 2012, plywood, fabric, glass,
photocopies, acrylic paint, 80 × 160 cm;
Private collection, New York

S./pp.: II - III
Erwachter Schlaf, 2006, fabric and synthetic
resin paint on MDF, 100 × 200 cm (closed),
100 × 400 cm (open); Goetz Collection

© 2013 Robert Elfgen; für das Werk von/
for the work by Giorgio de Chirico: VG Bild-
Kunst, Bonn; die Autoren/the authors und/
and DISTANZ Verlag GmbH, Berlin

Vertrieb/Distribution
Gestalten, Berlin
www.gestalten.com
sales@gestalten.com

ISBN 978-3-95476-000-8
Printed in Germany

Erschienen im/Published by
DISTANZ Verlag
www.distanz.de